DECOLONIZING EUROPEAN

Global Connections
Series Editor: Robert Holton, Trinity College, Dublin

Global Connections builds on the multi-dimensional and continuously expanding interest in Globalization. The main objective of the series is to focus on 'connectedness' and provide readable case studies across a broad range of areas such as social and cultural life, economic, political and technological activities.

The series aims to move beyond abstract generalities and stereotypes: 'Global' is considered in the broadest sense of the word, embracing connections between different nations, regions and localities, including activities that are trans-national, and trans-local in scope; 'Connections' refers to movements of people, ideas, resources, and all forms of communication as well as the opportunities and constraints faced in making, engaging with, and sometimes resisting globalization.

The series is interdisciplinary in focus and publishes monographs and collections of essays by new and established scholars. It fills a niche in the market for books that make the study of globalization more concrete and accessible.

Also published in this series:

Decolonizing European Sociology
Transdisciplinary Approaches

Edited by

ENCARNACIÓN GUTIÉRREZ RODRÍGUEZ,
University of Manchester, UK

MANUELA BOATCĂ
Catholic University of Eichstätt-Ingolstadt, Germany

SÉRGIO COSTA
Freie Universität Berlin, Germany

Routledge
Taylor & Francis Group

LONDON AND NEW YORK

First published 2010 by Ashgate Publishing

Published 2016 by Routledge
2 Park Square, Milton Park, Abingdon, Oxfordshire OX14 4RN
711 Third Avenue, New York, NY 10017, USA

First issued in paperback 2016

Routledge is an imprint of the Taylor & Francis Group, an informa business

British Library Cataloguing in Publication Data
Decolonizing European sociology : transdisciplinary
   approaches. -- (Global connections)
   1. Sociology--Europe. 2. Social sciences--Europe--
Philosophy.
   I. Series II. Gutiérrez Rodríguez, Encarnación.
   III. Boatcă, Manuela. IV. Costa, Sérgio.
   301'.094-dc22

Library of Congress Cataloging-in-Publication Data
Decolonizing European sociology : transdisciplinary approaches / [edited] by Encarnación Gutiérrez Rodríguez, Manuela Boatcă and Sérgio Costa.
    p. cm. -- (Global connections)
   Includes bibliographical references and index.
   ISBN 978-0-7546-7872-4 (hbk) -- ISBN 978-0-7546-9723-7 (ebook)
   1. Sociology--Europe. 2. Postcolonialism--Europe. I. Gutiérrez Rodríguez, Encarnación.
II. Boatcă, Manuela. III. Costa, Sérgio, 1962-

   HM477.E85D43 2009
   301.09182'1--dc22

                                                                            2009049225

ISBN 13: 978-1-138-24971-4 (pbk)
ISBN 13: 978-0-7546-7872-4 (hbk)

Contents

List of Tables

List of Contributors

Manuela Boatcă is Assistant Professor in the Department of Sociological Theory and Researcher at the Center for Latin American Studies (ZILAS), Catholic University of Eichstätt-Ingolstadt, Germany. Her research interests include macro-theories of social change, world-systems analysis, and postcolonial studies in historical-comparative perspective, with a regional focus on Eastern Europe and Latin America. She is author of *From Neoevolutionism to World-Systems Analysis: The Romanian Theory of 'Forms without Substance' in Light of Modern Debates on Social Change* (2003) and co-editor of *Geschlecht – Gewalt – Gesellschaft* (2003, with S. Lamnek); *Des Fremden Feind, des Fremden Freund. Fremdverstehen in interdisziplinärer Perspektive* (2006, with C. Neudecker and S. Rinke); and *Globale, multiple, und postkoloniale Modernen. Theoretische und vergleichende Perspektiven* (forthcoming, with W. Spohn). She is currently working on a monograph on the postcolonial continuities of global inequality relations.

Gurminder K. Bhambra is Associate Professor of Sociology at the University of Warwick. Her research addresses how, within sociological understandings of modernity, the experiences and claims of non-European "others" have been rendered invisible to the dominant narratives and analytical frameworks. In challenging the dominant Eurocentred accounts she argues for the recognition of "connected histories" in the reconstruction of historical sociology from a postcolonial perspective. Her monograph, *Rethinking Modernity: Postcolonialism and the Sociological Imagination* (2007) won the BSA Philip Abrams Memorial Prize for best first book in Sociology and was shortlisted for the European Amalfi Prize. She is co-editor of *Silencing Human Rights* (with Dr Shilliam), and *1968 in Retrospect* (with Dr Demir).

Heriberto Cairo, Dr. Phil in Political Sciences and Sociology, Complutense University in Madrid (UCM). He is Professor in Political Sciences and Administration in the UCM. He is director of the Master in Contemporary Studies of Latin America and main coordinator of the Interuniversity Doctorate Programme in "Latin American Studies: Political and Social Reality" at the UCM. His research area lies in political geography with a focus on the study of the geopolitics of war and peace, political identities and territorial ideologies and borders. Recent publications: *Vertientes americanas del pensamiento y el proyecto des-colonial* (2008) (with W. Mignolo); *La construcción de una región. México y la geopolítica del Plan Puebla-Panamá* (2007) (with J. Preciado y A. Rocha); *Geopolítica, guerras* *y resistencias* (2006) (with J. Pastor); *Democracia digital. Límites y oportunidades* (2002).

Franco Cassano is Professor of Sociology of Cultural Processes at the University of Bari, Italy. In the 1980s, he started a series of reflections on the South, reconsidering its cultural identity in relation to a modernity that was not produced. He thus paved the way to a debate about the autonomy of "Southern Thinking" (*pensiero meridiano*). He has been Director of the Peace Studies Center at the University of Bari and of the "Rassegna Italiana di Sociologia". Among his recent publications are: *Il pensiero meridiano* (Laterza, 1996); *Mal di Levante* (Libreria Laterza, 1997); *Paeninsula. L'Italia da ritrovare* (Laterza, 1998); *La Méditerranée italienne*, with Vincenzo Consolo (Maisonneuve e Larose, 2000); *Modernizzare stanca. Perdere tempo, guadagnare tempo* (Il Mulino, 2001); *Oltre il nulla. Studio su Giacomo Leopardi* (Laterza, 2003); *Homo civicus. La ragionevole follia dei beni comuni* (Dedalo, 2004); *L'alternativa mediterranea* edited with D. Zolo, (Feltrinelli, 2007); *Tre modi di vedere il sud* (Il Mulino, 2009).

Sérgio Costa is Professor of Sociology at the Free University of Berlin and a Senior Researcher at the Brazilian Centre of Analysis and Planning (São Paulo). His research interests include: contemporary social theory, cultural differences and democratic theory, racism and anti-racism, comparative migration studies. Selected monographs and edited volumes include: *Vom Nordatlantik zum Black Atlantic. Postkoloniale Konfigurationen und Paradoxien transnationaler Politik* (2007, also available in Portuguese); *As cores de Ercília: Esfera Pública, Democracia, configurações pós-nacionais* (2002); *Brazil and the Americas. Convergences and Perspectives* (2008) (co-editor with H. Nitschack and P. Birle); *The Plurality of Modernity: Decentring Sociology* (2006) (co-editor with W. Knöbl, J.M. Domingues and J.P. Silva); *Jenseits von Zentrum und Peripherie: zur Konstituition der fragmentierten Weltgesellschaft* (2005) (co-edited with H. Brunkhorst).

Sandra Gil Araújo is a Juan de la Cierva Research Fellow at the University of Granada and a member of the Latin American Migrant Researchers Interdisciplinary Group based in Spain. She was born within a migrant family in Buenos Aires and studied Sociology at the University of Buenos Aires. In 1992 she migrated to Madrid, where she completed a doctoral thesis in Sociology at the Complutense University of Madrid. She has participated in and coordinated numerous research projects and taught postgraduate courses on migration policies and international migration. She published extensively on these topics in renowned journals and books. She has been invited as a visiting lecturer and speaker to different European and Latin American universities, workshops and conferences. One of her recent publications is *Las periferias en la Metrópolis. Políticas migratorias, genero y estratificación de la población latinoamericana en España* (Melanges de la Casa de Velásquez, 2009).

Nilüfer Göle is Professor at the Ecole des Hautes Etudes en Sciences Sociales, Paris. Her work is dedicated to the study of new configurations between modernity and Islam, in particular to the emergence of new Muslim figures in public space in a comparative perspective. Among her main publications are: (with Ludwig Ammann (eds)), *Islam in Public: Turkey, Iran and Europe* (Istanbul, Bilgi University Press, 2006)/German edition: *Islam in Sicht. Der Auftritt von Muslimen im öffentlichen Raum* (Bielefeld, Transcript Verlag, 2004); *Interpénétrations. L'Islam et l'Europe* (Paris, Galaade Editions, 2005); *Musulmanes et Modernes. Voile et Civilisation en Turquie* (Paris, La Découverte, 1993, 2003 – also published in Turkish, English, German and Spanish). Her sociological approach aims to open up a new reading of modernity from a non-western perspective engaging a critique of Eurocentrism in the definitions of secular modernity. Currently she is conducting research on the controversies and confrontations engendered by visibility claims of Islam in Europe.

Encarnación Gutiérrez Rodríguez is Senior Lecturer in Transcultural Studies in the School of Languages, Linguistics and Cultures at the University of Manchester. She is co-director of the Migration and Diaspora Cultural Studies Network at the University of Manchester. She is the author of *Intellektuelle Migrantinnen* (1999) and *Migration, Domestic Work and Affect* (2010). Other publications include *Spricht die Subalterne Deutsch? Migration und Postkoloniale Kritik* (with H. Steyerl, 2003); *Gouvernementalität* (with M. Pieper, 2003); *Border, Frontiers, Homes* (with Caixeta, Tate and Vega, 2003) and the *FQS* special issue on "Method after Foucault" (2007). Currently, she is completing a monograph on affect, domestic work and migration.

Kien Nghi Ha, currently Postdoctoral Research Fellow at the University of Heidelberg, works in the field of Political Sciences and Cultural Studies. His research interests include Asian Diasporic Studies, postcolonial criticism, cultural hybridity, identity politics, colonial presences, and analyses of racism and migration. Selected monographs include: *Unrein und vermischt. Postkoloniale Grenzgänge durch die Kulturgeschichte der Hybridität und der kolonialen "Rassenbastarde"* (2010); *Ethnizität und Migration Reloaded. Kulturelle Identität, Differenz und Hybridität im postkolonialen Diskurs* (2004) and *Vietnam Revisited* (2005). He is also co-editor of *re/visionen. Postkoloniale Perspektiven von People of Color auf Rassismus, Kulturpolitik und Widerstand in Deutschland* (2007).

Jin Haritaworn is Helsinki Collegium for Advanced Studies Fellow and works intellectually, politically and creatively at the nexus of critical race, gender and sexuality theory. Current interests include transnational sexuality studies, feminist/queer/trans of colour theories, queer necropolitics, homonationalism, affect and intimate publics, "transgression" and "ambiguity", Thai diaspora and mixed race, representations of sex work migration, and other multi-issue theorizing. Work has appeared or is forthcoming in various journals, including *Social Justice, Sexualities, European Journal of Cultural Studies, European Journal of Women's Studies* and *Journal of Ethnic and Migration Studies*, and a monograph on sexual citizenship, gentrification and militarization is forthcoming in the Pluto series *Decolonial Studies, Postcolonial Horizons*.

Gregor McLennan is Professor of Sociology and Director of the Institute for Advanced Studies at the University of Bristol. He is the author of *Marxism and the Methodologies of History; Marxism, Pluralism and Beyond; Pluralism* and *Sociological Cultural Studies: Reflexivity and Positivity in the Human Sciences* (2006), and co-editor of several volumes in social and political theory, including *The Idea of the Modern State*. He is currently working on a critical assessment of postsecular social theories.

Jan Nederveen Pieterse is Mellichamp Professor of Global Studies and Sociology at University of California, Santa Barbara and specializes in globalization, development studies and cultural studies. Recent books are *Globalization and Culture: Global Mélange* (second edition, 2009); *Development Theory: Deconstructions/Reconstructions* (second edition, 2010); *Is There Hope for Uncle Sam? Beyond the American Bubble* (2008); *Ethnicities and Global Multiculture: Pants for an Octopus* (2007); *Globalization or Empire?* (2004).

Boaventura de Sousa Santos is Professor of Sociology in the School of Economics, University of Coimbra (Portugal), Distinguished Legal Scholar at the University of Wisconsin-Madison, and Global Legal Scholar at the University of Warwick. He is Director of the Centre for Social Studies of the University of Coimbra and Director of the Centre of Documentation on the Revolution of 1974, at the same university. He has published widely on globalization, sociology of law and the state, epistemology, democracy, and human rights in Portuguese, Spanish, English, Italian, French and German. He is author of 36 books and has co-edited 28 books.

Shirley Anne Tate is Senior Lecturer and Director in the Centre for Interdisciplinary Gender Studies, School of Sociology and Social Policy, University of Leeds. She is interested in exploring the intersections of "raced" and gendered bodies and "race" performativity within the Black Atlantic diaspora. Among her publications is her book *Black Skins, Black Masks: Hybridity, Dialogism, Performativity* (2005) which focuses on "race" performativity and on going beyond hybridity theorizing. Her new book *Black Beauty: Aesthetics, Stylization, Politics* (2009) looks at Black beauty within the Black Atlantic diaspora as affect-laden, performative "race" work that continues to impact on communal politics. Her research interests are varied and include the body, domestic and care work, beauty, Black identity, migration, the culture of Britishness, food and transracial intimacies.

Göran Therborn is Professor Emeritus of Sociology and Director of Research at the University of Cambridge, UK. Previously he was co-Director of the Swedish Collegium for Advanced Study in Uppsala, and University Professor of Sociology at Uppsala University. He is currently working on capital cities as representations of power; global processes of inequality, and other global processes and comparisons; contemporary radical thought and forces of possible change; roads to and through modernity. His recent publications include: *From Marxism to Post-Marxism?* (London, Verso 2008); "Eastern Drama: Capitals of Eastern Europe, 1830-2006", in *International Review of Sociology* no. 2 (2006) (guest editor and author); *Between Sex and Power. Family in the World 1900-2000* (London, Routledge 2004); *Inequalities of the World* (editor and co-author), (London, Verso 2006); *Asia and Europe in Globalization: Continents, Regions, Nations* (co-editor and coauthor), (Leiden, Brill 2006).

Immanuel Wallerstein is Senior Research Scholar at Yale University. He is the author of *The Modern World-System* (3 vol.); *Utopistics, or Historical Choices of the Twenty-first Century; Decline of American Power: The U.S. in a Chaotic World*, and most recently, *European Universalism: The Rhetoric of Power*. He was the founder and Director of the Fernand Braudel Center (1976-2005). He was President of the International Sociological Association (1994-1998). He chaired the international Gulbenkian Commission for the Restructuring of the Social Sciences, whose report is *Open the Social Sciences*. A collection of his work appears as *The Essential Wallerstein*.

Frontispiece: Vienna Academy of Arts, November 2009, during the student protests against Bologna University

Source: Image courtesy of Jens Kastner.

Introduction
Decolonizing European Sociology: Different Paths towards a Pending Project

Manuela Boatcă, Sérgio Costa and Encarnación Gutiérrez Rodríguez

In 1990 Robert Brym asked "are we at the end of sociology?" This was at a time when postmodernism seemed to be challenging the epistemic boundaries of sociology and the demise of Communism appeared to be heralding the end of history (Fukuyama 1992). Now, more than a decade later, we envisage a new project that does not announce the end of sociology, but a revision of this "rusty" discipline, predominantly populated by the spectres of a line of white European erudite males. What could happen to Weber, Marx, Durkheim, Giddens or Habermas, to just mention a few, if they were reminded by authors like Gloria Anzaldúa, Audre Lorde, Patricia Hill Collins, Raewyn Connell or Gayatri Chakravorty Spivak, of what they forgot to mention when they were analysing society, that is "the underside of modernity" (Dussel 1995)? This volume aims to read sociology against its grain – exposing and disposing of its conventional European genealogy of thought and revealing its national boundaries as limitations to knowledge of global interconnections. To this end, it brings together a critical set of essays that engage with the decolonial turn in European sociology from a "European" perspective. This might appear to be a paradoxical endeavour, as readers might be tempted to assume that, instead of de-centreing Europe, this project could produce the opposite effect. But, as this collection of essays demonstrates, sociology has evolved within the paradigm of "European modernity". To conceal or ignore this fact would be to disregard the basis on which this discipline still operates. This is therefore the starting point for our diagnosis as well as our critique.

Contesting European Modernity

Since its institutional beginnings in the nineteenth century, sociology, self-defined as a science of the modern (Western) world, has conceptualised modernity endogenously by taking the social norms, structures, and values characterizing the so-called Western societies as a universal parameter for defining what modern societies are and the processes of their emergence as the path to be followed by other, modernizing countries. Thus, under a sociological lens, "non-Western societies" appear as economically, politically and culturally incomplete and lacking in the face of *the* modern pattern, which is exclusively inferred from

"Western societies". Processes taking place on all structural levels in the non-Western world are generally interpreted sociologically as steps towards a drawn-out Westernization. The dichotomous division of the world in Western and non-Western societies has also moulded the historical narrative adopted by sociology: It is a meta-narrative centred on the "Western" nation-state that reduces modern history to a gradual and heroic Westernization of the world, without taking into account that, at least since the Western European colonial expansion of the sixteenth century, different "temporalities and histories have been irrevocably and violently yoked together" (Hall 1996: 252). This analytical blindness to identifying evident (post-)colonial entanglements in the constitution of (global) modernity is also shared by contemporary attempts to create a cosmopolitan sociology beyond methodological nationalisms (Randeria 1999). As Bhambra shows in this volume, some authors engaged in the cosmopolitism project still start from a "centred universalism", thus failing "to recognize contributions made in connections of which Europe had no part, as well as connections suppressed in the history of European uniqueness".

The critique of sociology's inherent methodological nationalism, undertaken in world-systems analysis since the 1970s and several strands of globalization theories in the 1990s, has been responsible for opening up both conceptualizations of space and of time for a global sociological approach. It thus became analytically possible, though by no means sociological common practice, to distinguish between different and entangled historical paths to modernity as a worldwide phenomenon, instead of lining up parallel modernities corresponding to distinct nation-states or civilizations (see Therborn in this volume). At the same time, viewing (capitalist) modernity as a global phenomenon allowed for the possibility of disentangling the different geopolitical projects embedded in the agenda of area studies of allegedly non-modern regions (see the chapters by Cairo and Wallerstein).

An idealized distinction between Western (modern) cultures and non-Western (pre- or non-modern) cultures has also marked sociological efforts of interpreting contemporary cultural dynamics. The dominant sociological understanding of culture is that of a set of common properties (identity) shared by individuals who constitute an "imagined community" at the local, regional or national levels. As Pieterse (2007 and also in this volume) convincingly demonstrates, these interpretations misconstrue a crucial aspect of global cultural dynamics: the generalization of cultural diversity. The imagination of a "Creolized Europe" or "Black Europe" is still neglected in analyses of European societies that ignore Europe's cultural transformation triggered by a colonialist, slavery and imperialist past, conditioning today's migratory movements.

In the wake of Edward Said's (1978) seminal contribution, Postcolonial Studies have largely taken upon themselves the task of exposing the extent to which such representations of culture(s) as sealed entities foster Orientalist representations of the Other. The project of decolonizing European sociology however requires that we complement the necessary critique of Orientalism with a clear conceptualization and separate treatment of Occidentalism, defined as "the expression of a constitutive relationship between Western representations of cultural difference and worldwide Western dominance" (Coronil 1996: 57). In this understanding, Occidentalism does not represent the counterpart of Orientalism, but its precondition, a discourse *from* and *about* the West that sets the stage for discourses about the West's Other(s). Most importantly, it is not a pan-European, but a pan-Western discourse, that constructs and downgrades European Others to the extent that their "Westernness" becomes questionable, manifested in constant appeals addressed to post/migrant and migrant communities to "integrate". This leads us to consider the production of European sociological knowledge within Walter Mignolo's (2007) framework of border epistemology, setting Europe at the epistemic juncture of coloniality and modernity, a project that therefore demands "decentring Occidentalism".

Decentering Occidentalism – Other Europes

Critiques of Eurocentrism often neglect the fact that the Western perspective on knowledge as it emerged with the establishment of Western hegemony as a global model of power is not a mere synonym of Eurocentrism. While Eurocentrism is an essential component of Occidentalism, and both can be treated as interchangeable in terms of their impact on the non-European world to a certain extent, it is imperative to differentiate with respect to the distinct range of the two within Europe.

During early modernity, when the secondary and peripheral Europe of the fifteenth century became the conquering Europe in the Atlantic (Dussel 1995) and at the same time the first centre of the capitalist world-system (Wallerstein 1979), both the European territorial dominance and the extent of its epistemic power were still partial. In contrast, as of the eighteenth century, hierarchies that structured Europe according to principles similar to those applied to the colonial world gradually started taking shape. If, for Anibal Quijano (2000), the propagation of Eurocentrism in the non-European world occurred with the help of two founding myths, evolutionism and dualism, the same also served to propagate Occidentalism in Europe once the change in hegemony from the old Spanish-Portuguese core to the Northwestern one had been effectuated. On the one hand, the evolutionary notion that human civilization had proceeded in a linear and unidirectional fashion from an initial state of nature through successive stages leading up to a singular Western form of civilization justified the *temporal* division of the European continent: while the East was still considered feudal, the South had marked the end of the Middle Ages, and the Northwest represented modernity. On the other hand, dualism – the idea that differences between Europeans and non-Europeans could be explained in terms of insuperable natural categories such as primitive-civilized, irrational-rational, traditional-modern (Quijano 2000: 543) allowed both a *spatial* and an *ontological* division within Europe. By being geographically inextricable from Europe, and at the same time (predominantly)

Christian and white, the European Southeast and especially the Balkans could not be constructed as "an incomplete Other" of Western Europe, as in the case of the Far East, but rather as its "incomplete Self" (Todorova 1997). Moreover, its proximity to Asia and its Ottoman cultural legacy located it halfway between East and West, thus giving it a condition of semi-Oriental, semi-civilized, semi-developed, in the process of "catching up with the West".[1] In the same vein, the European South, epitomized by the declining Spanish empire and its Moorish legacy, was gradually defined out of the Western core both for its proximity to Arab/Berber North Africa and for its reputation as a brutal colonizer of the New World, constructed as the opposite of England's own benevolent colonialism (Cassano 1995; Santos 2006).

Parallel to the construction of colonial difference overseas, we thus witness the emergence of a double imperial difference in Europe (stretching on to Asia): on the one hand, an external difference between the new capitalist core and the existing traditional empires of Islamic and Eastern Christian faith – the Ottoman and the Tsarist one; on the other hand, an internal difference between the new and the old capitalist core, mainly England vs. Spain:

> In this short history it is clear that the imperial external difference created the conditions for the emergence, in the eighteenth century, of Orientalism, while the imperial internal difference ended up in the imaginary and political construction of the South of Europe. Russia remained outside the sphere of Orientalism and at the opposed end, in relation to Spain as paradigmatic example of the South of Europe (Mignolo 2006: 487).

From this moment on, we have at least two types of European subalterns to the hegemonic model of power, as well as the first imperial map of multiple Europes (Boatcă 2010). In Spain and Portugal, the memory of lost power and the dominion of imperial languages induced the awareness of a decline from the core, i.e., an imperial nostalgia. Instead, in that part of the continent that had only emerged as "Europe" due to the growing demise of the Ottoman Empire – that is, Eastern Europe and the Balkans – the rise to the position of semiperiphery within the world system alongside the enduring position of periphery within Europe itself made the aspiration to Europeanness – defined as Western modernity – the dominant attitude.

Thus, the subdivisions underlying the imperial map of multiple Europes served to positively sanction the hegemony of the new core as "heroic Europe", the self-defined producer of modernity's main achievements: the Lutheran Reformation,

---

1   Maria Todorova speaks in this context of "Balkanism". Unlike Orientalism, which deals with a difference between (imputed) types, the European (Self) and the Oriental (Other), "Balkanism" as a discourse treats the differences within one type (Todorova 2004: 235), the civilized Western European and the semi-civilized, semi-Oriental Eastern European.

the Enlightenment, the French Revolution, and the British Industrialization (Dussel 1995). France, England, and Germany, as epitomes of what Hegel called "the heart of Europe", thus became the only authorities capable of imposing a universal definition of modernity and at the same time of deploying imperial projects in the remaining Europes or through them. Northwestern Europe's gradual rise to economic prosperity during which hegemony was disputed among Holland, France, and England, would use the territorial gains of the Spanish-Lusitanian colonial expansion in order to derive the human, economic and cultural resources that substantiated the most characteristically modern achievements – of which the "Industrial Revolution" is a paradigmatic example (Moraña et al. 2008). However, this will occur without integrating the contribution of either the decadent European South or of the colonized Americas in the narrative of modernity, which was conceived as being both of (North)Western and of inner-European origin.

On the other hand, and especially as of the mid-nineteenth century, the Western European core of the capitalist world-economy benefited from the end of Ottoman rule in the east of the continent by establishing neocolonies in the rural and agricultural societies of the region. The subsequent modernization of the Balkans and the European Southeast through the introduction of bourgeois-liberal institutions and legislation, while pursuing the goal of making the region institutionally recognizable to the West and financially dependent on it, at the same time involved the shaping of political and cultural identities of countries in the region in relation to the Western discourse of power. Consequently, not only Austria, but also Poland, Romania and Croatia defined their contribution to European history as "bulwarks of Christianity" against the Muslim threat, while every country in Eastern Europe designated itself "frontier between civilization and barbarism" or "bridge between West and East", thus legitimizing Western superiority and fostering the same Orientalism that affected themselves as Balkan, not Christian enough, or not white enough (see Wallerstein in this volume).

From such a perspective – that of the instrumentalization of the geopolitical location of "the other Europes" for the purposes of heroic Europe in the long durée – it becomes easier to understand that the Occidentalism directed at the subalterns never represented an obstacle to the Eurocentrism that the latter displayed on their part toward the non-European world. It was quite the contrary. Samuel Huntington accused the Orthodox and Muslim parts of Europe of marginality and passivity with respect to the achievements of modernity, situating them on the other side of one of the fault lines in the future clashes of civilizations. Re-mapping Eastern Europe and the Balkans in the context of a hierarchical model of multiple Europes reveals that the blindness to coloniality prevalent in these areas' political and identity discourses rather makes them accomplices of the colonial project of power underlying the emergence of modernity. In this sense, our project aims to propose different paths to decolonization.

Different Paths to Decolonization

The volume focuses on Europe as enduring centre, as subject of sociological production, on the one hand and as main point of departure, as object of theory-building, on the other. However, as our authors argue, this Europe is intrinsically a product of its colonial and imperial legacies, reflected in the discipline of sociology. The essays assembled here thus aim to "provincialize" (Chakrabarty 2000), deconstruct and de-centre Europe. This means confronting European sociology with its epistemological premises and complex societal movements, questioning it as a hegemonic centre.

Accordingly, the division of the book into five sections reflects the attempt to challenge disciplinary boundaries and voice submerged, marginalized or alternative proposals emerging from decolonial feminism and Queer Theory, Critical Migration Studies, Critical Geopolitics, World-Systems analysis, Postcolonial Critique, and the modernity/coloniality perspective. As they reflect ongoing and interrelated processes, the sections at times cross-reference each other in terms of content. Thus, in Part I, "Unsettling Foundations", the authors examine the challenges represented by postcolonial critique and/or the perspective of coloniality for sociology as a discipline. Concretely, Boatcă and Costa identify critical micro, meso and macrostructural approaches that, as a whole, entitle talk of an emerging, but as yet not unified field of postcolonial sociology with a clear decolonizing potential and a promising research agenda. For Bhambra, the Postcolonial Theories' promise of acknowledging the structural connections between core and periphery is best realized within a "provincialized", rather than global cosmopolitanism, and in a project of "connected sociologies", rather than in the currently advocated global or public sociology based on abstract universal categories. Gutiérrez Rodríguez discusses the pitfalls of the institutionalization of postcolonial sociology by asking how far a critical agenda can be pursued in the name of "Postcolonial Critique" at a time when the label has become merchandise in the competitive global market of Higher Education. Discussing the German and British situation, she addresses the paradox between the incorporation of critical thinking, which raises the question of global inequalities in an institutional setting, and the reproduction of these inequalities by the same institution. She argues for decolonizing sociology by starting with a stronger representation of Black and Ethnic Minority faculty, in particular, at professorial level, alongside fostering the access of local minoritized groups to Higher Education.

Following up on the discussion of the concept of modernity in the introductory section, the chapters in Part II, "Pluralizing Modernity", engage with one of the most prolific sociological debates of the past decade – the opening up of the conceptualization of Eurocentred modernity by such alternatives as multiple, global, or entangled modernities. Whereas all the authors in the section critique the label and the research programme behind the multiple modernities approach, their solutions and their respective focuses span a wide range. Göran Therborn denounces the notion of different modernities, defined on the basis of the set of institutions characterizing them, as a "descriptive cop out", and suggests instead conceiving of modernity as a time orientation tied to different modernist strivings. He consequently identifies four different historical paths to modernity function of their engagement with the colonial endeavour and goes on to examine the extent to which they still affect the social relations and the power asymmetries in the contemporary world.

Jan Nederveen Pieterse argues against current approaches that interpret the entire assortment of modernity models found in different world regions as varieties of *the* first, European modernity. Thus, he searches for framing new modernities in the global South as well as for disclosing entanglements between different modernities, finding out that Western modernity is merely a modernity among others and also includes "historical particularities that are not necessarily intrinsic to modernity per se".

Nilüfer Göle sees the challenge represented by Islam as the main critical potential for opening up understandings of European modernity, and at the same time for unsettling sociology's traditional disciplinary boundaries. In particular, Göle looks at how the current research interest in Islam and the corresponding consolidation of Islamic studies as an explicitly interdisciplinary field engaging political science, sociology, anthropology, and law, reopens debates about the universalist claims of secular modernity, European understandings of the relationship between religiosity and sexual emancipation, and the legitimacy of the nation-state as a unit of analysis of political dynamics.

Part III, "Questioning Politics of Difference", discusses the micro and macro politics of identity by unveiling the limits of dominant concepts of multiculturalism and cultural identity in the context of labour, migrant and sexual rights, queerness and raciality, global migratory flows, and the Communist collapse in Central and Eastern Europe.

Gregor McLennan opens this debate by critically reviewing new approaches concerning secularity and postsecularity, and multiculturalism in order to indicate an important turning point in postcolonial debates moving away "from the theory and politics of difference per se, towards a much more expansive humanism". This change expresses the ambivalent position of Postcolonial Studies to postsecularism highlighting the fact that sociology's modernist frame may well be (necessarily) limited, but perspectives that aim to be more receptive to "irreducibly plural" cultures and ontologies are typically stricken by conundrums stemming from their own continuing obligations to modernist thinking. McLennan recognizes a potential contribution of Postcolonial Studies for renewing sociology at the epistemological level but he emphatically rejects the idea of a postcolonial "revolution" aimed at reconstructing central analytical keys of sociology, as defended by Bhambra (2007).

From a different angle and focusing on "Muslim homophobia" in Germany, Jin Haritaworn traces the genealogy of a moral panic around "migrant homophobia" at two major construction sites – the Simon Study commissioned by the biggest gay organization, which compared homophobia among "migrant" and "German" school children in 2007, and the violent attack against a group of queer and transgendered people at the Drag Festival in Berlin in 2008. Engaging with the argument that "homophobic Islam" becomes the constitutive outside of a nation and a Europe which imagine themselves as intrinsically friendly towards gays, queers and transpeople, Haritaworn reveals the deep remaining ambivalences inherent in this discourse. The apparent discourse of liberation is very often underlined by the assumption of pre-modern attitudes, attributed to "Muslim migrants" impeding this process. A (con)fusion between homophobia and Islamophobia occurs, in which "Muslim migrants" are identified as unable to integrate into the "modern European society".

With the issue of the (re)creation of cultural boundaries within Europe, the section turns to the macro-structural dimension of the politics of difference. Rather than common cultural traditions, Immanuel Wallerstein argues, the subdivisions of Europe into Western, Central, Eastern Europe and the Balkans reflect the historical construction of a European hierarchy and its current geopolitical stakes at the global level. By culturally aligning themselves with (Western) Europe in the post-Communist era, Central and Eastern European countries not only reinforce the hierarchy, and, with it, the logic underlying the recurrent construction of European Others, but at the same time positively sanction Western Europe's geopolitical projects, thus siding with the North in the global North-South divide.

The section on "Border-Thinking" (Part IV) alludes to Mignolo's concept of border epistemology. Set within the confines of Europe, border epistemology as an analytical perspective interrogates the immanent colonial legacies and technologies of racisms operating in everyday culture. While Mignolo elaborates this concept within the analysis of Latin American coloniality, the translation of this analytical approach within the European context poses questions in regard to its "exteriority" (Dussel 1995) within its own borders. The exteriority of Europe within its borders is articulated by the discursive and institutional attacks on non-European and Eastern European migrants and refugees interpellated as the "Others" of modernity. These attacks are very often condensed in the appeal of "integration" and its institutional translation, an aspect that the essays of Kien Nghi Ha (in the case of Germany) and Sandra Gil Araújo (in the case of Spain) address.

While Ha discusses the violent effects of integration policies effected through the enforcement of German language courses and citizenship courses, Gil Araújo reveals how behind these programmes racialized and ethnocentric assumptions are in place through which non-European migrants are racialized and constructed as "uneducated", "unskilled" and "uncivilized". The construction of the nation's other as pre-modern, is also conceived in discourses on Black beauty, where the racialized Black body is projected as "nature". How Black women are supposed to style themselves is thus not a power-neutral question, but rather implies a thorough examination of its culturally racialized predication. Voicing decolonial voices within the midst of Europe, in Britain, Shirley Anne Tate demonstrates how beauty is territorialized and contextualized. While discourses on beauty seem to reflect an abstract concept of aesthetics, they represent a concrete, geopolitically and historically contextualized corporeality, confirmed by conventions of white beauty. In turn, discussing the representation of Black beauty reveals that we need to decolonize this discourse in order to perceive practices of beauty transcending the White/Black paradigm. In this regard, Tate illuminates an aesthetics departing from "the *epistemic priority* of the problem of the color line," (Maldonado-Torres 2008: 246) giving a preference to the voices of Black British women and their proposals on aesthetics and stylization.

Finally, the volume comes full circle with Part V, "Looking South". On the one hand, the authors in this section engage with the South as a metaphor for the global periphery and for an alternative epistemology of counter-globalization (Cassano, Sousa Santos). On the other hand, by literally looking (to the) South, they reveal structural hierarchies originating in historical subdivisions within Europe itself (Sousa Santos, Cairo), thereby pointing to the crucial insight that the process of decentering Europe must take into account the different colonialisms emanating from Europe, as well as the different processes of decolonization involving subordinated empires such as Spain and Portugal as opposed to hegemonic empires such as England and France. Heriberto Cairo, in particular, thoroughly dispatches the construction of an "Occident", "West", "Europe", what we mean by these divisions and what they imply in regard to the "East" or the "global South". Demonstrating how geographical labelling is a result of an imperial system of research, sometimes linked to military geopolitical strategies in the case of "Latin America", Cairo urges us to rethink the categorization of a world system in the light of a decolonial critique.

Rather than advocating one path to a uniformly defined decolonizing process, which we think would be reproducing the fallacy we criticize mainstream sociology for committing, our aim is to open up a space for a multiplicity of critical projects that may not use the same term for labelling themselves, but which pursue common goals. In this sense, we see the project of decolonizing European sociology as the mere beginning of a long journey in which such common pursuits can be negotiated.

Bibliography

Bhambra, G. 2007. Sociology and Postcolonialism: another "missing" revolution? *Sociology*, 41(5), 871-84.

Boatcă, M. 2010. The Quasi-Europes: World Regions in Light of the Imperial Difference, in *Global Crises and the Challenges of the 21st Century*, edited by T.E. Reifer. Boulder: Paradigm Publishers.

Brym, R.J. 1990. The End of Sociology? A Note on Postmodernism. *The Canadian Journal of Sociology/Cahiers Canadiens de Sociologie*, 15(3), 329-33.

Cassano, F. 1995. *Il pensiero meridiano*. Bari: Laterza.

Chakrabarty, D. 2000. *Provincializing Europe: Postcolonial Thought and Historical Difference*. Princeton: Princeton University Press.

Coronil, F. 1996. Beyond Occidentalism: Toward Non-Imperial Geohistorical Categories. *Cultural Anthropology*, 11(1), 51-87.

Dussel, E. 1995. *The Invention of the Americas: Eclipse of "the Other" and the Myth of Modernity*, translated by M.D. Barber. London: Continuum.

Fukuyama, F. 1992. The End of History?, in *The Geopolitics Reader*, edited by G. Ó Tuathail, S. Dalby and P. Routledge. New York/London: Routledge, 107-14.

Hall, S. 1996. When was the "Postcolonial"? Thinking at the Limit, in *The Postcolonial Question: Common Skies, Divided Horizons*, edited by I. Chambers and L. Curtis. London: Routledge, 242-60.

Maldonado-Torres, N. 2008. *Against War. Views from the Underside of Modernity*. Durham: Duke University Press.

Mignolo, W. 2002. The Geopolitics of Knowledge and the Colonial Difference. *South Atlantic Quarterly*, 101(1), 57-96.

Mignolo, W. 2006. Introduction. *South Atlantic Quarterly*, 105(3), Summer 2006, 479-99.

Mignolo, W. 2007. Delinking. The Rhetoric of Modernity, the Logic of Coloniality and the Grammar of De-Coloniality. *Cultural Studies*, 21(2), 449-514.

Moraña, M., Dussel, E.D. and Jáuregui, C.A. 2008. Colonialism and its Replicants, in *Coloniality at Large: Latin America and the Postcolonial Debate*, edited by M. Moraña, E.D. Dussel and C.A. Jáuregui. Durham: Duke University Press, 7-23.

Pieterse, J.N. 2007. *Ethnicities and Global Multiculture: Pants for an Octopus*. Lanham: Rowman & Littlefield.

Quijano, A. 2000. Coloniality of Power and Eurocentrism in Latin America. *International Sociology*, 15(2), 215-32.

Randeria, S. 1999. Jenseits von Soziologie und soziokultureller Anthropologie: Zur Ortsbestimmung der nichtwestlichen Welt in einer zukünftigen Sozialtheorie. *Soziale Welt*, 50(4), 373-82.

Said, E. 1978. *Orientalism*. New York: Vintage.

Santos, B. de Sousa 2006. Between Prospero and Caliban: Colonialism, Postcolonialism and Interidentity. *Review. Journal of the Fernand Braudel Center*, XXIV(2), 143-66.

Todorova, M. 1997. *Imagining the Balkans*. New York, Oxford: Oxford University Press.

Wallerstein, I. 1979. *The Capitalist World Economy*. Cambridge: Cambridge University Press.

PART I
Unsettling Foundations

Chapter 1

Postcolonial Sociology: A Research Agenda

Manuela Boatcă and Sérgio Costa

Twists and Turns – On the Usefulness of Paradigm Shifts

Both in its self-understanding as an academic field and in its demarcation from other social sciences, sociology is inseparably linked to its research aim – modernity. Disciplines in which the Western world served as both a speaking subject and a study object were a result of the intellectual division of labor that emerged in Western Europe towards the end of the nineteenth century. Each one of the supposedly autonomous spheres of human activity seen as characterizing the modern world – the market, the state and the (civil) society – was then assigned an academic field, thus yielding economics, political science, and sociology (see Wallerstein 1999: 2). In contrast, anthropology and Oriental studies were supposed to explain why the rest – basically, the non-European periphery – was not or could not become modern.

This geopolitical distribution of scholarly tasks in function of their pertinence to Western modernity has been true for the entire duration of sociology's institutional existence. This (now tacit) understanding of the scholarly division of labor still paves the way for present-day research. Whereas anthropology began its institutional existence by dealing with the non-European world – as an instance of the "premodern" – and therefore incorporated both colonial relations and postcolonial developments relatively early into its research field,[1] a sociology of global scope that goes beyond the analytical frame of modern Western(ized) nation-states still finds itself in need of legitimacy. Given that colonized or totalitarian countries were not on their way towards modernity, they were long denied the status of valid objects of sociological analysis; in turn, after gaining independence, they were allowed to become reception sites for European and North American social theories – yet not their production sites. The globalization of sociology as a discipline is therefore often regarded as (or reduced to) the successful implementation of the Western model in receptive national contexts:

---

1 This is not to say that anthropology adequately or critically addressed colonial relations of power at all times, but that the (however inadequate) treatment of colonial contexts was an integral part of its self-definition as a discipline – which was not the case for sociology. On the complicity of anthropology with colonial policy and the embeddedness of the anthropological perspective with colonial practices, see Asad 1973, Fabian 1983.

> Taking off from its principal holds strong in Germany, France and the United
> States, classical sociology spread throughout the world, everywhere that the idea
> of society as the creation of a nation-state came to the fore. [...] At the same
> time, because it is tied to the nation-state and to the existence of a civil society
> possessing autonomy within the framework of the nation-state, sociology
> remained absent from colonized countries as well as from those where traditional
> leaders continued to hold power (Touraine 2007: 185ff.).

In spite of differing emphases in the various national cultures of scholarship and
of successive epistemological and methodological paradigm shifts, such as the
cultural or the spatial turn, little has changed in terms of this – self-imposed –
analytical narrowing of the sociological gaze. Against this background, talk of a
postcolonial sociology seems rather like a contradiction in terms.

Advocating a postcolonial turn as a further trend would, in our view, be equally
wrong. Rather than a paradigm shift, we are interested in tracing back the colonial
turn that preceded the institutionalization of sociology and that has so far prevented
the emergence of a global sociology of colonial, neocolonial and postcolonial
contexts. Using examples from each of the three levels of the sociological analysis
– the macro-, the meso- and the micro-structural level – we subsequently intend
to point to the necessary corrections that a postcolonially sensitive sociology can
perform to the diagnoses of current social theory.

This already implies the thesis that postcolonial sociology in itself does not
represent an internally contradictory approach, but one that is both long overdue
and in need of programmatic systematization. Before turning to the latter, a double
terminological elucidation is necessary: on the one hand, what is it that makes
postcolonial theories particularly suitable for enhancing sociological knowledge,
on the other, what makes postcolonialism as an explicitly sociological perspective
useful.

Why postcolonial *sociology?*

The postmodern and the poststructural turn have brought the contingency of cultural
and historical knowledge, the discursive construction of social, as well as the end
of modern meta-narratives to the center-stage of social scientific debates as soon as
the 1970s and early 1980s. Postcolonial theories, whose criticism of the European
modernity's claim to universality in part builds on such debates and whose self-
designation necessarily harks back to the previous "posts", found themselves from
the very beginning under suspicion of selling similar contents under a slightly
different label. The tension between the need for the label "postcolonial" on the
one hand and its political ambivalence on the other therefore became a matter of
lasting debates among representatives of postcolonialism itself (see Shohat 1992;
Dirlik 1994; Hall 2002). Contrary to the assumption that it only accounts for the
temporal positioning of societies within colonial history, the term "postcolonial"
also refers to the reconfiguration of economic, social and political relationships

which colonialism has triggered in former colonies and metropoles, as well as to the tension between power and knowledge production in the context of imperial relationships (see Gutiérrez Rodríguez 1999; Coronil 2004; Costa 2005).

It thus becomes clear that postcolonialism as a concept and perspective, despite significant internal differences, underscores the historical context of (colonial) power considerably more than poststructuralism and postmodernism and draws from this position a political program which widely differs from both the postmodernist and the poststructuralist ones. While, for postmodernism, the end of the meta-narratives of Western modernity via *deconstruction* resulted in a juxtaposition of autonomous spheres (see Lyotard 1986), for postcolonialism, uncovering the connection between global power relationships established in the context of European colonial expansion and the historical and current inequality relations at the local, national and international levels is to be achieved through *decolonization*. The demarcation from postmodern strategies thus becomes an explicit step even in the formulation of the most prominent postcolonial ones. For Dipesh Chakrabarty,

> The project of provincializing Europe ... cannot be a project of cultural relativism. It cannot originate from the stance that the reason/science/universals that help define Europe as the modern are simply 'culture-specific' and therefore only belong to the European cultures (2000: 43).

The cultural relativism, that, within the postmodern celebration of sexual, cultural, racial, ethnic and religious difference, amounts to a "politics of image", is therefore increasingly confronted in the context of postcolonial approaches by an intercultural "politics of action" or "politics of despair" (Klein 2000: 124; Chakrabarty 2000: 45) aimed at disclosing the imperial and colonial history of repression and violence behind the establishment of the North-South divide. The different strategies consequently entail distinct policy implications, as reflected in the postmodern policy of multiculturalism on the one hand and the postcolonial plea for interculturality on the other. While the promotion of multiculturalism at the level of state policy and discourse relies on the principle of recognition and tolerance of racial, ethnic, religious, or sexual Others, interculturality – especially as defined and implemented by indigenous movements in Latin America – involves a questioning of the sociopolitical reality of (neo)colonialism reflected by the existing models of state, democracy, and nation and a transformation of these structures so as to guarantee full participation of all peoples in the exercise of political power (Walsh, forthcoming). Although the terms are often used interchangeably, they consequently stand for widely divergent agendas: multiculturalism, tantamount to the above-discussed identity politics of so-called "minority particularisms" in search of inclusion in the dominant system, aims at deconstructing present cultural hierarchies in exchange for a juxtaposition of cultural models; by contrast, interculturality is conceived as an ethical, political and epistemic project with the goal of decolonizing forms of social organization, institutional and government structures, as well as perspectives of knowledge originating in the sociohistorical context of the European modernity and imposed as universal during colonial and neocolonial times.

This becomes even clearer in the replacement of the unqualified postmodern notion of difference by the postcolonial concept of "colonial difference" (Chatterjee 1993; Mignolo 1995), employed both within Indian Subaltern Studies and Latin American decolonial thought[2] in order to explain the reorganization of differentiation criteria yielding the racial and ethnic structure of European colonies. Socio-economic and epistemic hierarchies out of which subaltern differences emerged in colonized territories are thus historically contextualized prior to considering possibilities for their transformation.

Why postcolonial sociology?

Part of the necessary contextualization of processes of hierarchization entails connecting institutionalized sociology to its location in the western world and its beginnings in the heyday of Western imperialism (see Seidman 2004: 261; Bhambra 2007a). Although the establishment of sociology as a discipline in Britain, Germany, France and Italy ran parallel to their race for African territories and the creation of their colonial empires in Asia and Africa, sociological categories, basic concepts and key explanatory models only reflected developments and experiences internal to Western Europe. Key moments of Western modernity, for which the sociological approach was supposed to offer an explanation, were considered to be the French Revolution and the English-led Industrial Revolution, but not Western European colonial politics or the accumulation of capital through the Atlantic slave trade and the overseas plantation economy.

The suppression of the colonial and imperial dynamics from the terminological toolkit of classical sociology applies to the respective national sociologies almost irrespective of the success of their states as colonial powers (see Bhambra 2007b: 872). The picture is slightly different as far as the period after the decolonization of Asia and Africa in the second half of the twentieth century is concerned. Unlike in the British context, in which the history of colonial rule plays a prominent role, in the German debate, the lesser colonial past as well as developments in

---

2   In contrast with postcolonial studies, the decolonial approach, originating in Latin America, departs from the critique of the primarily English-speaking field of postcolonial theory, viewed as having privileged British colonialism in India at the expense of other colonial experiences around the world. Decolonial studies consequently focus on manifold colonial and postcolonial contexts in an attempt to enforce "an epistemic diversality of world decolonial interventions" (Grosfoguel 2006: 142). While the distinction between postcolonial and decolonial is an important one, and debates about "decolonizing postcolonial studies" are ongoing, it is the common denominator of both approaches, i.e., the study of colonial relations of power and their present-day consequences, that we consider to be of particular relevance for sociology.

the postcolonial period are treated as negligible quantities at best (see Castro Varela/Dhawan 2005). Within German sociology, postcolonial perspectives thus have the reputation of being third-degree imports: firstly, from cultural or literature studies, secondly, from an Anglophone region, and thirdly, from a different, i.e., "genuinely" postcolonial context. As such, they are assigned a limited sociological relevance within German theoretical debates, but no independent sociological content (see Gutiérrez Rodriguez 1999: 21).

And yet postcolonial theories are aimed straight at the heart of sociology's central terminology. By criticizing binary oppositions such as West-Rest, First-Third World or modernity vs. tradition as essentialist and by drawing attention instead to the relationality between the concepts involved, they reveal the positively connoted ones – the West, the First World, modernity – as prescriptive and ahistorical universals (see Trouillot 2002: 848), to which no independent, objective social reality corresponds, and which therefore harbor strategies of exclusion. In turn, historical contextualization as a postcolonial method allows it to consider tradition

> not as an objective fact, as modern social theories all too easily presuppose, but as a set of projections from the perspective of theories of modernity onto everything from which one delimits oneself. At the same time, tradition is a necessary part of the discourse of modernity, without which modernity cannot exist or be mapped out. It makes up the field into which modernity penetrates and which it tries to subjugate. An end of [...] the idea of tradition would be the end of the discourse of modernity (Randeria et al. 2004: 18, our translation).

Postcolonial Macro-Sociology

The sociological globalization debate of the 1990s and the ensuing debate on multiple modernities seriously challenged both the national-centrism and the Western-centrism of conventional macro-sociological approaches. The globalized world ousted the nation-state as an analytical framework, and Western modernity was suddenly only one among many – though it (implicitly or explicitly) retained the flavor of historical starting point or at least key reference for subsequent non-Western variants – the Indian, the Islamic or the Latin American modernity. Yet the claim of the new macro-sociology to thus reach a global scope left the colonial gaze inherent in the available grand theories still untouched.

The common denominator – as well as the bone of contention – of theories of globalization and multiple modernities was the issue of convergence of societal patterns. Globalization theoreticists saw the emergence of a global civil society, of world culture and of global communication technologies as a sign of the worldwide assertion of Western development models (see Robinson 2001; Giddens 2002) – and therefore for the most part endorsed the convergence thesis. Multiple modernity scholars in turn stressed the diversity of institutional patterns, collective identities and socio-political projects created around the world as a result of the confrontation between the cultural program of Western European modernity and the social realities in the territories militarily and/or economically controlled by European powers (see Eisenstadt 2000) – and therefore emphasized divergence. At the same time, both diagnoses as well as the perspectives underlying them took the Western pattern of modernity as a reference point (see Spohn 2006). As Raewyn Connell (2007: 60) has demonstrated using the example of such central concepts as "global postmodernity" and "world risk society", most globalization theories do not evince a new research program tailored on the analysis of world society, but theoretical strategies we could reasonably describe as drawing on the "elevator effect" of macro-sociological explanations: trends originally observed and conceptualized in the context of metropolitan societies are scaled up one level and used to describe global processes. This makes globalization into the process by which risks, capital accumulation or hybridization literally become global in the conspicuous absence of any recognizable center of power or domination principle (see also Escobar 2007: 181ff.; Costa 2007: Chapter 4).

Such a position implicitly conveys the desire of many macro-sociologists after 1989 – in the wake of the delegitimization of Marxism as political and theoretical alternative – to take their distance from political economy as a social scientific approach, and thus delimit themselves from theories of imperialism, neo-colonialism and the world system (see Boatcă 2007). Tellingly for this tendency, the multiple modernities perspective tackled the analysis of divergence using a neo-Weberian approach which stressed the diversity of cultural programs associated with the expansion of Western modernity in the Americas, but not the structural dependencies and processes of hierarchization that accompanied colonization. By reducing the diversity of approaches to modernity to the cultural level, and by attributing a pioneering role to the Western European model in generating this diversity – i.e., "by not allowing difference to make a difference to the original categories of modernity" (Bhambra 2007b: 878) – multiple modernities authors paradoxically reinforced the very concept that they criticized – that of the self-sufficient, original Western modernity advocated in modernization theory. In the words of Shmuel Eisenstadt:

> While the common starting point was once the cultural program of modernity as it developed in the West, more recent developments have seen a multiplicity of cultural and social formations going very far beyond the homogenizing aspects of the original version (2000: 24).

To date, no unified postcolonial macro-sociology acts as a counterbalance to globalization and multiple modernities perspectives. Yet more and more approaches – only some of which are postcolonial by self-designation – attach central importance to the historical experience of colonialism for the explanation of global processes. On the one hand, neo-Marxist theories of globalization have pointed to the continuities between the liberal imperative of development determining the economic policies of ex-colonial countries after the Second World

War and the neoliberal postulate of globalization of the 1990s by emphasizing the neocolonial asymmetries of power that both helped reproduce. By identifying both development(alism) and globalization as projects or discursive strategies, they at the same time have shown how their naturalization ("there is no alternative") obscures the role played by colonialism in the construction of the models to be followed in each case (McMichael 2004; Wallerstein 2005). On the other hand, theoretical models situated at the intersection between anthropology, history and sociology, and which trace the emergence of "entangled modernities" and "connected histories" (Randeria 1999; Subrahmanyan 1997) back to the constitutive link between Western European patterns of modernity and (post)colonial modernization processes gain increasing attention within sociology (Costa 2007; Bhambra 2007a). Therein, tradition is not conceptualized as a rigid opposition to modernity, but as an integral part of an entangled colonial history, as a result of which the structural imbalance between "centers" and "peripheries" entailed the unequal distribution of definition power between the West and the "Rest" with respect to one's own degree of modernity (Therborn 2003; Knöbl 2007). In this case as well, there is no universal or first modernity acting as a guiding reference to latecomers, but several paths to entangled modernities.

The Latin American "decolonial approach" in turn raises the issue of entanglement by using the concept of "coloniality" in order to analyze the emergence of "tradition" in the context of the construction of difference from the alleged modernity of Western European colonial powers in those peripheral areas under colonial rule. Coloniality is therefore understood as a power relationship between (colonial) centers and (colonized) peripheries which outlasted administrative and political colonialism, the logic of which it continues to implement on the economic, social, cultural, and ideological levels. As such, it represents both the obverse (or dark side) and a necessary condition of Western modernity since the "discovery" of the New World. With the help of binary oppositions such as civilized-barbarian, rational-irrational, developed-underdeveloped or modern-traditional, modern identity could on the one hand be enclosed and demarcated from colonial alterity, and on the other the political intervention, the economic exploitation and epistemological paternalism towards the colonies be legitimized as a means of carrying the goods of modernity over to the periphery (see Quijano 2000; Dussel 2002; Grosfoguel 2002). The social imaginary of the modern world was therefore configured around a global classification system which elevated the Western European civilization to the status of a universal standard and through which the economic and political power asymmetries between centers and peripheries were reflected on the cultural and epistemological level (see Mignolo 2000: 13).

The corresponding Occidentalist rhetoric passed through several phases in which the construction of colonial difference from the Western European self was alternately organized around concepts of race, ethnicity, or both. In turn, hierarchization proceeded along a spatial dimension (Christians in the North vs. savages in the South), a temporal one (civilized in the core vs. primitives in the periphery), or a mixture of the two (developed vs. underdeveloped), depending on the dominant European worldview of the time (Mignolo 2000; Boatcă 2009). The coloniality of the resulting heterogeneous power structure – i.e., not merely of an economic, but of a political, cultural and epistemological nature – is revealed by the enduring character of global inequality dimensions of colonial origin:

> [...] If we observe the main lines of social domination and exploitation on a global scale, the main lines of power today, and the distribution of resources and work among the world population, it is very clear that the large majority of the exploited, the dominated, the discriminated against, are precisely the members of the 'races', 'ethnies', or 'nations' into which the colonized populations were categorized in the formative process of that world power, from the conquest of America and onward (Quijano 2007: 169).

While the approach of the "global postmodernity" remains trapped in Eurocentrism by pleading for a mere recognition of these differences, at the same time as it maintains globalization as their universal goal, the project of "transmodernity" (Dussel 2002) assumes the potential universality of all cultural elements representing the "excluded exteriority" of Western modernity, which can now be transformed from this very exteriority. Much like in the Indian Subaltern Studies approach (see Chakrabarty 2000), the critique of modernity from the subaltern position of coloniality unveils the West's universal history as a local history with particular character. Its global projects – whether civilization, development, or globalization – appear in this light as generalizations of Western Europe's local historical experience meant to underpin its own claim to power, and expose the (post)colonial continuities in the hierarchization of difference, rather than celebrate differences as such. Terms such as "transmodern" and "coloniality" are therefore not mere substitute categories, that could – or should – be swapped for "tradition", but they entail the possibility of reconceptualizing modernity in an historical perspective by uncovering its colonial counterpart. They thus allow us to address the mutual interdependencies between development and underdevelopment, inclusion and exclusion, instead of locating them in converging or diverging contexts of modernity on the one hand, and tradition on the other.

Meso-Analytic Level: The Political Sociology of Power Relations

Recent analyses dedicated to the research of disputes and asymmetries of power in various contexts allow us to identify a common set of critiques which forms the nucleus of what we call postcolonial political sociology. Unlike in conventional political sociology, in this case, national borders do not shape the central analytic unit, nor do national political institutions constitute the preferential focus of investigation. Instead, the emphasis lies on power relations, which involve actors of various natures (states, multilateral organizations, social movements) on different levels (local, regional, national, global).

The interest in power disputes also conditions the conceptual apparatus mobilized for these studies, to the extent that categories which do not emphasize asymmetrical relations between world regions and social groups are avoided or critically deconstructed. The first efforts of critical deconstruction in this field take aim at the evolutionist idea of development drawn from modernization theory, according to which modernization involves the simple transfer of ways of life and of social structures found in Europe to the rest of the world. Thus, various works in the field of postcolonial studies show that development does not represent a mere process of irradiation of modern forms from Europe, but an interdependent transformation that simultaneously produces prosperity in the wealthiest nations and disadvantages for the poorest (see Pieterse and Parekh 1995; Dussel 2000; Escobar 2004; for an overview: Manzo 1999).

In general terms, it can be argued that the critical effort undertaken by postcolonial political sociology is developing in two distinct directions: the first line of research includes studies about the political relations between the various regions of the world and can be interpreted as a reaction against approaches which, after the fall of real socialism, describe the new international order as a space no longer dominated by disputes and conflicts, but by horizontal relations and the search for the realization of supposedly universal interests (world peace, human rights, sustainable development etc). Concepts derived from this context, and, in particular, works based on the idea of governance,[3] are the target of sharp criticism from postcolonial studies (Ziai 2006; Randeria 2003; Eckert and Randeria 2006). According to this criticism, the emphasis on the concept of governance presents the illusion of an ecumenical and conflict-free international arena in the realm of which those objectives common to all of humanity always prevail. An analysis of the new configurations of global politics sensitive to power relations should provide precisely the opposite, that is, elucidate how asymmetries are reproduced and how new inequalities are produced in the international realm:

> In the new architecture of global governance, power appears in a diffuse and fleeting form, and the magnitude of sovereignty, in each case, appears strictly related to political fields, territories and specific population groups. [...]. It

---

3   These contributions seek to broaden the conventional concept of political steering used in the political sciences, including, in addition to the nation states and international and intergovernmental organizations, non-state actors as well as decision-making structures on different levels (a multilevel approach) as part of a complex process of governing beyond national frontiers. After its introduction in 1995 through the "Commission on Global Governance", the concept of governance acquired growing prominence both in academic discussions as well as in political praxis through its adoption by organizations ranging from the United Nations Development Program (UNDP) to the European Commission (see, among many others, Brand et al. 2000).

is necessary to base the study of globalization on distinct ethnographies and historic case studies that link the micro and macro levels. This allows working with the specificities present in the various forms of transnationalization in the different regions and in the different "epochs" (Eckert/Randeria 2006: 16ff. our translation).

The concretization of the postcolonial research program in terms of the perspective described is already under way, at least in part. One example is the careful deconstruction of the role of the concept of the sovereign within the history of international law developed by B.S. Chimni (2004) or the critical treatment conferred by A. Anghie (2004) to the new tools of international administrative law. These works represent exemplary efforts of questioning the universalism professed in legal discourses. They indicate that institutions of international law also play a role in the perpetuation of colonial forms of domination and of the legal and real privileges that the wealthiest segments enjoy in various parts of the world.

The second development line of postcolonial political sociology is related to the studies about the processes of democratization that take place in Latin America, Africa, Asia and South and Eastern Europe since the 1970s.

The transition paradigm, dominant since the 1980s (O'Donnell, Schmitter and Whitehead 1986), applies the fundamentals of modernization theory to politics, transforming the research about democratization into an implicitly comparative field, within which the models of transformation observed in the consolidated "hyperreal" (Chakrabarty 2000) democracies of Western Europe are treated as the only valid model for democracy. Actors and structures found in "other" societies are signified as deficits of or obstacles to democratization.

With the development of democracy in "non-Western" societies, it however became evident that the theoretical premises and the methods of analysis of transition research were not suitable for either identifying the difficulties encountered or even adequately framing positive developments. Civil societies and local public spheres have shown different dynamics than the one supposed by transition research. Thus, actors and structures such as ethnic movements or neighborhood associations, which, according to the concepts of politics used in transition research, are not the first carriers of democratic values, perform a central role in furthering democracy in these societies (Costa and Avritzer 2004). At the same time, legal and decision-making structures implemented according to the molds of similar institutions in North America or Europe do not fulfill the expected functions: the new parliaments prove to be chronically vulnerable to corruption and the abyss between formal law and social reality seems to be an unconquerable problem (Méndez, O'Donnell and Pinheiro 1999). Nevertheless, transition research continues to seek a solution for its own analytical-theoretical insufficiencies in the realm of implicit comparison with "mature" Western democracies, while treating the new democracies as "defective democracies", ruled by "failed states" and characterized by "low intensity citizenship" (O'Donnell 2007).

Various contributions in the realm of postcolonial research in different continents have shaped a sociology of democratization that in part complements and in part corrects the transition paradigm. Following these contributions, the local structures found in the various regions are no longer presented as a late copy of the corresponding structures observed in Western Europe or North America, but interpreted considering the socio-historical context that gives them meaning.[4] At the same time, postcolonial research attempts to overcome the endogenism of transition research, by investigating local transformations in the context of their interrelations with the interventions of multilateral organizations (Macamo 2006; Walsh 2005), with transnational conflicts around the use of local natural resources (Escobar 2004; Randeria 2003) and of the connections established by regional democratic actors on the global plane (Costa 2007; Randeria 2005).

In sum, postcolonial research in the field of political sociology supplies crucial impulses for critical reflection about the constellations of power that are formed in the local and national realms and how they are articulated globally. While classical political sociology is gradually losing ground due to its limitation to national borders and its exclusive concentration on institutionalized forms of politics, postcolonial research supplies new reasons and motivations for sociology's interest in politics. Moreover, by bringing the question of power once again to the center of the research interest, postcolonial political sociology also fills the cognitive gaps left by political science in its recent process of specialization and growing orientation towards problem-solving.

For a Micro-Sociology of Cultural Relations

At least since the second half of the twentieth century, the constructivist concept of culture has become the sole concept of culture accepted as valid by contemporary sociology. Previous primordialist attempts to define culture based on metaphysical or supposedly natural ties (race, climatic dispositions, predestination) have thereby lost legitimacy. Although such definitions can still be investigated as self-representations of certain actors, they no longer count as sociological explanations.

According to sociology's constructivist concept of culture, the constructed character of cultures can be observed both in the constitution of individual identities as well as in the differentiation of cultural units. While, according to this reading, individual cultural identity is an intersubjective process through which societal dispositions are internalized and processed in the form of a stable individual identity (see Mead 1969: 86ff.), the constitution of broad units, such as ethnicities, nations, and cultural minorities implies a long term historical development marked by the consolidation of a specialized communicative infrastructure in

---

4   The convincing study by Randeria (2005) about the political contribution of castes as actors in Indian civil society constitutes a good example of how to investigate local development on the basis of its own social semantic.

the processing and transmission of common experiences. It is in the realm of these processes of symbolic transmission that both the cultural groups to which a concrete (sociological) existence is attributed – the British, the Europeans, the Muslims – as well as the different *cultural units* (British culture, German culture, etc.) are formed.

Culture, in this conception, is exemplarily defined by Habermas, as a

> set of conditions of possibility for activities related to the solution of problems. It offers to the subjects that grow within it not only linguistic and cognitive capacities, as well as those for action, but also grammatically pre-structured worldviews and archives of accumulated knowledge (2005: 313, our translation).

For postcolonial studies, this way of defining culture as involving demarcated and separated units in the realm of which common elements are produced and reproduced comes with theoretical, empirical and methodological insufficiencies. According to postcolonial criticism, the sociological concept of culture supposes homogenizing identity constructions nearly always defined by a link to a territory and associated to one's place of birth or residence, cultural and social surroundings, etc. This concept of culture does not take into account the separation between the social and the territory and is blind to the growing deterritorialization of the processes of cultural circulation in the contemporary world (Hall 2000: 99; 1994: 44).

From a theoretical point of view, postcolonial studies reproach the dominant sociological concept of culture with not being suited to detect the power relations inscribed in cultural contacts. That is, to the degree to which sociology uses cultural units defined by social actors themselves as descriptive and politically neutral categories, the discipline is insensitive to the fact that cultural ascriptions presuppose asymmetric power relations and at the same time contribute to their reproduction.

Pieterse's research on the tensions between national identities and ethnicity formation illustrates this well:

> To understand how cultural difference is constructed is to understand the formation and politics of national identity [...]. National identity is a historical process; ethnicity, identity politics, and multiculturalism are phases in this ongoing process. From a historical point of view, nation formation is a dominant form of ethnicity. In short, nationhood is *dominant ethnicity* and minorities or ethnic groups represent *subaltern ethnicity* (Pieterse 2007: 16. emphasis in the original).

From a methodological point of view, the way that sociology treats culture(s) is equally problematic for postcolonial studies, given that the self-representations of social actors are not critically deconstructed, but accepted as evidence of the existence of cultural identities. The established sociological concept of culture does not take into account that even the reference to an original and authentic tradition is part of the performance – understood in the linguistic sense as action and in the sense of mise-en-scène – of difference and can only be understood based on an analysis of the social-discursive context in which it is inserted:

> Terms of cultural engagement, whether antagonistic or affiliative, are produced performatively. The representation of difference must not be hastily read as the reflection of pre-given ethnic or cultural traits set in the fixed tablet of tradition (Bhabha 1994: 2).

Through its criticism of the sociological concept of culture and of preceding approaches of the sociology of culture, postcolonial studies provide sociological research with a set of categories and methodological procedures that can be understood as pieces of an innovative micro-sociology of the negotiations of cultural differences. Particularly relevant here are contributions in the realm of British Cultural Studies, supported by Stuart Hall and Paul Gilroy.

While Hall (1994) basically concentrates on the internal tensions of British anti-racist movements, Gilroy (1995, 2000) introduces a comparative dimension by searching for political and cultural interactions within the imagined space of the "Black Atlantic".[5] The starting point of the two authors is the idea of difference that they borrow from poststructuralism and, more precisely, the concept of *différance* used by Derrida. They use the notion of *différance* to deconstruct the antinomic discourses that counter the "I" and the "other", the "we" and the "they" (Hall 1994: 137ff). In this context, the construction of cultural identities is understood as a dynamic political process in which identity, or, as Hall prefers, identification, is not expressed in the interior of a closed system of cultural signs. To the contrary: identification is, for Hall, built in the realm of politics itself and follows the possibilities of recognition offered by the social context.[6]

This is not to say that the evocation of cultural units such as "the British" or "the Americans" is irrelevant for the cultural constructions observed. Nevertheless, these cultural identities do not function as a computer program that defines *a priori*

---

5   In the variation emphasized by Gilroy, the concept of Black Atlantic presents a dual definition. Empirically, the Black Atlantic concerns the process of diffusion and reconstruction of a "black culture" that accompanies the routes of the African diaspora. Politically, the Black Atlantic refers to a dimension based in modernity, to the degree to which it illuminates the nexus between slavery and modernity, and in addition, reveals modern political institutions as spaces particularly suited for the reproduction of visions and interests of the white man (Gilroy 1993).

6   The key concept used by Hall to describe the position of the subject in the realm of a determined discursive formation is "articulation", understood in a dual manner, that is, both the idea of expression as well as the link between two elements which may come together. The principle of contingent articulation can, according to Hall, be observed both in the formation of the individual subject as well as in the production of collective subjects (Hall 1996).

behavior models; they are first discursive interpellations in front of which those involved in a social interaction are obliged to position themselves. The identification is constituted dynamically and interactively in a realm of negotiations involving ascriptions, discriminations and private interests.

Conclusions: Towards a Postcolonial Sociology

Our very attempt at delineating a program for a *postcolonial sociology* is in itself indicative of our epistemological position. Unlike McLennan (2003), for example, we do not understand postcolonial analysis as involving the end of sociology as a discipline. Rather, in the approximation between sociology and postcolonial studies, we see a chance at completing and expanding sociology at precisely those turning points where it appears to reach its epistemological limits. When we speak of complementarity in this context, we mean that both the conceptual apparatus and the methods of postcolonial studies are compatible with a sociological approach. Above all, we find the epistemological interests of sociology on the one hand and postcolonial studies on the other to be overlapping in a decisive aspect: in their claim of being able to situate social relations and societal structures within complex analytical matrices.

The faults that postcolonial criticism finds with sociology are not irreparable and inevitable deficiencies of an academic discipline, but rather consequences of a particular institutionalization process. As shown above, both sociology's focus on the nation-state and its "colonial gaze" on non-Western societies derive from this institutional history. At the same time, reflexivity, openness, self-criticism and the capacity for changes in perspective are also part of the self-understanding of sociology, they are constitutive elements of its raison d'être. Recognizing the need to react to the narrowing of its own critical perspective should therefore be part of the dynamics of sociology. This is precisely where postcolonial studies enter the field.

At the macro-sociological level, the results of postcolonial analysis lead to an overcoming of the conventional history of linear evolution of modern societies, without falling into the particularism of infinitely multiplied modernities. To this effect, the postcolonial concept of entangled modernity as well as the concept of shared and connected histories point to the entanglements but also to the ruptures and asymmetries in the constitution of the modern and (post-) colonial world.

On the meso-analytical level, postcolonial studies shed light on the interpenetrations between actors and historically constructed power structures tied to contexts of action on different levels (local, regional, transnational and transregional), thereby contributing a considerable epistemological potential. These heuristic possibilities are neither accessible to conventional political sociology, which concentrates on the national space and on established political actors, nor to the field of international relations, which has largely turned blind to power relations.

At the micro-sociological level, the contribution of postcolonial studies lies, above all, in an expanded and more dynamic sociological concept of culture. Accordingly, the relevant constituting pieces of social interactions are not cultural repertoires originating in hermetically closed cultures bound to a determined geographic space, but spontaneously articulated cultural differences. Unlike in the postmodern interpretation of poststructuralism, however, the articulation of differences in the postcolonial reading has nothing to do with the exercise of a hyper-liberal freedom of identity. Postcolonial studies treat differences in the context of societal structures, understood as structures of power and thus contain a clear sociological scope.

In this sense, postcolonial sociology would be the equivalent of a context-specific, history sensitive sociology of power, the subject matter of which is not the Western world, or a host of modernities endlessly pluralized in postmodern fashion, but the "entangled modernity" (Randeria 1999) emerged at the intersection of military power, capital expansion and transculturality; not the North Atlantic civilization, but the transmodernity of the twenty-first century (Dussel 2002) resulted from the North's interactions with the Black Atlantic as well as with other diasporic and minority experiences of the "majority world" (Connell 2007).

Bibliography

Anghie, A. 2004. *Imperialism, Sovereignty and the Making of International Law.* New York: Cambridge University Press.

Asad, T. (ed.) 1973. *Anthropology and the Colonial Encounter.* London: Ithaca Press.

Bhabha, H. 1994. *The Location of Culture.* London/New York: Routledge.

Bhambra, G. 2007a. *Rethinking Modernity: Postcolonialism and the Sociological Imagination.* London: Palgrave Macmillan.

Bhambra, G. 2007b. Sociology and Postcolonialism: Another 'Missing' Revolution? *Sociology*, 41(5), 871-84.

Boatcă, M. 2007: Macrosociology, in *Blackwell Encyclopedia of Sociology*, edited by G. Ritzer, [Online]. Available at: http://www.sociologyencyclopedia.com/public/LOGIN?sessionid=003607f9450b9af544e07279d1800e6d&authstatus code=414 [accessed 20 September 2009].

Boatcă, M. 2009. Lange Wellen des Okzidentalismus. Ver-Fremden von Geschlecht, Rasse und Ethnizität im modernen Weltsystem, in *Kritik des Okzidentalismus. Transdisziplinäre Beiträge zu (Neo-)Orientalismus und Geschlecht*, edited by G. Dietze, C. Brunner and E. Wenzel. Bielefeld: transcript, 233-50.

Brand, U., Brunnengräber, A., Haake, M., Stock, C. and Wahl, P. 2000. *Global Governance. Alternative zur neoliberalen Globalisierung?* Münster: Westfälisches Dampfboot.

Burawoy, M. 2008. Rejoinder: For a Subaltern Global Sociology? *Current Sociology*, 56(3), 435-44.

Caillé, A. 2007. Introduction to Symposium. *European Journal of Social Theory*, 10(2), 179-83.

Castro Varela, M. and Dhawan, N. 2005. *Postkoloniale Theorie. Eine kritische Einführung*. Bielefeld: transcript.

Chakrabarty, D. 2000. *Provincializing Europe. Postcolonial Thought and Historical Difference*. Princeton: Princeton University Press.

Chatterjee, P. 1993. *The Nation and its Fragments*. Princeton: Princeton University Press.

Chimni, B.S. 2004. International Institutions Today: An Imperial Global State in the Making. *The European Journal of International Law*, 15(1), 1-37.

Connell, R. 2007. *Southern Theory: The Global Dynamics of Knowledge in Social Science*. Crows Nest: Allen & Unwin.

Coronil, F. 2004. Latin American Postcolonial Studies and Global Decolonization, in *Postcolonial Studies Reader*, edited by N. Lazarus. Cambridge: Cambridge University Press, 221-40.

Costa, S. 2005. (Un-)Möglichkeiten einer postkolonialen Soziologie, in *Jenseits von Zentrum und Peripherie: Zur Verfassung der fragmentierten Wertgesellschaft*, vol. 2, edited by H. Brunkhorst and S. Costa. München/Mering: Rainer Hampp Verlag, 221-50.

Costa, S. 2007. *Vom Nordatlantik zum "Black Atlantic". Postkoloniale Konfigurationen und Paradoxien transnationaler Politik*. Bielefeld: Transcript. Portuguese: *Dois Atânticos*. Belo Horizonte: Ed. UFMG.

Dirlik, A. 1994. The Postcolonial Aura: Third World Criticism in the Age of Global Capitalism. *Critical Inquiry*, Winter 1994, 328-56.

Dussel, E. 2000. Europa, modernidad y eurocentrismo, in *La colonialidad del saber: eurocentrismo y ciencias sociales*, edited by E. Lander. Caracas: Unesco/UCV, 59-78.

Dussel, E. 2002. World-System and Trans-Modernity. *Nepantla: Views from South*, 3(2), 221-44.

Eckert, A. and Randeria, S. 2006. *Vom Imperialismus zum Empire? Globalisierung aus außereuropäischer Sicht*. Frankfurt am Main: Suhrkamp. Revised version of Introduction [Online] available at: http://www.ethno.uzh.ch/publications/pdfs/2009VomImperialismusZumEmpire.pdf [accessed: 5 September 2009].

Eisenstadt, S.N. 2000. Multiple Modernities. *Daedalus*, 129, 1-30.

Eisenstadt, S.N. 2003. *Comparative Civilizations and Multiple Modernities*. Brill: Leiden.

Escobar, A. 2004. Beyond the Third World: Imperial Globality, Global Coloniality and Anti-Globalisation Social Movements. *Third World Quarterly*, 25(1), 207-30.

Escobar, A. 2005. *Más allá del Tercer Mundo. Globalización y diferencia*. Bogotá: ICANH.

Escobar, A. 2007. Worlds and Knowledges Otherwise: The Latin American Modernity/ Coloniality Research Program. *Cultural Studies*, 21(2-3), 179-210.

Fabian, J. 1983. *Time and the Other: How Anthropology Makes its Object*. New York: Columbia University Press.

Friedrichsmeyer, S., Lennox, S. and Zantop, S. (eds) 1998. *The Imperialist Imagination: German Colonialism and Its Legacy*. Ann Arbor: University of Michigan Press.

Giddens, A. 2002. *Runaway World: How Globalization is Reshaping Our Lives*. London: Profile.

Gilroy, P. 1993. *The Black Atlantic: Modernity and Double Consciousness*. Cambridge: Harvard University Press.

Gilroy, P. 1995. Roots and Routes: Black Identity as an Outernational Project, in *Racial and Ethnic Identity: Psychological Development and Creative Expression*, edited by H. Harris, H. Blue and E. Griffith. London/New York: Routledge, 15-30.

Gilroy, P. 2000. *Against Race: Imagining Political Culture Beyond the Color Line*. Cambridge: Belknap/Harvard.

Grosfoguel, R. 2002. Colonial Difference, Geopolitics of Knowledge and Global Coloniality in the Modern/Colonial Capitalist World-System. *Review*, 15(3), 203-24.

Grosfoguel, R. 2006. Preface. *Review,* special issue 'From Postcolonial Studies to Decolonial Studies: Decolonizing Postcolonial Studies', 19(2), 141-43.

Gutiérrez Rodríguez, E. 1999. Fallstricke des Feminismus. Das Denken 'kritischer Differenzen' ohne geopolitische Kontextualisierung. *polylog. Zeitschrift für interkulturelles Philosophieren*, 4, 13-24, [Online]. Available at: http://them. polylog.org/2/age-de.htm [accessed 5 September 2009].

Habermas, J. 2005. *Zwischen Naturalismus und Religion. Philosophische Aufsätze*. Frankfurt am Main: Suhrkamp.

Hall, S. 1994. *Rassismus und kulturelle Identität*. Hamburg: Argument.

Hall, S. 1996. On Postmodernism and Articulation, in Stuart Hall, *Critical Dialogues in Cultural Studies*, edited by D. Morley and C. Kuan-Hsing. London/New York: Routledge, 131-50.

Hall, S. 2000. *Cultural Studies. Ein politisches Theorieprojekt*. Hamburg: Argument.

Hall, S. 2002. Wann gab es 'das Postkoloniale?' Denken an der Grenze, in *Jenseits des Eurozentrismus. Postkoloniale Perspektiven in den Geschichts – und Kulturwissenschaften*, edited by S. Conrad and S. Randeria. Frankfurt am Main: Campus, 219-46.

Klein, N. 2000. *No Logo*. New York: Picador.

Knöbl, W. 2007. *Die Kontingenz der Moderne. Wege in Europa, Asien und Amerika*. Frankfurt am Main/New York: Campus.

Lyotard, J.-F. 1986. *Das postmoderne Wissen. Ein Bericht*. Wien: Edition Passagen.

Manzo, K. 1999. The International Imagination: Themes and Arguments in International Studies. *Review of International Studies*, 25, 493-506.

McLennan, G. 2003. Sociology, Eurocentrism and Postcolonial Theory. *European Journal of Social Theory*, 6(1), 69-86.

Macamo, E. 2006. The Hidden Side of Modernity in Africa – Domesticating Savage Lives, in *The Plurality of Modernity: Decentring Sociology*, edited by S. Costa, J.M. Domingues, W. Knöbl and J.P. Da Silva. München/Mering: Rainer Hampp, 161-78.

McMichael, P. 2004. *Development and Social Change: A Global Perspective*. Thousand Oaks: Pine Forge Press.

Mead, G.H. 1969. *Geist, Identität und Gesellschaft*. Frankfurt am Main: Suhrkamp, (orig. 1934).

Méndez, J.E., O'Donnell, G. and Pinheiro, P.S. (eds) 1999. *The (Un)Rule of Law and the Underprivileged in Latin America*. Notre Dame/Indiana: Notre Dame University Press.

Mignolo, W. 1995. *The Darker Side of the Renaissance. Literacy, Territoriality, and Colonization*. Ann Arbor: University of Michigan Press.

Mignolo, W. 2000. *Local Histories/Global Designs: Coloniality, Subaltern Knowledges, and Border Thinking*. Princeton: Princeton University Press.

O'Donnell, G. 2007. *Dissonances: Democratic Critiques of Democracy*. Notre Dame: University of Notre Dame Press.

O'Donnell, G., Schmitter, P. and Whitehead, L. 1986. *Transitions from Authoritarian Rule*. Baltimore/London: John Hopkins University Press.

Pieterse, J.N. 2007. *Ethnicities and Global Multiculture: Pants for an Octopus*. Lanham: Rowman & Littlefield.

Pieterse, J.N. and Parekh, B. 1995. Shifting Imaginaries: Decolonization, Internal Decolonization, Postcoloniality, in *The Decolonization of Imagination: Culture, Knowledge and Power*, edited by J.N. Pieterse and B. Parekh. London: Zed Books, 1-20.

Quijano, A. 2000. Coloniality of Power and Eurocentrism in Latin America. *International Sociology*, 15(2), 215-32.

Quijano, A. 2007. Coloniality and Modernity/Rationality. *Cultural Studies*, 21(2-3), 168-78.

Randeria, S. 1999. Geteilte Geschichte und verwobene Moderne, in *Zukunftsentwürfe. Ideen für eine Kultur der Veränderung*, edited by J. Rüsen. Frankfurt am Main: Campus, 87-96.

Randeria, S. 2003. Glocalisation of Law: Environmental Justice, World Bank, NGOs and the Cunning State in India. *Current Sociology*, special issue 2003, 305-28.

Randeria, S. 2005. Verwobene Moderne: Zivilgesellschaft, Kastenbindungen und nicht staatliches Familienrecht im (post)kolonialen Indien, in *Jenseits von Zentrum und Peripherie: Zur Verfassung der fragmentierten Wertgesellschaft*, vol. 2, edited by H. Brunkhorst and S. Costa. München/Mering: Rainer Hampp Verlag, 169-96.

Randeria, S., Fuchs, M. and Linkenbach, A. 2004. Konfigurationen der Moderne: Zur Einleitung, in *Diskurse zu Indien*, Sonderheft der "Sozialen Welt", edited by S. Randeria, M. Fuchs and A. Linkenbach. München: Nomos, 9-34.

Robinson, W. 2001. Social Theory and Globalization: The Rise of a Transnational State. *Theory and Society*, 30(2), 157-200.

Seidman, S. 2004. *Contested Knowledge. Social Theory Today*. Malden: Blackwell.

Shohat, E. 1992. Notes on the "Post-colonial". *Social Text*, 31-32 (Spring), 99-113.

Spohn, W. 2006. Multiple, Entangled, Fragmented and Other Modernities. Reflections on Comparative Sociological Research on Europe, North and Latin America, in *The Plurality of Modernity. Decentring Sociology*, edited by S. Costa, W. Knöbl, J.M. Domingues and J. Pereira da Silva. München/Mering: Hampp, 11-22.

Subrahmanyan, S. 1997. Connected Histories. Notes Toward a Reconfiguration of Early Modern Eurasia. *Modern Asian Studies*, 31(3), 735-62.

Therborn, G. 2003. Entangled Modernities. *European Journal of Social Theory*, 6(3), 293-305.

Touraine, A. 2007. Sociology after Sociology. *European Journal of Social Theory*, 10(2), 184-93.

Trouillot, M.-R. 2002. North Atlantic Universals: Analytical Fictions, 1492-1945. *The South Atlantic Quarterly*, 101(4), 840-58.

Wallerstein, I. 2005. After Developmentalism and Globalization, What? *Social Forces*, 83(3), 321-36.

Walsh, C. 2005. (De)Construir la interculturalidad. Consideraciones críticas desde la política, la colonialidad y los movimientos indígenas y negros en el Ecuador, in *Interculturalidad y política. Desafíos y posibilidades*, edited by N. Fuller. Lima: Red para el Desarollo de las Ciencias Sociales.

Walsh, C. 2007. Shifting the Geopolitics of Critical Knowledge. Decolonial Thought and Cultural Studies "Others" in the Andes. *Cultural Studies*, 21(2-3), 224-39.

Walsh, C. (forthcoming). Interculturality and the Coloniality of Power. An Other Thinking and Positioning from the Colonial Difference, in *Coloniality of Power, Transmodernity, and Border Thinking*, edited by R. Grosfoguel, J.D. Saldivar, and N. Maldonado-Torres. Durham: Duke University Press.

Wittrock, B. 2000. Modernity: One, None, or Many? European Origins and Modernity as a Global Condition. *Daedalus*, 129, 31-60.

Ziai, A. 2006. *Zwischen Global Governance und Post-Development. Entwicklungspolitik aus diskursanalytischer Perspektive.* Münster: Westfälisches Dampfboot.

Chapter 2

Sociology After Postcolonialism: Provincialized Cosmopolitanisms and Connected Sociologies

Gurminder K. Bhambra

Recent debates on 'public sociology', sparked off by Michael Burawoy's (2005a) ASA Presidential Address on the subject, have addressed sociology in a global world with a view to reconnect sociological accounts with normative claims.[1] The first of these concerns has also been influenced by the emergence of postcolonial critiques, as well as earlier arguments from the field of development studies, which, as Leela Gandhi argues, 'attempt to reassert the epistemological value and agency of the non-European world' (1998: 44). Increasing recognition of the global context of sociology is similarly evident in recent arguments against the supposed methodological nationalism of the past (Beck 2000). These arguments attempt to unify explanatory and normative concerns in a cosmopolitanism for the twenty-first century. For Beck and Sznaider, for example, 'what cosmopolitanism *is* cannot ultimately be separated from what cosmopolitanism *should be*' (2006: 4). This conjunction of arguments about global sociology and normative claims about cosmopolitanism, and the problematic relation of each with postcolonial critiques, is the topic of this chapter.

Briefly, postcolonialism is perceived to involve a form of particularism, which is in conflict with a necessary universalism required by critical social science. In the first part, I shall look at the historiographical assumptions and explanatory lacunae in mainstream sociological accounts of modernity from a postcolonial perspective. This will be followed by a discussion of the implicit and problematic sociological assumptions in the normative arguments about 'global' cosmopolitanism. It is the combination of two 'flawed' sociologies (that of the classical tradition and its contemporary residue, and that which underpins claims for a new cosmopolitanism), that produces, for their proponents, a failure to recognize that it could indeed be possible to learn from postcolonialism without a need for universal categories to ground any dialogue. I shall argue that the period of sociology's disciplinary formation was also the heyday of European colonialism, yet the colonial relationship has usually not figured in the development of sociological understandings. Further,

1   I should like to thank Rodrigo Cordero-Vega, Robert Fine, John Holmwood, Robbie Shilliam and the editors of this volume for helpful comments on this chapter.

recent attempts to address global issues from an other-than-Western perspective have continued to rest upon a universalistic cosmopolitanism grounded in the Western tradition. The voice of non-Western others continues to be displaced. I shall argue for a form of cosmopolitanism – 'provincialized cosmopolitanism' – that is sensitive to the voice of non-Western others and flattens the hierarchies of knowledge implicit in 'global cosmopolitanism'.

Sociology and Modernity

Modernity is arguably the central concept of sociology. Regardless of the different interpretations put forward by sociologists about the nature of modernity, the timing of its emergence, or its continued character today, all agree on its role in the establishment of sociology as a discipline (see, for example, Nisbet 1966, Giddens 1973, Heilbron 1995).[2] Indeed, setting out the parameters of 'the modern' has been defined as a key task of sociology both conceptually and methodologically. The world historical implications of the French and Industrial Revolutions stimulated debate about the emergence of a *modern* world and this world was held to require a distinctively *modern* form of explanation. In the process, ideas of rupture and difference became the paradigmatic assumptions that framed both the standard methodological problems posed by social inquiry and the explanations posited in resolving them.

Ideas of temporal and spatial disjuncture at the heart of understandings of modernity have, however, come to be challenged by many theorists and, correspondingly, there is an increasing hesitancy in equating westernization with progress. Despite this, it is my contention that the 'West' is still seen as the 'lead society', to use Parsons's (1971) significant formulation, albeit the lead society within what is now characterized as a plurality of 'multiple modernities' (for example, Wittrock 1998, Eisenstadt 2000) as opposed to the lead society within the linear model of development of earlier modernization theory (for example, Lerner 1958, Rostow 1960). The idea of modernity *as the new* continues to require the specification of a temporal break – between the agrarian pre-modern and the industrial modern – also to be mirrored in spatial terms. This occurs, as Bhabha argues (1994: 243-6), with the colonial space becoming the 'non-place' set against the colonialists' place in, and of, the modern.

The history of modernity, then, comes to rest on 'the *writing out* of the colonial and postcolonial moment' (Bhabha 1994: 250). Further, with the spatial ordering of the time of modernity, a particular theory of cultural difference is instituted – one which installs 'cultural homogeneity into the sign of modernity' (Bhabha 1994: 243). For postcolonial theorists, this ultimately demonstrates the ethnocentric limitations of the concept; specifically, the way in which a particularism becomes transformed into a universal. Sociological theorists of modernity (and of multiple

---

2   The arguments of this section are developed in more detail in Bhambra (2007a).

modernities), put forward ideas of the modern world emerging out of the twin processes of economic and political revolution located in Europe, thus conflating Europe with modernity and rendering the process of becoming modern, at least in the first instance, one of endogenous European development. Accordingly, the rest of the world is assumed to be external to this world-historical process and, concretely, colonial connections significant to the processes under discussion are erased, or rendered silent.[3]

This is evident in the historiography of the Industrial Revolution whereby all achievements within the geographical space of Europe are seen to have emerged as a consequence of the endogenous efforts of Europeans alone. The British production of cotton textiles is one such instance, and is often put forward as a leading example of the success of the emerging factory mode of production. Yet, what is missing from this narrative is the simultaneous destruction of the cotton textile industry elsewhere which opened up external markets for the export of British goods, namely in India and Ireland. The impact of a mutual process of industrialization at 'home' and de-industrialization elsewhere upon the subsequent success of British industry is rarely discussed. David Washbrook (1997) is a notable exception arguing, as he does, that the mechanization of the cotton textiles manufacture in Britain has to be understood as part of 'a much longer "global" history of the fabric itself' (1997: 417). Cotton, as Washbrook argues, first came to Britain from India, as did the knowledge of how to design, weave, and dye it. Further, it was largely grown in the southern plantations of the United States by Africans brought over as slaves and was part of the triangular trade that linked Africa to the Americas to Europe. To understand the global success of the mechanization of the cotton industry simply in terms of an evolution from a pre-existing British domestic system of production without recognizing the context of its relationships with other parts of the world is seriously to distort its history.[4]

A similar process of exclusion is evident in the dominant accounts of the 'Democratic Revolutions'. For example, we see that the dates and names associated with it, as Fischer (2004) argues, most often include 1789, 1848, Robespierre, Napoleon, Hegel and so forth – the colonies, and, in particular, Haiti,[5] rarely make it into the canonical histories of the concept. As Trouillot (1995) argues, texts as far apart politically as Hobsbawm's (1962) *Age of Revolution* and the Penguin *Dictionary of Modern History* ignore the Haitian Revolution. Further, the abolition of slavery which was an integral aspect of both the Haitian Revolution and its impact on the French Declaration of Rights, are not even mentioned in the

---

3   For further elaboration on the concept of silence and silencing, see Bhambra and Shilliam (2009).

4   See, also, Sidney Mintz (1986) on the history of sugar as a commodity and its instrumental role in fuelling the Industrial Revolution.

5   Haitian independence was proclaimed in 1804 as a consequence of a successful slave revolution against the French colonial overseers, making it the first country to abolish slavery as well as declare independence (see Trouillot 1995, Fischer 2004).

main classical studies of the French Revolution, be they those of Michelet (1967 [1847]) or the more recent studies by Rudé (1988) and Schama (1989).[6] This silence complements, and exacerbates, the exclusion of slavery and colonialism from European historiographical traditions. Modernity becomes identified with political emancipation, but it is an emancipation structured by those very exclusions (including internal exclusions – for example, around gender [Kelly 1984]).[7]

I characterize these positions within historiography, not in order to say that historical accounts remain unchanged (indeed, they have been modified quite significantly in the light of postcolonial critiques), but rather to identify the kind of historiography that is embedded in the standard sociological accounts of modernity. These, I argue, are framed by a particular historiography, one which is Eurocentric in character. As Seidman remarks, sociology's emergence coincided with the high point of Western imperialism, and yet, 'the dynamics of empire were not incorporated into the basic categories, models of explanation, and narratives of social development of the classical sociologists' (1996: 314). Outside the canonical 'twin revolutions', then, the potential contribution of other events (and the experiences of non-Western 'others') to the sociological paradigm has rarely been considered (see Chakrabarty 2000, Bhambra, 2007a). This in itself is, in part, a consequence of the erasures that are implicit when the remit of sociology is understood to be 'modern societies' – that is, societies engaged in processes of modernization – where the 'postcolonial' is necessarily associated with 'pre-modern' societies, societies that have traditionally fallen to anthropology, or to the interdisciplinary area of development studies. Shifting the frame through which we view the events of 'modernity', however, forces us to consider the question of subaltern agency and ask: 'what is this "now" of modernity? Who defines this present from which we speak?' (Bhabha 1994: 244).

If we can now understand dominant approaches as Eurocentric, however, it is because of new voices emerging in wider political arenas and in the academy itself. The demise of colonialism as an explicit political formation has given rise to understandings of postcoloniality and, perhaps ironically, an increased recognition of the role of colonialism in the formation of modernity. Postcolonial scholarship, as has been demonstrated, has been integral to the opening out and questioning of the assumptions of the dominant discourses. It has further provided, as Spivak argues, the basis from which to reclaim 'a series of regulative political concepts, the *supposedly* authoritative narrative of whose production was written elsewhere' (1990: 225). The task here, then, is less about the uncovering of philosophical

---

6   It was not until a delegation from Saint Domingue (later Haiti) made the case for the abolition of slavery to the Constituent Assembly in Paris in November 1794 that it was included in the Declaration. However, Sonthonax, the French Jacobin commissioner, had proclaimed emancipation in Haiti in 1793 and the Assembly simply ratified this decision and extended it to all French colonies (see Trouillot 1995, Fischer 2004).

7   The way in which sociology has addressed 'internal', compared with 'external', exclusions is addressed in Bhambra (2007b).

ground than in 'reversing, displacing, and seizing the apparatus of value-coding' itself (Spivak 1990: 228). This, I shall argue, involves accepting the possibility, in times of the postcolonial, of a critical realignment of colonial power and knowledge through a methodology of 'connected histories and sociologies'. This will be taken up and discussed in more detail in the conclusion.

Multiple Modernities and Postcolonial Criticism

As postcolonial criticisms have become more familiar, proponents of the dominant view make minor adjustments and suggest that this is all now very familiar and, that while the critique may once have had cogency, its force is only in relation to positions that are now superseded. This, for instance, is how arguments about multiple modernities function, namely to disarm criticism while maintaining the fundamental structure of the original argument. In developing their approach, theorists of multiple modernities believe that two fallacies are to be avoided. The first, associated with earlier modernization theories, is that there is only one modernity. The second is that of Eurocentrism, or: 'that looking from the West to the East legitimates the concept of "Orientalism"' (Eisenstadt and Schluchter 1998: 2). Here the argument is that, while the idea of one modernity, especially one that has already been achieved in Europe, *would be Eurocentric*, theories of multiple modernities must, nonetheless, take Europe as the reference point in their examination of alternative modernities (Eisenstadt and Schluchter 1998: 2). Thus, while they point to the problem of Eurocentrism, they do so at the same time as asserting the necessary priority to be given to the West in the construction of a comparative sociology of multiple modernities.[8]

In a similar fashion to the proponents of modernization theory, theorists of multiple modernities identify modernity with 'the momentous transformations of Western societies during the processes of industrialization, urbanization, and political change in the late eighteenth and early nineteenth centuries' (Wittrock 1998: 19). As such, it is understood simultaneously in terms of its *institutional constellations*, that is, its tendency 'towards universal structural, institutional, and cultural frameworks' (Eisenstadt and Schluchter 1998: 3), as well as a *cultural programme* albeit 'beset by internal antinomies and contradictions, giving rise to continual critical discourse and political contestations' (Eisenstadt 2000: 7). Understanding modernity in this way permits them to situate European modernity – seen in terms of a unique combination of institutional and cultural forms – as the originary modernity and, at the same time, allows for different cultural encodings that result in modernity having become *multiple*. This explains the paradox whereby they can apparently dissociate themselves from Eurocentrism at the same time as self-consciously embracing its core assumptions, namely, 'the Enlightenment

---

8   The arguments of this section are developed in more detail in Bhambra (2007a: Chapter 3).

assumptions of the *centrality of a Eurocentred type of modernity*' (Eisenstadt and Schluchter 1998: 5, my emphasis).

The focus on different, non-European civilizational trajectories involves the (apparently positive) acknowledgement that, as Wittrock (1998) argues, these societies were not stagnant, traditional societies, but were developing and transforming their own institutional and cultural contexts prior to the advent of Western modernity. However, for Wittrock, it was not until the institutional patterns associated with Western modernity were *exported* to these other societies that multiple modernities were seen to emerge within them. Thus, it is the conjunction between the institutional patterns of the Western civilizational complex with the different cultural codes of other societies that creates various distinct modernities. By maintaining a general framework within which particularities are located – and identifying the particularities with culture (or the social) and the experience of Europe with the general framework itself – theorists of multiple modernities have, in effect, neutered any challenge that a consideration of the postcolonial could have posed. As Dirlik argues, by identifying 'multiplicity' with the cultural aspect, 'the idea of "multiple modernities" seeks to contain challenges to modernity' – and, I would argue, to sociology – 'by conceding the possibility of culturally different ways of being modern' (2003: 285), but not contesting *what it is to be modern* and *without drawing attention to the social interconnections in which modernity has been constituted and developed.* Those who defend the dominant approach to comparative historical sociology frequently accept that Eurocentrism is a problem that has sometimes distorted the way in which modernity has been conceived, they also argue that 'Eurocentrism' cannot be denied as 'fact', that, put simply, the European origins of modernity cannot be denied. However, it is precisely that 'fact' that is denied when global interconnections are recognized.

'Global' Cosmopolitanism

Recently, Beck (2000, 2006) has argued that a cosmopolitan approach is necessary to engage critically with globalization and to go beyond the limitations of state-centred disciplinary approaches typical of sociology and political science. He suggests that sociology continues to delimit the object of its inquiry within national boundaries rather than in the more appropriate context of 'world society'. As a consequence, it is less well able to engage with the 'increasing number of social processes that are indifferent to national boundaries' (2000: 80). He argues for a transition from the 'first age of modernity', structured by nation-states, to the cosmopolitan paradigm of the second age of modernity in which 'the Western claim to a monopoly on modernity is broken and the history and situation of diverging modernities in all parts of the world come into view' (2000: 87).

This I argue, is as limited as the state-centred approaches it criticizes precisely in the way that it sanctions the appropriateness of their concepts to the past, arguing that it is simply their application to the present and the future that is at issue. At a minimum, 'first modernity' could be argued to be as much characterized by empires as by nation-states and so the concepts of the 'first age' of modernity were as inadequate in their own time as they are claimed to be today. There is no acknowledgement that if certain understandings are problematic today, they are likely also to have been problematic in the past and thus require a more thorough overhaul than Beck proposes.

Equally significant, the engagement of others within this new cosmopolitan age is to be circumscribed to particular issues identified by Beck. He writes: 'the West should listen to non-Western countries *when they have something to say* about the following experiences' (2000: 89, my emphasis).

He then goes on to list four main themes: (1) the possibilities for coexistence in multi-religious, multi-ethnic and multicultural societies; (2) the question of tolerance in a confined space where cultural differences are prone to lead to violence; (3) 'highly developed' legal and judicial pluralism in non-Western countries (his use of scare quotes); (4) experience of dealing with multiple sovereignties as a consequence of empire (although this word is not used). The implication is that, when non-Western countries are not speaking about these issues, it is not necessary for the West to listen. This appears to be less a form of cosmopolitan engagement, new and distinct from the nation-state hierarchies of the first age, and more like 'business as usual'.

Beyond the simple arrogance of listing areas where 'we' should listen to 'them', there is also much to comment on in the substance of the list itself; not least, the aspect that the West and the non-West are presented as two homogenous blocs confronting each other as equals in a world that is not recognized to have been structured by hierarchical relations (for example, of imperialism and slavery among others). Further, the assumption is that the European 'social settlement' presents the apex of negotiating the contradictions of the modern world order with little recognition of other constructions of social solidarity that have existed (see Shilliam 2006) and that where there is some acknowledgement of 'development' in other places it has to be relativized through the use of scare quotes. The implication is that legal and judicial pluralism is only necessary in otherwise complex and developed Western societies because of the migration of populations to them from places that have such pluralism due to the presence of ethnic and religious differences.

This is then compounded by Beck's subsequent list of areas in which the West is 'beginning to adopt non-Western standards of reality and normality *which do not bode well*' (2000: 89, my emphasis). Presumably, the point is that they do not bode well for the West since, in his own terms, they are the everyday conditions of existence for the non-West – on which there is no comment. In particular, Beck identifies the de-regulation of the labour market in the West as leading to the 'abandonment of the co-operatively organized employee society that froze the class conflict between work and capital' (2000: 89). This is methodological nationalism given that he does not comment on the conditions of the international division of labour, and the hierarchies between the global north and south, which were themselves part of this 'frozen' settlement.

In another, again un-reflexive, example, Beck uses the image of a sand-pit to address the current world situation. He argues that the first age of modernity involved capital, labour and state 'making sand cakes in the sandpit' (where the sand pit is the national community), and attempting 'to knock the other's sand cake off the spade in accordance with the rules of institutionalized conflict' (2000: 89). The situation in the second age of modernity is akin to business having been given a mechanical digger which was being used to empty out the whole sandpit (2000: 89). The metaphor is peculiarly inept, given the association of infancy with the sandpit and the use of adult-child metaphors to understand colonial relations and responsibilities from a Western perspective. What is clear is that Beck's construction is itself an example of the methodological nationalism he opposes. He appears ignorant of the processes of colonialism, imperialism and slavery, which 'emptied out' from the sand pit of the colonized, not only mineral resources, but also human bodies, and not 'according to rules of institutionalized conflict'.

For Beck, then, cosmopolitanism is seen as an issue of the present and the future and there is no discussion of thinking cosmopolitanism back into history (for discussion, see Chernilo 2007; Fine 2007). While I have also argued that sociological concepts are inappropriately bounded – specifically, that they are 'methodologically Eurocentric'[9] – this is not something that is *only now* becoming problematic as a supposedly 'first modernity' has given way to a contemporary now-globalized world. Beck's (2000; 2006) argument for cosmopolitanism is part of a long line of social theory that takes Western perspectives as the focus of global processes, and Europe as the origin of a modernity which is subsequently globalized. A cosmopolitan sociology that was open to different voices would, I will suggest in the conclusion, be one that provincialized European understandings.

Cosmopolitanism and Europe

What appears striking in not just the sociological, but also the wider academic literature on cosmopolitanism, is the extent to which 'being cosmopolitan' (as a practice) is associated with being *in* the West and cosmopolitanism (as an idea) is seen as being *of* the West. As noted earlier in my discussion of Bhabha, by writing out the wider contexts within which ideas and practices are located, a particular cultural homogeneity is assumed and this becomes a standard of universal significance. Anthony Pagden, for example, writes,

> it is hard to see how any form of 'cosmopolitanism' can be made to address the difficulties of the modern world if it does not in some sense begin where Kant [and the Stoics] … began, that is with some vision of a community of 'the wise'

---

9   I owe the coining of this term to Peo Hansen.

whose views must in the end triumph ... In the modern world it is equally hard to
see, at least in the immediate future, that those views can be anything other than
the reflection of the values of western liberal democracies (2000: 19).

With this, Pagden asserts the origin of 'cosmopolitanism' – both as idea and as
practice – in the history of what he claims as European, or, more generally, Western,
thought and draws a direct link between that history and our present – again, here,
in the West. If he reaches out to others, primarily ancient Greeks, it is to reclaim
them as the origins of something truly European. This is a parochial reading of
cosmopolitanism which betrays the very ideals that the concept expresses. If this is
a contradiction, it is one that Pagden is prepared to embrace. He concludes that

> it must be an error to suppose that 'cosmopolitanism' can be detached from
> the history of European civilization, or the history of European philosophy ...
> To put it another way, it is an error to hope that we can ever achieve a truly
> cosmopolitan vision of the cosmopolis (2000: 20).

Note that Pagden says that if cosmopolitanism is of European civilization, it cannot
be *truly* cosmopolitan and yet it cannot *not* be of European civilization. Rather
than engage with this apparent contradiction, it is presented as Pagden's self (that
is, European self) congratulatory close to his article. In other words, he accepts a
particularism of Europe that presents itself as universal and does not think that that
requires further comment. Yet, as I observed at the start of the chapter, when those
who promote cosmopolitanism attribute particularism to the arguments of their
postcolonial 'others', they condemn it.

The issue with the claims made explicitly by Pagden – and implicitly by other
authors working in this area – is twofold. First, there is a refusal to acknowledge
that there have been cosmopolitan practices and the development of cosmopolitan
ideas in other parts of the world outside of European contact, in relation to European
contact, and not subordinate to it. Second, there is no engagement with the
problematic tension brought to the fore when we (*if, we*) address contemporaneous
European domination over much of the world as the very real negation of the idea
and ideals of cosmopolitanism otherwise put forward. For Pagden, there simply
are no cosmopolitan practices in other parts of the world worthy of discussion and
certainly no instances beyond Europe of intellectual engagement with the idea.
And as for the practices of slavery, imperialism, dispossession and colonialism
contemporaneous with the development of the 'European' idea of cosmopolitanism,
being such to call into question the values of European or Western civilization, he
has very little to say.

The field of cosmopolitanism is not limited to Pagden or Beck and there
are also a number of critical engagements in this area. Scholars such as Muthu
(2003), Jacob (2006), and Fine (2007) in different ways, have put forward counter-
histories, histories of other voices and other places and, in doing so, have provided
the basis both of contesting previously held parochial versions as well as widening

the scope of the debate. Muthu (2003), for example, develops a sustained argument for 'Enlightenment against Empire', the title of his monograph, in which he uses the relatively lesser known (or 'underappreciated') resources of Enlightenment thinkers to elucidate the largely unacknowledged anti-imperialist strand within their philosophies of cosmopolitanism. The early modern historian, Jacob (2006), similarly seeks to fill a lacuna. In her case, it is the 'temporal vacuum' in many histories of the Enlightenment which skip from the Stoics to Kant without examining the cosmopolitan 'cultural practices and de facto mores' of early modernity. As she suggests, 'long before Kant wrote, early modern Europeans were having new experiences we may legitimately describe as cosmopolitan' (2006: 11).

Fine, in turn, presents a critical engagement with modern cosmopolitanism and seeks to reinstate it within the tradition of *social* theory as distinct from the natural law tradition from which it is said to emanate (2007: 133-4). Yet, while opening up the space to consider the standard histories of cosmopolitanism differently, these histories also remain circumscribed to a particular geographical territory and intellectual tradition and, as a consequence, limit the possibility of cosmopolitanism properly to be understood 'cosmopolitan-ly'.

Counter histories can also reproduce what it is that they are counter to and, in many cases, what *is* reproduced – even in the work of scholars who may not wish consciously to do so – is a European genealogy.[10] It is not that forms of universalism are particular to Europe, but that Europe seems to have real difficulties with the universalism it espouses. While scholars argue for the universalism of what are assumed to be European categories, they then rarely acknowledge the processes through which that universalization is enacted, processes of colonization and imperialism for the most part. Even as sympathetic a scholar as Venn, who has argued for the recognition of colonialism as 'a necessary condition of the possibility ... to produce a cosmopolitan culture' (2002: 68), simultaneously argues that it is not possible to examine cosmopolitanism 'without locating it within the discourse of the Enlightenment and its inscription in the project we call modernity' (2002: 77). In a similar fashion to Beck, he also emphasizes the importance of cosmopolitanism in shaping the world to come and as something peculiarly European which is only contingently related to the rest of the world through the impact of colonialism. There is little discussion of cosmopolitanism as a concept, or as practices, that may already be present elsewhere.

Provincialized Cosmopolitanisms/Connected Sociologies

If we were to take cosmopolitanism as a way of looking at the world, this would require us to take the perspective of the world; that is, to be cosmopolitan in our very practices in understanding what it was and is to be cosmopolitan. As Pollock

---

10   The use of the term, 'European genealogy', similarly hides other exclusions within Europe such as the place of Eastern Europe or then the Balkans (see Boatcă 2007).

et al. (2000) argue, cosmopolitanism, as a historical or a sociological category, should be considered as open and not pre-given in form or content: it 'is not some known entity existing in the world, with a clear genealogy from the Stoics to Immanuel Kant, that simply awaits more detailed description at the hands of scholarship' (2000: 577).

Rather, they suggest, we should look at 'how people have thought and acted beyond the local' (2000: 586) in different places and across time to generate new descriptions of cosmopolitanism.[11] This would suggest new practices, which in turn 'may offer a better understanding of the theory and history of cosmopolitanism' (2000: 578). The primary argument made by Pollock and others is that the very phenomenon of cosmopolitanism is threatened by the work of purification that insists on regarding it as the product of one culture, emerging from a centre and diffusing outwards. If we wish an inclusive cosmopolitanism, it would have to be one outside a centred universalism.

A 'provincialized' cosmopolitanism would be made up of dialogues among a series of local perspectives on cosmopolitanism, with no unifying centre. We would need to 'provincialize Europe', in Chakrabarty's (2000) resonant phrase, that is, to de-centre Europe in our considerations. We would need to recognize contributions made in connections of which Europe had no part, as well as connections suppressed in the history of European uniqueness. Contra Pagden, we do need to think of cosmopolitanism as something other than the values emerging from a reflection on western liberal democracy (though, this is not to say that there is nothing to be learned from such reflection). The task now is a cosmopolitanism that can learn from others where we recognize that what 'they' contribute is not a confirmation of what 'we' already know, but the bringing into being of new understandings relevant to the worlds we inhabit together.

The idea of 'global sociology' has recently been promoted as a way in which sociology can redress its previous neglect of those represented as 'other' in its construction of modernity. The arguments of Michael Burawoy (2005b, 2008) and Raewyn Connell (2007) are indicative here with their calls for, respectively, a *provincialized* social science and *Southern* theory, which have culminated in a common call for global sociology. For Burawoy, a global sociology constructed from above would be ignored or would 'justify particularistic reactions and isolationist projects' and, as such, 'has to be constructed from below' (2008: 442). In discussing the feasibility of such a 'subaltern' global sociology, however, he suggests that three questions need first to be answered: (1) whether there is a common project around which sociologists could unite; (2) whether there is a community of discourse within which to communicate; and (3) how to address

---

11   See Lamont and Aksartova (2002) for one example in which this has been successfully undertaken. Acknowledging that much of the literature on cosmopolitanism is either implicitly or explicitly associated with elites, they seek 'to explore ordinary cosmopolitanisms, defined as the strategies used by ordinary people to bridge boundaries with people who are different from them' (2002: 1).

the international inequalities that structure the social world (2008: 442). He is cautiously optimistic in response to these questions and concludes his article by suggesting that a subaltern universality could be forged 'from the connections among particular sociologies' in the address of 'the common challenges we face in defending society' (2008: 443).

Connell similarly argues for the necessity of engagement with scholars from the global South in the construction of global sociology. She argues that the 'global scope of sociology' was lost in the 1920s and 1930s with the collapse of the evolutionary framework that had structured it in the nineteenth century (2007: 50) and suggests that the main problem facing the construction of a global sociology today is 'to connect different formations of knowledge in the periphery with each other' (2007: 213).[12] However, global sociology, in her terms, seems to be constructed through the simple association of disparate theorists, traditions, and disciplines. This not only homogenizes the variety of scholars and texts discussed, a variety that is otherwise valorized, into a mundane grouping of 'Southern theorists', but it also disconnects ideas and thought from the social contexts within which they emerged and disconnects those ideas from the 'mainstream' as well as from each other. Global sociology is implicitly presented as a conglomeration of disaggregated entities, unknown and unaffected by any form of interconnection that may have previously existed, and it is left to Connell herself to create the means by which these unconnected authors would be brought into conversation with each other.

While both Burawoy and Connell argue for a global sociology, then, the means of pursuing it are different. However, neither has a strong conception of interconnections either historically, or in the present, which might inform their understanding of the global. Rather, global sociology is to emerge through the accretion of 'new' knowledge from different places with little consideration of the interconnections among the locations in which knowledges are constructed and produced. Nor is there recognition that global sociology would require sociology itself to be re-thought backwards, in terms of how its core categories have been constituted, as well as forwards in terms of the further implications of its reconstruction. Burawoy's calls for a subaltern global sociology, for example,

---

12   With relation to sociology's 'global scope' in Connell, I would argue that to the extent this is related to the existence of an evolutionary framework then it has to be recognized that such a sociology continued till at least the 1960s through modernization theory with its implicit if not, more usually, explicit evolutionary framework which encapsulated some aspects of global interconnections. While much of the literature on modernization theory is problematic for the reasons outlined earlier in the chapter, it was globally oriented in substance and practice (with collaborations with scholars in other parts of the world). Moreover, since this was the highpoint of comparative sociology, while the framework within which it was developed might have been flawed, there was much greater interest in building the range of cases and thereby incorporating local knowledges in those cases (for further discussion see Bhambra 2007a: 61-4).

in which voices from the periphery would be allowed to enter into debates with the centre (2008: 443; see also 2005a) are based on the idea that sociology could be different in the future with little acknowledgement that, in order for this to happen, sociology would also need to relate differently to its past. As Holmwood notes, although Burawoy allows for new (postcolonial) voices within sociology, his understanding of the sociological endeavour is such that these new voices 'do not bear on its previous constructions' (Holmwood 2007: 55). Connected sociologies must operate from all directions across time and place in their construction and reconstruction of sociology's objects, relations, and identities.

Bibliography

Beck, U. 2000. The Cosmopolitan Perspective: Sociology of the Second Age of Modernity. *British Journal of Sociology*, 51(1), 79-105.

Beck, U. 2006. *Cosmopolitan Vision.* Cambridge: Polity Press.

Beck, U. and Sznaider, N. 2006. Unpacking Cosmopolitanism for the Social Sciences: A Research Agenda. *The British Journal of Sociology*, 57(1), 1-23.

Bhabha, H.K. 1994. *The Location of Culture.* London: Routledge.

Bhambra, G.K. 2007a. *Rethinking Modernity: Postcolonialism and the Sociological Imagination.* Basingstoke: Palgrave Macmillan.

Bhambra, G.K. 2007b. Sociology and Postcolonialism: Another "Missing" Revolution? *Sociology*, 41(5), 871-84.

Bhambra, G.K. and Shilliam, R. 2009. Introduction: 'Silence' and Human Rights, in *Silencing Human Rights: Critical Engagements with a Contested Project*, edited by G.K. Bhambra and R. Shilliam. Basingstoke: Palgrave Macmillan, 1-19.

Boatcă, M. 2007. The Eastern Margins of Empire. *Cultural Studies*, 21(2), 368-84.

Burawoy, M. 2005a. For Public Sociology. *American Sociological Review*, 70, 2-28.

Burawoy, M. 2005b. Conclusion: Provincializing the Social Sciences, in *The Politics of Method in the Human Sciences,* edited by G. Steinmetz. London: Duke University Press, 508-25.

Burawoy, M. 2008. Rejoinder: For a Subaltern Global Sociology. *Current Sociology*, 56(3), 435-44.

Chakrabarty, D. 2000. *Provincializing Europe: Postcolonial Thought and Historical Difference.* Princeton: Princeton University Press.

Chernilo, D. 2007. *A Social Theory of the Nation-State: Beyond Methodological Nationalism*. London: Routledge.

Connell, R.W. 2007. *Southern Theory: The Global Dynamics of Knowledge in Social Science.* Cambridge: Polity Press.

Dirlik, A. 2003. Global Modernity? Modernity in an Age of Global Capitalism. *European Journal of Social Theory*, 6(3), 275-92.

Eisenstadt, S.N. 2000. Multiple Modernities. *Daedalus: Multiple Modernities*, 129(1), 1-29.

Eisenstadt, S.N. and Schluchter, W. 1998. Introduction: Paths to Early Modernities – A Comparative View. *Daedalus: Early Modernities*, 127(3), 1-18.

Fine, R. 2007. *Cosmopolitanism*. London: Routledge.

Fischer, S. 2004. *Modernity Disavowed: Haiti and the Cultures of Slavery in the Age of Revolution*. London: Duke University Press.

Gandhi, L. 1998. *Postcolonial Theory: A Critical Introduction*. Edinburgh: Edinburgh University Press.

Giddens, A. 1973. *Capitalism and Modern Social Theory: An Analysis of the Writings of Marx, Durkheim and Max Weber*. Cambridge: Cambridge University Press.

Heilbron, J. 1995. *The Rise of Social Theory*. Cambridge: Polity Press.

Hobsbawm, E.J. 1962. *The Age of Revolution: Europe 1789-1848*. London: Weidenfeld and Nicolson.

Holmwood, J. 2007. Sociology as Public Discourse and Professional Practice: A Critique of Michael Burawoy. *Sociological Theory*, 25(1), 46-66.

Jacob, M.C. 2006. *Strangers Nowhere in the World: The Rise of Cosmopolitanism in Early Modern Europe*. Philadelphia: University of Pennsylvania Press.

Kelly, J. 1984. *Women, History, and Theory: The Essays of Joan Kelly*. London: University of Chicago Press.

Lamont, M. and Aksartova, S. 2002. Ordinary Cosmopolitanisms: Strategies for Bridging Racial Boundaries Among Working-Class Men. *Theory, Culture and Society*, 19(4), 1-25.

Lerner, D. 1958. *The Passing of Traditional Society: Modernizing the Middle East*. New York: The Free Press.

Michelet, J. 1967 [1847]. *History of the French Revolution* edited by G. Wright. Chicago: University of Chicago Press.

Mintz, S.W. 1986. *Sweetness and Power: The Place of Sugar in Modern History*. London: Penguin Books.

Muthu, S. 2003. *Enlightenment against Empire*. Princeton: Princeton University Press.

Nisbet, R.A. 1966. *The Sociological Tradition*. New York: Basic Books.

Pagden, A. 2000. Stoicism, Cosmopolitanism, and the Legacy of European Imperialism. *Constellations,* 7(1), 3-22.

Parsons, T. 1971. *The System of Modern Societies*. New Jersey: Prentice-Hall.

Pollock, S., Bhabha, H.K., Breckenbridge, C.A. and Chakrabarty, D. 2000. Cosmopolitanisms. *Public Culture*, 12(3), 577-89.

Rostow, W.W. 1960. *The Stages of Economic Growth: A Non-Communist Manifesto*. Cambridge: Cambridge University Press.

Rudé, G. 1988. *The French Revolution: Its Causes, Its History and Its Legacy after 200 Years*. London: Weidenfeld and Nicolson.

Schama, S. 1989. *Citizens: A Chronicle of the French Revolution*. London: Random House.

Seidman, S. 1996. Empire and Knowledge: More Troubles, New Opportunities for Sociology. *Contemporary Sociology*, 25(3), 313-16.

Shilliam, R. 2006. What about Marcus Garvey? Race and the Transformation of Sovereignty Debate. *Review of International Studies*, 32(3), 379-400.

Spivak, G.C. 1990. Post-structuralism, Marginality, Postcoloniality and Value, in *Literary Theory Today*, edited by P. Collier and H. Geyer-Ryan. Cambridge: Polity Press, 219-44.

Trouillot, M.-R. 1995. *Silencing the Past: Power and the Production of History.* Boston: Beacon Press.

Venn, C. 2002. Altered States: Post-Enlightenment Cosmopolitanism and Transmodern Socialities. *Theory, Culture and Society*, 19(1-2), 65-80.

Wittrock, B. 1998. Early Modernities: Varieties and Transitions. *Daedalus: Early Modernities*, 127(3), 19-40.

Chapter 3

Decolonizing Postcolonial Rhetoric[1]

Encarnación Gutiérrez Rodríguez

The title of this chapter appears to be a tautology. How can the "postcolonial" be decolonized, if it already indicates a posterior stage to colonialism? And we might need to ask what do we mean by "rhetoric"? I will discuss here "rhetoric" in relation to "critique". Critique becomes rhetoric when it detaches ideas from practices, finding its ultimate goal in rewording concepts, rather than in the transformation of institutional practice. For Adorno, critique necessitates that we look at both the consistency (fabric) and conceptualization (textuality) of society (Adorno 1977). Yet the end of social critique is not a hermeneutic understanding of society. Rather, a critical analysis of society begins where understanding finds its limits, where the focus on discontinuities and multiple antagonisms complicates our view and drives us to interrogate the epistemic pillars of our scientific presuppositions.

Applying this notion of critique to postcolonial studies prompts us to interrogate its epistemological foundations as well as its institutional translation. In this chapter I will trace the epistemological contributions of decolonial voices, subjugated knowledge, represented by Black, Chicana and Third World feminist and queer theorists of the 1980s in the United States. I will address the absence of their theory production from the curricula in Sociology departments in Western Europe. Their liminal or non-existent representation in introductory Sociology textbooks, but also within the area of Gender Studies in Sociology, symptomatically signals the increasing under-representation of critical theory in this discipline. While the emergence of British Cultural Studies revolutionized at least British Sociology in the 1980s, producing a new perspective on how to connect and analyze the symbolic with the social, this view has become liminal or obsolete in today's discipline. Further, poststructuralist and post-Marxist approaches have become less attractive, while postcolonial and decolonial approaches remain at the margins. A decolonial feminist-queer epistemology[2] is very much needed

---

1   I would like to thank Shirley Anne Tate, Manuela and Sérgio Costa for the insight comments to this chapter.

2   I refer here amongst others to debates in the United States, attached to the Combahee River Collective (1977), Gloria T. Hull, Patricia Bell Scott and Barbara Smith (1982), Barbara Smith (1983), Angela Y. Davis (1981), Audre Lorde (1984), bell hooks (1984), Gloria Anzaldúa (1987, 1990, 2000), Chandra Talpade Mohanty, Ann Russo and Lourdes

in order to understand the complexities, multidimensionality and intricacies of postcolonial societies.

The emergence of postcolonial critique in the late 1980s and decolonial approaches in the 1990s in the West is tied to specific societal conditions, informing the local production of knowledge and its global embeddednes (Gutiérrez Rodríguez 2003). Significantly, a decolonial perspective brings us back to reconsidering theory as embodied, embedded in history and geopolitically contextualized. Decolonizing European Sociology needs to depart from one of the foundational principles of decolonial feminist-queer epistemology, embodied knowledge.

Embodied Knowledge

In the 1980s, the role of the "universal objective scholar" was challenged by feminist standpoint theory (Harding 2004, 2008).[3] From an African American feminist perspective Patricia Hill Collins (2000), for example, criticizes the presumption of disembodied knowledge rooted in the principle of scientific objectivity, based on the presumption of the socially detached and omniscient scholar. Numerous introductory books on foundational concepts and ideas in Sociology reproduce this assumption, representing an almost exclusive lineage of white male European scholars as the founders of this discipline. By accident, sometimes we might find the portrait of a female scholar, and more recently, an exclusive selection of a few Caribbean or African American male scholars. Female or queer scholars with an Asian, African, Caribbean or Latin American background are almost absent in these foundational narratives. Still, in the twenty-first century, Social Sciences are institutionally thought within the paradigm of European modernity, omitting what Enrique Dussel (1996, 2003) has coined the "underside of modernity", its interpenetration with coloniality.

Against the perception of the production of knowledge as a geopolitically and socially unmarked moment, decolonial feminists such as Collins demonstrate that knowledge productions are linked to knowledge positions, a heuristic position, a standpoint (Collins 2000). Demonstrating the ontological dimension of epistemology, standpoint theory evokes the historical and material conditions from which knowledge emerges. Informing the fabric of knowledge, geographical, social and political conditions pervade our creative and intellectual potential, configuring a specific angle towards the world, people and things, reminiscent of their place and time. Scientific knowledge as such is always situated, as Donna Haraway (1996) argues, always partial and located. Every scholar, every intellectual is a product of the discourses and material conditions of their time. They are embedded in a historical, geographical and social context, in which their ability to speak is (in)formed by their access to economic and public resources. The access to jobs

---

Torres (1991), Trin T. Minh-Ha (1989), Gayatri Chakravorty Spivak (1987, 1993, 1999), Chela Sandoval (2000), to name just a few.

3   For further discussion see Gutiérrez Rodríguez (2010).

in Higher Education, research funding, professional networks and publishers is fundamental to the generation and public dissemination of ideas.

As Pierre Bourdieu (1988) emphasizes in *Homo Academicus*, this access is governed by mechanisms of social distinction, through which social belonging to the hegemonic group is guaranteed or denied. The ability to share and exercise a common cultural codex, imposed by the dominant group, is a prerequisite for acceptance into circles of power. Social and cultural capital, as Bourdieu notes, are indispensable for becoming part of a national project in which a leadership position can be realized (Bourdieu 1987, 1990). Through the example of the French case, Bourdieu demonstrates how French academia is ruled by a traditional elite that presupposes its "habitus" as the model for public behavior (Bourdieu 1988).

While Bourdieu instigates a sophisticated analysis of the interpenetration between culture and society, pondering on the role of symbolic power and symbolic violence and demonstrating the persistence of economic and social inequalities, his analysis omits how gendered and racialized mechanisms of exclusion and inclusion pervade the field of academic knowledge production. Although Bourdieu is aware of the colonial repertoire of the French nation as he demonstrates in his work on the Kabylie (1958), this structural moment is silenced in his analysis of social distinctions.[4] Thus, the role of "race" and gender in the organization of social inequalities is not perceived. However, his observation regarding the corporeality of power or embodied social structure (Bourdieu 1988), is useful to relate the concept of "embodied knowledge" to the materiality of knowledge production, played out in and through hegemonic power struggle.

As Antonio Gramsci (2007) notes, academia plays a fundamental role in establishing a hegemonic national project. He emphasizes the roles of "traditional intellectuals" and "organic intellectuals" in forging the future of the nation in his analysis of the status quo and hegemony. The position of the "organic intellectual" was inflected by a new social struggle, from which "he" re-emerged as its representative or public voice. The "organic intellectual" voices the need for change and a new common sense, supported by new subjectivities, the factory workers, determined by a new mode of production, Fordism. This new class represents a new moment in history, which counters traditional elites and challenges their hegemonic position. While the relevance of Gramsci's analysis of hegemony is necessary for understanding the power dynamics in "embodied knowledge", this perspective also disregards the colonial context and gender asymmetries ingrained in hegemonic power struggle.

Though Gramsci engages with the role of knowledge production in the forging of a hegemonic national project, he does not link this project to Italian colonial imperialism in Eritrea. This is interesting as he is attentive to the colonizing mechanisms within Italy itself, when he tackles the immanent contradiction driving the Southern question (Gramsci 2006). In his analysis of Italian Southern labor migration for the Northern car industry, Gramsci delivers an analysis of the

---

4   For further critique on Bourdieu's work in this regard, see Connell (2007).

paradox of modernity and its immanent negation. This perspective resonates with the "perspective of coloniality" in some aspects. The exploitation of the Southern car factory workers in the North accentuates the ambiguous relationship of modernity to coloniality. While the factory workers do not represent the colonized or indentured labor force, the discussion of the Southern migration to the North conjures up the dualism of modernity and coloniality.

Modernity for Gramsci is inextricably caught in the antinomy of progress and misery. This immanent contradiction, which Marx referred to as the immanent antagonism between capital and labor, is put in a different light, when we consider the "perspective of coloniality" (Mignolo 2000, 2005) and Black, Chicana and Third World feminist epistemology. Coming back to the production of knowledge, this is a field organized by different social antagonisms, through which access is guaranteed or denied to the authorized field of knowledge production. This is the fabric in which knowledge is situated.

Locality Matters – Situated Knowledge

Within the Western European context, the production of institutionalized knowledge was largely defined by a white, male upper and middle class until the second half of the twentieth century. The "canon" of social theory has, until very recently, ignored contributions by female and/or racialized scholars (Reed 2006). Charles Mills goes as far as interpreting the ontological foundation of social sciences as "white supremacist" (Mills 1994).[5] While white upper and middle class women have been gaining access to leading positions in research and teaching in European universities since the 1990s, scholars with a non-White European background are hardly represented, for example, in the UK (Wakeling 2007), the Netherlands and France, and almost completely absent in countries such as Germany (Gutiérrez Rodríguez 2000b), Spain and Austria. Universities in Western Europe are projects of national elites. Whilst some countries' research ambitions have opened the doors to international competition as is the case in the UK and the Netherlands, in most countries Universities remain in the hands of the national White elites.

Moreover, on an international scale, the geographical situatedness of institutional knowledge production and the hegemony of the English language in the academic world (Ortiz 2004) prioritize and favor research coming from the United States, Australia or Britain. Consequently, research from the global South and in other languages is hardly noticed by the Anglo-Saxon world, if they are not published in English and in high impact journals, mostly located in Britain and the United States. "Universal" academic knowledge production is so sustained by global and local inequalities, by what Gayatri C. Spivak (1987, 1993, 1999), discusses as the "geopolitical" embeddedness of knowledge production. This

---

5   An interesting critique on "white supremacist" in sociology is also formulated by Ladner (1973).

geopolitical situatedness is marked by the "dark side" (Mignolo 1995) of European modernity, coloniality. In this context, coloniality (of power, knowledge, and being) does not refer to the prevalence of a colonial administration, rather it points to "a modality of being as well as to power relations that sustain a fundamental social and geopolitical divide" (Maldonado-Torres 2008: 239).

Decolonizing Epistemology – Ontologizing Knowledge

Decolonial epistemology, while focusing on "embodied knowledge", is also interested in challenging the foundational myth of European modernity (Dussel 1994, 1995; Grosfoguel 2002, 2006; Maldonado-Torres 2006; Quijano 2000; Mignolo 1995, 2000). Introducing the "perspective of coloniality" as an epistemological point of departure in order to understand European modernity, authors like Dussel and Mignolo reveal the negation of modernity in modernity itself. The other side is the colonial and imperial experience negated by celebratory accounts of European progress and civilization. Coloniality, however, is entangled with modernity and constitutes it in an inextricable way.

Coloniality's discursive positioning "outside" of Europe and the North Atlantic, disregards the fact that the origins of coloniality lie within and depart from Europe. Situating colonialism outside Europe and the North Atlantic enables a division of the world into modern/developed and traditional/under-developed societies. Through the discourse of modernity in European and North Atlantic Philosophy and Social Sciences, an "ontology of continental divides" (Mignolo 2005) has been produced, in which a hierarchical and judgemental classification of the world is at work (Wallerstein 2001). This classification reflected in the division of the world into first, second, third and fourth, is rooted in Eurocentric paradigms of economic, political and cultural development. Covering the entanglement between modernity and colonialism, these categories obfuscate the origins of these divisions as a result of European colonialism and its aftermath. Social Sciences, and in particular, Sociology, engages with this perception, by situating the origins of modernity in Europe.

If we look at just two classical works in Sociology, Habermas (1981) and Luhmann (2006), we can see the parochiality of these highly sophisticated thinkers. They develop a differentiated methodology for understanding deliberate democratic systems (Habermas 1981) and social systems (Luhmann 2006), relating to a complex epistemological framework and detailed analysis of European societies from the eighteenth century onwards. However, when it comes to non-European societies we simply encounter a Eurocentric anthropological rhetoric about "Hochkulturen" (Luhmann 2006) in reference to India and Japan; or "Stammesgesellschaften" (Habermas 1981: 242) in regard to indigenous communities in the Americas. Interestingly, through this perspective, Europe's societies are represented as highly complex, individualized and differentiated, whilst the reference to non-European societies exposes little knowledge about the intricate civilizations of Mesopotamia, Persia, China, Mesoamerica (Aztecs and Mayan) and the Andes (Incas and Aymaras). In sum, European societies are represented as modern and complex, while other societies are thought as "primitive" or "inferior" to their "civilized European" counterparts. Nonetheless, these accounts reveal a liminality in Europe itself, where little attention is paid to the role of Spain and Portugal in the project of modernity.

Modernity and civilization are identified with France or England and, to some extent, due to the intellectual debates in the nineteenth century, with Germany. Mercantilism, the French Revolution and the Industrial Revolution in England are the historical references for the emergence and development of modernity that we encounter in numerous philosophical and sociological writings (Wallerstein 2001). In contrast, the "perspective of coloniality" sets the emergence of modernity within the colonization of the Americas in 1492. For Dussel, Spain's absence is indicative of its liminality as a nation which also encompasses Africa. This liminality makes its role as the first European colonizing nation invisible. With the same vigor as it used to destroy the plurality of religious beliefs and kinship models in the Peninsula, imposing Catholicism and with it the nuclear, monogamous, heterosexual, patriarchal family, the Spanish Crown colonized amongst others the Caribbean, Central and South America.[6] Thousands of years of Amerindian knowledge and traditions were destroyed. Guided by an ideological matrix sustained by the construction of the "Other" in regard to the dominant Self (Dussel 1995: 39), Spanish colonization evolved not only on the level of territorial annexation and labor exploitation, but also on the level of the colonization of knowledge. As Dussel notes, the "'Other' is obliged, subsumed, alienated, and incorporated into the dominating totality like a thing or instrument" (ibid). On the basis of this epistemological construction, the colonized was enslaved or reduced to an exploited labor force.

While Spain is situated at the fringes of the Northern European project of modernity, Latin America, Asia, Africa and Oceania are completely absent from it. It was not until the English Empire became the new hegemonic global force that modernity would be linked to the second pivotal event for European societies, capitalism. In the mid-seventeenth century the Spanish Empire was weakened

---

6   The colonization of the Americas extended the violent expansive and oppressive character of the Spanish crown, enforcing a Catholic nation, predominantly Castilian, culminating in the defeat of Boabdil, the last Sultan of Granada, on January 6, 1492, the inauguration of the Spanish inquisition in 1481, expulsion of the Spanish Jews on 31 March 1492, the forced conversion and cultural repression of Spanish Muslims in 1502, resulting in the Edict of Expulsion in 1609. This signalled the end of a rich intercultural intellectual encounter in the Peninsula, in which global knowledge circulated from Bagdad to Córdoba to Toledo (Menocal 2003). The expulsion and genocide of the Muslim and Jewish population, but also the persecution and execution of other religious communities, matriarchal enclaves and female healers branded as witches, happened parallel to the colonization of the Americas.

by colonial rivals such as England, the Netherlands and France. Industrialization brought a relatively rapid transformation of society, reflected also in the emergence of new academic disciplines such as Sociology. Significantly, German (Marx, Weber, Tönnies, Mannheim, Simmel) and French intellectuals (Comte, Durkheim) laid out the paradigms of this discipline, embracing and reproducing assumptions about Europe's central role. From this Eurocentric angle, European Sociology developed its "universal paradigms" of modernity, civilization, evolution and progress. For Max Weber, as Dussel (2005) points out, Europe represents the cradle of civilization and culture. It is from here that the "signs of evolutionary advance and universal validity" are created (Weber 1950: 340). This presupposition laid out the foundations for European Sociology, which will be significantly altered in the twentieth century. It was not until the late twentieth century that new voices reached European and North Atlantic academia, challenging its predominant androcentric White European focus.

Decentering European Sociology

In the late twentieth century, feminist epistemology questioned the colonizing effects of academic knowledge. Decolonial queer-feminism introduced an intersectional perspective on domination, a critical analysis of the persistence of colonial power and racism in Western societies, and the geographical situatedness of knowledge and knowledge production into feminist theory. While the gender/sex debate reached Sociology departments in the 1990s (Butler 1994), the decolonial perspective from Black, Chicana and postcolonial feminists remains largely absent from Sociology curricula. If we consider that society is the main key concept in Sociology, the resistance that an intersectional analysis of society, proposed by Black feminists such as Angela Davis or Audre Lorde or Chicana feminists such as Chela Sandoval or Gloria Anzaldúa, experienced in regard to its inclusion into the teaching canon of Sociology is remarkable. I remember how I used to have tedious debates as an Assistant Professor in the Department of Sociology at the University of Hamburg regarding the seriousness of Cultural Studies or Gender Studies as specialist areas of this discipline. To teach Black feminism or Chicana feminism or postcolonial critique was deemed inadequate and placed me at the margins. Black and Chicana feminist social and cultural theorists were branded as "not serious" academics and not properly situated within disciplinary boundaries. Due to their creative and innovative writing techniques, their analyses of society were reduced to the field of literary studies or women's history. The particularization of this critical perspective on society and culture diminishes the contributions of these thinkers to key concepts in social theory such as social change, transformation, agency, social inequality and processes of differentiation, to name just a few. Occasionally, some contributions find their way into gender or postcolonial studies curricula, though not always referenced back to the source. Let me illustrate this argument further through the example of the debate in German Gender Studies on "intersectionality", a concept conceiving of the simultaneity and interlocking nature of various relations of domination and power.

In the last few years, German Gender Studies seems to have re-discovered "intersectionality", as numerous workshops and conferences with international guest speakers were organized. From a British or US American Gender Studies perspective this might seem a little bit odd, considering that the debate took place at least 25 years ago. Also, from an activist's perspective, the belated reception of this debate in German Gender Studies seems surprising, given that this discussion had already taken place in the 1980s led by migrant, exilic, Jewish and Black feminists. Referring to Critical Legal Studies and the debates on critical "race" studies in the United States, the debate on "intersectionality" in Germany simulates a genuine interest in understanding the multidimensionality of gender, at the same time that it ignores the local debates which had already proposed this perspective.[7] How can we interpret this silencing within German Gender Studies?

The answer could lie in the academization of a debate that might consider the contributions of these feminists as interesting testimonies of their times, but lacking in a thorough analysis. Perhaps using theory from the United States or Britain enables the theoretical insight that is assumed to be absent from German feminism. But maybe the problem lies somewhere else. Maybe these protagonists, Jewish, Black, diasporic and migrant German feminists, are not perceived as members of the German women's movement or even as feminist theorists. Elsewhere I have discussed how through racialization these women are constructed by the official discourse as "objects", but not "agents" of knowledge (Gutiérrez Rodríguez 1999, 2000a). The antagonism of the moment of emergence of "intersectionality" in Germany in the 1980s is thus bypassed, avoiding its inclusion into the canon of German Gender Studies.

This academic approach to epistemology detaches knowledge production from its ontological dimension. The adaptation of debates happening in other parts of the world creates the perception of "intersectionality" as a foreign problem, which needs first to be translated into and through its own academic context. What this perspective disregards is that this translation already happened, long before an academic debate started in 2005 (Erel, Gutiérrez Rodríguez, Haritaworn and Klesse 2008). Prevalent forms of racism, orientalism and xenophobia in Germany led to Black, migrant and exilic women's movements from the late 1970s on. In the course of their struggle these movements have looked for explanatory models adopting them to their specific societal circumstances. In the debate on "intersectionality", this detail is overlooked, reducing a critical concept emerging from and engaging with political struggle, to a mere object of scientific contemplation. Critical analysis is thus robbed of its transformative potential for society.

A similar situation can be observed in regard to the increasing interest in Postcolonial Studies in German Sociology. Here the debate is detached from

---

7   See Oguntoye et al. (1986); Kalpaka, Räthzel (1985); Hügel et al. (1999); FeMigra (1994); Popoola, Sezen (1999); Gelbin, Konuk, Piesche (2000), for example.

social actors, who have translated and critically questioned the adaptation of this theoretical framework into the German context. The uncomfortable debate about Germany's colonial past and colonial patterns of governing and knowledge production as well as the existence of racism are foreclosed by immunizing local voices. Instead, an apparently "purely" academic, depoliticized approach is followed and adapted. This brief insight into the German context illustrates how the reception and critical adaptation of decolonial epistemology and postcolonial critique in the 1990s is tied to specific societal conditions and political struggle, in which knowledge production takes place. It also reveals the material conditions in which critical theory is produced.

The Materiality of Knowledge

Decolonial feminism, postcolonial critique and the "perspective of coloniality" are not just motivated by the discontent with insufficient paradigms and models of analysis to understand complex social realities based on a heteronormative social order, configured within the tension between modernity and coloniality. Their claims emerged in regard to a modern-colonial world-system, in which access to wealth distribution and to knowledge production is unevenly organized along the lines of "race", gender, sexuality, able-bodiedness and class. Knowledge is produced under these conditions and is fuelled by the experience of exclusion, appropriation and marginalization. While elements of feminist-queer decolonial thought, postcolonial critique and the decolonial Latin American epistemology project in the United States could enter some niches of the English publishing market, within academia these voices come from Area Studies, Languages departments, Gender and Women's Studies. Thus, these debates are taking place in what some see as the fringes of academia, leaving Sociology departments almost untouched. What happens when these theoretical approaches, textured by specific conditions of knowledge production and power struggle between dominant and marginalized groups, become part of the curricula?

This question has been repeatedly raised in Women's and Gender Studies regarding the professionalization of knowledge.[8] What happens when knowledge produced in social protest movements and understood as political intervention sustains disciplinary curricula, neutralizing the claims for social change and institutional transformation? Inclusion into the mainstream agenda very often ensures a silencing of the question of who has access to Higher Education and also who is part of the faculty.[9]

---

8 See, for example, Smith (1990), Yamato (1990) and Baca Zinn et al. (1990).

9 As Eva Hartmann critically notes in her study on the transnationalization of Higher Education (2003), the tertiary education system has become a commodity in the age of information. In the context of the knowledge, information and communication society "education" has a commodity value, which is negotiated on an international scale. In 1994,

The privatization of Higher Education, the increase in student fees, the decrease in grants for disadvantaged students and students from the Southern peripheries, reinforces the inequalities structuring academic institutions. A paradoxical situation emerges in which advanced critical thinking is promoted in the classroom without questioning for whom this teaching is made available. Thus, in research institutions and postgraduate programmes a situation is encountered in which a situation in which the internal, local, cosmopolitan configuration from below is almost absent in the class room, while debates on cosmopolitanism might stand at the heart of curricula. A similar constellation can be noticed in the recruitment level of academic staff, although altered by systemic regional differences.

Regarding Sociology, for example, it can be noticed that the struggle for coherent disciplinary boundaries is also reflected on the level of recruitment policies. The demarcation of disciplinary boundaries very often reflects national political agendas. Sociology departments in Europe recruit their staff in general from the local national elites, mostly white men and a few white women, very often sharing the "habitus" of what Bourdieu terms the *Homo Academicus*.[10] Though not deliberately, Sociology departments subtly engage with what Gramsci has defined as a national project. For example, Spanish or German universities, as Bourdieu discusses in the French case (Bourdieu 1988) usually recruit their academic staff from their immediate midst. Nonetheless, some European countries such as Britain and the Netherlands have left the traditional recruitment pathway and adopted themselves to the needs of a global Higher Education market which has resulted in numerous international appointments. However, this development does not always include the promotion of local Black and Ethnic minorities into Higher Education (Wakeling 2007).

In contrast to British universities, German universities are resistant to an internationalization of their faculty, on the levels of the inclusion of members from local minorities and international recruitment. Germany also lacks an efficient and transparent system of recruitment (Zimmermann 2000). Procedures against racial discrimination or the principle of equality in regard to individuals of diasporic and migrant backgrounds are non-existent. Criteria for person specifications and job descriptions can be changed in the course of the selection process by the recruitment committee without any further consultation with or control by an external body. There is neither an obligation to give feedback to the candidates, nor transparency in the selection process.

Under these conditions Sociology departments may develop their research agendas and strategies solely in terms of their own personal networks. These

---

the World Bank published a strategy paper in which it noted the relevance of the education sector for the global economy. It recommended the introduction of tuition fees and a loan system for students to regulate public spending on education (Hartmann 2003, 4).

10   See research for example Zimmermann (2000) and Monroe et al. (2008) on gender inequality in German and United States higher education; see also Jones (2006) on Black female academics in the UK.

discriminatory procedures may leave candidates who are external to the local professional networks out of the selection process. While research on the recruitment of Black scholars and scholars with a migration and diasporic background is underdeveloped, some preliminary observations suggest that racial discrimination might be an issue (Gutiérrez Rodríguez 2000b). Remarkably, scholars with a diasporic or migrant background are amongst the first in leaving the country in search of academic job opportunities, for example, to Britain or the United States. Significantly, it was this generation, who in the 1980s and 1990s started to adapt a postcolonial framework of analysis to the German context. While their contributions have been widely read, this is rarely cited in publications on "postcolonial Sociology".

It is this paradoxical situation of inclusion of knowledge production on the one side and exclusion of the local translators and originators of these debates on the other, in which a perspective on coloniality unravels. Yet to decolonize European Sociology entails not only scrutiny of the epistemic foundations of European thought. Rather, it involves attending to the ontological dimension of knowledge production itself. Relating the material conditions of knowledge with its ontology requires an interrogation of the paradigms that persist in re-establishing disciplinary boundaries, reiterating androcentric and Eurocentric knowledge traditions. Countering the hegemonic representation of sociological knowledge entails not only that we cross disciplinary boundaries, enabling interdisciplinary practices, but also that we revise our epistemological foundations. Such an attempt can be approached by decolonizing the discipline, proposing a project of liberation (Dussel 1996, 2003) that involves de-linking from coloniality and modernity (Mignolo 2007).

"Decoloniality" involves generalizing the experience of decolonization and anti-colonial struggles in Asia, Africa, and Latin America as well as the experience of subalternity in the global economic centers. The decolonial project aims to foreground subjugated knowledge, creative and intellectual foundations in the "global South" and within the margins of the "global North" as I suggest here. Decolonizing European Sociology could contribute, at least on an academic level, to unmasking the limitations of this discipline and its link to coloniality. This could also trigger a debate on the global but locally experienced inequalities intrinsic to this field which organize access to "authorized" knowledge, prevalent in an androcentric Eurocentric angle. Mignolo's strategy of de-linking refers to Gloria Anzaldúa's notion of "Nepantla – borderlands" (Anzaldúa 1987, 2000).

Beyond Sociological Boundaries – Border Thinking – Nepantla

Gloria Anzaldúa's notion of *borderlands* underlines the epistemic condition which she defines as "la facultad", "the capacity to see in surface phenomena the meaning of deeper realities, to see the deeper structure below the surface" (Anzaldúa 1987: 60). This "faculty" arises out of existential experiences of abjection and subjugation at the juncture of different systems of domination, when as Anzaldúa argues "when you're against the wall – when you have all these oppression coming at you – you develop this extra faculty" (Anzaldúa 2000: 123). "La facultad" discerns a special faculty emerging out of the epistemic and ontological conditions of living at the borderlands between the United States and Mexico, epitomizing the intersection between the fluidity and invasive force of capital, on the one side, and the violence of military border control stopping the flow of people, on the other; in short, between imperialism and coloniality. Under these conditions a specific knowledge is produced, acquired through the struggle for liberation, a knowledge conditioned by the historical and material circumstances circumventing this context. Knowledge is accompanied here by wisdom, as Hill Collins has observed in regard to subjugated knowledge.

"La facultad" as Anzaldúa describes in her later work is shaped in the "in-between space", where boundaries break down, where identity categories dissolve and new ways of understanding ourselves, the world and the cosmos emerge, "Nepantla" (Anzaldúa 2000). The Nahuatl word *Nepantla* is the "liminal state between worlds, between realities, between systems of knowledge" (Anzaldúa 2000: 235). This is the space inhabited by the subject at the borderlands, a subject that Anzaldúa metaphorically conceives as the "borderwoman" – the "*mestiza*". The *mestiza* figure is a kind of a trickster, somebody that unites the moon and the sun, the night and the day. She has *mestiza consciousness*, created at the crossroads of simultaneous systems of domination, in which ambivalent lines of belonging and the ambiguous position of inside-outsider are created. She describes herself as a *mestiza*, someone who "is in all cultures at the same time, *alma entre dos mundos, tres, cuatro, me zumba la cabeza con lo contradictorio. Estoy norteada por todas las voces que me hablan simultáneamente*" (Anzaldúa 2000: 235). It is this state of consciousness that Anzaldúa describes as the epistemic condition of the borderlands. This consciousness is caught in the paradox of the border as the site of rigid boundaries and the trespassing of them, at the same time. Thus, the *mestiza*

> has discovered that she can't hold concepts or ideas in rigid boundaries. The borders and walls that are supposed to keep the undesirable ideas out are entrenched habits and patterns of behaviour; these habits and patterns are the enemy within. Rigidity means death. Only by remaining flexible is she able to stretch the psyche horizontally and vertically. *La mestiza* constantly has to shift out of habitual formations; from convergent thinking, analytical reasoning that tends to use rationality to move toward a single goal (a Western mode), to divergent thinking, characterized by movement away from set patterns and goals and toward a more whole perspective, one that includes rather than excludes (ibid, 79).

Whilst "la facultad" is imbued with the experience of dispossession, persecution and violence, living at the borderlands also unleashes new strategies of coping and transgressing boundaries. Transgression represents the driving force of border consciousness, an aspect that Walter Mignolo (2007) develops further in regard to "border thinking". Border thinking accentuates the "de-linking from the colonial matrix of power" (Mignolo 2007: 455).

It traces the threshold between modernity and coloniality in that it acknowledges the centrality of Western traditions of thought for the development of modern sciences and the dominant conceptualization of the world, at the same time that it makes clear the limitations and epistemic violence of this perspective. Border thinking is liminal thinking, a juggling of cultures, as Anzaldúa puts it, turning contradictions into ambivalences (Anzaldúa 1987: 79). Border thinking occurs where phenomena collide as instead of perpetuating the divide, it embraces the crossing, the living on multiple shores.

From this perspective of transversality, Anzaldúa suggests that we "disengage from the dominant culture, write it off altogether as a lost cause, and cross the border into a wholly new territory" (ibid). This transgressive and transversal movement in which contradictions are dissolved into myriad infinite series of differences resonates with Gilles Deleuze and Felix Guattari's (2004) rhizomatic movement. But, in contrast to Deleuze and Guattari's concept of deterritorialization as nomadic thinking, Anzaldúa's notion of *Nepantla* – borderlands comprises the experience of forced and violent displacement, enforced by border and migration regimes, in which the ontology of *mestiza* knowledge is based. The heuristic standpoint for knowledge is not the rhizomatic movement of ideas and practices, but the constant tension between agentic transgression and violent sublimation. At this threshold, the "new common logic of knowing: border thinking" (Mignolo 2007: 497), composed of the "pluriversality" of local colonial histories entangled with imperial modernity arises (Mignolo 2007: 497). Thus, "critical border thinking is the method that connects pluriversality (...) into a universal project of delinking from modern rationality and building other possible worlds. Critical border thinking involves and implies both the imperial and colonial difference" (Mignolo 2007: 498).

Following Anzaldúa's Nepantla-*borderlands* and Mignolo's critical border thinking, European Sociology needs to be read against its grain. To read it against the grain means to destabilize disciplinary boundaries and its Eurocentric paradigm by confronting it with colonial difference.

Conclusion: Countering Monolingual Cosmopolitanism

Going back to our previous argument, the perspective of de-linking or *Nepantla*-borderlands is crucial to the project of decolonizing European sociology. It is a project that has its roots in decolonial feminist-queer epistemology, a perspective that is consistently ignored in androcentric receptions of postcolonial and decolonial theory or is at best marginal in Gender Studies curricula in Sociology departments. Including the perspective of *Nepantla*-borderlands within Sociology curricula, Gender and Postcolonial programmes could be conducive to deepening critical perspectives on the colonial and imperial legacies informing current academic knowledge. Such an approach might challenge the institutionalization of Postcolonial Studies which favors an androcentric, heteronormative representation of knowledge. Instead, a queer-feminist decolonial angle, for example as proposed by Cherrie Moraga, Gloria Anzaldúa, Audre Lorde and Jacqui Alexander, could contribute to a broader analysis of the heterosexual matrix and economies of desire pervading the modern/colonial world system.

Further, Anzaldúa's paradigm of *Nepantla*/borderlands drives us to reconsider the disciplinary constraints imposed on a project such as "postcolonial Sociology". The habit of the *Homo Academicus* to restrict and seal his specialist knowledge by constructing strict disciplinary boundaries as a basis for an indisputable coherent identity, reproduces an inability to grasp the complexity and fluidity of social phenomena in a modern/colonial world system. De-linking or border thinking, instead, promotes interdisciplinarity and dialogue between institutionalized and non-institutionalized knowledge practices. These unravel "the geo-politics of knowledge from the perspective of coloniality, the untold and unrecognized historical counterpart of modernity" (Mignolo 2005: xi).

From this perspective, the commodification strategies jeopardizing the critical potential of Postcolonial Studies can be addressed by welding its epistemological premises to its ontology. Becoming merely an attractive commodity in the global market of postgraduate degrees, Postcolonial Studies can lose its political edge as a position of critical social enquiry. Critique may be reduced to rhetoric, easily consumable as part of an educational package without promoting transformative practice. Interrogating this transmutation of critique to commodity, we need to be aware of the consequences that might arise when critical movements of thought become data and frozen events held in archives and in books. When Postcolonial Studies is limited to disciplinary views, branded with different labels such as "Postcolonial Literature" or "Postcolonial Sociology", a re-colonization of knowledge takes place, dissipating the potential of critique through disciplinary domestication.

In sum, I have argued here for the need for a critical decolonial feminist-queer perspective in Sociology. This perspective relates the question of knowledge to the coordinates of hegemony and subalternity. Following Gramsci, hegemony is achieved when an alliance between political representation and civil society is forged. For Gramsci, the question of hegemony was crucial in order to understand how a national project could be pursued and realized. Therefore, he was intrigued by the role of intellectuals as allies or opponents of social change. Translating these observations to decolonizing European Sociology, we could say that this project foregrounds a new/old social constellation articulated by a group of intellectuals, originally from non-European countries or members of minoritized groups within Europe. While these groups of intellectuals are not subalterns, they articulate the power relations between the center and the periphery of power-knowledge, between subalternity and hegemony. This group of intellectuals are not only interrogating the foundational epistemic grounds of European modernity, but also articulating their discomfort with a Eurocentric matrix of representation and distribution of resources.

Specifically, in regard to academia, English monolingualism reveals more than just a lingua franca, it denotes the symbolic and factual power exercised by the hegemonic position of the Anglo-Saxon economic and political centers. Within these parameters, a standardization of academic knowledge occurs, set not only by language, but by the tools of institutional quality evaluation established through it. For example, one of these is the increasing rhetoric linked to prestige and acceptance in the global academic community of "high-impact" journals, mostly based in Britain and the United States. Here English works not just as a global language of communication, but as a method of effacing the local complexity of intellectual debates. Translation into English follows what I have called elsewhere a "uniform market logic" (Gutiérrez Rodríguez 2008), reducing the intricacies of the original text to the standards of the receiver. Of course, I do not want to demonize the language of Shakespeare or Joyce here, what I would like to emphasize though is what I have discussed elsewhere as the politics of transversal translation (Gutiérrez Rodríguez 2006).[11]

In this spirit, times are changing; new proposals and challenges are being made. In the North, Area Studies and Languages departments are considering their creative and theoretical potential for *border thinking* and *multilingualism*. We might find some traces of the project of decolonizing European Sociology here while Sociology departments might maintain disciplinary monolingualism.

Bibliography

Adorno, T.W. 1977. *Kulturkritik und Gesellschaft I*. Frankfurt am Main: Suhrkamp.

Anzaldúa, G. 1987. *Borderlands. La Frontera*. San Francisco: Aunt Lute Books.

Anzaldúa, G. 1990. *Making Face, Making Soul. Haciendo Caras*. San Francisco: Aunt Lute Foundation Books.

Anzaldúa, G. 2000. *Interviews – Entrevistas*, edited by A. Keaton. New York/ London: Routledge.

Anzaldúa, G. and Moraga, C. 1981. *This Bridge Called my Back*. New York: Kitchen Table.

Baca Zinn, M., Weber Canno, L., Higginbotham, E. and Thornton Dill, B. 1990. The Cost of Exclusionary Practices in Women's Studies, in *Making Face, Making Soul. Haciendo Caras*, edited by G. Anzaldúa. San Francisco: Aunt Lute Foundation Books, 29-41.

---

11 Some attempts in this direction are followed, for example, by the on-line journal transversal (http://eipcp.net/transversal/) or by the networks of Latin American, Caribbean, Portuguese and Spanish journals Latindex.

Bourdieu, P. 1958. *Sociologie de l'Algérie*. Paris: PUF.

Bourdieu, P. 1987. *Distinction: A Social Critique of the Judgement of Taste*. Harvard: Harvard University Press.

Bourdieu, P. 1988. *Homo Academicus*. Stanford: Stanford University Press.

Bourdieu, P. 1990. *In Other Words: Essays Toward a Reflexive Sociology*. Stanford: Stanford University Press.

Butler, J. 1994. Feminism by any other name (Interview with Rosi Braidotti). *Differences: A Journal of Feminist Cultural Studies*, 6(2-3), 27-35.

Collins, P.H. 2000. *Black Feminist Thought: Knowledge, Consciousness, and the Politics of Empowerment*. New York/London: Routledge.

Combahee River Collective 1977. *A Black Feminist Statement*. Boston.

Connell, R. 2007. *Southern Theory: Social Sciences and the Global Dynamics of Knowledge*. London: Polity.

Davis, A.Y. 1981. *Women, Race and Class*. New York: Random House.

Deleuze, G. and Guattari, F. 2004. *A Thousand Plateaus. Capitalism and Schizophrenia*. London/New York: Continuum.

Dussel, E. 1994. *1492: El encubrimiento del Otro: Hacia el origen del "mito de la modernidad"*. La Paz: Plural Editores.

Dussel, E. 1995. *The Invention of the Americas: Eclipse of "the Other" and the Myth of Modernity*, translated by Michael D. Barber. London: Continuum.

Dussel, E. 1996. *The Underside of Modernity: Apel, Ricoeur, Rorty, Taylor and the Philosophy of Liberation*, edited and translated by Eduardo Mendieta. Amherst: Prometheus Books.

Dussel, E. 2003. *Beyond Philosophy: Ethics, History, Marxism, and Liberation Theology*, edited by Eduardo Mendieta. Lanham: Rowman and Littlefield.

Erel, U., Haritaworn, J., Gutíerrez Rodríguez, E. and Klesse, C. 2008. On the Depoliticisation of Intersectionality Talk: Conceptualising Multiple Oppressions in Critical Sexuality Studies, in *Out of Place. Interrogating Silences in Queerness/Racialities*, edited by A. Kuntsman and E. Myake. York: Raw Nerve Books, 265-92.

FeMigra (Akin, S., Apostolidou, N., Atadiyen, H., Güran, G., Gutiérrez Rodríguez, E., Kanat, A., Kutz, L. and Mestre Vives, L.) 1994. Wir, die Seiltänzerinnen, in *Gender Killer*, edited by C. Eichhorn and S. Grimm. Amsterdam: Edition ID-Archiv, 49-63.

Gelbin, C.S., Konuk, K. and Piesche, P. 2000. *AufBrüche*. Taunusstein/Main: Ulrike Helmer Verlag.

Glick Schiller, N. and Wimmer, A. 2002. Methodological Nationalism and Beyond: Nation-State Building, Migration and the Social Sciences. *Global Networks*, 2(4), 301-34.

Gramsci, A. (orig. 1926) 2006. *The Southern Question*. Toronto: Guernica Editions.

Gramsci, A. (orig. 1937) 2007. *Prison Notebook*, vol. 3. New York: Colombia University Press.

Grosfoguel, R. 2002. Colonial Difference, Geopolitics of Knowledge and Global Coloniality in the Modern/Colonial Capitalist World-System. *Review*, 25(3), 203-24.

Grosfoguel, R. 2006. La descolonización de la economía política y los estudios postcoloniales: Transmodernidad, pensamiento fronterizo y colonialidad global. *Tabula Rasa*, 4, 17-48.

Gutiérrez Rodríguez, E. 1999. *Intellektuelle Migrantinnen: Subjektivitäten im Zeitalter der Globalisierung. Eine dekonstruktive Analyse von Biographien im Spannungsverhältnis von Ethnisierung und Vergeschlechtlichung*. Opladen: Leske & Budrich.

Gutiérrez Rodríguez, E. 2000a. Fallstricke des Feminismus. *Polylog. Forum for Intercultural Philosophy*, 2 [Online]. Available at: http://them.polylog.org/2/age-de.htm [accessed: 2 July 2009].

Gutiérrez Rodríguez, E. 2000b. Akrobatik in der Marginalität. Zu Produktionsbedingungen intellektueller Migrantinnen im Kontext der Arbeitsmigration, in *AufBrüche*, edited by C. Gelbin, K. Konuk and P. Piesche. Taunustein am Main: Ulrike Hellmer Verlag, 207-23.

Gutiérrez Rodríguez, E. 2003a. Repräsentation, Postkoloniale Kritik und Subalternität, in *Spricht die Subalterne deutsch? Migration und Postkoloniale Kritik*, edited by E. Gutiérrez Rodríguez and H. Steyerl. Münster: Unrast, 17-37.

Gutiérrez Rodríguez, E. 2003b. Gouvernementalität und die Ethnisierung des Sozialen. Arbeit, Migration und Biopolitik, in *Gouvernementalität*, edited by E. Gutiérrez Rodríguez and M. Pieper. Frankfurt am Main: Campus, 161-78.

Gutiérrez Rodríguez, E. 2006. Translating Positionality. On Post-Colonial onjunctures and Transversal Understanding. *Translate: On-line Journal for Cultural Theory and Cultural Studies* [Online]. Available at: http://translate.eipcp.net/transversal/0606/gutierrez-rodriguez/en [accessed: 1 July 2009].

Gutiérrez Rodríguez, E. 2008. Lost in Translation: Transcultural Translation and Decolonialization of Knowledge. *Translate: On-line Journal for Cultural Theory and Cultural Studies* [Online]. Available at: http://translate.eipcp.net/transversal/0608/gutierrez-rodriguez/en [accessed: 1 July 2009].

Gutiérrez Rodríguez, E. 2010. *Migration, Domestic Work and Affect*. New York: Routledge.

Habermas, J. 1981. *Theorie des kommunikativen Handelns*, vol. 2. Frankfurt am Main: Suhrkamp.

Haraway, D.J. 1996. *Simians, Cyborgs and Women: The Reinvention of Nature*. New York/London: Routledge.

Harding, S. 2004. *The Feminist Standpoint Theory Reader: Intellectual and Political Controversies*. New York/London: Routledge.

Harding, S. 2008. *Sciences from Below: Feminisms, Postcolonialities, and Modernities*. Durham: Duke University Press.

Hartmann, E. 2003. The Transnationalization of Tertiary Education in a Global Civil Society, in *Agents of Change: Virtuality, Gender, and the Challenge to the Traditional University*, edited by G. Kreutzner and H. Schelhowe. Opladen: Leske & Budrich, 25-42.

hooks, b. 1984. *Feminist Theory: From Margin to Center*. Boston: South End Press.

Hügel, I., Lange, C., Ayim, A. and Bubeck, I. 1999. *Entfernte Verbindungen: Rassismus, Antisemitismus, Klassenunterdrückung*. Berlin: Orlanda Frauenverlag.

Hull, G.T., Scott, P.B. and Smith, B. 1982. *All the Women are White, All the Blacks are Men, But Some of Us Are Brave*. New York: The Feminist Press.

Jones, C. 2006. Falling Between the Cracks: What Diversity Means for Black Women in Higher Education. *Policy Futures in Education*, 4(2), 145-59.

Kalpaka, A. and Räthzel, N. 1985. Paternalismus in der Frauenbewegung?!. *Informationsdienst zur Ausländerarbeit*, 3, 21-27.

Ladner, J.A. 1973. *The Death of White Sociology*. New York: Random House.

Lorde, A. 1984. *Sister Outsider*. Freedom: The Crossing Press.

Luhmann, N. 2006. *Die Gesellschaft der Gesellschaft*, vol. 2. Frankfurt am Main: Suhrkamp.

Maldonado-Torres, N. 2008. *Against War: Views from the Underside of Modernity*. Durham: Duke University Press.

Menocal, M.R. 2003. *The Ornament of the World: How Muslims, Jews and Christian Created a Culture of Tolerance in Medieval Spain*. Boston: Little, Brown and Company.

Mignolo, W. 1995. *The Darker Side of the Renaissance: Literacy, Territoriality, and Colonization*. Ann Arbor: University of Michigan Press.

Mignolo, W. 2000. *Local Histories, Global Designs*. Princeton: Princeton University Press.

Mignolo, W. 2005. *The Idea of Latin America*. Oxford: Blackwell.

Mignolo, W. 2007. Delinking. *Cultural Studies*, 21(2), 449-514.

Mills, C. 1994. Revisionist Ontologies: Theorizing White Supremacy. *Social and Economic Studies*, 43(3), 105-34.

Mohanty, C.T., Russo, A. and Torres, L. 1991. *Third World Women and the Politics of Feminism*. Bloomington/Indianapolis: Indiana University Press.

Monroe, K., Ozyurt, S., Wrigley, T. and Alexander, A. 2008. Gender Equality in Academia: Bad News From the Trenches, and Some Possible Solutions. *Persperctives on Politics*, 6(2), 215-33.

Oguntoye, K., Opitz, M., Schultz, D. and Lorde, A. 1986. *Farbe bekennen: Afro-Deutsche Frauen auf den Spuren ihrer Geschiche*. Berlin: Orlanda Frauenverlag.

Ortiz, R. 2004. As ciências sociais e o inglês. *Revista Brasileira de Ciencias Sociais*, 19(54), 5-22.

Popoola, O. and Sezen, B. 1999. *Talking Home: Heimat aus unserer eigenen Feder, Frauen of Color in Deutschland*. Amsterdam: Bloom Moon Press.

Quijano, A. 2000. Coloniality of Power, Eurocentrism, and Latin America. *Nepantla: Views from South*, 1, 533-80.

Reed, K. 2006. *New Directions in Social Theory: Race, Gender and the Canon.* London: Sage.

Sandoval, C. 2000. *Methodology of the Oppressed.* Minneapolis: Minnesota University Press.

Smith, B. 1983. *Home Girl. A Black Feminist Anthology.* New York: Kitchen Table: Women of Color Press.

Smith, B. 1990. Racism and Women's Studies, in *Making Face, Making Soul: Haciendo Caras*, edited by G. Anzaldúa. San Francisco: Aunt Lute Foundation Books, 25-9.

Spivak, G.C. 1987. *In Other Worlds.* New York/London: Routledge.

Spivak, G.C. 1993. *Inside Outside the Teaching Machine.* New York/London: Routledge.

Spivak, G.C. 1999. *A Critique of Postcolonial Reason.* Cambridge/London: Harvard University Press.

Trinh T. Minh-Ha. 1989. *Woman, Native, Other: Writing Postcoloniality and Feminism.* Bloomington/Indianapolis: Indiana University Press.

Wakeling, P. 2007. White Faces, Black Faces: Is British Sociology a White Discipline? *Sociology*, 41, 945-60.

Wallerstein, I. 2001. *Unthinking Social Science: The Limits of Nineteenth-Century Paradigms.* Philadelphia: Temple University Press.

Weber, M. and Winckelmann, J. 1950. *Soziologie, weltgeschichtliche Analysen, Politik.* Stuttgart: Kröner.

Yamato, G. 1990. Something about the Subject Makes it Hard to Name, in *Making Face, Making Soul. Haciendo Caras*, edited by G. Anzaldúa. San Francisco: Aunt Lute Foundation Books, 10-13.

Zimmermann, K. 2000. *Spiele mit der Macht in der Wissenschaft.* Berlin: Sigma.

PART II
Pluralizing Modernity

Chapter 4

Different Roads to Modernity and Their Consequences: A Sketch

Göran Therborn

Meanings of Modernity

Space is a crucial parameter of social imagination, a little conscious frame of reference of social thinkers and scientists as well as of every (wo)man. The history of sociology and of anthropology, mutatis mutandis also of other social sciences, may be summed up as a trajectory from the "classical" nineteenth century-early twentieth century social universe, and its evolution of course, to the post-World War I focus on the local – Malinowski overtaking Westermarck in anthropology, and sociology modelled from Chicago, instead of by Weber or Durkheim – to be followed by the national, of the representative survey in sociology, of belated anthropological interest in "development". A global perspective was pioneered by Immanuel Wallerstein and "world system analysis" from the mid-1970s, and became mainstream in the 1990s, on the surf of "globalization". Geopolitical changes and methodological developments have driven these mutations of the social, from a universal to a global.

Modern and modernity are time concepts, but their spatial location has become increasingly problematized. Few scholars today would find Anthony Giddens' (1990: 1) almost disarmingly Eurocentric definition of modernity fruitful: " ... 'modernity' refers to modes of social life or organization which emerged in Europe from about the seventeenth century onwards and which subsequently became more or less worldwide in their influence". The so far most powerful challenges have come from the revisionist Parsonsianism of Shmuel Eisenstadt (2000), with a program of "multiple modernities", and from postcolonial studies (e.g. Conrad and Randeria 2002). An original alternative is provided by the anthropologist Jack Goody (2006: 297), envisaging a basically common Eurasian history, and modernity as "a regular evolutionary change".

For two decades, on and off, these issues, of the space of social imagination and the most fruitful meaning of modernity have preoccupied me. So far, my conclusion has been that modernity has to be put into a global context, but not as different modernities, which would be a descriptive cop out, but as something produced and experienced differently by different, but linked, pathways to modernity. Therefore my sympathy with, and my recognition of the importance of, the project of the editors of this volume, of transcending Eurocentrism.

But collective publication projects and individual schedules of obligation do not always fit. The following is then a compromise, between the desires of the editors and of myself, on one hand, and my scheduled duties on the other, a rapid, freehand sketch.

Modernity, then, had better be defined as one, but as a culture capable of appearing not only in different places but also, conceivably, at different times. While modern societies do look differently, that had better not be seen as a plurality of modernities, but as the outcome of different modernist strivings. You should avoid defining modernity, in plural or in singular, as a set of institutions, which would never allow you to escape from arbitrariness, about what is modern, pseudo-modern, or non-modern. Instead, modernity had better be defined in non-arbitrary, etymological terms as a time orientation, a culture, an epoch, a society, a social sphere oriented to the future, as something new and makeable, disavowing the authority of the past, of tradition, questioning ancient wisdom.

Such orientations can best be studied empirically with respect to specific practices, such as cognition, art, economics, and politics. There is no reason to expect changes in the different fields to be synchronic. The contrary should be expected. In Western Europe, there was a breakthrough of a scientific modernity in the first half of the seventeenth century, theorized in the works of Francis Bacon and Descartes, and soon institutionalized in the British Royal Society and the French Academy of Science. The modern cognitive development was strengthened by the discovery of a New World, unknown to Antiquity, but it seems to be an unwarranted Americo-centrism to claim that the latter was decisive. The breakthrough came principally in physics and its philosophy, not in anthropology and botany.

In late seventeenth century France there was a major aesthetic battle, "the Quarrel of the Ancients and the Moderns", mainly in literature – won by the moderns. It is only by mid-eighteenth century that a conception of a new economics is asserted, the rise of a post-agrarian "commercial" society, heralded by the Scottish Enlightenment, in John Millar's notion of economic evolution and in Adam Smith's *Wealth of Nations*.

Political theory was still mainly backward-looking in the eighteenth century. The concepts of "reform(ation)" and "revolution" still referred to a glorious past of purity and freedom – like the English "Glorious Revolution" of 1688 – and in a sense rightly so, given the return meaning of the prefix "re". Alternatively, revolution could refer to cyclical motion, as Copernicus' work on planetary motion *Revolutionibus planetorum*, or in the main article on revolution in the French *Encyclopédie*, the *summa* of Enlightenment knowledge, which deals with the revolution of wheels in clocks and watches. It was the French Revolution that obliterated the meaning of the prefix and turned revolution and reform into keys to the future. While the Founding Fathers of the American Revolution had their Classical European ideals, in politics as well as in architecture, they were consciously constructing a novel polity.

Table 4.1   Roads to/through modernity by the location of forces and cultures for and against

Pre/Anti-Modernity	Pro-Modernity		
	Internal	*External Forced*	*Imported and Learnt*
Internal	Europe	Colonial Zone	Reactive Modernization
External	New Worlds		

Note: Countries of reactive, or externally induced, modernization, e.g., Japan, China, Ottoman Empire/Turkey, Iran, Siam/Thailand.

A breakthrough of modernity may then occur at different times in different fields of the same culture area. But from the perspective of an understanding of the social geological formation of the contemporary world, it seems that it is the victory of a future-oriented conception of politics, as a concentration of a society's collective force, which is crucial.

Four Roads to Modernity

The modern political rupture with the past took different forms and occurred at different times in different parts of the world. In an empirical work on the history of the right to vote (Therborn 1992) it dawned upon me that all these differences may be summed up into four major pathways into modernity, defined by the conflict lines for and against the new, between modernity and tradition, between modernity and anti-modernity. They can be distinguished in general analytical terms, and therefore used not only to sort groups of countries but also as ideal types, two or more of which may have been taken by a particular country. How was the new political culture generated? Internally, in the given society, or imposed or imported from outside? Who were the forces of the new? A new stratum with the given society, an external force, or a part of the old internal elite? Where were the main forces of anti-modernity, of traditional authority and submission, inside or outside?

In this vein, we may distinguish four main conflictual configurations in the world. Originally they emerged as empirical generalizations, but, especially as they can be located in a logical property space, they can also be used as ideal types. Not all logical combinations have been empirically significant, but the four main actual roads to modernity were opened up in the following ways.

The new future orientation of the last centuries first emerged in Europe, not as a natural emanation of European civilization, but out of conflicts internal to Europe, to Northwestern Europe primarily. In other words, the European route was one of civil war, violent or not, which pitted the forces of reason, enlightenment, nation/people, innovation, and change against those of the eternal truths of the Church, of the sublime wisdom and beauty of Ancient philosophy and art, of the divine rights of kings, of the ancient privileges of aristocracy, and of the customs of fathers and grandfathers.

In the New Worlds of European settlement, anti-modernity was, in the first rise of modern currents, perceived as mainly external, in the conservative metropolis, in Britain to North America, in Spain and Portugal to Latin America, *and*, increasingly, in the local Others of the settler societies, the natives, the slaves, and the ex-slaves. Independence got rid of the external metropolis, but what to do with the local Others was to haunt the moderns of the New Worlds for a very long time. It still does.

To the Colonial Zone, from North-western Africa to Southeast Asia, modernity arrived literally out of the barrel of guns, with the colonial conquest, subduing the internal forces of tradition. Colonialism by modern states, such as by nineteenth and twentieth century European states, meant an imposition of modernity from outside, after having defeated native traditional authorities. But imposed European colonial modernity was in fact a mixture of a very delimited modernist thrust and neotraditionalism – of bolstered "indirect rule" and codified ethnic identities and customary law. Japanese twentieth century colonialism in Taiwan, Korea, and Manchuria was much more consistently modernist, pushing mass education and industrialization. Modernity was not carried further by settlers, but by new generations of natives, of "évolués" who turned what they had learnt from their conquerors – about the possibility of change and development, about nations, peoples, rights – against their masters and created anti-colonial nationalism. This is the road to modernity by anti-colonial rebellion. The countries of Reactive Modernization were challenged and threatened by colonial domination, and in the face of these threats a part of the internal elite started to import innovation. Here modernity developed as pre-emptive reaction by a part of an internal elite perceiving their realm being under acute foreign threat, and imposed from above on the population, still following traditional orientations. The modernist project was in this case conservative in intent, aiming at enhancing the population's capacity to defend an existing state. Initially this was generally conceived only in military terms, of acquiring modern arms, arms technology, and military organization, but that program was soon widened to economic technology, education, transport, public health, and political institutions. A new and stronger form of social cohesion was a central aim, seen as a key to the overwhelming strength of the threatening imperialist powers. Meiji Japan is the most successful and clear-cut example, but several pre-modern polities embarked upon it, Qing China, Joson Korea, Siam of Chlulongkorn, The Ottoman empire, Egypt of Muhammed Ali and his successors, Qajar Persia, Abyssinia.

As was said above, the roads to modernity can be seen as abstract types, implying that we may find countries taking two or more roads. The contemporary world has two major hybrids in this respect, Russia and China. This hybrid development set its own limits to Communism as an alternative modernity.

Russia is a European power, and its revolution in 1917 was very much in the European modernist trajectory from the French Revolution of 1789, a reference constantly on the minds of the revolutionaries of 1917, of the February as well as of the October Revolution. The Bolshevik revolution was a European-type revolution by an urban industrial working-class, organized and rallied by a party that developed as a section of the international European labour movement. However, Lenin and the other Bolshevik leaders were well aware of the fact, that they and their following constituted only a minority in a mainly rural and agrarian country. Their modernist reading of historical development entitled them nevertheless, as they saw it, to start a profound social transformation from above. The ruthless industrialization under Stalin was a move of defence of an isolated underdeveloped country with many powerful enemies, as well as a program of social change. There was a precedent in Russian history, the reign of Tsar Peter I, generally known as Peter the Great, who wanted Russia to catch up with Western Europe.

The hybridity of China's twentieth century road to modernity stems above all from two features, the country's ambiguous national status, and the character of its most successful political import. From the last nineteenth century decades of the Qing dynasty and during the Republic, China was neither independent and sovereign nor a colony, or rather it was both at the same time. There was a Chinese state, without a viceroy or a governor-general above it. But foreign powers held a number of "treaty ports", most importantly Shanghai, and had asserted various extra-territorial rights in the country. A major source of public revenue, the customs, was run by a foreign imperialist consortium. Anti-imperialist nationalism in the face of a long series of foreign humiliations created the first modern political party, still usually transcribed as the Kuomintang, and modern mass movements in China. Of landmark importance was the May Fourth (1919) Movement against the post-World War I settlement handing over the colony of defeated Germany, Tsingtao, to Japan. Out of this anti-colonial nationalism came a generation of iconoclastic intellectual modernism, and a political radicalism, which in the early 1920s allied the Kuomintang government with the Soviet Union. Directly out of a part of the May Fourth Movement came also the Chinese Communist Party, founded in 1920. On the other hand, as China was never fully colonized, the ideologies of the colonial powers did not penetrate much of China, outside the swinging circles of Shanghai or the few pupils of American missionaries.

After the failure of Reactive Modernization in the last decades of the Qing dynasty, the colonial/anti-colonial road became important to Chinese modernity, but it was not the only one. There was the road of social revolution. The ancient empire had fallen to an indigenous revolution in 1911, and the turn to the Soviet example after May 1919 led to a protracted revolutionary process. The Chinese Communists under Mao's leadership became successful because they turned a European-type working class party and class politics into a party of rural class struggle, and because they wedded their class politics to anti-imperialist, first of all anti-Japanese, nationalism.

Experiences on the Road

The pathways to modernity have left enduring, though not necessarily perpetual or unchangeable consequences. So far they are clearly discernible. Without any claim to exhaustiveness, four such historical consequences will be briefly touched upon here. Each of them challenges European and North Atlantic views of politics and of society. The different routes to modernity generated different notions and different experiences of political rights and representative government, nation, religion, and inequality.

Representative government

My discovery of the four main roads to and through modernity occurred during a study of the right to vote in the world (Therborn 1992), in turn following upon two regional studies of the suffrage, one of the OECD countries, the other of Latin America.

The European questions of modern representative government were: who has the right to represent the people? How many political rights should be accorded the people and its representatives?

In spite of the inclusion of democracy and other forms of deliberative government in Europe's revered Antiquity, in spite of the Roman law concept of *representatio*, spreading from business to politics, and in spite of the medieval traditions of representative government, with the two highest offices elected, of Pope and Emperor, those questions took a very long time to be finally answered. 350 years in fact, from the English Civil War of the 1640s to Swiss universal suffrage in 1971, the democratization of the Iberian peninsula in the mid-1970s, and the belated Communist acceptance of competitive elections by the end of the 1980s. Even the principles of popularly elected government and of "democracy", allowing for ambiguities of interpretation, took a long time to conquer the European mainstream, until the end of World War I by the former, and till the defeat of Fascism in 1945 of the latter. Why it took so long, and so many revolutions is a story too complex even to be summarized here. But underlying the whole process was that modern representative government in Europe concerned the fundamental internal socio-economic ordering of society, around which there were many conflicting interests, well organized, the old ones from European medieval traditions, new ones from a rapidly evolving industrial class society.

In the New World of the Americas, rights and representations of the people were asserted in the wars of independence. Here the crucial questions were: who are the people? How should political rights be implemented?

Were slaves, ex-slaves, and Indians part of the people, whose rights the Enlightened declarations of independence and new constitutions boldly proclaimed? No, obviously not. When the last British governor of Virginia promised freedom to all slaves who escaped from their American owners and joined the British, George Washington called him "that arch-traitor to the rights of humanity" (!) (Schama

2005: 18). Despite the defeat of the Southern slave-owners in the American Civil War, racially universal suffrage was not established in USA until 1968-70, after almost two centuries of independence. Latin Americans were less rabidly racist than North Americans, but slavery persisted longer in Brazil (until 1888) than in the US, and explicit exclusion of illiterates from the right to vote was maintained in Chile, Ecuador, and Peru until the 1970s, and in Brazil until 1989.

The possibility of exercising political rights was a special problem of the Americas, and not only due to Latin American coups and dictators. In contrast to Europe, the crucial dates of democracy in the Americas are not acceptance of democracy, but of the exercise of formally recognized rights. In the US, this was around 1970, a century after the slave states were defeated in the Civil War, when democratic rights could be exercised in the South, in Argentina it was the secret ballot of the Saenz Peña Law of 1912. The tremendous Mexican Revolution in 1910 broke out under the slogan of "Effective suffrage and no re-election [of the President]".

In the Colonial Zone the key question was the representation of the colonized in the government of their country. Gradually, this was conceded by British and the French, while rejected by the Portuguese and by the African settler regimes of South Africa and Rhodesia. In the latter cases independence came from war – or protracted struggles and international sanctions – but in the former through constitutional negotiations. Independence was not a direct democratic conquest – it was rejected by referendum in all French Africa except Guinea in 1958 – but a deal negotiated by a political elite who had come to the fore through an electoral process, with variable constituency arrangements, as the legitimate representatives of the colonized people. Representative government in the Colonized Zone centred around the rights of the colonized to represent their land, little about the rights and relations of the people and their representatives in government.

Shrewd rulers of countries of Reactive Modernization, of Meiji Japan, for instance, or the Young Ottomans in Istanbul noticed that the powerful, threatening imperial powers had constitutional representative governments. This was interpreted as a key to their force and cohesion. So, in this fourth pathway to modernity, popular political rights and representative government emerged as a response to the question, How can national cohesion be strengthened?

The Japanese government in 1881 announced its plan to octroi a constitution by 1889 and to hold elections (with a very restricted suffrage) in 1890, and kept its promises. Rights of representation were given from above with a view to having "the people satisfied and able to cooperate actively with the administration, in order to reach the goal of modernization and full national sovereignty" (Mason 1969: 24). Democracy, however, ensued only after national defeat and disaster, in the 1940s. In Turkey not even national disaster was enough. Upon the crumbling Ottoman empire followed a much more vigorous and forceful modernization from above under Kemal Atatürk, with more political participation, but no democracy.

Nation

The nation and the nation-state were European inventions, which like representative government spread around the world. But, again, a similar concept took on different meanings, and was deployed for different reasons, with different consequences.

In a global perspective two aspects of the European nation stand out. One is its anchorage in a popular and territorial history, distinguished from the writ of princely power. The other is its heavy, distinctive cultural load, with spoken language at its core. The political dimension of the nation – important to the nation of "free-born Englishmen" – was most developed in the French Republican current from the Revolution, as a nation explicitly open to non-natives. However, after the Revolution's embrace of all sympathizers, mastering the French language became required of all citizens of France, generating a large-scale program of turning "peasants into Frenchmen". The creation of national languages, i.e., through standardization among several dialects and by grammatical and orthographic codification became a major task of European small nation intellectuals of the nineteenth century, from the Balkans to Norway. Where possible, minority languages were driven out of national culture.

The settler states of the Americas had to create new nations, which mythologically and emblematically of course drew upon historical examples as symbolic resources – Ancient European Republicanism in the case of the US, historical Catholic experiences and pre-Columbian, e.g., Inca and Aztec, high culture in Hispanic America – but which claimed no national history, and which shared their language with the colonial metropolis. Most distinctive of the New World, however, was its conception of the nation as a club, to which desirable members could and should be recruited. Targeted immigration from Europe was a major dimension of nation-formation. Particularly in Latin American, Brazilian as well as, for instance, Argentine, discourse, this club member recruitment was explicitly referred to as "whitening" or "civilizing" the nation (cf. Quijada 2003; Zea 1965: 65ff, 103ff). For a long time, only people of external, European descent were regarded as a full citizens of the new nations of the Americas and Australia.

Nations of the Colonial Zone constitute a third variety. There were no historical territories, no singular historical peoples, only colonial boundaries. In a rare wise decision, African nationalist leaders decided to accept them all, however arbitrary and culturally divisive. Ali Jinnah did not, and British India, larger than any pre-colonial state of India, broke up into India – which Nehru refused to call Hindustan – Pakistan, and Bangladesh, through terrible pogroms and wars of divorce. The great linguistic diversity of most postcolonial states has meant a widespread maintenance of the language of the former colonial masters as the official or officious language of politics and business. Indonesia and Malaysia are among the exceptions, using their modern codifications of Malay as their national language. Basically, the postcolonial nation is a colonial product, which implies a tendential reproduction inside the nation of the colonial divide of colonizer and colonized.

The nation of Reactive Modernization is the pre-modern realm, as seen by the princely court. This was how the successful modernizers of Meiji Japan saw it, the less successful rulers of Siam and Abyssinia, and the soon defeated modernizers of Joson Korea, Qing China, and of the Ottoman Empire. This was a historical legacy, but synonymous with its rulers, and the significant language was scriptural, Chinese ideographic script in East Asia, classical Arabic in the Ottoman Empire, the sacred script of Abyssinia and the more secular Thai one.

Religion

Religion is everywhere an ancient, pre-modern institution. Religion, the rules and rites of the sacred, was the core of most pre-modern societies, and very much so of Europe. But in the breakthrough to the modern political era, it played very different roles.

In the internal conflicts of Europe the established Christian churches, Protestant as well as Catholic and Orthodox, were on the losing side of anti-modern tradition. The pattern was set by the English Civil War and by the French Revolution, and in the nineteenth century the Papacy became the centre of European anti-modernism. Protestantism fissioned, between conservative High Church, and often moderately progressive Dissent, but there did also develop a reactionary Protestant fundamentalism, best represented by the Calvinist Dutch Anti-Revolutionaries, who started out as enemies of the French Revolution and of all subsequent ones, including the anti-colonial of the "East Indies".

This anti-modernist stance cost the European churches dearly, and Europe is today the most secularized part of the world. But there have been exceptions, when the Church became the main spokeswoman of the nation. This happened in Catholic Croatia, Ireland, Lithuania, Poland, Slovakia, in the Orthodox Balkans, and in Protestant Northern Ireland.

In the Americas, the Dissenting Protestants of New England saw themselves as a vanguard of social modernity, and there was no established high church identified with British rule. North America today is the rich world centre of religiosity. Ironically, that religiosity has also in the twentieth century spawned a militant postmodern Christian fundamentalism. Whereas almost all modern isms are of European origin – from monarchism to anarchism – "fundamentalism" is an American invention of the 1920s.

In Hispanic America, nationalism was often led by priests, like Hidalgo and Morelos in Mexico, or receiving its formulations from them (Brading 2003: 43ff; Demélas 2003: 353ff). The Mexican nationalists fought under the banner of the Virgin of Guadalupe. The Church had been harassed by the Spanish Bourbons of the second half of the eighteenth century, and was no bloc in defence of royal Spanish power. The Enlightenment had entered part of the clergy, who often also identified more with the Indians than with the Spanish power. Though European-inspired anti-clericalism later reached Latin America, religiosity has remained a central feature of Latin American social life.

In the Colonial Zone, missionary religions, Christian much more than Muslim, have been conveyors of modernity, of modern education and health care, in particular. Many of the anti-colonialist leaders had been educated in missionary schools. Native organized and codified religions, like Buddhism, Hinduism and Islam, on the other hand, have benefited from nationalist promotion. The ex-colonial world is today among the most religious parts of the globe.

In pre-modern East Asia, religion was always clearly subordinated to the secular rulers, and usually to a this-worldly official ethical culture, which might be summed up as Confucianism. This secular political subordination did not change with Reactive Modernization, although supplemented in nationalist Japan by state Shintoism. East Asia today appears as relatively secular by Euro-American religious belief and practice, but it is hardly secular-*ized*. In the Ottoman empire by contrast, the Muslim clergy formed a bastion of reaction, overcome only by the shattering of the empire and the assertion of Mustafa Kemal pasha, creating a secular Turkish state from above, with a subdued but pervasive religiosity below. While the Siamese and Abyssinian monarchies successfully managed to enlist Buddhism and Christianity, respectively, as royal supports, the post-Second World War Shah of Iran was finally felled by an Islamic revolution.

Inequality

The open futures of modernity challenged hereditary inequalities, but in what direction and to what extent was very variable.

In Europe, the modern thrust focused on the hereditary privileges of the aristocracy and the high clergy, and on the estates society in general. The latter was gradually and unevenly followed by an industrial class society. The French Revolution replaced the rights and privileges of estates with a common national citizenship, and its land redistribution changed the distribution of income and wealth. "Class" emerged as a central concept of European social analysis in the aftermath of the French Revolution, referring to the economically based new internal inequality of national societies. On the whole, Western European income distribution seems to have been remarkably stable for centuries up until World War I, after which a significant economic levelling took place until the end of the century. Industrial capitalism did increase economic inequality, as Marx claimed, in Britain in the second half of the eighteenth century, in Prussia and Germany in the second half of the nineteenth century, and in France from the July monarchy to the Third Republic (Lindert 2000; Morrisson 2000). But from the dialectics of industrial capitalism came also, later, the force of equality – if not of socialism, as Marx had envisaged. Europe is the least unequal region of the world, in particular Europe east of the British Isles, west of Poland, and north of the Alps.

In the Americas, human equality was held to be "self-evident", as the American Declaration of Independence put it. The key question then became: who are the equals? And the answer was also self-evident: white men. White North America in the eighteenth and nineteenth centuries was clearly less unequal than comparable

European countries, not only lacking an aristocracy but also having a less skewed distribution of income and wealth than Britain. The liberal French aristocrat de Tocqueville (1835/1961: 41) was so overwhelmed by it in the 1830s, that he came to see the "gradual development" of equality as "a providential fact", reading it back into French history from the eleventh century on. But White equality coexisted with Black slavery, and the racial divide is still visible today in the urban ghettoes. And the White equality which mattered to the Founding Fathers of the USA referred to "life, liberty, and the pursuit of happiness", and did not include economics. It was existential and social. "Class" has always had difficulties to coagulate in a society of settler individualism, ethnic immigration, and race.

Latin America was always more hierarchical than Anglo-America, and also racially hierarchical, from Québec to La Plata, rather than dichotomized. The great German scholar Alexander von Humboldt (1811) was struck by the enormous income inequality in New Spain (soon to become Mexico), but contrasted it with much more egalitarian Lima. Ibero-America was primarily a land of conquistadores, rather than of settlers and immigrants. It is now one of the most unequal parts of the planet, combining Latin social hierarchies with legacies of extensive Indian servitude and of Black slavery, recently augmented by massive "informalization" of postindustrial, neoliberal labour markets. But at least until the full onslaught of neoliberalism in late twentieth century, the two Latin countries most shaped by nineteenth century mass immigration, Argentina and Uruguay, were markedly less unequal than the rest of the region.

In the Colonial Zone, the demand for equality was above all for equality with the colonizers. This set the stage for a postcolonial social division between the majority of the population, the poor, and the new political elite. Class organization has been confined to small modern enclaves, of dockers, railwaymen, miners, plantation workers, few industrial workers. Many countries of Sub-Saharan Africa are now similar to the Latin American ones in inequality, with even larger, marginalized urban slum populations. Corresponding to the racial divides of the Americas are ethnic ones in Africa, following locations in the colonial structure and/or the ethnic composition of the rulers.

While the elite-population bifurcation is a common feature of postcoloniality, national politics can, of course, make a major difference. In India, important equalizing steps were taken after independence, most importantly land reform and a vast program of affirmative action for the lower castes. An organized industrial working class began to develop, centre in the textile industries of Bombay, although always a small minority – largely smashed in late twentieth century– in the overwhelming non-industrial postcolonial economy.

To the ruling elites of Reactive Modernization, equality was above all equality among modern nations.

This was directed against the humiliating unequal treaties which China, Japan, the Ottoman empire, and other pre-modern states had had forced upon them by the imperial powers of Europe and North America, providing special trade and port concessions and extra-territorial jurisdiction to those powers. At the Versailles

Peace Conference in 1919, Japan proposed a clause of "racial equality" in the covenant of the League of Nations, of equality among nations regardless of race. The White settler dominions, Australia shrillest of all, opposed it, and US President Wilson had it thrown out of the preparing commission (Shimazu 1998).

However, the fact that today Japan and the two other Northeast Asian national development states most inspired by it, South Korea and Taiwan, constitute one of the least unequal regions of the world economically, may also follow from the concerns of national cohesion and the notion of noblesse oblige characteristic of Reactive Modernization. Although South Korea, after its belated democratization, has some rather strong trade unions, Northeast Asian income equality is hardly explainable by internal class relations of force, although fear of Communism was conducive to postwar land reform. Existential status is another matter – the basically conservative Reactive Modernization wanted to preserve pre-modern hierarchy, etiquette, and deference. While class organization and class conflict have had limited importance in both regions, the current Northeast Asian pattern of inequality is the opposite of the North American.

Patriarchy and the rights of women could not break through as issues in the first decisive openings of political modernity, and gender equalization has its own trajectories, which can also be connected to the main historical pathways to modernity (Therborn 2004). But that is another story. Women played a significant part in the early period of the French Revolution and in Paris, and some courageous female revolutionaries tried to push the "Rights of Man" further. But they never managed to get a fair hearing in the male sites of power. The Revolution ended with an affirmation of a secularized patriarchy in the Napoleonic Civil Code of 1804, with its notorious clause of the husband being the "*chef de famille*", kept in France until 1970. Powerful women's movements were pioneered in USA and in other White settler countries, such as Australia and New Zealand in the 19th century. The first egalitarian marriage legislation came in Northern Europe right after World War I, by reform in Scandinavia, by revolution in Russia.

Through colonial settlement, colonial rule, and colonial threat, Europe left its imprint on the whole modern world. But the world cannot be understood from the western tip of the Eurasian continent. Even worldwide Europe-generated concepts like representative government and nation have acquired different meanings and rationales in other parts of the world. Key notions of sociological analysis, like religion and class, have vastly different significance in different parts of the modern capitalist world.

References

Brading, D. 2003. La monarquía católica, in *Inventando la nación. Iberoamérica. Siglo XIX*, edited by A. Annino and F-X. Guerra. México: Fondo de cultura económica, 15-26.

Conrad, S. and Randeria, S. (eds) 2002. *Jenseits des Eurozentrismus*. Frankfurt am Main: Campus.

Demélas, M-D. 2003. Estado y actores colectivos. El caso de los Andes, in *Inventando la nación. Iberoamérica. Siglo XIX*, edited by A. Annino and F-X. Guerra. México: Fondo de cultura económica, 347-78.

Eisenstadt, S. et al. (eds) 2000. Multiple Modernities. *Daedalus*, 129(1).

Giddens, A. 1990. *The Consequences of Modernity*. Stanford: Stanford University Press.

Goody, J. 2006. *The Theft of History*. Cambridge: Cambridge University Press.

Humboldt, A.v. 1811. *Political Essay on the Kingdom of New Spain* vol. 1. London: transl. J. Black.

Lindert, P.H. 2000. Three Centuries of Inequality in Britain and America, in *Handbook of Income Distribution* vol. 1, edited by A. Atkinson and F. Bourguignon. Amsterdam: Elsevier, 167-216.

Mason, R.H.P. 1969. *Japan's First General Election, 1890*. Cambridge: Cambridge University Press.

Morrisson, C. 2000. Historical Perspectives on Income Distribution: The Case of Europe, in *Handbook of Income Distribution* vol. 1, edited by A. Atkinson and F. Bourguignon. Amsterdam: Elsevier, 217-60.

Quijada, M. 2003. Qué nación? Dinámicas y dicotomías en el imaginario hispanoamericano, in *Inventando la nación. Iberoamérica. Siglo XIX*, edited by A. Annino and F-X. Guerra. México: Fondo de cultura económica, 287-315.

Schama, S. 2005. *Rough Crossings*. London: BBC Books.

Shimazu, N. 1998. *Japan, Race, and Equality: The Racial Equality Proposal of 1919*. London: Routledge.

Therborn, G. 1992. The Right to Vote and the Four Routes to/through Modernity, in *State Theory and State History*, edited by R. Torstendahl. London: Sage, 62-92.

Therborn, G. 2004. *Between Sex and Power: Family in the World, 1900-2000*. London: Routledge.

Tocqueville, A. de. 1835/1961. *De la démocratie en Amérique* 2 vols. Paris: Gallimard.

Zea, L. 1965. *El pensamiento latinoamericano*. Vol. 2. México: Pomarca.

Chapter 5

New Modernities: What's New?

Jan Nederveen Pieterse

'Modernities' is an increasingly fashionable terminology, but what does it mean? Is the shift from modernity to modernities important? Is it just one of these label changes that enables sociologists to recycle familiar material under a different heading, new and improved? Does it represent an anthropological turn in sociology – climbing down from grand theory into the minutiae of local differences? Is it a capitulation to postcolonial studies, a modish extension of the repertoire, a slight variation in the curriculum as a genuflection to new postcolonial intelligentsias? In other words, is modernities really *modernity plus local franchises*, or is something more fundamental at issue?

That the theme of modernities is on the agenda makes sense for various reasons. First, the discourse of development and transition – as in developing countries – is future oriented and in effect places them in everlasting limbo in the waiting room of history. After several 'development decades', is 'development' still an appropriate or sufficient heading for these numerous societies? Are they only entitled a future and not the dignity of a present? Are they ever to be on the margins of or en route to an already defined state, modernity, and is their destiny ever to be an approximation, a building in construction – an 'incomplete modernity', as in a classic label for Latin American societies? Does their condition not also intimate truths about contemporary modernity? Moreover, several developing countries have changed status. The London Stock Exchange upgraded South Korea and Taiwan to 'the status of "developed markets" – on a par with the UK and US' with momentous consequences for international financial markets. As the economies change status, so do the societies and understandings of modernity must accommodate these realities as well. At Microsoft, in view of outsourcing software programming, the motto is 'Think India'.

History is changing too and some of the most radical perspectives emerge not in sociology or social theory but in history. Consider some fundamentals.

> In 1500, Europe was a peripheral economic power: it had only three of the world's twenty largest cities (the rest were in Asia, the Middle East or Africa (Frost 1998: 52).

and

> In 1697 Giovanni Careri, a merchant from Naples, Italy, considered Mexico City
> equal to Italian towns. With nearly 100,000 inhabitants it was the largest city in
> the Americas (Hoerder 2002: 203; cf. Frank 1998: 12).

Janet Abu-Lughod (1989) pushed the time line of the modern world-system back
from Wallerstein's 'long sixteenth century' to the thirteenth century, more in line
with Fernand Braudel's periodization of capitalism and recentering early capitalism
in the Levant and the Middle East. K.N. Chauduri (1990), Andre Gunder Frank
(1998) and Kenneth Pomeranz (2000) push the timing still further back and centre
the early world economy in East and South Asia. This has profound implications
for our thinking about modernity and capitalism.

This reorientation applies to current trends too. Westernization is gradually
being overtaken by easternization, in its various meanings such as the spread of
Japanese management techniques (Kaplinksy 1994), the East Asian development
model, Asian diaspora economies, the orientalization of everyday culture in the
West, Malaysia's Look East policy, and the emergence of China as a force in the
world economy. The emerging economies are epicentres of economic growth and
renewal. The world cities of the twenty-first century may no longer be New York
and Tokyo but Changzhou and Beijing. These developments are acknowledged
in business media, and to some extent in economics and development studies,
but sociology continues to be spellbound by the vicissitudes of modernity in the
West, in the process advertising the provincial character of western sociology.
Western sociology is the sociology of modernity. Modernity spawned sociology
and modernity is sociology's baby. Modernity has been a western panopticon, a
watchtower and cosmology in which the world is comprehended, ordered and
ranked from an occidental point of view. This applies to the classics, from Marx to
Weber, for whom the locus of modernity is the West while its dynamics, whether
capitalism or rationalization, have a universal vocation. It applies to Habermas
who seeks to prolong the program of the Enlightenment, to Giddens who views
globalization as one of modernity's consequences and turns the globe into an annex
of the West, to the postmoderns most of whom are hardcore occidentalists, and it
applies to those who enunciate the end of modernity. 'If an historical era is ending,
it is the era of modernity itself' (Toulmin 1990: 3). Faced with this modernity
without windows one wonders, where is the exit?

The critique of Orientalism has not been matched by or developed into a
critique of Occidentalism, that is, a critique of the self-understanding and self-
presentation of the West. Conventional understandings of modernity are steeped
in Occidentalism; industrialism, modernity and sociology originate in the same
nineteenth-century epoch and classical theory is embedded in the tacit framework
of western imperialism (Connell 1997). Western social science still dominates
social science globally, even as it remains entrenched in occidental narcissism.

In *The Closing of the American Mind*, Allan Bloom cautions that the nonwestern
cultures are all ethnocentric:

Only in the Western nations, i.e., those influenced by Greek philosophy, is there
some willingness to doubt the identification of the good with one's own way
(1987: 36).

This kind of stubborn reification of the classics has long been left behind in
European classical studies but remains virulent in American conservative discourse.
Occidental narcissism is a keynote of elite conservatism that runs through Leo
Strauss and his University of Chicago acolytes and has found a contemporary
translation in the political agendas of neoconservatives (cf. Drury 1997).

Modernities may be an increasingly fashionable terminology, but does the current
literature do justice to the depth of this theme? A special issue of *Public Culture
on Alternative Modernities* (published as Gaonkar 2001) is a quasi-postmodern
rereading of mostly European texts of modernity and offers little that is alternative.
A special issue of *Daedalus* devoted to Multiple Modernities lists several new
destinations, but does the train really leave the station? What precisely is *new* about
these destinations? Interesting as the treatments are, they are mostly descriptive or
rework local or regional theory, rather than reflecting on fundamentals. Ironically the
issue is edited by one of the stalwarts of modernization theory, Shmuel Eisenstadt.
In his introduction Eisenstadt notes that 'Western patterns of modernity are not the
only "authentic" modernities, though they enjoy historical precedence and continue
to be the basic reference point for others' (2000: 3). This angle is woven throughout
his account with passages such as 'As the civilization of modernity developed first
in the West...' (2000: 7). In this view,

> Practically from the beginning of modernity's expansion multiple modernities
> developed, all within what may be defined as the Western civilizational framework.
> It is important to note that such modernities, Western, but significantly different
> from those in Europe, developed first not in Asia – Japan, China or India – or
> in Muslim societies where they might have been attributed to the existence of
> distinct non-European traditions, but within the broad framework of Western
> civilizations (ibid.: 13).

Here the reference is to the development of modernity in the Americas. So the
theme is modernities, but in effect we never leave the West. Contrast this with
Subrahmanyam (1998):

> Having taken away so much from the societies of South Asia, it seems to be high
> time that social science at least gave them back what they had by the sixteenth
> and seventeenth centuries – their admittedly very ambiguous "early modernity"
> (Subrahmanyam 1998: 100).

So here are two opposed views: modernity and multiple modernities start in the
West, and alternatively, 'early modernity' has its beginnings in Asia. What is at
stake in this argument?

Eisenstadt's perspective is most common in the literature and represents a weak argument on modernities. In this discussion I will present a continuum of views on modernities from weak to strong arguments. The weak versions don't dispute the western claims to precedence and present new modernities essentially as add-ons to modernity, variations on the theme. Strong arguments, in contrast, no longer privilege the West and critique or deconstruct modernity and western perspectives on modernity. I argue that the latter perspective is both more appropriate and more interesting.

Dirlik, Bahl and Gran's *History after the Three Worlds* (2000) signals ambivalence: it is part praise of new themes and methodologies (in particular subaltern studies) and part revindication of Marxism *vis-à-vis* cultural studies; that is, the new is incorporated (or repudiated) in order to regain lost territory in the old. So the old is not settled, is never settled, and variations will inevitably be enlisted to rework the theme.

This is a large argument that concerns making sense of epochs, so by its nature it is high trapeze work. When doing mountain views let's not complain about the air being thin for it comes with the scenery. One question is whether this argument can be settled in theory at all, or is the construction of social theory, dominated by western inputs, too circular in the first place?

Modernities is one option among three broad choices: postmodernism, which is a familiar enough avenue; reworking or reinventing modernity – here Beck's new modernity or risk society is the most influential formulation; and third, modernities, which is a theoretically weak choice by comparison to the other two. As a theme modernities is much less developed, and this is where this discussion comes in. I will first discuss the antecedents of the idea of modernities and then turn to the implications of revisionist history such as Frank's *ReOrient*. The next section deals with the question of how to frame the new modernities in the global south, on the argument that what matters are not the specifics and the minutiae, but the way the discussion is framed. The closing section addresses the interaction of modernities.

Antecedents of Modernities

How do we locate the general turn towards the plural? In several ways it evolves from and is framed by earlier analyses of modernity in the West. The fundamental move from modernity to modernities took place in western sociology following the recognition of the diverse growth paths of various countries and regions and the difference between early and late (and late-late) industrializers. Differences between northern and southern Europe, Western, Central and Eastern Europe are part of this understanding. But the theme and magnetism of modernity was so prominent and compelling that the notion of different modernities only surfaced much later.

Western thinking has long been steeped in critiques of modernity such as Freud's *Civilization and its Discontents*; Frankfurt School cultural pessimism and its ripples through Erich Fromm, Marcuse (*One Dimensional Man*), David Riesman (*The Lonely Crowd*); Popper's critique of large-scale social engineering; Habermas' colonization of the life-world; Foucault's society of disciplinary normalization; and Bauman's work on modernity and the Holocaust.

Familiarity breeds contempt and sustained familiarity with modern times generates new problematizations and a move from modern sociology to sociology of modernity: from a generic category, modernity, to really-existing modernity, and from treating modernity in the future tense or as blueprint, to viewing it as a condition, and thus the finding that French, Italian modernity etc. is different in significant ways and so is modernity in the 'peripheries' of Europe (e.g. Calinescu 1987). We can describe this shift as an ethnographic turn in sociology (Bauman 1991, 1992; Featherstone et al. 1995). The redeployment of anthropologists in 'modern' and urban settings (as part of critical anthropology) contributes to retooling sociology and to deepening the puzzle of modernity.

The idea of multiple modernities in the West is familiar and includes American modernity as distinct from European, as mentioned by Eisenstadt (and Taylor 1999). This notion carries a conservative subtext for it resonates in a subtle way with the theme of American exceptionalism (Lipset 1996).

Postmodernism emerged from these and other problematizations of modernity and, likewise, involves a shift in the observers' gaze from programmatic modernity and modernity as incomplete project à la Habermas to modernity as present or, indeed, as past.

The landscape changed over time; the 'American challenge' could still be conceived within the Eurocentric framework, but how about the 'Japanese challenge'? The era of decolonization generated fundamental critiques of Eurocentrism (Amin 1989; Nederveen Pieterse and Parekh 1995). The sprawling frame of modernity comes up again in relation to the newly industrialized countries, in particular the East Asian challenge.

These trends are all relevant and under each heading there are insightful contributions, which can be described as a decentering of modernity. Yet I think the literature is unsatisfactory in fundamental ways. The core problem is that modernities tend to be thought of as modernity plus, i.e. modernity plus variations, and modernity itself is not fundamentally in question. The theme remains essentially the script of Marx, Durkheim, Weber, along with Comte and Tönnies, reworked by Parsons and the modernization theorists, Habermas, Norbert Elias (the civilizing process) and Wallerstein (the modern world-system). Renegade voices such as Foucault (regimes of truth) and Lyotard (the postmodern condition) are being accommodated *outside* modernity, tucked away under the headings of poststructuralism or postmodernism.

How modernities are understood is, of course, a function of the general understanding of modernity. Two major angles on modernity are universalist and historicist (Table 5.1). The shift in perspective from modernity to modernities

Table 5.1   Angles on modernity

Angles	Variants	Sources
Universalist	An overall evolutionary dynamic.	General.
	Unilinear evolutionism.	Colonial anthropology.
	Evolutionary universals.	Structural functionalism.
	Convergence theory.	Modernization theory.
Historicist	Modernity takes particular forms according to historical and initial conditions.	Nonwestern views.
	Multilinear evolution.	Much current sociology.

represents a shift from a universalist to a historicist approach. The historicist view essentially broadens unilinear evolution to multilinear evolution. All along this has been the main approach in nonwestern sociology, in particular in South and East Asia (Singh 1989); so the general shift to *modernities* signifies that the historicist view is now being adopted also in western sociology. Yet incorporating modernities in the historicist view of modernity leaves modernity itself essentially untouched; we merely add variations to the repertoire. This is a weak argument on modernities.

If, on the other hand, we think of modernities as a potentially radical new departure several tasks or opportunities emerge. European culture and modernity are, of course, wired to non-European worlds in many ways (e.g. Bernal 1987). The prosperity and cultural efflorescence of the Renaissance in Italy and beyond was conditioned and inspired by the Levant trade and cultural flowering in the Islamic world. C.L.R. James argued that growing bourgeois prosperity in Bordeaux and Nantes was made possible by the wealth generated by the slave trade: without African slaves, no revolution in Europe and no 'age of democratic revolution'. The emergence of the Westphalian interstate system in the seventeenth century was made possible by alliances between the Ottoman Empire and the Protestant powers, outflanking the Habsburgs and Rome (Atasoy 1999): without the Ottomans, no Westphalia, no 'modern interstate system'.

Anthony King (1995) argues with delectable irony that postmodernism *preceded* modernity notably in the colonial cities in the global south where the experience of fragmented and multicultural social space had been common long before it came to the West: 'the culture, society, and space of early twentieth century Calcutta or Singapore prefigured the future in a much more accurate way than did that of London or New York. "Modernity" was not born in Paris but rather in Rio. With this interpretation, Euro-American paradigms of so-called "postmodernism" have neither much meaning nor salience outside the narrow geographical confines of Euro-America where they developed' (King 1991: 8). In this assessment modernity is not simply being reinvented in the global south but originated there in the first place. This would make colonial modernization a prototype of modernization and the predecessor of postmodernism. However, showing that European culture and modernity hold ample non-European traces (e.g. Nederveen Pieterse 1994, 2009) doesn't necessarily affect the precedence and status of European modernity; that requires more fundamental reassessments.

Ex Oriente Lux

Frank (1998), Pomeranz (2000) and Hobson (2004) argue that most of the attributes we associate with modernity – market production and intensive and long-distance trade, high rates of economic growth and productivity growth, high rates of population growth, urban densities, extensive transnational divisions of labour, etc. – existed in China and South Asia centuries before they existed in Europe. This has profound implications. Most western social science has been concerned with explaining the lead of Europe and the backwardness of other regions, as in Marx's Asian mode of production, Weber's Protestant ethic, Wallerstein's modern world-system, modernization theory, David Landes' arguments, and so forth. But what if the task becomes, rather, to explain the backwardness of Europe, the precedence of Asia and the ramifications of the Afro-Eurasian world economy?

This reorientation enables us to understand how early science and technology, philosophy, and examples of urbanity and modernism, luxury and sensuousness, all originate in the Orient. Thus, this path leads from the oriental bazaar and the Kasbah to the Arcades of Milan and Paris and thence to the department store. In science and technology, it leads from China and South Asia via Mesopotamia to Venice and European crafts and technologies (porcelain, paper, fireworks, etc.). In art, it leads from Ukiyo-e via displays of Japanese works in Paris salons to Japonisme to impressionism and beyond.

By this reckoning, early capitalism, markets and manufactures all go back to the East. This reorientation accounts for the historical antecedents of western modernity much more effectively than the usual intra-European view. This implies a complete and fundamental reworking of the premises of 'modern' (i.e. nineteenth century) social science. We must then explain Europe's lead over time in quite different terms (on the basis of geography, the triangular trade, etc.). A further implication is that we must strip modernity of its specifically European complexes such as rationalism, secularization, liberalism. The European *Kulturkampf* and the particular contests between church and state, between absolutism and people's sovereignty and democracy, are but one way in which modernity takes shape. Antagonism between religion and science (which Needham 1981 noted was absent in Confucian China) is not a necessary feature of modernity. Thus western modernity becomes *a* modernity and loses its model status. By the same token this also casts a different light on the recent emergence of the Asian economies and in fact their reemergence as forces in the world economy. The rapid rise of East and South Asia is based on centuries-old experience and resumes older patterns.

Against this backdrop the Mediterranean and Atlantic eras appear as but transitory phases in the global *longue durée*.

Framing Modernities

In the global south modernity is the corollary of 'development'. Despite dependency theory and other criticisms of modernization thinking, modernity and modernization have been quite alive in public discourse, social science and policy formulation in the south. Here modernity is still often thought of in future tense, as a programmatic concept which serves both as carrot and stick, as promise and critique, and in both modalities is fraught with ambivalence. While the divergence between the program and the realities of western modernities is common knowledge, this has not obliterated the project of modernity itself but has affected its definition and course. In developing countries a downside of the plural relativization of modernities is that *modernity* loses its critical edge; on the other hand, the dark side of modernity (ecological damage, social engineering, alienation, McDonaldization, consumerism) is familiar enough.

Touraine (1992) notes that development is always a combination of universal attributes of modernity, which are notoriously difficult to isolate, as well as of distinct types of modernization corresponding to specific cultures and nations. This articulation is shaped by the nature of the governing elite's relationship to established social forces and to the most advanced nations. Countries with dualist and inarticulated economies experience a separation of political-cultural mobilization from technological and economic transformations.

The idea of 'transition', the usual entry point in discussions of 'modernizing' societies, keeps social analysis in the future tense and keeps us from undertaking a sociology and ethnography of modernity in the present tense; it is a form of 'coevalness denied' (Fabian 1983). Common self-descriptions of developing societies are *abortive* or *truncated modernity* (Latin America), societies *in transition* with modernity as the destination, or hybrid societies mixing traditional and modern sectors and values. Tradition is a salient theme: 'the internal model of traditionalism exerts a powerful influence over the contours of modernity taking shape in the developing countries' (Lee 1994: 32). Following extensive debates on the impact of colonialism, the character of capitalism and the absence of independent entrepreneurs or a national bourgeoisie, questions of good governance, civil society and political democratization have been on the horizon in most of the global south.

Conceptually what does it mean to speak of alternative modernity or 'modernities'? 'Alternative modernity' is limited in that alternative may imply better (as in alternative development), which is questionable and old fashioned in sentiment, as if looking for utopias on different shores. Consider this observation about the south in the United States: 'Traditional Southern elites represent a different political economy, but to classify this as "premodern" as Lind does, is too easy; it may well be considered an alternative modernity. This means to acknowledge that it has dynamics of its own and is not simply locked in a premodern pattern' (Nederveen Pieterse 2004: 6). Here 'alternative modernity' means to acknowledge social formations in their own terms and not as derivative of or measured in relation to a finished state somewhere in the West. In fact, this methodological caution is the ABC of anthropology.

There are distinct regional differences among modernization discourses in the south. Thus, in Asia, prominent themes are the value of cultural traditions and the *historicity* of modernity, which involves a recognition of historical depth. In Latin America, *periphery* is a central theme, as in dependency theory's peripheral capitalism and dependent development; which involves a geographical sensibility and a comparative understanding of cultures in spatial framework.

In his work on Zambia, James Ferguson uses 'modernism',

> first, to underline the point that the dismantling of linear teleologies of emergence and development remains an unfinished task ... in African studies and elsewhere; and second to suggest that current debates about modernism and postmodernism need not only "take account of Africa," but to be fundamentally qualified in the light of the contemporary African experience (Ferguson 1999: 17).

In the Zambian copper belt, *The Expectations of Modernity* have not been met. To discuss these experiences Ferguson introduces themes such as 'counter-urbanization' and quotes a local who says, 'From now on, it's just down, down, down' (ibid.: 13).

> New modernities' may be the most common terminology, but modernities in the south can be analyzed from several points of view, each with its radius of relevance: in terms of difference (but not really), newness, hybridity, and distinctiveness. These perspectives range from weak to strong arguments on modernities. These terminologies and emphases imply various registers of comparison with western modernities, so indeed, how modernities are framed is already a matter of the 'entanglement of modernities (ibid.: 13).

Different, but not really

The argument of difference has merits but is a limited view. Difference, after all, has been argued by Orientalists as well as by Asian chauvinists. *Different, but not really* may serve as a criticism of essentialist positions whether in the form of western Orientalism or Asian claims to uniqueness. Under this heading, for instance, we can consider the Confucian ethic thesis as a form of 'Asian Protestantism': different, but not really. In similar fashion we could address themes such as Asian bureaucratic capitalism and developmental states – as an Asian neo-mercantilism, authoritarian modernization – as instances of conservative modernization (as in Bismarck's Germany) and as fetishisms of 'simulated modernity'.

This is the tenor of many self-descriptions of modern societies in the global south: we are historically and culturally different, yet structurally we increasingly resemble the modern societies in the north. This perspective is ultimately assimilationist for it assumes that in the end differences can be subsumed under a single explanatory framework. It rehearses the convergence thesis of industrialized and industrializing countries converging on the same patterns, or East and West meet and in time difference slips away. Difference, in this view, is a matter of timing and rhythm. In an alternative reading, this angle intimates an understanding of deeper structures of modern life, which *are* similar regardless of cultural differentiation. Thus cultural texts recede as the script of modernity takes over.

New modernities

Just what is new about the modernities that are taking shape in the global south? First, the effect of newness itself, or the revitalization and reinvention of modernity; according to the Malaysian sociologist Raymond Lee,

> If modernity is undergoing a serious crisis in the West, it seems to be enthusiastically promoted and celebrated in those Third World countries that are enjoying improved standards of living, vibrant economies and more tolerant political attitudes. ... If modernity in the West needs revival, it may have to look towards Asia through trade and cultural exchanges to be instructed on what a revitalized modernity entails (Lee 1994: 3).

The revitalization of modernity has its roots in growing middle classes who constitute new markets for consumer durable goods at a time when in the West and Japan mainly replacement markets exist. The great Asian bazaar is booming at the confluence of multinational and regional capital. As *The Economist* noted in the nineties,

> With astonishing speed, many Asian countries are embracing a retail revolution which in Europe and the United States took decades to develop. It is powered by the emergence of a middle class newly able to shop for more than bare necessities. But different places are at different stages: China, India and Indonesia are just starting, while in Taiwan and Thailand the changes are well under way and in Malaysia retailing is at take-off point (4 March 1995).

Part of the vitality of Asian modernities stems from a contrast effect to the 'end of modernity' in the West. 'Third World modernization at the edge of the 21st century is unique because it borrows from Western modernity but occurs at the confluence of the latter's decline and what augurs as the postmodern age' (Lee 1994: 37 and 4).

New modernity also implies a *renewal* of modernity. In Asia, 'the outcome is not a simple local adaptation of the modernity paradigm, but possibly a revivification of traditional life-worlds to alter modernity beyond its original image' (ibid.: 37). Thus, newness involves several nuances: *reinventing* modernity, *reflexivity* in relation to western modernities, and *revitalization* of modernity, which matters also to the West as rejuvenation, growth stimulus and competition. With renewal also comes redirection in the flow of investments and a growing momentum of East Asian investments in North America and Europe. In several American states, Japanese and Korean manufacturers are now the leading companies. A further nuance of newness is distinctiveness – which is discussed below.

A recurring theme is *simulated modernity* or *mimesis*. 'Modernity experienced by non-Western consumers through the postmodern commodity form is a simulated modernity because it thrives on the free-floating signifiers of the global culture industry and not necessarily on the historical referents of Western society' (Lee 1994: 29). With respect to Chile, Christian Fernandez makes a similar point: 'Mimesis because the gesture is represented without any awareness of its context: we copy the imported image without knowing about how it originally came into being, and also without any great concern as to whether or not it happened to be relevant to our reality' (quoted in Richard 1993: 465).

This may be a one-sided appraisal, not just in view of deep history but also of current trends. Part of the reinvention of modernity is a circulation effect. Modernity is migrating, traveling East and South, and with this comes feedback: modernity reinvented in the East revitalizes and reshapes modernity in the West. Given that the main dynamos of economic growth are now in Asia, its importance to the West is growing steeply. Also postmodernism in the West is influenced by the south:

> Immigrants from the Third World to the First World provide a hidden, under-reported source of change to modernity through the traditions, lifestyles and ethnic organizations they import into the First World. ... It is a postmodern 'culture of revenge' in which the excesses of modernity (as witnessed in colonial expansion and conquests) paved the way for the destruction of its exclusiveness, to bring others into the game and disorient the teleology of power and control (Lee 1994: 40, 42).

It follows that the other side of mimesis is transformation and East-West, South-North flows of influence, which is another dimension of Easternization.

> In other words, mimesis of modernity is dialectical: it is absorbed, syncretized and regurgitated by the recipient countries, but in the process it comes to resemble a form of resistance to capitalist forces of the First World. It is as though the Third World in mimicking the First World is reinventing modernity to challenge that very force that penetrated their social and cultural boundaries in the first place (ibid.: 45).

Bricolage modernities

In Raymond Lee's assessment of new modernities in the East, bricolage is a central feature:

> The intermingling of Western values (including the Protestant ethic) and Confucianism within general contexts of centralized political control and tight kinship networks has probably resulted in the creation of a type of modernity unlike that experienced in the West. ... The uniqueness of this Eastern modernity lies in the bricolage of values bounded by an authoritarian ethos which, contrary to the expectations of Western liberalism, has provided a necessary impetus for economic take-off, expansionism and relentless growth not witnessed elsewhere in the Third World. (Lee 1994: 40)

Viewing Asian modernity as 'a unique conglomeration of East-West values and practices' is a common trope, as in 'western technology, Asian values' (Mahathir and Ishihara 1995). Mahbubani speaks of 'a fusion of Western and East Asian cultures in the Asia-Pacific region. It is this fusion, not a renaissance of ancient Asian glories, that explains the explosive growth of the Pacific and provides the possibility of continued peace and prosperity in the region' (1995: 102). In this view, Asian modernities are intrinsically syncretic and hybrid; they are mélange modernities (Nederveen Pieterse 1998).

The idea of bricolage as enabling modernization is strikingly different from the traditional Latin American notion of *mestizaje* as an affliction, which has only recently given way to more affirmative assessments (Ortiz 2000; Canclini 2001). In Latin America, mixture was conventionally interpreted in racial terms and followed pessimistic nineteenth-century European ideas that race mixture leads to decadence, yielding to another project of mixing as whitening or Europeanization. In contrast, Asian ideas view fusion all along in *cultural* terms and as, overall, willed and chosen. This is bricolage with agency.

The Asian self-awareness of mélange modernity is also strikingly different from western views. According to conventional occidental self-awareness, European modernity sprang from what was taken to be a relatively homogeneous civilizational frame – the Renaissance and Enlightenment, with the classics and Christianity as antecedents. Influences from 'the Orient', from the Far East to Africa, shaped Europe's civilization, much more than was recognized from nineteenth century points of view, but these influences were taken to come from an *external* geographical space (with the exception of Andalusia and the Ottoman Balkans).

Asian modernities stem from syncretic civilizational backgrounds involving multiple transcultural religions, multi-ethnic societies and cultural crosscurrents. They are developed hybrids. It would follow that projects of monocultural zealotism and *mission civilisatrice* such as drove the West in its spirit of expansion and conquest are less likely in Asia. This fundamentally different self-perception may explain why in contemporary Asia there is less interest in an 'Asian century' than in a global century, at a time when American elites continue to be obsessed with creating 'Another American Century'.

African modernization has been aborted. Slavery and the gun-slave cycle followed by colonialism interrupted and side-tracked the development of African societies (as in Walter Rodney's classic thesis, 1972). The experience of colonialism has been fresher and more destructive than anywhere else and decolonization has been most recent. In sub-Saharan Africa, key themes in relation to modernity have been traditional institutions and values virtually in a restorationist and indigenist fashion and reworked as négritude, African socialism and ujama. Revisionist history inspires Afrocentric readings of Egyptian civilization and the ancients, and indigenization in language politics (Thiong'o 1986, 1993) and Afrocentric ethnosociology (Akiwowo 1999).

In the Middle East, debates on modernity tend to be framed by discussions of Islam and the West and whether to interpret and frame Islam as anti-modernity, alternative modernity or postmodernism (e.g. Ahmed 1992). In the process it gives rise to new hybrids such as Islamic feminism (e.g. Karam 1999).

Distinctive modernities

Which features besides newness are distinctive about the modernities in the global south? Distinctiveness implies a strong argument on modernities; it may refer to social structure, historical patterns or collective reflexivity. Points for discussion in this brief sketch are that the new modernities are not imperialist, not military-driven and less nationalistic.

Feudalism plays an important role shaping the Asian modernities, but there is no common regional feudal background. In this respect Asia differs from Europe which did possess a transnational aristocracy and from the North American pattern which is not post-feudal (and is based on a profound rupture with feudalism). Funabashi notes that 'Asia, which lacks a common heritage of aristocratic classes and culture, has increasingly become a hotbed of middle-class globalism' (1993: 78).

The new modernities in Asia emerge on the other side of empire. They have been on the receiving end of predatory colonialism, civilizational proselytizing, missionary modernization and developmental narcissism from the West or Japan. Except for Thailand which like Ethiopia, Persia and Turkey was never colonized, they are postcolonial societies.

The new modernities in Asia are not expansionist in an imperial, territorial sense but are market-driven forms of modernization. To the extent that they are driven by export-oriented growth their expansionism is economic, aimed at acquiring market share. Military industries play a minor role (except nuclear technology). In the modernization of the early and late industrializers (Britain, the American Republic, France, Germany, Russia, Japan) there was a close connection between the state, the military and industry. Soviet modernization and its emphasis on heavy industry fit this pattern.

In Asia, the Korean War and the Vietnam War were a tremendous boost to industrial development. But military capabilities have not played a big part in industrialization, even in countries where the military have been in command (as in Indonesia, the Philippines, Thailand, Vietnam and still in Pakistan, North Korea and Myanmar). In part this is a function of the Cold War and the American military umbrella extending over the Pacific. This feature Asia shares with Germany's postwar reindustrialization. It is reflected in the character of Asian industrialization, with the emphasis on light industry and commerce.

Nation building and nationalism in the new modernities are less territorialized and more translocal than the previous wave of modernizations. There are intense border disputes between India and Pakistan (Kashmir) and China and its neighbours. Yet, coming to maturity at a later historical period, the Asian modernities have not been as intensely nationalistic as the European, American and Japanese modernities. This by historical standards relatively moderate nationalism may be related to the factor of fusion culture mentioned earlier, and it may reflect the role of transborder commerce and exports in their mode of industrialization.

This makes it possible to recognize, rather than suppress, the role of diasporas in the new modernities in the East, although the status of the Chinese diaspora is problematic in much of Southeast Asia. Indian, Muslim, Central Asian and European diasporas have been active throughout Asia (Hoerder 2002). Parsees from Bombay laid the foundations for Hong Kong's role as a financial centre (Kotkin 1991).

During the Asian crisis of 1997 the IMF blocked the creation of an Asian Monetary Fund proposed by Japan; now Thailand proposes an Asian bond fund. East and Southeast Asian countries are increasingly joining Japan in becoming significant foreign aid donors. They export a different model of development than the West, tuned to their own experiences. Japan places a strong emphasis on human resource development. The human development approach owes much to East Asian experiences. Asian perspectives involve a different global horizon from western development discourse.

The various ways of framing new modernities reflect different takes on the theme of modernities: 'different, but not really' represents convergence theory plus local variations; newness refers to pluralism in modernity, or modernities-lite; hybridity refers to plural sources of modernity; and distinctiveness represents radical pluralism or modernities in a strong sense. The implication of modernities in a strong sense is that western modernity becomes *a* modernity. Accordingly, western complexes – such as the French preoccupation with *laicité* and headscarves – reveal historical particularities that are not necessarily intrinsic to modernity *per se*.

The Interaction of Modernities

The ascendance of new modernities usually means the nadir of old modernities. Encounters between old and new modernities are a recurring thread in history, such as the encounter between Britain and Germany at the turn of the century.

Germany, which had been united as recently as 1871 and within one generation had become an awesome industrial and military power, was, on the eve of the war, the foremost representative of innovation and renewal. She was, among nations, the very embodiment of vitalism and technical brilliance... Britain was in fact the major conservative power of the fin de siècle world (Eksteins 1989: xv).

About the same time another such encounter was unfolding between the Old World of Europe and the New World of America – witness Kafka's America, Lenin's Taylorism and Gramsci's 'Americanism and Fordism'. Witness the influence in Europe of jazz, the impact of Lindbergh, and the general aura of 'Americanization' (ibid.: 268-76). 'Yesterday, European Culture! Today, American Technology!' (Wollen 1993) Witness, further, European anti-Americanism and ambivalence in relation to *Le défi Américain*. Germany and the United States were rivals in the struggle for succession of the British Empire. Hegemonic rivalry, also featuring Russia and Japan, was the backdrop of the two world wars.

The USSR was another alternative modernity; the rivalry between modernities occasioned the Cold War and lasted through most of the twentieth century. The two world wars and the Cold War were contestations between rival modernities. The 'American challenge' was followed by the 'Japanese challenge' and now faces a Chinese challenge.

In the long script of history the alternation of easternization/westernization may be viewed as a cyclical affair. East meets West meets East, and so forth (Nederveen Pieterse 2009). Each cycle takes place under different circumstances. Each period is framed by the overall level of technology and social organization. Berkeley's 'westward march of empire', given that the earth is round, is bound to land in the place where it started.

First came a long period of easternization of the world – the world of the Silk Routes, the caravan trade, the world that bequeathed us the 'world religions', the 'axial age' and much else. The period of westernization ranges from the ages of reconnaissance, expansion, colonialism and empire to US hegemony. It stretches, arguably, from the (unsuccessful) Crusader Kingdom of Jerusalem to the Iraq war, from the fifteenth century maritime explorations to Disney world.

In the 1920s, anticipating world revolution, Lenin looked towards developed capitalist countries such as Germany and to the colonized countries, particularly in Asia. Sultan Galiev went further and announced a time when 'East wind will prevail over West wind'. Mao Zedong took up this theme which became part of Lin Biao's strategy of 'encirclement of the cities by the countryside'. Anouar Abdel-Malek writing after the Arab oil boycott revived this notion. Since the late twentieth century a new Asian dynamic emerges, entirely different from the earlier anticipations under the sign of revolution: as a powerhouse of capitalism.

Now observations such as the following are increasingly common: 'They (the peoples of the presumed backward East) have become more modern (or indeed postmodern perhaps) than Us (the peoples of the supposedly advanced West)' (Morley 1994: 135). This brings to mind the theme of the 'rise and decline of the

West', *Der Untergang des Abendlandes*, which is now coupled with a comeback of the Morgenland. Western 'endism' echoes this litany – the end of empire, end of hegemony, end of modernity, end of history. It falls within the long tradition of western cultural pessimism, going back to the decline of the Roman Empire and Tacitus' sorrows, echoed by Edward Gibbon amidst the growing status anxieties of the European aristocracy and by Paul Kennedy in the late-twentieth century.

Yet part of this is a recentring of modernity – just *where* is the 'end of history'? Presumably, following Foucault, as the centre of power or hegemony shifts, so does the centre of truth. Reflecting on modernities invites a reassessment of modernity in the West, an undertaking that may be termed the deconstruction of modernity. If the centre of hegemony and truth shifts to Asia, in time this will hold implications for Asian modernities too. The significance of the theme of modernities is that it takes us beyond western social science and invites a global conversation on new terms.

References

Abu-Lughod, J.L. 1989. *Before European Hegemony: The World-System A.D. 1250-1350.* New York: Oxford University Press.

Ahmed, A.S. 1992. *Postmodernism and Islam.* London: Routledge.

Akiwowo, A. 1999. Indigenous Sociologies: Extending the Scope of the Argument. *International Sociology* Special issue, 14(2).

Amin, S. 1989. *Eurocentrism.* London: Zed.

Anderson, P. 1998. *The Origins of Postmodernity.* London: Verso.

Atasoy, S. 1999. Globalization and Turkey: From Capitulations to Contemporary Civilization, in *Globalization: Policies, Challenges and Responses*, edited by S.T. Ismael Calgary. Alberta: Detselig Enterprises, 257-70.

Bauman, Z. 1991. *Ambivalence and Modernity.* Cambridge: Polity.

Bauman, Z. 1992. *Intimations of Postmodernity.* London: Routledge.

Bernal, M. 1987. *Black Athena: Afroasiatic Roots of Classical Civilization: The Fabrication of Ancient Greece 1785-1985.* London: Free Association Press.

Bloom, A. 1987. *The Closing of the American Mind.* New York: Schuster.

Calinescu, M. 1987. *Five Faces of Modernity.* Durham/NC: Duke University Press.

Canclini, N. 2001. Contradictory Modernities and Globalisation in Latin America, in *Through the Kaleidoscope: The Experience of Modernity in Latin America*, edited by V. Schelling. New York: Verso.

Carrier, J. (ed.) 1995. *Occidentalism: Images of the West.* Oxford: Clarendon Press.

Chauduri, K.N. 1990. *Asia before Europe: Economy and Civilization of the Indian Ocean From the Rise of Islam to 1750.* Cambridge: Cambridge University Press.

Connell, R.W. 1997 Why is Classical Theory Classical? *American Journal of Sociology*, 106(6), 1511-57.

Dirlik, A., Bahl, V. and Gran, V. (eds) 2000. *History after the Three Worlds: Post Eurocentric Historiographies*. Boulder: Rowman & Littlefield.

Drury, S.B. 1997. *Leo Strauss and the American Right*. Houndmills: Macmillan.

Eisenstadt, S. 2000. Multiple Modernities. *Daedalus*, 129(1), 1-29.

Eksteins, M. 1989. *Rites of Spring: the Great War and the Birth of the Modern Age*. New York: Bantam.

Fabian, J. 1983. *Time and the Other: How Anthropology Makes its Objects*. New York: Columbia University Press.

Featherstone, M., Lash, S. and Robertson, R. (eds) 1995. *Global Modernities*. London: Sage.

Ferguson, J. 1999. *Expectations of Modernity: Myths and Meanings of Urban Life on the Zambian Copperbelt*. Berkeley: University of California Press.

Frank, A.G. 1998. *ReOrient: Global Economy in the Asian Age*. Berkeley: University of California Press.

Frost, L.F. 1998. Coming Full Circle: a Long-Term Perspective on the Pacific Rim, in *Studies in the Economic History of the Pacific Rim*, edited by S.M. Miller, A.J.H. Latham and D. O'Flynn (eds). London: Routledge, 45-62.

Funabashi, Y. 1993. The Asianization of Asia. *Foreign Affairs*, 72(5), 75-85.

Gaonkar, D.P. (ed.) 2001. *Alternative Modernities*. Durham: Duke University Press.

Hobson, J.M. 2004 *The Eastern Origins of Western Civilisation*. Cambridge: Cambridge University Press.

Hoerder, D. 2002. *Cultures in Contact: World Migrations in the Second Millennium*. Durham: Duke University Press.

Hopkins, A.G. (ed.) 2002. *Globalization in World History*. New York: Norton.

James, C.L.R. 1938. *The Black Jacobins*. London: Secker and Warburg.

Kaplinsky, R. 1994. *Easternisation: the Spread of Japanese Management Techniques to Developing Countries*. London: Frank Cass.

Karam, A. 1999. *Islam, Women and the State in Egypt*. London: Macmillan.

King, A. 1991. Introduction: Spaces of Culture, Spaces of Knowledge, in *Culture, Globalization and the World-System*, edited by A. King. Basingstoke: Macmillan, 1-18.

King, A. 1995. The Times and Spaces of Modernity (Or Who Needs Postmodernism?), in *Global Modernities*, edited by Featherstone et al. London: Sage, 108-123.

Kotkin, J. 1991. *Tribes*. New York: Random House.

Lee, R.L.M. 1994. Modernization, Postmodernism and the Third World. *Current Sociology*, 42(2).

Lipset, S.M. 1996. *American Exceptionalism: A Double-Edged Sword*. New York, Norton.

Mahathir, M. and Ishihara, S. 1995. *The Voice of Asia*. Tokyo: Kodansha International.

Mahbubani, K. 1995. The Pacific Way. *Foreign Affairs*, 74(1), 100-11.

Morley, D. 1994. Postmodernism: The Highest Stage of Cultural Imperialism? in *Altered States: Postmodernism, Politics, Culture*, edited by M. Perryman. London: Lawrence and Wishart, 133-57.

Nederveen Pieterse, J. 1989. *Empire and Emancipation.* New York: Praeger.

Nederveen Pieterse, J. 1994. Unpacking the West: How European is Europe? in *Racism, Modernity, Identity: on the Western Front*, edited by A. Rattansi and S. Westwood. Cambridge: Polity, 129-49.

Nederveen Pieterse, J. 1998. Hybrid Modernities: Mélange Modernities in Asia. *Sociological Analysis*, 1(3), 75-86.

Nederveen Pieterse, J. 2004. *Globalization or Empire?* New York: Routledge.

Nederveen Pieterse, J. 2009. *Globalization and Culture: Global Mélange.* Lanham: Rowman & Littlefield.

Nederveen Pieterse, J. and Parekh, B. (eds) 1995. *The Decolonization of Imagination.* London: Zed.

Needham, J. 1981. *Science in Traditional China.* Cambridge: Harvard University Press.

Ortiz, R. 2000. From Incomplete Modernity to World Modernity. *Daedalus*, 129(1), 249-60.

Pomeranz, K. 2000. *The Great Divergence: China, Europe and the Making of the Modern World Economy.* Princeton: Princeton University Press.

Richard, N. 1993. Postmodernism and Periphery, in *Postmodernism: a reader,* edited by Thomas Docherty. New York: Harvester Wheatsheaf, 463-70.

Rodney, W. 1972. *How Europe Underdeveloped Africa.* London: Bogle-L'Ouverture.

Singh, Y. 1989. *Essays on Modernization in India.* New Delhi: Manohar, orig. ed. 1978.

Subrahmanyam, S. 1997. Connected Histories: Notes Towards a Reconfiguration of Early Modern Eurasia. *Modern Asian Studies*, 31(3), 735-62.

Subrahmanyam, S. 1998. Hearing Voices: Vignettes of Early Modernity in South Asia, 1400-1750. *Daedalus*, 127(3), 75-104.

Taylor, P.J. 1999. *Modernities: A Geohistorical Interpretation.* Cambridge: Polity.

Thiong'o, N.W. 1986. *Decolonising the Mind: The Politics of Language in African Literature.* London/Nairobi/Portsmouth: James Currey/Heinemann.

Thiong'o, N.W. 1993. *Moving the Centre: The Struggle for Cultural Freedoms.* London/Nairobi/Portsmouth: James Currey/Heinemann.

Touraine, A. 1992. *Critique de la modernité.* Paris: Fayard.

Toulmin, S. 1990. *Cosmopolis: The Hidden Agenda of Modernity.* Chicago: University of Chicago Press.

Wade, R. 1996. Japan, the World Bank and the Art of Paradigm Maintenance: the East Asian Miracle in Political Perspective. *New Left Review*, 217, 3-336.

Wollen, P. 1993. *Raiding the Icebox.* Bloomington: Indiana University Press.

Chapter 6

European Self-Presentations and Narratives Challenged by Islam: Secular Modernity in Question

Nilüfer Göle

The discipline of sociology, which has shaped the comprehension of modernity as intrinsically a secular process of change, faces today new challenges raised by the revival of religion in general and Islam in particular. European sociology confronts these challenges in a more significant and dramatic way to the extent that Europe becomes a site where particular modes of encounter between the principles of secular modernity and Muslim religious claims are taking place at the level of everyday life practices and are debated in different national publics. In the last three decades, by means of religious claims of Muslim migrants and new controversies in the public life, Islam, an external reference, is becoming an indigenous one in European public life. We can speak of the re-territorialization of Islam in Europe, its "Europeanization" and indigenization which however does not follow a dynamics of assimilation in conformity with European secular modernity. In other words, Islam is becoming contemporary with Europe both in terms of proximity in time and in space (making part of a European "chronotope" [Bakhtin 1978]) but in confrontation with the principles of European secular modernity. "De-centering" European sociology, or displacing the sociological gaze with an anthropological sensibility for difference in non-Western territories and cultural habitations of modernity have helped to engage a critical stand in social sciences (Chakrabarty 2002; Ashcroft 1994). But the present forms of encounter between Islam and Europe take place in the same chronotope (correlation between time and space) without the geographical distance and time lag between the Western colonizer and the colonized, between the modern European and the traditional Muslims, which in turn necessitate framing the relation in terms of transnational and intercultural (read intercivilizational) terms. Consequently, the intimate encounters between Islam and Europe engender a mutual transformation that call for a two-way mirroring and intercultural reflexivity, only possible by means of liberating European narrative of modernity – and sociology – from their colonial frame and universalist claim.

Over the last two decades, the studies on Islam started to occupy a central place on the social science agenda. Such a resurgence of interest in Islam is related to the revival of religious claims and movements that have transformed the political and public scene in Muslim-majority countries as well as in Western contexts. The use of Islam as a reference for the self-presentation by diverse social groups such as youth, women and migrants in the contemporary world poses a challenge to the Western narratives of secular modernity. With the emergence of contemporary forms of Islam that range from the Iranian revolution and women's veiling to jihadist movements, studies on Islam cease to be a field reserved exclusively to Orientalists, theologians or area studies specialists and move to the center of the research agenda of political sciences, sociology, anthropology, and law. Increasingly, interdisciplinary approaches are used to study contemporary forms of Islamic religiosity and agency. The entry of Islam on the research agenda brings forth new horizons of critique in social scientific agenda. We can speak of a new configuration of "Islamic studies" that unsettles the disciplinary frontiers and opens-up critical readings of European modernity and sociology from the vantage point of Islam.

Whether Islamic studies can have an impact on introducing the vantage point of the "subaltern" Muslim and decolonizing European sociology. Whether universalist claims of European sociology can give way to new ways of articulating secularity and modernity and therefore contribute to the "opening of the social sciences" (Wallerstein et al. 1996). All emerge as questions that need to be addressed. Indeed Islamic studies increasingly expand to different disciplines and transform their research agenda. I will evoke three major, broad and cutting edge research topics, namely, globalization, the public sphere, and gender, in order to elaborate on the ways Islam enters on these research agendas and thereby unsettles the established frames of thought. I use the notion of Islam to the extent that Muslim actors in their present day practices articulate their faith and agency in ways that challenge Western hegemony on definitions of modern global order, European public life and gendered self.

The contemporary forms of Islam are studied and framed differently depending on whether the emphasis is on religion, modes of governance, social norms and values, or on modes of mobilization and confrontation. Different conceptualizations, such as religious revivalism, Islamic Sharia, cultural conservatism, terrorist-jihadist movements, and the "clash of civilizations", all designate the cross-disciplinary efforts to depict and comprehend the contours of contemporary Islam. However, the latter raise problems of conceptualization and labeling. Islamic Studies have in fact attempted to name and conceptualize the imprint of Islam in the actions and interpretations of diverse actors. The notion of Islamism has had an advantage of establishing a distinction between Islam as a religion and its forms of political radicalization. The political science approaches to Islam have allowed us to understand contemporary forms of religious contestation that are not separable from the mobilization of masses, the seizure of state power and the application of Sharia law. Nonetheless, political science approaches have tendency to reduce the role of religion to its instrumentalization by groups of political power. Anthropological approaches, on the other hand have underscored the importance of faith, studied the formations of religious subjectivities yet dissociated them from questions of agency and social problems. Sociological studies provided depictions of the role of urban groups, educated youth, women and intellectuals in Islamic movements, but remained within the limits of the state vs. society dichotomy. The study of contemporary Islam calls for depicting the diversity of praxis and the transnational dynamics in which Islamic religion is reinterpreted and reactivated with the aim of shaping the intimate, public and political lives of Muslims. Islamic movements do not merely target juridical governance and political life, but equally affect the public and private spheres, that is to say, gender regimes, social morals and spatial arrangements. The complexities of contemporary Islamic modes of expression and the new re-compositions between faith and agency, secular and religious, personal and public requires an interdisciplinary approach but furthermore a critique of the already established frames of Western sociological thought.

As sociological theories about secularization undergo a critical revision, the studies on the "return of religion" have gained a real interest. The two pillars on which the narrative of modernity was constructed, namely, secularization and the idea of progress, are challenged by the concomitant desire for the return of religion and for the forces of the immutable (Dozon 2007). However, contemporary Islam is far from being a continuation of the chains of the historical past, and witnesses on the contrary a radical rupture and change. The imprint of the past, the religious and the traditional can only be captured within the prism of contemporary social forms of criticism and contestation. The Islamic movements are "rejuvenated" by the adherence of young and educated urban populations and "feminized" by the presence of girls and women that have begun to take on the veil since the 1980s (following a period of unveiling in the 1920s, in conformity with the secular reformist movements of elites in many Muslim countries such as Turkey, Iran and Egypt). The revival of Islam means for many of its young and female followers a relearning of religious knowledge, studying the precepts, and re-thinking the present issues from the prism of the religious past. The immutability promised by religion and the power of its *long durée* history create a veritable magnetism for those who seek guidance in a world governed by "presentism" (Hartog 2003). Islamic fundamentalism revalorizes the golden age of Islam, drawing on a model in the past, rather than an unrealized ideal, a utopia. The text of the Koran and the life of the Prophet Muhammad serve as guidelines and sources of example for sorting out the grammar of leading a "truly" pious existence at the level of everyday life practices as well as for finding the right path in modern life.

Hence, framing contemporary Islam as the "return of religion" reveals to be a more complex phenomenon than it appears. The notion of "religion" embodies and carries a plethora of meanings and praxis that requires unpacking and criticism in the light of practices and interpretations of contemporary actors. Islam(ism) is the name that refers to the conscious and collective ways of refashioning religion from the prism of contemporary issues in modern life politics and in a globalized world. In doing so, contemporary Islam enters on the historical stage of the present in debating and confronting the Universalist claims of secular modernity and European social thinking. The entry of Islam into the realm of global politics, European publics and sexual modernity, unsettles the established power relations and frames of thought. The three realms correspond to three different scales on which Western modernity disputes over its hegemony, namely over the rules of the world order, the morals of the public life, and the sexual norms of the self. The three realms and scales operate on different temporalities but they exemplify the most central sites in tracking and debating the changes of Western European modernity. The social scientific agenda in general and sociology in particular search for understanding the new patterns of globalism and transnational dynamics, the cultural and religious difference in the public sphere and the forms of sexual emancipation and feminism. Islamic studies enter these three pioneer areas and transform the intellectual agenda in challenging the definitions of transnational publics and self.

First, one has to be reminded that studies on globalization and Islam came to be related only recently, especially in the aftermath of 9/11. There is an increasing awareness that Islam cannot be studied as if it were confined to political dynamics within a given nation-state (as was the case with the Islamic revolution in Iran in 1979); neither can it be identified with one single region (such as the Middle East). It circulates among different publics, nations and regions and becomes a global affair whether it is related to the phenomenon of immigration, to public controversies, or to terrorist acts. Secondly, Islam becomes public, meaning that religion, which is supposed to be contained within the private domain, claims visibility in the public arena. Thirdly, questions of gender and sexuality are central in the course of contemporary Islamism but also in the process of confrontation with European publics. The Islamic veiling in public is a sign of transgressing spatial and gendered boundaries of the sacred private domain. Furthermore, staging the Islamic difference by means of the symbolism of the veil in the European public spheres carries an ambivalent message: Muslim women claim their access and presence in the secular public life yet provokes a discord in unsettling the tacit rules and cultural codes of European public life.

The controversies on Islamic headscarves of Muslim students in French public schools or of teachers in Germany[1] indicate clearly the way Islam ceases to be a Muslim-Muslim question and becomes a concern for European public. Contemporary Islam provokes cultural "malaise", mobilizes collective passion to the extent that the very foundations of secular modernity is thought to be threatened by the religious claims in public life. Islam is perceived as a threat to the most contemporary and highly valued achievements of European liberal democracies, such as sexual liberation, gender equality and the freedom of expression. The public presence and staging of Islam in European democracies

---

1   For the French and German controversies see Amir-Mozami 2004, Bowen 2007 and Scott 2007. For the British context, see Joppke 2009.

trigger a debate on the presence of Muslims in Europe, and well beyond that, on the cultural values of Europe. In the course of these debates, the values that govern the public order (secularism, freedom of expression and tolerance) as well as the ones concerning the private or personal sphere (women's status, religious faith) come to be confronted with one another and then renegotiated, bringing about a displacement of boundaries between public and private, secular and religious, and Europe and Islam.

Islam on the Global Scene

The process of globalization brings people and cultures in closer contact. The anthropological distance and the frontiers between the self and the others, between the moderns and the indigenous, between the colonizers and the colonized are blurred, if not erased within an increasingly interconnected globe. The reduction of time and space between different parts of the world brings together cultures, countries and people, however not necessarily creating a better understanding between cultures. Globalization accelerates the speed with which information, goods, and people circulate among different publics, markets and nations, but the blurring of frontiers equally provokes national anxieties, social frictions and cultural clashes. These propositions are also valid for Islam.

Globalization does not stop short of changing the lives and minds of Muslims; but furthermore Islam becomes an active component in the acceleration and amplification of globalism. Political Islam does not operate exclusively on a national scale, but enters into a new phase of circulation at a planetary scale. In an earlier phase, the politicization of Islam, that has led to the Iranian Revolution of 1979 was studied on a national scale as a mode of popular mobilization inspired by an ideology and a religious lexicon that condemn the authoritarian and "impious" powers of the Middle East. Islamic radicalism was explained as an outcome of several factors, such as immigration, economic poverty and political regimes, as a "reaction" to a situation of "crises". The vertical relations of power between state and society were privileged in this earlier phase of Islamic studies. However, the scale of analysis shifted to a more transnational and global one following the terrorist attacks of 9/11 in 2001 that marked a turning point in the analysis of "global Islam" (Roy 2002). Mainly the terrorist dimensions of Islamic movements are explained in conformity with the forces of globalism. The jihadism of Al-Qaeda is taken to be the most dramatic illustration of globalized Islam; its nebulous mode of organization, the profile of its terrorist-martyrs, the transnational life-trajectories in their military training, as well as the targets of attack can all be seen as the product of a transnational logic. The global imprint is quite obvious in the logic of terrorist acts or in the life trajectories of the terrorists. However, the jihadist attacks did not only follow and profit from global dynamics, but also in an unexpected and unwilling way brought the United States to join the global world and suffer its destructive effects (Göle 2002a).

The centrality of the notion of "umma", the community of believers in the Islamic faith, predisposes Muslims to think and act beyond national borders, i.e., globally. Although it is quite unrealistic to evoke a unified Muslim community at a moment in history when confessional differences and national interests continue to divide Muslims (Kepel 2004), contemporary Islamism does participate in the production of a common imaginary. It elaborates itself by mutual borrowings and hybridizations: the traditions and norms of a confession (such as the martyr figure in the Shiite tradition) are continuously re-adapted and transformed by those of other confessions, hence producing a religious and political syncretism (Khosrokhavar 2003). One might argue that the production of Islamic social imaginary takes place through micro-practices, performative and visual acts that circulate between different publics and take roots in different national contexts (Göle 2002b). It is possible to sort out a mapping of an Islamic imaginary following a series of constitutive events that provide a common reference, repertoire of action and collective memory. The formation of an Islamic imaginary transgresses national boundaries and pre-established confessional distinctions; it works as a collage, an assemblage bringing together distinct elements, composing with different fragments and producing a new pattern of action. Globalization accelerates the elaboration of a social religious "imaginary" and its promises, providing a virtual sense of belonging, a social bondage even between those who do not share the same communitarian, confessional or national distinctions. The "sorority" between veiled women or the "fraternity" between martyrs – even though they represent two very distinct and opposing forms of religious agency and religious figures – pious-self or self-sacrifice – embody the micro practices constitutive of this imaginary.

The notion of social imaginary (Taylor 2004) is elaborated by means of religious performances, symbols, and narratives; it is mediated by means of a visual and popular culture. Islamic social imaginary is shaped by religious piety, memory and a repertoire of action that is both religiously and politically oriented among actors who are connected to each other by religious and "imaginary" ties, forming an "imagined community" (Anderson 1991). The radicalization of Islamic political movements in the end of 1970s was closely related with a new ideological framework that was elaborated by thinkers and ideologists of Islam. These authors were widely translated and read by the generation of Muslims who have followed the ideas of politicization of Islam and embraced the criticism addressed to orthodox religious thinkers ("ulema"). But in distinction from Islamic theology and ideology, both being shaped by the knowledge of few, by a group of theologians and political activists, Islamic social imaginary is shaped by new forms of visual and performative culture and is shared by persons and groups who do not have necessarily a sense of belonging to a political structure or to a religious institution. However globalized forms of Islam participate in the elaboration of a religious imaginary and cultural performance that unsettles and challenges the European secular imaginaries and gendered performances.

If the political and the national are not the decisive mediators of conflict and consensus, how can we frame the question of religious and cultural difference? The debates on globalization necessitate a rethinking of the place of the national (Calhoun 2007), but likewise of the public sphere.

Islam in Public

The nature of the relationship between the political and the public spheres, their mutual interdependence undergoes a change with the impact of globalism. By means of global communication networks, the public sphere, participates in a transnational realm, whereas the political sphere is constrained and confined within the boundaries of a nation-state. Globalization instigates the autonomization of the public *vis-à-vis* the political realm. Whereas publics have the tendency to become transnational, politics remain national.

The public domain hence becomes the privileged site for the manifestations of a globalized Islam in Europe (Allievi and Nielsen 2003). The search for the public visibility of religion triggers public controversies in different national contexts and across the borders. Islam participates in the formation of a transnational European public, but in confrontation with the norms and morals of European secular modernity. The emergence of a transnational public space is accompanied by the deepening of the cleavages: national publics, cultural codes and religious referents are brought in spatial proximity while cultural differences are at the same time staged, accentuated and amplified by symbols, clichés or grotesque images. In the age of globalism, the public sphere favors circulation rather than mediation (whether political, intellectual or artistic), the figural rather than the textual, the affective, sensorial and scandalous rather than the rational and discursive. Hence symbols, images, icons or cartoons travel faster than words, penetrate personal and collective imaginaries, and propagate by amplification of their significations and perceptions. The public sphere becomes the site for the confrontational proximity and co-penetrations between different Muslim and "European" cultural and religious codes.

In late modernity, the spectacular and the visual figural attributes of public communication are privileged. New forms of Islamic agency follow and furthermore amplify the performative, symbolic, sensorial and affective dimensions of expressing religious difference. Islam is staged in public by means of religious rituals and symbols, by gendered modes of address, by manifestations and collective prayers, and by new forms of jihadism and violence that challenge and threaten the consensual values and civilizational attributes of Europe. These acts and agencies, less discursive and more performative, employ a sort of grammar of silence, a non-verbal communication and yet have the power of provoking and unsettling the established relations of cultural difference and power.

A new frame of thought is necessary to conceptualize the ways European publics relate to Islamic difference. It necessitates unsettling the hegemony of the

European self-presentation and conceptualization of a transversal bond without excluding the role of the confrontation, violence and discord; namely a process of "interpenetration" between the two in which the definitions of sexuality and the sacred plays a central role (Göle 2005).

A mapping of events, incidents and controversies can highlight the zones of contact and confrontation, the zones that we can also designate as "frontier spaces" (Sassen 2006) between Europe and Islam. The fatwa against Salman Rushdie, the public debate on the Islamic veiling in France, Ayan Hirsi Ali's film on "Submission" and the assassination of Theo Van Gogh, the cartoon controversy in Denmark, the attacks of Al-Qaeda in the European cities and the debates on the Turkish candidacy to the European Union are all examples of the antagonistic nature of this encounter. Each of these events, in different ways, has carried Islam into European publics and provoked a larger debate on the cultural values and frontiers of Europe in distinction with Islam; ranging from the place of religion in public life, principles of secularism, freedom of expression and gender equality.

The relationship that has been established between an ideal-public sphere and the functioning of a pluralistic democracy, particularly in the work of Jürgen Habermas, has been revisited from an interdisciplinary perspective in view of a more pluralistic conceptualization of the public sphere. The critiques of the public sphere have demonstrated the ways the latter reassembles and includes as well as the way it excludes by means of drawing boundaries and establishing criteria of access in terms of education, class, age, gender and race. However Islam has been disregarded in these conceptualizations of the public sphere (Habermas 1992; 2002). Adding Islam on this list does not imply simply the broadening of the boundaries of the public sphere. The irruption of Islam within European publics reveals new boundaries of exclusion but also the public doxas, namely a set of shared secular imaginaries and feminist presuppositions that are constitutive of the contemporary European public mind. Islam carries religion into public life and disrupts the pre-established boundaries between privatized religion and public rationality on the one hand and gendered definitions of agency on the other hand. The Islamic veiling of the young school girls disrupts the criteria of age, education and gender in proscribing access to public citizenship and debate. The arguments that have favored the ban of the religious signs in French public schools were based generally upon the denial of agency (they are minor) and individuality of Muslim girls (they are religious) in adopting the headscarf. Furthermore, fathers, brothers, militant Islam or the community pressure are designated as the oppressor behind the symbol of the veil. Secular narratives of modernity have expected religion to withdraw into the private realm and disappear as an actor of change, of history. Consequently, the definitions of citizenship rights – namely, equal access to the public sphere, freedom of expression, liberty and agency – are all thought to be the outcome of secular formations of individualism and power. Muslim women's claim for religious covering disrupts the equation between secularism and political agency, but also between feminism and emancipation. Religious gendered agency reveals a series of ambivalences – faith and agency, woman and public life, age and decision – that can not be acknowledged within the secular European frames of thinking in terms of "either-or" categories (either religious or secular, either feminist or Islamist, either European or Muslim). Public Islam blurs and unsettles not only the personal-public frontiers, and religious-secular oppositions, but moreover brings forth new borrowings, mixings, re-compositions between these binary oppositions.

Sexuality and Islam

In shifting the boundaries between the personal and the political, contemporary Islam ironically joins Western feminism in many ways. The realm that is considered to be closest to the personal, corporal, intimate and sacred is carried into public life; wearing religious symbols in public schools, construction of mosques in European cities, dietary regimes in cafeterias, Islamic holidays, rooms for prayer in work settings, all examples that inscribe a religious imprint in the European public spaces. The European presence of Islam takes religion into the agenda of politics, but more profoundly unsettles the established boundaries between the private and the public. A religious reminder of the personal, private and public makes its way into new agencies and imaginaries. A sacred notion of the private parts of the body and space is at work in modern public life; a process that I have designated as "modern-mahrem", as this Arabic word "mahrem" signifies the interior, sacred, gendered space which is both spatial and corporeal (Göle 1996).

The veiling of women is a reminder of an alternative ways of linking femininity and sexuality in public. While feminine traits are expressed and distinguished from male outlook and male appearances (veiling is supposed to set a difference from male dress codes), woman's sexuality is contained within the values of modesty. In contrast, the secular feminist modes of self-fashioning blurs gender differences by borrowing from men's clothing and appearance (unisex and short hair as emblems of feminism) and expose the liberty of sexual disposition and interaction with the other sex. The opposition and confrontation between two figures of women, reveal the differences of corporeal management of feminity and sexuality in public life. The battleground involves alongside the orientation of ethical values that of esthetical ones. Inventions of new modes of Islamic covering point to the changes in the domain of fashion, through which new elaborations between beauty, feminity and sexuality are manifested.

The question of woman and sexuality occupies a central place in these controversies because late modernity is shaped by gender equality and by emancipatory regimes of body and sexuality. The European self-fashioning and self-presentation embodies the equality of gender relations, between women and men as well as between persons of the same sex. In the eyes of the European publics, Islamic veiling as a symbol of religious submission and gender segregation becomes a reminder of a pre-feminist past. However the veiling is carried into public life by young women who by means of education and political engagement have distanced themselves from traditional roles of women and found themselves in social mixing with men. The veiling publicly stages a form of feminine personality and sexuality that enters into confrontation with the European self-presentations of woman and secular modernity. Islamic veiling is contemporary with secular feminism and yet in oppositional distinction with the pre-established norms of secular emancipation.

For the feminists of post-1968, the body was central in the struggles for emancipation of women (as the slogan "our bodies belong to us" illustrates); a body liberated from the chains of biological difference (the right for abortion and contraception), from sexual violence and harassment, and from the male desire and gaze; a body that was taking its revenge by displaying its new liberty in public. Feminism has profoundly altered not only the relationship between women and men, but also the relationship of women with their own bodies. This process is also synonymous with the entrance of women's bodies in the spiral of an accelerated secularization in which the culture of "care of the self", "pleasing one's own self" and "taking good care of one's body" show that the body has not only turned into a place of cult for personal liberty, but also become conform with the imperatives of neo-liberalism. Yesterday's rights to contraception and abortion and today's "genetic engineering" have displaced the realm of reproduction from the universe of natural constraints to that of personal choice, thereby shifting the cursor from nature towards culture. This process is an undeniable sign of a larger personal liberty and plurality of options of choice in life, but also opens up significant questioning in moral and ethical terms. The "return of religion" in contemporary world is not a relic of the past but an indicator of the contemporary problems and limits raised by late or ultra-modernity.

Religion in general and the act of veiling in particular recall the submission of the self to divine will, and valorize the feeling of humility against the will of the secular and omnipotent modern subject. Once more it is woman's body – as the marker of values of modesty or pleasure, submission or emancipation – that comes to intersect the patriarchal power relations and the confrontation among religious and secular women. In other words, the Enlightenment project can be read as an incessant displacement of the frontiers between nature and culture, progressively displacing the realm of religion, reproduction and nature into the domain of the cultural and thus turning religion into a matter of individual choice; woman's body follows the imperatives of this meta-project and delineates the cursor between the religious and the mundane, the patriarchal and the personal, the natural and the cultural.

In the act of wearing the Islamic veil, one can read a critique addressed to the logic of extreme emancipation, in which the body is the locus. Without always being the master of the signification of this act, a woman that covers her hair conveys a sense of preservation of self, a resistance to the spiral of secularization – a spiral that encompasses all domains of life from procreation to aesthetics, and that offers a distressing promise of incessant changes and innovations. In counter distinction with Western woman's body – considered as a symbol of aesthetic prestige and liberty, an object of idolatry – Muslim women re-introduce in their subjectivity a part of abstraction through obedience to the divine order, to religious rituals and constraining mundane and carnal pleasures. (The training of the *nafs* – an Arabic word that means the flesh, the spirit of concupiscence, and symbolizes the carnal impulses – so as to make it obedient to pious impulses is central for the construction of Muslim subject).

Islamic veiling allows Muslim women to make their appearance on the public scene as much as it conceals and confines them. It accentuates the battle of social mores by means of adopting performative but silent/nonverbal communication. It is the incarnation of Islamic religious precepts, of the social grammar of interdiction between the gaze and the body as well as of the exposition of what is at stake in clothing and effects of "stylization". Georg Simmel argues that clothing is an "appeasing response to the exaggerated subjectivism of the époque, the place of 'retreat', of individual's taking distance and a manifestation of a sense of modesty and discretion" (Simmel 1998). For clothing is about the connection of particular to the general, the personal to the impersonal, and the subjective to the inter-subjective. It distinguishes and creates a distance as much as it allows the individual to enter into a form that is shared by the others. It is with these modern ways of clothing that the veiling is situated in this "in-between-ness": it is both "modern and Muslim" (Göle 1993; 2003). Being a modern Muslim is a state of being "in-between" because it reveals both proximity and alterity through the clothing of emancipated religious women and thus seeks to subvert the aesthetical definition of femininity and that of subjectivity.

Islamic Studies are inseparable from the studies on modernity in its multiple, alternative and non-occidental forms. The more the definition of modernity is separated from the Enlightenment paradigm, the more our reflection opens up on the new forms and criticisms that modernity takes on today. This fact weakens the Western narratives on modernity at work in the social sciences today. While at the same time it blurs the frontiers between the social sciences of the "other" (Orientalism, Area Studies, Anthropology, Postcolonial Studies) and the social sciences of the (Western) "self" (History, Sociology, Political Sciences and Feminism). Islamic Studies is at the heart of this metamorphosis in social sciences: it is both subject and instigator of this transformation. The gendered, public and global manifestations of Islam challenge the studies on Islam to open up a new space for reading Western modernity and decolonizing European sociology. Islam and Islamic studies can be thought as a necessary antinomy, as the "constitutive outside" (Derrida 1991) to the public doxas of secular-sexual modernity. To the extent they contribute to the unpacking of these Eurocentric doxas of sexual norms, public morals and global order, Islamic studies have the potential to subvert social scientific agenda and reorient social criticism.

References

Allievi, S. and Nielsen, J.S. (eds) 2003. *Muslim Networks and Transnational Communities in and Across Europe*. Leiden and Boston: Brill.

Amir-Mozami, S. 2004. *Discourses and Counter-Discourses: The Islamic Headscarf in the French and German Public Spheres*. Unpublished PhD Dissertation. Florence: European University Institute, Department of Political and Social Sciences.

Anderson, B. 1991. *Imagined Communities: Reflections on the Origins and Spread of Nationalism*. London and New York: Verso.

Ashcroft, B. (ed.) 1994. *The Post-colonial Studies Reader*. London: Routledge.

Bakhtin, M. 1978. *Esthétique et théorie du roman*, translated by Daria Olivier. Paris: Gallimard, 384-50.

Bowen, J.R. 2007. *Why the French Don't Like Headscarves: Islam, the State, and Public Space*. Princeton: Princeton University Press.

Calhoun, C. 2007. *Nations Matter: Culture, History and the Cosmopolitan Dream*. New York: Routledge.

Chakrabarty, D. 2002. *Habitations of Modernity: Essays in the Wake of Subaltern Studies*. Chicago: The University of Chicago Press.

Derrida, J. 1991. *L'Autre Cap*. Paris: Les editions de Minuit.

Dozon, J.P. 2007. Les Temps des retours, in *Les Sciences Sociales en Mutation*, edited by M. Wieviorka. Paris: Editions Sciences Humaines, 371-8.

Göle, N. 1993. *Musulmanes et Modernes*. Paris: La Découverte (Second Edition 2003, La Découverte Poche).

Göle, N. 1996. *The Forbidden Modern: Veiling and Civilization*. Ann Arbor: University of Michigan.

Göle, N. 2002a. Close Encounters: Islam, Modernity, and Violence, in *Understanding September 11*, edited by C. Calhoun, P. Price and A. Timmers. New York: The New York Press, 332-44.

Göle, N. 2002b. Islam in Public: New Visibilities and New Imaginaries. *Public Culture*, 14, 173-90.

Göle, N. 2005. *Interpénetrations: L'islam et l'Europe*. Paris: Galaade Editions.

Göle, N. 2007. L'islam à la rencontre des sciences sociales, in *Les Sciences Sociales en Mutation*, edited by M. Wieviorka. Paris: Editions Sciences Humaines, 417-26.

Göle, N. and Amman, L. (eds) 2004. *Islam in Sicht. Der Auftritt von Muslimen im öffentlichen Raum*. Bielefeld: Transcript (published in English 2006. *Islam in Public*. Istanbul: Bilgi University Press).

Habermas, J. 1992. *Droit et democratie, Entre faits et norms*, translated by R. Rochlitz and C. Bouchindhomme. Paris: Gallimard.

Habermas, J. 2002. *Apres l'Etat-nation, Une nouvelle constellation politique*, translated by Rainer Rochlitz. Paris: Fayard.

Hartog, F. 2003. *Regimes d'historicité*. Paris: Seuil.

Joppke, C. 2009. *Veil: Mirror of Identity*. Cambridge and Malden: Polity Press.

Kepel, G. 2004. *Fitna, guerre au coeur de l'islam*. Paris: Gallimard.

Khosrokhavar, F. 2003. *Les nouveaux martryrs d'Allah*. Paris: Flammarion.

Roy, O. 2002. *L'Islam mondialisé*. Paris: Seuil.

Sassen, S. 2006. *Territory, Authority, Rights: From Medieval to Global Assemblages*. Princeton: Princeton University Press.

Scott, J.W. 2007. *The Politics of the Veil*. Princeton: Princeton University Press.

Simmel, G. 1998. *La parure et autres essais*. Paris: Maison des sciences de l'homme.

Taylor, C. 2004. *Modern Social Imaginaries*. Durham and London: Duke University Press.

Vinas, F. 1998. *Entre oui et non: Simmel, Philosophe de l'Ame moderne, La parure et autres essais*. Paris: Editions Maison des Sciences de l'Homme.

Wallerstein, et al. (eds.) 1996. *Open the Social Sciences: Report of the Gulbenkian Commission on the Restructuring of the Social Sciences*. Stanford: Stanford University Press.

PART III
Questioning Politics of Difference

Chapter 7

Eurocentrism, Sociology, Secularity

Gregor McLennan

From Postcolonialism to Postsecularism

In previous reflections on the concerns of this volume (McLennan 2000, 2003), my starting point was to underline the fact that, by comparison with other disciplines, sociology had been slow to engage with postcolonial thought. Whether posed in terms of the lack of journal special issues, presentations of the classics, authoritative theoretical overviews, or in the content of textbooks, the case could be made that sociology – at least until the later 1990s, and at least in the 'mainstream' – did not take to heart the postcolonial critique of Eurocentrism in the human sciences. Since that time, however, things have changed for the better. Even if direct encounters with postcolonialist authors have remained a minority pursuit, most sociologists have had to face the central issues in innumerable ways – in debates about globalization, for example; in interconnection with discourses coming from cultural studies, human geography, history and anthropology; in discussions around re-imagining 'public sociology' in a plural world; and in the greater emphasis given nowadays to the *normative* and *rhetorical* fabric of every sociological framework and intervention. The changing timbre of the textbooks and collections of readings reflects this greater awareness, though undoubtedly to varying degrees, and more notably when placed under the rubric of 'social theory' than under sociology *per se*.

A trawl through the pedagogic and specialist literature quickly reveals that if much has indeed been achieved, more still needs to be done to counter unacceptably Eurocentric inclinations, and to expand substantive working knowledge of non-western histories and cultures. But it is also important to be realistic, and to resist any overbearing moralism: *all* thought systems are inevitably ethnocentric in focus, style, and available expertise. Moreover, what it even *means* to 'de-colonize', or to 'postcolonialize' sociology is far from crystal clear. Over a decade has passed since commentators were already agreeing that postcolonial thought itself had gone into 'impasse' (Slemon 1994: 29, Young 1995: 163, Moore-Gilbert 1997: 186), and during the intervening time, some standard features of early postcolonial critique have come to seem more like weaknesses than strengths. For example, sociology and other western discourses were routinely pilloried for their underlying humanism and universalism – 'Eurocentric!' – and for their associated lack of commitment to a narrowly conceived identity politics, the latter often legitimated by gestural reference to 'standpoint epistemologies' that are now agreed to be problematical. Nowadays, even theorists as central to identitarian multiculturalism and anti-Orientalism, respectively, as Bhikhu Parekh (2008) and Edward Said (2004), have moved sharply away from the theory and politics of difference *per se*, towards a much more expansive humanism. As Said puts it, 'we must begin to rid ourselves, consciously and resolutely, of the whole complex of attitudes associated not just with Eurocentrism but with identity itself' (Said 2004: 55).

Thus, one reason for the 'impasse' in postcolonial thinking is that the politics of identity/difference has lost its earlier doctrinal status. Another is that no consensus was found concerning how closely in content and spirit *postcolonialism* mapped on to *postmodernism*. As a result, the critique of Eurocentrism, and the development of postcolonial critical theory, took very diverse forms. And today a further complication arises as to how far these two 'posts' – whether taken together or separately – map on to a third, namely *postsecularism*. This theme of postsecularism was always there to an extent in the earlier theorizations, but it is only very recently that the full dramatic scenario has emerged: that *all along*, the deepest problem with Eurocentric social thought, even/especially in its critical variants, was its presumption of the truth and inevitability of secularist humanism. Troubled by the resurgence of 'religious enthusiasm', both in intellectual life and in society generally, Said reaffirmed that 'it must be a major part of the humanistic vocation to keep a fully rounded secular perspective' (Said 2004: 51). But others are much less sure about this, and seek to deepen the *problematization* of western secular thought, perhaps to the extent of revitalizing intellectual *anti*-secularism, such that 'religious' ways of comprehending social life are perceived to have, at the very least, equal standing with 'scientific' or 'materialist' approaches.

For example, Charles Taylor's recent heavyweight opus, *A Secular Age*, implicates sociology in a number of negative ways. Firstly, for Taylor, the 'modern social imaginary' that has defined sociology's central focus – 'modernity' itself – is characterized primarily in terms of *secularity*. Secularity for Taylor does not mean secular*ism* as such; rather, it signals the historical situation in which believing in God has become only one option amongst others, and in which the 'default' option – at least amongst critical academics – is 'unbelief' (Taylor's term for atheism). But whether it is secularity or secularism that is hegemonic within modernity and the modern social imaginary, this bundle of terms is systematically associated in Taylor's presentation with profound and pervasive moral 'malaise'. Second, Taylor sees modern social science as grounded in a background dogmatic 'unthought', namely the assumption of a purely 'immanent' reality, in which open-ness to a 'transcendent' beyond is closed off – wrongly in his opinion. This presumption of immanence, Taylor thinks, is what ultimately, but falsely, motivates traditional sociological expectations of growing secularization, whether in current empirical terms or as a matter of theoretical principle over the very long run.

Third, there is a striking lack of *sociological* description and explanation across the 870 pages of Taylor's book. Rather, it is a history of *ideas*, and indeed a quasi-Hegelian meta-narrative of the dialectic of *consciousness*. Instead of sociological reasoning about the relation of religious beliefs to the socio-economic structures and cultural practices in which they are embedded, Taylor prefers to tell a 'phenomenological' story of how 'we' came into secular modernity and its definitively 'flat' spiritual universe that leaves us all aching for a greater sense of 'fullness'. This minimizing of social causality makes it considerably easier to *imagine*, and then *approve*, how we might subsequently take ourselves *out of* secular modernity and into a higher phase of collective self-empowerment in terms of spiritual transformation and a 'converted' apprehension of divine manifestations in the mundane world.

Now the first thing we might want to do in response to Taylor (2007) is to impress upon him the fact that many sociologists, of wildly different temperaments, would dissent from the view that sociology is (variously) a scientific, materialist, modernity-complacent, or religion-unfriendly tradition. Just to snapshot two American doyens of the discipline on this: Robert Bellah (2007) in a US Social Science Research Council blog calls Taylor's postsecular centrepiece 'one of the most important books to be written in my lifetime', and Daniel Bell in an interview states plainly that 'for me, the foundation is religion' (Beilharz 2006: 102). So we must be careful not to falsely *anthropomorphize* the institutional figure 'Sociology' and declare it to be definitively hostile to religious belief. On the other hand, if one is committed to the view, as I am (McLennan 2006), that the very idea of sociology cannot be sustained *except* in some *broadly* 'naturalistic' sense, and thus in some *broadly* scientific-materialist and 'secular' sense, then these sentiments issuing from senior people in philosophy and sociology represent something to be alarmed about. Fortunately, there are large cracks in Taylor's whole edifice of explanatory and normative argument, and the emerging space of postsecularism contains variants that are decidedly more ambivalent (for substantiation, see McLennan 2008, 2009). But even so, the point stands that the question of *postcolonialism* is – and perhaps always has been – nowadays tied up with the question of *postsecularism*, as long as the perception stands that secularism in thought is a) rationalistically hostile to religious cultures, and b) forms a necessary part of the hegemonic western disparagement of the 'backward' non-West. The overlap between these two posts makes it even more difficult to establish what is required for sociology to become fully postcolonial.

In that context, I think we need to be cautious about, and seek to complicate, the continuing view that sociology has always been *intrinsically* 'Eurocentric', and that being Eurocentric always signals something primordially *bad*. The shadow of that sort of negativist essentialism falls over fellow-contributor to this volume Gurminder Bhambra's recent argument that if there was a 'missing revolution' in the discipline of sociology in relation to gender and sexuality, sociology has had at least as much difficulty even *recognizing* the absence of a missing revolution around postcoloniality/ism. This, Bhambra maintains, is not just a matter of repairing sociology's 'neglect of colonial relations' as such. Rather, sociology will only become postcolonially-adequate when it completely '*reconstructs*' its 'core categories of analysis' (Bhambra 2007: 782-783). As the phraseology here indicates, this represents a root-and-branch challenge to sociology, and raises some interesting conceptual issues about just how far the basic concepts of a discourse can be 'reconstructed' before we are obliged to call it something entirely different. Before following up on that, let us first see whether there can be any simplistic recourse to 'anti-Eurocentrism' as a corrective to sociology's deficits.

Problematizing Anti-Eurocentrism

The view that sociology can be speedily tutored into a coherent postcolonialist standpoint ignores dilemmas which strafe the whole field of debate, not least on basic questions of *definition and application*. For such an elementary matter, the postcolonial literature contains surprisingly few specifications of what the problem of Eurocentrism actually involves. Amongst the most developed is Wallerstein's (1997) five-fold criterion, which Said finds useful enough to take over wholesale in the text already referred to. Eurocentrism, in Said's words, is characterized by 'its misleadingly skewed historiography, the parochiality of its universalism, its unexamined assumptions about Western civilization, its Orientalism, and its attempts to impose a uniformly directed theory of progress' (2004: 53). In fact, this is a significant dilution of Wallerstein's original formulation, because Said's rendition implies, for example, that the problem is not universalism *per se* – a view held by many anti-Eurocentrics – but *parochial* universalism. And feasibly, it is the *un-examinedness* of the assumptions about Western civilization that is objectionable, rather than their existence as such. Furthermore, Wallerstein himself does not state whether being Eurocentric requires committing *all* of the five 'sins', or whether just any *one* of them will do. This prevarication is damaging, because few scholars can be found guilty under the maximal five-count charge, whilst if anyone breaches just one of them, no one is going to demand blood exactly.

In any case, we might wonder whether there are precisely five component charges here at all. The second, third and fourth charge seem to mutually define each other, whilst the commission of the first – skewed historiography – is usually bound up with how far it supports the fifth – a 'uniformly directed theory of progress'. Focusing on this, it is abundantly clear not only that, within western social theory, 'progress' has for many years been placed under erasure, but also that historical scholarship is now well supplied with complex and reflexive understandings of the emergence of western modernity. This healthier state of affairs is unquestionably due to postcolonialist pressure, but not exclusively, and anyway the sense that there is a continuing urgent deficit to make good needs to be deflated as a result.

Moreover, it cannot be expected or demanded, *a priori*, that all credible positions on the history must necessarily disavow every element of the traditional 'rise of the West' storyline. Michael Mann, for example, is perfectly willing to take on board many of the 'good points' that 'anti-Orientalist' critics make against previous accounts of the 'European Miracle'. In particular, he fully accepts that Europe 'exported' its liberalism, science and industry by way of 'mass killing, slavery, racism and authoritarian government' (Mann 2007: 51, 54). But Mann's work equally discourages thinking about this process as an abstract unified Eurocentric *project*, firstly because, prior to global expansion, European states bitterly fought it out amongst themselves in a first phase of imperial struggle; and, secondly, because Mann does not think that the evidence available to us supports any strong counter-story. The dramatic 'lead' taken by the West over the rest in material and organizational development was *not* late and 'accidental', as anti-Orientalists tend to maintain, but 'deep-rooted' and systemic. Mann also notes, surely correctly, that no value judgment necessarily accompanies such an assessment. Systematically scouring out the same debate in terms of the meta-theory of socio-historical enquiry, Joseph Bryant (2006) comes to more emphatic conclusions. Postcolonial revisionist arguments, he cogently demonstrates, tend to attribute a wholly implausible equivalence across civilizational contexts to every socio-technical factor that could be held to differentiate between large-scale social formations. Even more importantly, they also prioritize episodic, contingent and discontinuist explanatory motifs that 'effectively annul or suspend the workings of anterior structural arrangements' (Bryant 2006: 436). This kind of politically-driven historical accidentalism, Bryant insists, is profoundly flawed, reversing hard-won methodological gains in our understanding of societal 'path-dependency' over the *longue duree*, and arbitrarily denying the 'combinatorial' logic of systemic change.

Finally, in this sector of discussion, we need to ask whether the notion of Orientalism itself, regarded by Wallerstein and everyone else as constitutive of Eurocentrism, is fully viable. Pathbreaking though Said's *Orientalism* was, it has been treated uncritically, even hagiographically, in subsequent postcolonial commentaries. This seems unwarranted, because there are important weaknesses in its framing and detail. The internal friction, for example, between its Gramscian and Foucauldian theoretical strands was evident from the outset, generating very different sorts of postcolonial analysis and politics. But more than this, Said's founding articulation of Orientalism has been forcefully queried by Johann Arnason (2003: 336-9) as involving 'extraordinary conceptual and historical looseness'. First, Said oscillates between 'emphatic definitions and loose associations'; giving essentialist formulations whilst at the same time stressing that his project is 'explicitly anti-essentialist' (Arnason 2003: 336, Said 1995: 331). Second, it is very difficult to sustain an all-encompassing institutional or 'corporate' conception of the Orientalist 'system of knowledge', whilst also freely accepting that work falling into this mould is not only highly varied, but carries the 'determining imprint' of 'almost uncountable individual writers' (Arnason 2003: 336, Said 1995: 8, 23).

Third, Said's historical placement of Orientalism is 'vague and cavalier', generally dating its emergence around 1800, only to suggest in addition, variously, that it has a 4000-year history, an ancient Greek provenance, and a grounding in the workings of the Roman empire. A fourth criticism shows how Said shuttles between very broad and much narrower parameters in terms of the geography of Orientalism's remit (sometimes the Middle East, sometimes everywhere from China to the Mediterranean), and its cultural specificity (sometimes reckoned to be trained overwhelmingly on Islam, sometimes bringing into play anything generally non-Western). Arnason's impatience with this kind of imprecision partly lies in his conviction that the classical sociological tradition, and above all *Weber*, contains many resources with which the debate could be pinpointed to more constructive ends. But even Weber is summarily, and without any textual examination, dismissed by Said and numerous followers as Orientalist.

Having entered the detail of one central set of issues, we can turn more snappily to related dilemmas that trouble postcolonial theory:

- Is it 'Eurocentrism', exactly, that stands as the main offence to progressive discourse, rather than more generic ills, which can also be found in other cultural locations: racism, slavery, imperialism, capitalism, industrialism? Of course, thanks to postcolonialism, we cannot now think of those substantive problems as though they are abstract universals, *disconnected* from their historical and geographical conditions of existence/emergence. But neither can 'Eurocentrism' be taken in a formalistic, stand-alone way.
- If the West and its apologists are legitimately accused of failing to comprehend the plurality and heterogeneity of other cultures, doesn't the construction of the West as a regressive block universe commit exactly the same error, only in reverse?
- No coherent consensus exists within postcolonial or anti-Eurocentric thought. In particular, a poststructuralist-influenced strand of thought (Bhabha 1994, Venn 2000) runs sharply against a more traditionally Leftist 'anti-imperialist' wing (Amin 1989, Ahmad 1992). These serious conceptual tensions of the 1980s and 1990s have been relieved neither by the uptake of 'activist' rhetoric on the part of some previous deconstructionists (Young 2003), nor by the significant efforts of others to find a satisfactory middle way (Hall 1996, Chakrabarty 2000). This is partly because the whole postcolonialism debate has merged in inchoate fashion with themes and arguments around multicultural identities, cultural hybridity and cosmopolitanism.
- Whilst the reliance of anti-imperialist postcolonialists on analytical frameworks and tools derived from the western social and philosophical tradition was both obvious and undisguised – including versions of scientific universalism and the figure of Progress – poststructuralist disruptions of 'Eurocentric' conceptions of social time and cultural experience, such as Homi Bhabha's, appeared to thoroughly breach familiar rationalist and sociological norms. However, upon closer inspection (see McLennan 2003), such disruptions themselves, a) rely upon a background historical sociology of movements of peoples, practices and ideas; and b) tend to replace one kind of universalist understanding (eg sociological) with another (eg. psycho-somatic economies), rather than bolster a sense of

permanent 'dislocation' amongst contingent temporalities, urgings and performances.

- There is no current agreement about the terminology that can best progress anti-Eurocentric work. One recurrent coinage is that of 'multiple modernities', another is 'provincializing Europe'. But the first, some think, is merely the latest way that mainstream social science adjusts to, and thereby incorporates, the anti-Eurocentric challenge. This is because the master concept, 'modernity', remains at the centre of attention, and the western experience still stands as the original template that Others either reproduce or deviate from. 'Provincializing Europe', on the other hand, despite its coiner's insistence that this 'cannot be a project of cultural relativism', nor a 'nativist' one (Chakrabarty 2000: 43) has inevitably been taken in just such ways, resulting in an excessive pluralism of stand-alone mentalities and traditions. Eurocentrism is de-centred and contextualized alongside various equivalents (Afrocentrism, Asian values and so on), but at the cost of forgiving *all* of them their local obscurantisms as well as experiential particularities.

- Many of the wrangles around the nature of Eurocentrism cannot be resolved, or even clearly specified, as long as a central and difficult issue persists, something that confronts *all* social theorists: the divergent implications of the *concept of ideology*. In its restricted meaning, 'ideology' refers to an interest-driven, power-related body of ideas that distorts and masks the social reality it describes and invokes. Yet in its more 'relaxed' sense, ideology is about *making sense* of our lives, and the world, from within general orientations of cultural value, some of them intangible. No one can hope to escape such an 'ethnocentric' formation, the experiential quality and uncertain effect of which cannot directly be converted into the coinage of truth, reality, or material interests.

Historicism, Temporalities, Ways of Being

The purpose of the previous section was to question whether, when the demand is made that sociology be revolutionized along postcolonial lines, postcolonial thought is coherent enough to bear all the weight being placed upon it. The dilemmas identified are weighty, and the lack of intellectual and political consensus amongst postcolonialists is real. Now I want to bring the issue of postsecularism fully into the mix. It would appear that you do not have to be a postcolonialist to be a postsecularist, and *vice versa*. But there are important connections to be drawn out, connections that can be presented as intrinsic. In sociological discourse, at least as depicted by Gurminder Bhambra, 'the "postcolonial" is necessarily associated with "pre-modern" societies' (Bhambra 2007: 875). But what exactly is it about the pre-modern that sociology de-selects, given that it cannot be a matter of gender, or embodied sexuality, or anything else readily absorbed in the modern subject? The answer – though Bhambra does not say this explicitly – is: whatever is 'non-rational' or incommensurably 'different' in the experience and cultures of other societies, in particular, 'religious' and 'supernatural' ways of understanding the world. Sociology, therefore, in refusing to give proper regard to these things in their own right, declares itself to be definitively secular, indeed secularist. Derridean Ananda Abeysekara extends this line of thinking as follows: 'If we are to counter this prior notion of secularism, we ought to abandon thinking of secularism as a site in which religion remains located in a traditional past from which a de-divinized modernity has liberated itself' (Abeysekara 2008: 177). The proposal here is not only to 'rescue' pre-modern 'religious' understandings from the condescension of modernism, but to dispute that modernity itself has been 'de-divinized', and to further contest the assumption that de-divinized discourses are 'liberated'. Thus it is that postcolonialism and postsecularism become thoroughly fused, spelling double disaster, apparently, for modernist sociology.

It seems to me, however, that this scenario is seriously overstated, though fully to bring this out would require re-running almost every important argument – on all sides – in the 'rationality and relativism' debates of the 1970s and 1980s (Wilson 1970, Hollis and Lukes 1982). Suffice to say that having a 'rational' perspective on other cultures and societies simply means that we want to explain how they work, and that whilst, of course, our 'secular' sense of explanation and its validity will cognitively over-ride, if necessary, 'their' values for our purposes, this does not mean that local values and actions are not perfectly valid and rational in their own way. We then achieve, at least in principle, a proper sense of cultural *relativity* without succumbing to cultural *relativism*. We should also note that, in the modern present itself, whilst a scientific outlook necessarily undermines 'fundamentalist' religious visions of the world, rationalistic explanations are necessarily limited in scope and depth, and are always changing in substance. So there is still plenty room available for those who remain committed to ostensibly 'non-rational' or religious beliefs. Such beliefs, it could be said, are not so much *negated* as *postponed* when we engage in sociological explanation. We might also, finally, simply reject as mistaken the proposition that sociology is committed to regarding *post*colonial issues in essentialist fashion as expressions of the *pre*-modern.

These are important qualifications. Yet perhaps, in the end, the issue *is* intractable. *If* postcolonialism really is anti-secularist, and *if* the combination of these two discourses represents a complete bracketing out of the concept of modernity, plus the obliteration of any link between modernist thinking and societal liberation, then this would surely spell the end for sociology. At that point we just have to take a stand, one way or the other. But to see, one more time, whether these matters can be more satisfactorily negotiated, let us turn to the formulations of Dipesh Chakrabarty, who is heavily relied upon by both Bhambra and Abeysekara, yet also respected by historical sociologists sceptical of full-scale postcolonialism (Arnason 2003: 346).

In his book *Provincialising Europe*, Chakrabarty makes it clear that he has no interest in engaging in 'postcolonial revenge', either by rubbishing Eurocentric traditions of thought or by pretending postcolonial theorists have not themselves been definitively influenced by them. Chakrabarty is not, therefore, simply *against* the typically universalizing and analytical mode of sociology and history. In particular, he accepts that the concern with a common human future characterized by *social justice* – a veritable 'condition of political modernity' that is utterly shared by postcolonialism – is unthinkable except through conceptual schemas 'forged in Eighteenth century Europe' and still definitive of modern secular social science (Chakrabarty 2000: 4-5). But he does argue that those theories, traditions, and conceptual schemas, whilst 'indispensable', are also 'inadequate' (2000: 6, 16, 88, 254). They are inadequate because they are *historicist*.

Historicism involves the assumption that all events, agencies, and societies exist in the same temporality, a 'homogeneous' space that is treated as a 'natural' mode of existence. With history naturalized in this way, all forms of social practice and consciousness can be laid out according to the same temporal parameters, reflecting a singular ontological status, such that their differential features and relations can be expressed through an encompassing totality of pasts undergone and possibilities opened up. This analytic shows the influence of modern science on social and historical thinking, and historical sociology would indeed seem compelled to operate under some such guidelines. But Chakrabarty's suggestion is that, even if we feel that compulsion, the 'naturalization' of history and its reductive ontology should be resisted, partly because they entail a teleological political imperialism in which *the* past is necessarily tied to a modern/modernist present and future, whose privileged origin and source of dissemination is the West. A conceptual register in which society develops and spreads to other places *over time* thus becomes intrinsically bound up with the condescending, racist politics of the 'not-yet' – whether this takes the form of Mill's theoretical withholding of India's right to liberal self-government, or to Hobsbawm's notion that peasant consciousness, being 'pre-modern' is also 'pre-political' (Chakrabarty 2000: 6-13).

Chakrabarty accepts that postcolonial scholars, too, tend to gloss radical cultural differences and incommensurable temporalities in terms that are ultimately developmental-modernist. This happens, for example, when religiously-motivated peasant mobilization is re-described as a matter of 'power and resistance', or when the worship of tools and machinery is treated as just one instance of capital's subsumption of 'real' labour, or when the perception of active spirits within a servile community is translated in terms of their 'logic of ritual practice'. Chakrabarty's own previous work, he confesses, similarly brought a 'huge elaborate panoply of iconography and rituals' under overarching master concepts like 'culture' or 'religion', thus failing to go 'beyond historicism' entirely. For that to happen, we need to deliberately eschew 'sociological' understanding, since the latter is incapable of witnessing and affirming 'irreducible plurality' (2000: 16, 78, 81).

What is involved in this 'anti-sociological' effort? First, receptivity to radically different ontologies, the validity of which we cannot unilaterally decide. Gods, spirits and other supernatural entities are *agents* in 'premodern' lives and practices, and the sociological imagination cannot just deem them either to be illusions, or to re-constitute them as 'social facts' by dint of the logical priority of the social over the divine. Gods and spirits should therefore be taken to be 'co-eval' with the human (2000: 16, 74-6). Then, we need to develop a new politics of 'translation', such that different sorts of cultural phenomena, belief and experience do not have to pass through some neutral, superior set of terms that establish not only their general equivalence, but also their subordination (2000: Chapter 2). Instead, differences should be directly 'bartered' in a rough and ready way. Third, we need to produce 'conjoined and disjunctive genealogies' that do justice to the 'permanent tension' between different temporalities, and different futurities (2000: 254-5).

Chakrabarty's postcolonial discourse is complex and subtle, requiring careful attention to the different modulations present within it. But that complexity, and those divergent modulations, are mostly indicative of inconsistency and hiatus rather than integration of multiple desiderata.

1. The overall intellectual mood is *ambivalence* rather than outright *pluralism*. Chakrabarty has to engage in anti-sociology to give other possibilities breathing space, not because he really does want to abandon social science historicism – he tells us often enough that this is neither feasible nor desirable. Now, whilst ambivalence may be a virtuous state of mind at important junctures, it doesn't ultimately resolve key issues, and so the 'dilemmas' of postcolonial thought sketched earlier, after Chakrabarty, are compounded rather than relieved. In particular, the argument that analytical historicism is forever condemned to be concomitant with the teleological political moralism of the 'not yet', remains far from secure.

2. Ambivalence reigns because, in effect, strict pluralism – thinking about and intellectually accepting 'irreducible plurality' – is *impossible* to sustain. Once inside the historicist frame, for example, there can be no 'multiple temporalities'. As Roberto Unger bracingly argues, in work that I would classify as postsecular, we have to accept 'to the hilt' the *utter historicity* of things – ourselves as 'dying organisms', our societies and ideas, indeed nature itself, and even nature's laws (Unger 2007: 78). This does not mean that people even today, never mind in 'premodern' societies, cannot be receptively *imagined* as living their lives in different and multiple times. If their lives are deeply marked by that sense of another ontology, then we must take good stock of this. But, those people are not, otherwise, *actually* living in a different time and world.

   Similarly, in the secular frame, gods and spirits can certainly be *conceived* as 'co-eval' with human actions, just because many humans *themselves* think in this way, and then act on that basis. But only in a theologico-religious frame, and *not* in a social-scientific one, can we directly take gods and spirits *to be* agents in the world. Chakrabarty's articulation of these matters systematically wavers between these two very different possibilities, a wavering that rules out any productive and lasting resolution.

3. Chakrabarty's argument that the work of translation between different schemas should take the form of 'barter' rather than 'generalized exchange' is brilliantly phrased, triggering a number of interesting homologies between types of understanding and the logic of social formations (a very modernist and sociological sense of homology, we might add). But the underlying thought is nevertheless flawed, and its implications are unworkable, as can easily be shown in relation to Chakarabarty's own chosen re-descriptions. The fault lies in thinking that what is going on in 'bartered' translations – for example between Hindu and Islamic deities – is a 'natural' case of 'singularities trading with singularities' (2000: 84-5). This surely cannot be so: the direct, if only ever approximate, translations only 'work' because of a background shared *generality* – notions of the most holy, sin/offence, God's agents, the light, and so on. The fact that these generalities are untheorized and treated as absolute singularities in those particular cultures does not mean that they *are* uniquely singular, at least for purposes of translation. If they *were* totally singular, then they would not be even roughly translatable. Chakrabarty indirectly acknowledges this, in somewhat contradictory fashion, when meditating on Paul Veyne. The thought is this (2000: 82-3): Historians often play up *specificity*; but specificity is structurally tied to *generality*, whereas what is really 'occluded' by generality is singularity. Singularity in that sense amounts to whatever 'defies the generalizing impulse of the sociological imagination', the most obvious examples of this being gods and the like. This evidently circular or tautological piece of reasoning, however, is quickly cancelled out by Chakrabarty's prompt admission that 'of course, nothing exists out there as a singular-in-itself'. He then tries to ease this paralysing conundrum by construing the singular not *existentially* but as a kind of 'limit concept', since 'language itself mostly speaks of the general'. But this again compounds the problem rather than relieving it. Not only do we remain fully in the grip of a further generality, language, but the case against sociology as the fingered culprit in singularity's 'occlusion' necessarily falls.

In any case, Chakrabarty's appreciation of singularity and ontic difference, as with his arguments against sociology, are themselves shot through with quasi-sociological mediations, only comprehensible within a conceptually reflexive modern mentality. Thus, when he says that what was left out of his earlier historiography was a 'huge elaborate panoply of iconography and rituals', he is not, as intended, obviating the generality of master concepts such as culture or religion; he is simply offering different (but related) aspects of such generality. And just to assert that the agencies of gods and spirits are 'not merely symbolic', because such agencies or belief in such agencies are 'part of the network of power and prestige' in non-modern, non-secular cultures, demonstrates the necessity and value of the very form of thought we are being urged to unthink (2000: 14). There is, finally, considerable irony in the whole exercise, since Chakrabarty is striving to reach a higher form of *generality* within which ways of being that are focused on singularity can 'spontaneously' trade with those that are not.

4. It is important to see that Chakrabarty's postcolonial concern is bound up with a philosophical problem that has little to do with Eurocentrism or secularism as such, because, as he readily acknowledges, it reflects a deep 'fault line' definitive of the European tradition itself (2000: 18). This is the problem that in the relation between knowing subject and observed object, between abstraction and the concrete world, between theory and lived experience, between the universal and the local, between spare generalization and the teeming singularities of mind and being that it transposes, a certain *violence* is committed. There is thus nothing less than a 'scandal', Chakrabarty suggests, in every secular, historicizing assimilation into the modern 'imperious, all-embracing code' of worlds in which gods and spirits are agents (2000: 89-93).

    But what is the (specifically postcolonial, postsecular) force of this observation? As stated, the 'scandal' is by no means unique to the 'assimilation' of the religious pre-modern – the same could probably be said for analytical re-readings of the thoughts and feelings of contemporary teenagers, mothers, gamblers, and lovers. And it is not necessarily a 'scandal' at all, as Chakrabarty himself intimates, as long as the boundary between scientific analysis and its object (for example 'premodern superstition') does not get 'overdrawn' (2000: 238). But Chakrabarty then wobbles once more between this wise modulation, and the obscurantist proposal that analytical thought gives us *no* better penetration than everyday understanding into the deeper workings of things (2000: 239). Experience and its modes may not be fully captured *just* in terms of generalized sociological (and other such) explanations, but the greater intellectual 'scandal' lies in the romanticist fantasy that somewhere beneath and beyond the reaches of analytical reason, a deeper, mute, mysterious truth exists, glimpsed only through intuition and revelation.

5. That last 'metaphysical' consideration, we should further grasp, is not isomorphic with Chakrabarty's useful distinction-opposition between 'analytical' and 'affective' histories. The metaphysical issue concerns the necessary *modal* disjuncture between what is analysed and the act of analysis, and this is something that applies to *all* modes of analysis, including the hermeneutical and affective. You are no less 'distant', *modally speaking*, from your object of thought just because you seek to provide a 'loving grasp of detail in search of the diversity of human lifeworlds' (2000: 18).

Despite their subject-friendly and directly-divulgent appearance, terms such as 'lifeworld', 'cultural diversity', 'singular ontology' and so forth are first and foremost *theoretical* tools of analysis and assessment.

Conclusion: Postcolonial Discourse and Sociological Categories

Chakrabarty's position, whilst interestingly reflective, is neither fully convincing in itself, nor necessarily outside 'Eurocentric' discourse. Nor does it demand the wholesale reconstruction of sociological categories. Rather, it refers us to the necessary limits of all analytical-historicist thinking, and not only in special relation to pre-modern or religious ways of being. Chakrabarty's discourse, moreover, is intended to be *therapeutic* rather than logically watertight. We may wish somehow to reconcile historicist and non-historicist, secular and non-secular, analytical and expressive modes of understanding, but nevertheless these modes stand in 'permanent tension' just because they are *not* completely compatible. For certain purposes at least, we still have to choose between them; and if our purposes are *cognitive*, there is good reason to choose the first term in each of those pairs. We can also perhaps re-jig the entire problem in pursuit of a more relaxed sense of the relationship between analytical positivity and appreciative receptivity. Within sociology itself, for instance, there has been a long-standing discussion about 'the two sociologies': in Weber's terms, these relate to, respectively, adequacy at the level of *causality*, and adequacy at the level of *meaning*. Now it is only – another Weberianism – as *ideal types* that these projects, along with related distinctions (such as the nomological and the ideographic, positivism and hermeneutics), stand in the starkest contrast to one another. Moreover, within current postpositivist philosophical thinking, there are numerous resources for reworking and integrating these different aspects of comprehension. Talk of 'permanent tensions' (Chakrabarty) or 'aporias' (Abeysekara) in understanding the lived and structural characteristics of religious cultures, or any other socio-cultural phenomenon, is therefore excessive.

Returning, in that light, to the question of the 'missing postcolonial revolution' in sociology, this rhetorical framing seems guaranteed both to understate what is being ongoingly achieved, and to set an almost impossible benchmark for success. We should think here of how remarkable the feminist impact on sociology has been, even if 'only' at the level of what *constitutes* 'the social', and in terms of the institutional *politics* of the discipline. Some feminist theorists, it is true, continue to think that this is not nearly revolutionary enough. Thus, in a recent discussion, Ann Witz and Barbara Marshall insist that the 'imaginative architecture of the social…both presumes and erases the masculine'. Yet, in the last instance, the imperative is *not* after all to reject the category of 'the social' *itself* as intrinsically inadequate to feminist concerns, but rather to 'rethink' it, 'reworking it to make it more inclusive' (Witz and Marshall 2004: 33-4).

Exactly the same can be said in relation to postcolonial discourse. The 'neglect of colonial relations' can be further repaired, and the basic sociological categories can be further re-thought and made more inclusive – as long as this rethinking is not *solely* driven by political or moralistic considerations. We can also constantly seek to find ways of appreciating non-modern ontologies, and people's past and present sense of spiritual agency in the world. But modern social science thinking cannot, and should not feel obliged to, accept, endorse, or – *per impossible* – *enter* ways of being that are so radically other that we have to think of them as 'irreducibly plural'. If that is what the postcolonial revolution is about, then sociology, along with every other 'secular' intellectual endeavour, will be waiting in vain.

References

Abeysekara, A. 2008. *The Politics of Postsecular Religion: Mourning Secular Futures*. New York: Columbia University Press.

Ahmad, A. 1992. *In Theory*. London: Verso.

Amin, S. 1989. *Eurocentrism*. London: Zed Books.

Arnason, J. 2003. *Civilizations in Dispute: Historical Questions and Theoretical Traditions*. Boston/Leiden: Brill.

Beilharz, P. 2006. Ends and Rebirths: An Interview with Daniel Bell. *Thesis Eleven*, 85, 93-103.

Bellah, R. 2007. A Secular Age: Secularism of a New Kind. [Online]. Available at: http://www.ssrc.org/blogs/immanent_frame/2007/10/19/secularism-of-a-new-kind/ [accessed: 6 July 2009].

Bhabha, H. 1994. *The Location of Culture*. London: Routledge.

Bhambra, G. 2007. Sociology and Postcolonialism: Another 'Missing' Revolution? *Sociology*, 41(5), 871-84.

Bryant, J.M. 2006. The West and the Rest Revisited: Debating Capitalist Origins, European Colonialism, and the Advent of Modernity. *Canadian Journal of Sociology*, 31(4), 403-44.

Chakrabarty, D. 2000. *Provincializing Europe: Postcolonial Thought and Historical Difference*. Princeton: Princeton University Press.

Hall, S. 1996. When was 'the Post-colonial'? Thinking at the Limit, in *The Post-Colonial Question: Common Skies, Divided Horizons*, edited by L. Curti and I. Chambers. London: Routledge.

Hollis, M. and Lukes, S. (eds) 1982. *Rationality and Relativism*. Oxford: Blackwell.

Mann, M. 2007. Predation and Production in European Imperialism, in *Ernest Gellner and Contemporary Social Thought*, edited by S. Malesevic and M. Haugaard. Cambridge: Cambridge University Press.

McLennan, G. 2000. Sociology's Eurocentrism and the 'Rise of the West' Revisited. *European Journal of Social Theory*, 3(3), 275-91.

McLennan, G. 2003. Sociology, Eurocentrism and Postcolonial Theory. *European Journal of Social Theory*, 6(1), 69-86.

McLennan, G. 2006. *Sociological Cultural Studies: Reflexivity and Positivity in the Human Sciences*. Houndmills: Palgrave Macmillan.

McLennan, G. 2008. Among the Unbelievers. *New Left Review*, 52, 139-48.

McLennan, G. 2009. Postsecular Social Theory: A New Global Debate, in *Globalization and Utopia*, edited by C. El-Ojeili and P. Hayden. Houndmills: Palgrave Macmillan.

Moore-Gilbert, B. 1997. *Postcolonial Theory: Contexts, Practices, Politics*. London: Verso.

Parekh, B. 2008. *A New Politics of Identity: Political Principles for an Interdependent World*. Houndmills: Palgrave Macmillan.

Said, E. 1995. *Orientalism*. London: Penguin.

Said, E. 2004. *Humanism and Democratic Criticism*. Houndmills: Palgrave Macmillan.

Slemon, S. 1994. The Scramble for Post-colonialism, in *De-scribing Empire*, edited by C. Tiffin and H. Lawson. London: Routledge.

Taylor, C. 2007. *A Secular Age*. Harvard: University/Belknap Press.

Unger, R.M. 2007. *The Self Awakened: Pragmatism Unbound*. Cambridge: Harvard University Press.

Venn, C. 2000. *Occidentalism: Modernity and Subjectivity*. London: Sage.

Wallerstein, I. 1997. Eurocentrism and its Avatars: The Dilemmas of Social Science. *New Left Review*, 226, 93-107.

Wilson, B.R. (ed.) 1970. *Rationality*. Oxford: Blackwell.

Witz, A. and Marshall, B.L. 2004. The Masculinity of the Social: Towards a Politics of Interrogation, in *Engendering the Social*, edited by B.L. Marshall and A. Witz. Buckingham: Open University Press.

Young, R.J.C. 1995. *Colonial Desire: Hybridity in Theory, Culture and Race*. London: Routledge.

Young, R.J.C. 2003 *Postcolonialism: A Very Short Introduction*. Oxford: Oxford University Press.

Chapter 8

Wounded Subjects: Sexual Exceptionalism and the Moral Panic on 'Migrant Homophobia' in Germany

Jin Haritaworn

The effort represented by this volume, to bring together different margins of sociology, is timely. It is rendered critical by the unevenness with which various 'differences' have been taken up by the discipline's centre, as well as the social contexts which it aims to describe.[1] In Britain, for example, sociologists of sexuality have had some success in securing an institutional basis. The gay relationship and family, and the 'intimate citizenship practices' which it gives rise to, has been an especially productive area of scholarship (see Weeks, Heaphy and Donovan 2001). This is partly enabled by straight sociology's discovery of sexuality as a legitimate object in the 1990s (Giddens 1992, Beck and Beck-Gernsheim 1995).[2] Most prominently, Anthony Giddens' *Transformation of Intimacy* treats gay sex as symptom and forerunner of a 'late modern West' where sexuality is equalized, democratized and liberated from the constraints of reproduction and tradition (Giddens 1992: 15, 130, see Klesse 2007 for a critique).[3] Outside the academy, too, formerly privatized, pathologized and criminalized intimacies are increasingly invited into the public realm. Nevertheless, this circulation is differential – brown and white, disabled and non-disabled, transgendered and non-transgendered intimacies move at different volumes and speeds, and strike different affective registers.[4]

These celebratory accounts have sometimes remained indifferent to their wider political context. Jasbir Puar (2007) broke important ground by drawing our attention to the sexual productiveness of the global 'war on terror' and its

---

1   This is partly a reflection of a colonial division of labour which assigned sociologists with the study of the so-called 'modern' societies (Randeria 1999). As this chapter will show, this modernity/traditionality divide is not only racialized but also heavily sexualized.

2   See also the special issue on love and eroticism in *Theory, Culture and Society* 15(3/4).

3   Outside the academy, this is mirrored by the extension of partnership and adoption rights to gay couples and an increase in media representations of gay relationships.

4   My framework is influenced by the idea that publics are intimate and shot through with emotions (Cvetkovich 2003, Berlant 1997, Ahmed 2004).

domestic equivalences in racism and state violence. Drawing on Mbembe's (2003) radicalization of Foucault's biopolitics (1976), she coins the idea of a 'queer necropolitics',[5] where who gets assigned to life and who is discarded from it are radically reshuffled. At the basis of this is a sexual exceptionalism which is really an outflow of earlier colonial missions which were imagined as 'saving brown women from brown men' (Spivak 1999: 284ff). More precisely, Puar argues that the sexual subject formerly associated with death (through Aids) is now invited, officially at least, to leave the realm of death, and of the perverse, by vacating it for other 'populations targeted for segregation, disposal, or death' (Puar 2007: xii). Thus, Puar shows how the discourse on gay rights joins that on women's rights in justifying, and calling for, the disenfranchisement of racialized populations in both the peripheries and the metropoles.

This forces us to critically revisit the rhetorics of citizenship and inclusion. Rather than celebrating a sexually liberated or democratized Europe/West, a decolonial sociology might question how imagined entities such as the nation/Europe/the West come to cohere in the first place. We could start by showing curiosity towards the new affective languages, aesthetics, rituals, and symbols that mark this fictional entity as friendly towards women and gays, in the face of a barely ended institutional violence which remains unmourned. Finally, a decolonial sociology would attend to those figures that haunt[6] our happy story of diversity, and constitute its outside: the homophobic racial Other, who will not be missed from the community, and who in this narrative of care and intimacy becomes utterly disposable.

My chapter examines this with the emergence of the 'homophobic migrant' in Germany. It traces the genealogy of a moral panic around 'migrant[7] homophobia' at two major construction sites – the Simon Study commissioned by the biggest gay organization, which compared homophobia among 'migrant' and 'German' school children in 2007, and the violent attack against a group of queer[8] and

---

5   Mbembe's (2003) 'necropolitics' radicalizes Foucault's concept of 'biopolitics' by pointing to the centrality of death (social, cultural, literal) to sovereignty and population control. On 'Queer Necropolitics', see also the panel convened by Adi Kuntsman for the *American Anthropological Association* meeting in Philadelphia in 2009.

6   Avery Gordon (1997) encourages sociologists to attend to ghosts: those 'seething presences' which act and 'often meddl[e] with taken-for-granted realities'. She describes the ghost as a social figure 'investigating [which] can lead to that dense site where history and subjectivity make social life. The ghost or the apparition is one form by which something lost, or barely visible, or seemingly not there to our supposedly well-trained eyes, makes itself known or apparent to us, in its own way, or course' (Gordon 1997: 8).

7   The category 'migrant' was first forged as a term of solidarity by people of various diasporic origins and generations of post/migration. It has more recently been mainstreamed as a polite euphemism designed to replace older racist terms such as *Ausländer* ('foreigner', the category long used for migrants and their children regardless of birthplace or nationality).

8   I both adopt and contest a political notion of 'queer'. On the one hand, queer has served as an umbrella term comparable to 'Black' or 'of colour', to politicize the abjection

transgendered people at the Drag Festival in Berlin in 2008, which was instantly 'recognized' as the deed of 'Turks'.[9]

At the time of writing (in early 2009), these nascent sexual knowledges of race, culture and religion have culminated in new and, in Germany, unprecedented demands for hate crimes legislation along the American and British models. We are witnessing, then, a direct convergence between the enfranchisement of new sexual and gendered subjects and the disenfranchisement of post/migrants, whose displacement, policing and incarceration become synonymous with the protection of vulnerable intimacies. While the consequences of this new development cannot be fully anticipated, I am hoping that my analysis will provide a useful snapshot.

Innocent Kisses: The Respectable Gay Subject of the *Simon* Study

The Simon Study was disseminated in a series of articles which broke the usual silence about sexuality in the public debate in Germany. The article in the *Süddeutsche*, one of the biggest daily newspapers in Germany, is illustrative of the way in which the study's findings were debated (Grassmann 2007). The title 'Migrant youth against Gays: Homophobic Berlin' conjures a sense of crisis, of violence, emanating from a certain place (multiethnic Berlin), and certain bodies (migrant youth who immediately become readable as men of Turkish origin), which are pitted in struggle against gays, in a non-overlapping, necessarily conflictual relationship. 'Migrant' has moved in this description, from a category once coined in political solidarity between people of various diasporic origins and generations of migration, to one that politely replaces but does not supplant the discourse of the perennial *Ausländer*, or foreigner, who is forever excluded from the law of German blood. The journalist cites the quantitative results as evidence for the fact that homophobia is a problem 'especially with migrant youth':

---

of non-normative sexualities and gender expressions. However, this unity often causes epistemic violence, by collapsing differential positionings into each other and evading power, such as that of white queers over queers of colour, and non-trans people or gender conforming people over transgendered or gender non-conforming people.

9   Besides the socio-psychological Simon Study, which was commissioned by the LSVD, the biggest gay organization in Germany, a second sociological study into experiences of homophobic violence was conducted by the Berlin gay anti-violence project Maneo (Maneo 2007). While ethnicity did not appear to be a criteria in the design of the lengthy questionnaire, the singular finding highlighted was that '16% of the respondents stated in an open box that the perpetrators had been persons of non-German origin' (ibid.: 6). There are strong political overlaps between Maneo and the LSVD. The significance of academic knowledges of 'Muslim homophobia' has increased with the introduction of the hate crimes discourse into the German context, and the homophobia action plan by the Green Party demanded 'regular (at least every five years) online surveys of lesbians, gays and transgenders on experiences of violence' (Bündnis 90/Die Grünen (2008: 1).

On a five-point scale of homophobia the German pupils, according to the leader of the study Bernd Simon, scored 0.96, the Russian-descended ones 1.82, and the Turkish-descended ones 2.08 (ibid.).

These findings, we learn in the first and last sentence of the article, should be a cause of concern in a cosmopolitan city like Berlin, where 'a gay politician has been elected mayor twice', and where 'there should be a certain tolerance towards homosexuals' (ibid.).

The sign of diversity, in this discussion, moves from the racialized body (who becomes the 'migrant homophobe') to the sexualized one (who becomes the 'injured homosexual' in need of protection from the 'migrant homophobe'). The sexual subject is nevertheless mostly absent in the article, which foregrounds the cultural proclivity towards homophobia among, especially, migrants of Turkish origin – the 'Russian' ones quickly drop away from the discussion. Nevertheless, it is visually present through the photo of a kissing gay couple which accompanies the article.[10]

The two young men seem incidental to the narrative. Their gym-built, white bodies open up towards us. Their kiss takes place in public, on a square maybe. To a queer observer like myself, the spectacle evokes nostalgia. It 'reminds' me of the kiss-ins of the late 1980s (when I was just a teenager): that icon of radical queer history and Aids activism which, I was later told, was one of midwives of Queer (Seidman 1996). That ultimate symbol of transgression, of in-your-face direct action, which claims space in a hostile public that is far from friendly towards queers and transpeople, that would carelessly watch 'us' die (Cvetkovich 2003).

The public kiss in front of our eyes, too, has onlookers, but onlookers who are far from hostile. 'We' are positioned close-by, with more witnesses gathered opposite in the background, facing in the same direction as us, gathering around the two lovers. As readers and onlookers, we become witnesses to their queer love. We approve of it, would protect it even, from Others who *lack* our openness, who are excluded from view.[11] In Jasbir Puar's terms, the two gay men, formerly marked for death (through Aids), are 'folded (back) into life' (Puar 2007: 36).[12]

In contrast to 1980s kiss-ins, these performances of queer sexuality draw their spectators in without repelling them or calling for repression or pathologization.

---

10   http://www.sueddeutsche.de/panorama/artikel/965/134708/.

11   Reclaiming a non-ontological, phenomenological concept of sexual 'orientation' for a critical queer project, Sara Ahmed (2006) argues that politics involve orientation: Which well-trodden paths do we follow, which bodies do we turn towards? And which do we leave behind, or exclude from view?

12   This aesthetic inclusion of queer intimacy is not singular; besides the Süddeutsche, the left-wing *tageszeitung*, too, chose an image of gay male intimacy (the hugging protagonists of *Brokeback Mountain*), to represent the discourse on 'Muslim homophobia'. There is a veritable proliferation of a certain kind of gay (male) kiss in the German media. In the parallel debate on 'Muslim homophobia' in Hamburg, the local daily *Hamburger Morgenpost* even staged a kiss-in in front of the local mosque, for an article entitled very similarly, 'Muslims Against Gays' (see Eicker 2007, Peter and Schimkus 2008).

The kiss 'we' are watching is not diseased, pornographic or repugnant, but nice, out in the open, uncensored from the approving eye of the public. It is gender-conforming, aesthetic but not sissy. It is drawn-out and savoured, no quick fumble hidden away in a public toilet, or indeed, a closet. It appears both spontaneous and deliberate. Placed proudly under the rainbow flag, it also looks defiant.

The defiant stance of the kissers appears to contradict their public surroundings, which self-consciously identify themselves as welcoming. In Germany as in other Western European contexts such as Britain and the Netherlands, politicians have pronounced gay rights to be the 'core values' of the nation, and expressions of a specifically 'Western' and 'European' tradition of sexual freedom (Haritaworn, Tauqir and Erdem 2008, Haritaworn 2008, Kuntsman 2009, Petzen 2008). This re-signification has taken place within wider debates about 'integration' and its national variations, such as 'cohesion' in Britain, or the demand for a *Leitkultur* ('lead culture') in Germany. Both white gay activism, and official responses such as the Dutch Civic Integration exam and the Muslim Test of German nationality, explicitly target 'Muslims' as the constitutive outside of this re-imagined community. This also reflects a globalization of racism in the 'war on terror'. Rallying around a common enemy, Western Europeans increasingly imagine their heritage as shared, often even part of a trans-Atlantic West. This is partly enabled by a recategorization of the largest European post/migrant populations along religious lines: Britain's 'Asians' and Germany's '*Ausländer*' are increasingly becoming 'Muslim'. The pronunciation of queer love as desirable and belonging is thus deeply interwoven with processes of war, migration, backlash and exclusion.

The defiance of queer love in the face of apparent acceptance only makes sense if we take account of these continuing anxieties around non-heteronormative intimacy, and the ways in which these become displaced onto Others. 'We' are able to witness queer love communally because of Others who abstain from this communing, who may even need to be kept away, because their fear and hatred of this love makes them want to injure it. Our stance, therefore, is not necessarily a loving one (nowhere in the article are we asked to love queer people). It is, rather, a protective one. 'We' can come closer to them despite our continuing ambivalence because others plainly hate them. By positioning its heterosexual audience as oppositionally divided (white bodies which open up close-by, v. brown bodies which shrink back, or backwards even; which come close only in order to attack), the spectacle of the kiss thus also affects a turn towards a new kind of membership ideology, which enfranchises a new (sexual) subject but in the same breath disenfranchises (racial/religious) Others.

While spectacular, queer intimacy nevertheless remains unspoken in the article. In the Simon Study, too, it is conspicuously absent. This contrasts with the hyper-visibility of 'migrants' as an object of dissection. While performing 'migrants' as naturally different from 'Germans', the categories nevertheless require careful delineation. Thus, 'Germanness' is defined by Simon through birth in Germany and descent from four 'German' grandparents (ibid.: 90). This definition is stricter than current nationality laws, and more akin to the Nuremberg laws. By attesting to their unalloyed German blood, participants are reminded that hybrid, bicultural or hyphenated identities are meaningless. The need for such an elaborate definition of Germanness – the same category which 'migrants' are apparently refusing to integrate into – reflects a certain categorical insecurity. For how can we tell 'Them' from 'Us', in the face of multigenerational settlement and inter-ethnic family formation?

If ethnicity is defined anxiously, sexuality is not. It is simply taken for granted. We already know who the subject of sexuality is: 'the homosexual'. On the other hand, 'homophobic attitudes' are defined as

> a psychological tendency to react to homosexuals or homosexuality with a negative attribution. Such an attribution may include or find expression, *inter alia*, in negative affects or emotions (e.g. disgust), negative cognitions (e.g. devaluing stereotyping) and negative behavioural tendencies (e.g. avoidance tendencies) (ibid.: 88, my translation).

This definition of sexual oppression again occludes its history of contestation. Earlier gay liberation struggles identified this problem not simply as the attitudes of individuals but as the pervasiveness of norms, structures and hierarchies around gender and sexuality, including for instance the forcible adherence to a monogamous, nuclear family model based in oppositional gender roles. Such activisms did not work simply toward inclusion in a tolerant society, but critiqued the bases of society as part of wider movements, e.g. for civil rights and against the war in Vietnam (Duggan 2003).

In contrast, Simon's definition assumes that assimilation has already taken place. In fact, his stated rationale for the study is that homophobic attitudes should have no place in a country that is open to diversity and has politicians and other public figures who are gay (ibid.: 87). Again, post/migrants are displaced as symbols of diversity. Instead, they become the bearers of homophobia, which is redefined as threat to diversity, and alien to the imagined community.

It is worth examining this displacement in greater methodological detail. Sexual oppression here becomes a pathological affect understood to be residing in particular bodies, which can be clearly identified as homophobic. This affect can further be measured through a given set of attitudes and behaviours, which are quantifiable through 'items', or statements which respondents have to agree with or disagree with on a five-point scale from 0 (not true) to 4 (very true). There is no sense here of gender and sexuality as constituted in social encounters and power relations, or as subject to cultural or historic variation. This becomes even more problematic when we take a look at the 'items' used to measure homophobia and its correlates. Thus, the first item measuring 'homophobic attitudes' reads: 'When two gay men kiss in the street I find this repelling' (ibid.: 91). This already assumes the universality of public and private expressions of sexuality (cf. Klauda 2007). More problematically, this is then correlated with other variables, including *traditional masculinity*, *degree of religiosity*, *personal contacts with homosexuals*, *perceptions of discrimination*, and *integration* (all within a single-variable analysis, i.e.: the more traditional your masculinity, the more homophobic you are hypothesized to be). All of these variables and correlations perform a racialized definition of the homophobic body. Thus, *religiosity* is measured through an item such as 'Religion plays an important role in my life' (p. 91). In a context of anti-Muslim racism and 'war on terror', religion would naturally be more salient for Muslims as a marker of racism and resistant identity (e.g. Butler 2008). *Perceptions of discrimination* are measured through such items as 'Germany prefers to look after its "own people" rather than foreigners and migrants (people who have immigrated) and their children' (p. 91) – a rather accurate perception if one looks at the ways that life-chances and entitlements are distributed in the country (OECD 2008). *Traditional masculinity* is assessed through an item such as 'A man who is not prepared to defend himself against violence is a wimp' (p. 90-1). This disregards how people of colour, as well as many queers and transpeople who *lack* gender, class or race privilege, disproportionately have to defend themselves from violence, and are often pathologized and punished for this. Both the variables which the Simon Study proposes, and the items designed to measure them, are thus racially biased and categorically performative of the very 'homophobic Muslim' subject which they claim to objectively describe. 'Homophobia' is designed to be a 'migrant' problem.

There are further methodological problems with the study. In his description of the research, Simon states that his study is 'limited exclusively to Berlin' and hence 'not representative'. Having briefly delimited his findings, Simon then abandons all attempts at modesty in the discussion – the part which journalists and opinion makers are most likely to read. Instead he claims validity for the whole of the country:

> The study delivers robust clues that *in Germany*, youth with migration backgrounds differ significantly in their attitude to homosexuality from youth without migration backgrounds (ibid.: 97, my italics).

The local thus comes to stand in for the national, as if both were one and the same. There is no attempt to ground the findings in any social, spatial and temporal context (see Binnie et al. 2006: 21). However, in late 2000s Berlin, the idea of homophobia is highly salient in local discourses on ethnicity. Where discussions of homophobia enter into the public discourse, it is regularly identified as a 'migrant', more specifically a 'Muslim' problem (see Haritaworn and Petzen forthcoming). This needs to be historicized with the changing politics of the LSVD (Lesbian and Gay Federation Germany), the biggest surviving gay organization in the country which describes itself as 'the biggest civil rights, self-help and welfare organization for lesbians and gays in Germany' (LSVD n.d.a). Fatima El Tayeb (2003) shows how the LSVD adopted the 'integration of migrants' as its new *raison d'être*, after winning the campaign for the Life Partnership Act 2001. This shift in politics, from 'German' to 'migrant' homophobia, proved lucrative for the Federation, which receives public funding from the state. The Federation managed to insert itself into a globalized 'integration' debate which increasingly imagined its constitutive outside as 'Muslims' who segregate themselves and endanger multicultural harmony and world peace. As result, it effectively rose from a gay, local, to a national and, after being granted UN observer status in 2006, international player.[13]

This background information is not incidental, as the Simon Study was in fact commissioned by the LSVD. The Federation is likely to be the main beneficiary of its policy recommendations, which in 'complementary integration efforts that need to begin both with the migrants and the recipient society' and 'encouragement of personal contacts between homosexuals and migrants' closely match the work it currently undertakes (Simon 2007: 98, LSVD n.d. b). 'Homosexual' and 'migrant' do not overlap in this policy recommendation. They are constructed as adversarial: the former a vulnerable body, the latter a phobic, hateful perpetrator. The former the new symbol of a tolerant society, whose tolerance is nevertheless under threat, the latter its constitutive Other from whom we all must be protected.

Vulnerable Intimacies: Assimilating the Transgendered Body

It is against this background, of a new, intertextually crafted discourse on 'migrant homophobia', that the incident at the Drag Festival was received and debated. The anti-racist concept of the moral panic remains relevant for understanding this debate (Sudbury 2006, Hall et al. 1978): a problem is identified (migrant homophobia), which appears to call for academic and policy attention. This then leads to a sharp increase in the number of problematic acts, as new attacks are easily 'recognized' as 'migrant homophobia' – and in turn necessitate more public attention, and further political responses. As we shall see, the debate, which ultimately led to demands for hate crimes legislation, was both 'moral' and 'panicked'. The drama of the 'injured homosexual' and the hateful 'Muslim homophobe' has its own speed and affective economy. It urgently calls for, and climaxes with, 'our' intervention. 'We' rush to step in protectively, to take the injured bodies into the body of the nation (an urge which overrides our continuing ambivalence). As the event become re-narrated as a hate crime, the necessary course for action becomes crystal clear: the 'Muslim homophobe', that foreign body which threatens the well-being of the community, must be kept out, locked in, or expelled.[14]

Nevertheless, the actual occurrences at the Drag Festival were highly contested. On the last night of the festival, a group of visitors and performers, including drag kings, trans and genderqueer people, as well as queer women, were beaten up on their way home from the closing party at SO36, the popular gay club at the heart of the gentrifying area. The perpetrators were variously characterized as 'Turkish

---

13 We have argued elsewhere that the production of 'Muslim homophobia' as a new social problem partly occurred in metonymy with much older knowledges of 'Muslim sexism' (Haritaworn, Tauqir and Erdem 2008).

14 I am drawing on Sara Ahmed's (2004) ideas on the cultural politics of emotions.

men' (e.g. *tageszeitung* ibid., *Jungle World* ibid.), or as members of the 'Grey Wolves', the right-wing pan-Turkish youth group which is frequently described as fascist (*Drag Festival* 2008, *Indymedia* 2008, *Jungle World* ibid.). Which descriptor authors foregrounded seemed mostly a function of their own political orientation. While the Drag Festival organizers themselves, as radical queers who overlapped with the autonomous Left, laboured hard to be seen to avoid racist ascriptions, the evocation of the figure of the Grey Wolf did not stop an army of journalists, activists and politicians from disseminating the Drag Festival's press release as the latest proof of 'homophobia among Turks' (*Jungle World* 2008: 1).[15]

How did the sign 'Turkish' come to stick, in Sara Ahmed's (2004) terms, to the bodies of the 'attackers'? Neither their ethnicity nor their politics seemed clear in the accounts of the 'victims' themselves, who did not all position the events in the same way. The following quotes are from an email exchange with one of the people who got beaten up. According to this person, some of the attackers were conspicuously 'blonde'. While there is of course no obvious relation between hair colour and ethnicity, his choice to describe the attackers thus is nevertheless significant given the privileging of hair colour in German practices of phenotyping (with 'blonde' being an implicitly 'white' marker). Even the Grey Wolf membership of the attackers was in this narrative largely based on the account of one of the queers involved in the incident. As my interlocutor put it, the person had provoked the attackers in 'a "game" to see who is more macho, but this game got lots of us beaten up'. To cover up their responsibility in escalating the violence, the person then claimed to have seen a Grey Wolves sticker on the car of the attackers, and thereby began a 'conspiracy theory' which quickly became the source of new knowledges of 'Kreuzberg' and 'migrant homophobia'.

Even though the 'Turkishness' of the perpetrators was thus contested, it soon became common knowledge. Affect sticks to certain bodies, is read as residing within them, and emanating from them: fear, or fearsomeness, is already in the bodies of 'Turkish' men, so that the mere mention of gender violence alongside Turkishness (the location of a club, a faint imagining of a sticker) is enough to 'recognize' the perpetrators as Turkish (Ahmed 2004). As Ahmed explains in her earlier work, the thing about the stranger is that he is not strange at all; 'we' already know him, which is why 'we' easily *re*-cognize him (Ahmed 2000). We may add that it is through debates such as this that people of migrant parentage are reproduced as strange.

The narrative of Otherness forged in the debate, while culminating in appeals to the protectionist state, was not a mainstream one. On the contrary, it was born largely in the kind of spaces which identify themselves as pro/minoritarian: left-wing newspapers and online spaces, as well as gay, queer, drag and feminist e-lists. It marked a shift in the local and national politics of representation, which for maybe the first time included positions marked as intersectional. In some instances, as in the Simon Study, this occurred within a single-issue frame of representation,

---

15   The sign 'fascism' does more work in the German post-Holocaust context than I have space here to examine.

where sexuality and ethnicity appeared as conflictual and competitive subject positions. In others, multiply minoritized and oppositional voices were consciously sought out and incorporated, in ways which nevertheless served to strengthen and authenticate the hegemonic discourse on 'migrant homophobia'.

The special issue by the left-wing weekly newspaper *Jungle World*, entitled 'Homophobia among Turks and other Germans', illustrates this well. One year after the Simon Study, the *Jungle World* authors could take for granted the existence of 'Turkish homophobia' as an object which can be known, defined, described and acted upon. The Turkishness of homophobia is authenticated in the subtitle: 'Bissu schwül oder was?' – You gay or what?, which is misspelt, with additional *Umlaute* on the 'schwul' (*gay*), in a mockery of Turkish-German slang.[16] Not only can homophobes be known at first sight – they are, of course, Turkish, it's in their culture, they cannot even say 'gay', lack a vocabulary for homosexuality. In contrast, 'we' know 'them' intimately. We speak their language, while they can only ever mimic ours.

Such cultural imperialism threads itself through the whole issue. The five articles repeat and build on an Orientalist archive of gender and sexuality which should by now be familiar. The main article 'Homophobic Turkish youth and the fear of racism allegations' (Bozic 2008) quotes the Simon Study as a) stating that homophobic attitudes among migrant youth are 'significantly more wide-spread', and b) citing 'religiosity' and the 'acceptance of traditional norms of masculinity' as causes of homophobia. Further sources of expert knowledges include the LSVD, as well as other gay organizations which have been central to crafting the 'migrant homophobia' discourse for years (see Haritaworn and Petzen forthcoming).

The issue further contains an interview with Bali Saygili, the migrant worker at the LSVD ('It does not stop with verbal violence', Akrap 2008). As the only gay and Turkish-identified author, his contribution illustrates the particular pressures on queers who are marked as 'Muslims' (whether they want to or not) to mimetically repeat hegemonic knowledges of their communities (Puar 2007, Chow 2002). Minoritized people are given a voice as long as they are willing to serve as mouthpieces for dominant agendas. In a 'progressive' forum such as *Jungle World*, they are allowed to express what 'politically correct' left-wing people do not want to say themselves. Thus, Kumrovec's short article on the same page calls 'demands to deny naturalization of homophobes or deport honour killers' 'counter-productive'.[17] Saygili, on the other hand, does not shy away from this:

---

16 There is an additional play on *schwul/schwül* (English: gay/humid) at the bottom of the cover: 'It's becoming *schwül* (unpleasantly hot). The European Championship is almost over. On Saturday there will be Pride and the Transgenial (Alternative) Christopher Street Day, which is also protesting against sexist attacks in Kreuzberg. How homophobic are Turkish youth? What is being criticized? What is silenced?'

17 The new Orient competes with the old one in this representation: While the former is essentially homophobic and sexually repressed, the latter is essentially homoerotic and

I have become quite extreme and hold the view that those who do not wish
to accept the democratic rules in this country shouldn't be naturalized either
(Akrap 2008: 5).

The second Turkish-authored contribution is by the academic Ahmet Toprak
('The Masculinity of Turkish Youth', p. 4), whose book *The Weak Gender:
Turkish Men* (my translation) joined in the recent success of other pedagogues of
Turkish origin to enter into mainstream publicity (especially Kelek 2005). The
concentration of migration studies in pedagogy and anthropology in Germany
reflects a racialized division of academic labour which reserves sociological
debate to those working on so-called 'modern' societies (Randeria 1999). This
disciplinary bias partly explains the hegemony of a culturalist rather than anti-
racist model in Germany, which constructs post/migrants as essentially different
and deficient. Homophobia easily enters this list of deficiencies. Thus, Toprak
identifies a higher incidence of both homophobia and 'increased criminality
and anti-social behaviour' in migrant youth. Sexuality is thus metonymically
added onto an existing archive of educationalist problems, which have a clearly
defined cause (Turkish culture) and clearly defined solutions ('sexual and ethics
lessons') and areas of expertise ('social workers, teachers and others who have
experiences working with gay men (sic) and young people', ibid.).

Toprak follows the lead of the Simon Study and the LSVD by explaining
homophobia through problematic gender and cultural identities: it is again the
result of 'traditional masculinity', 'failed social mobility', and 'rural-patriarchal'
upbringings by immigrant parents who fail to 'prepare their children for the
globalized industrial society' (ibid.). I am struck by the spatial metaphors and
ideas in this description. Migrants, particularly working-class migrants, appear
as fixed and motionless. They do not change, do not assimilate, do not move
up. They stay down. When they do move – as in migration – this movement is
pathological: it is turned backwards, locked and frozen by bad experiences in the
recipient culture, melancholically attached to the rural culture (which is itself
backward). Toprak's migrants are like Sara Ahmed's (forthcoming) 'melancholic
migrants', who become affect aliens to a 'happy multiculturalism' which likes
diversity but only if it moves on, and moves up. Toprak's migrants, in contrast,

---

excessively sexual (see Puar and Rai 2002, Massad 2007). The *Jungle World* issue is
ostensibly about the former, yet the latter remains an important source of (homoerotic and
homophobic) Orientalist fantasy. Toprak's article (discussed below) is accompanied by
a photo of two naked, glistening torsos whose hands are intimately entwined. The photo
carries the title: 'Grease reduces friction, but it is unsuitable for lubrication: Oil wrestlers in
the Balkans'. While queerly abjected, the Oriental can never be properly gay. For another
example of this discursive competition in gay knowledges of the Orient, see the lead article
in the Berlin gay magazine Siegessäule in November 2003 (with the contentious title *Türken
raus: Vom Coming Out in 2 Kulturen/Turks Out: Coming Out in 2 Cultures*).

are neither hybrid nor cosmopolitan. They combine not the best, but the worst of both worlds: the 'rural-patriarchal' with the problems of the inner city.

The theme of mobility frames the whole *Jungle World* issue. On the cover image,[18] in front of a cartoon urban silhouette, 'queers' are beating up 'Turks', two opposing groups whose stark contrasts are marked through their colouring and shape. While the 'queers' are wearing colourful clothes – three wear little dresses, one wears leather – the 'Turks' are grey, monochrome, and covered. Several of them are labelled as *Graue Wölfe* ('Grey Wolves', again misspelt with additional *Umlaute* on 'grey'). The 'queer' diversity of features and hairstyles – long, blond, curly, red, shaved – contrasts with the 'Turkish' uniformity of styles and expressions – moustache, short hair, monotonous face. The 'queers' are painted in lively, moving swings and strokes – they kick, punch, bite, threaten their adversaries with red, green, purple, shiny sex toys. The 'Turks', on the other hand, are in straight lines – they are square and rigid, leaning *back*wards – or immobile, fixed – standing still. They look primitive, and this ascription appears to be racial: the big noses, bent bodies, long arms, which hang at the height of the genitals, seem suggestive of a right-wing iconography, rather than a left-wing newspaper.

The two groups move in different directions: while the 'queers' are moving towards the 'Turks' (albeit with force), the latter move backwards. Their homo/transphobia appears to be at the same time a refusal, in Sara Ahmed's (2006) terms, to orient themselves towards the 'right' objects. The passivity of the Oriental, who can only be shaken up by force, has of course a long genealogy, from Karl Marx's (1968) writings on India and China, to Raphael Patai's *Arab Mind* (1976), whose anthropological 'findings', we were told, informed the sexual abuse of Iraqi men in the military prison in Abu Ghraib (see Puar 2005).

In fact, the image covering the *Jungle World* uncannily reminds me of Abu Ghraib, the prison torture scandal which was allegedly inspired by Patai's 'findings'. Jasbir Puar (2005) has, of course, helped us understand Abu Ghraib as a spectacular performance of Orientalism, rather than a mere instance of cultural offensiveness. Abu Ghraib created knowledges of Orientalized sexuality, knowledges which the debate on 'migrant homophobia' implicitly cites and repeats: the idea that Muslim men have a particular, 'traditional' masculinity, that they are especially homophobic, but also eternally sodomized (there is a trace of the old Orient in here, the one that is homoerotic rather than homophobic, see Massad 2007).[19] At the same time, this racializing performance rests on a certain knowledge of 'queer' sex. Anal sex is at once a tool of liberation and indistinguishable from rape (Puar 2007). On the *Jungle World* cover, this double signification is extended to other

---

18   http://jungle-world.com/images/000/000/703/2008-26-cover-a.gif (last accessed 14/02/2009).

19   Puar and Rai (2002) argue that this repressed Orient differs from the one described by Said, which was in need of repression. While differing in its agents ('Europe' v. 'the West') and its intervention (sexual liberation v. sexual control), the civilizatory mission nevertheless remains the same.

queer and transgendered practices and identities: the use of vibrators, BDSM, leather, and drag.

This euphemizing of sexual violence (as freeing rather than violating) is of course enabled by the medium of the cartoon, which characteristically lives off humour and exaggeration. The cartoon allows the event to be staged as a battle which brings the 'war on terror' home. While the winners are clearly the queers, the imagery is nevertheless unflattering: the drag queens especially catch our eye with their big build, their bad style, their furry bodies and faces. The drag spectacle highlights the contradictions of the LGBT participation in racism and war. It has little of the normalcy and attractiveness of the gay kiss. It is, on the contrary, a freak show, a freak show, which amuses, draws us in voyeuristically, but repels us at the same time. The war is here waged sexually: its weapons are anal plugs which are still fuming, a rubber baton which is forced into a bottom, high heels which aim between the legs. The most effective weapon (judging from the atypically emotional face of the 'Turkish victim') is the cock of a drag queen or MTF, which is equipped with a big piercing. This transphobic representation – which characteristically aims at the disgust evoked by modified genitals in non-trans people – nevertheless blends seamlessly with the claim of 'German' progressiveness and 'Turkish' regressiveness.

Who is served by this kind of spectacle? We should note that white gay, lesbian, trans and drag knowledges are not on the same level in this discussion. While the victims of the attacks were female-assigned (albeit partly trans-identified), the central characters on the cover image appear male-assigned. Further, in the lead article, 'transphobia' is mentioned only once, but 'homophobia' or *Schwulenfeindlichkeit* (hostility towards gay men) 22 times. The central agents in the lead article are non-trans gay men, the same activists who have invested in the 'migrant homophobia' discourse for years and are likely to reap its benefits in the form of any policy changes.

Nevertheless, transphobia made it into both the action plan against homophobia by the Green Party and the counter-motion by the leading 'red-red' coalition between the Social Democrats and The Left which was passed by the local parliament and, at the time of writing, is being translated into increased funding for both gay and transgender projects. The genderqueer participants in the Drag Festival discussion, while misrepresented and marginalized, nevertheless managed to perform membership, ownership even, over a Kreuzberg figured as the home of colourful counter-cultures. The 'war on terror' and its attendant territorial contestations in the gentrifying post/migrant neighbourhood thus constitute a productive space for multiple assimilatory moves which each give rise to their own kind of exceptionalism: The unambivalent assimilationism of the new sexual citizen, who enters into sovereignty by assuming himself an assimilatory position towards ethnic/religious Others. The first-time entry into publicity by queer and transgendered people, who at once critique gay assimilation and mimic it. And the unassimilability of the post/migrant subject, whose may move only in order to exit the migrant community, and speak only in order to authenticate its irrecuperable pathology.

Conclusion: The Gay-Friendly Nation and its Affect Aliens

I have argued in this chapter that we are witnessing new forms of disciplining in which sexual rights activists and sexualities studies academics, once considered marginal to their epistemic and intimate publics, are closely collaborating. In these new imaginings of community, older ideas of diversity which centred around ethnicity are displaced. Migrants, especially straight people of Turkish origin, appear both stuck and out of place. Backward, melancholic, they orient themselves to the wrong objects. They refuse to move on, by moving towards whiteness/queerness (which become one and the same in this exceptionalist logic). When they do so, it is always in a threatening manner. Straight migrants become, in Ahmed's (forthcoming) terms, 'affect aliens' in Kreuzberg.

This relies on the mobilizing of a highly essentialist notion of affect, as residing in particular bodies: Simon's 'Turkish migrants' who are disgusted by homosexuals and therefore compelled to attack. By locating homophobic affect firmly elsewhere, in the body of 'Turkish migrants', new publics are imagined which are able to fantasize themselves as queer-friendly. By sticking 'violence' to 'their' bodies, 'we' are not only able to negate our homophobia. 'We' are able to re-imagine ourselves as benevolent witnesses and protectors to queer lovers and queer bodies. Because 'they' attack, 'we' defend. 'Homophobic Islam' thus becomes the constitutive outside of a nation, a Europe and, arguably also, a West which imagines itself as intrinsically friendly towards gays, queers and transpeople even – in the face of deep remaining ambivalences, not only towards ethnic minorities, but also towards the very sexually and gender non-conforming subjects who the discourse on 'migrant homophobia' purports to enfranchise.

Bibliography

Agamben, G. 2005. *State of Exception*. Chicago: University of Chicago Press.
Ahmed, S. 2000. *Strange Encounters: Embodied Others in Post Coloniality*. London: Routledge.
Ahmed, S. 2004. *The Cultural Politics of Emotions*. Edinburgh: Edinburgh University Press.
Ahmed, S. 2006. *Queer Phenomenology*. Durham: Duke University Press.
Ahmed, S. (forthcoming). *The Promise of Happiness*. Durham: Duke University Press.
Akrap, D. 2008. Es bleibt nicht nur bei verbaler Gewalt: Bali Saygili im Gespräch über Homophobie in Deutschland, queere Muslime und türkischen Nationalismus. *Jungle World*, 26 June, 5.
Beck, U. and Beck-Gernsheim, E. 1995. *Das ganz normale Chaos der Liebe*. Frankfurt am Main: Suhrkamp.
Berlant, L. 1997. *The Queen of Washington Goes to America*. Durham: Duke University Press.

Binnie, J. et al. 2006. Introduction: Grounding Cosmopolitan Urbanism. Approaches, Practices and Policies, in *Cosmopolitan Urbanism*, edited by J. Binnie et al. London and New York: Routledge, 1-34.

Bozic, I. 2008. Das große Schweigen: Homophobe türkische Jugendliche und die Angst vor Rassismusvorwürfen. *Jungle World*, 26 June, 3.

Bündnis 90/Die Grünen 2008. *Berliner Aktionsplan gegen die Homophobie.* Abgeordnetenhaus Berlin, Drucksache 16/1966, 1/12/2008, 16. Wahlperiode.

Butler, J. 2008. Sexual Politics, Torture, and Secular Time. *British Journal of Sociology*, 59(1), 1-23.

Chow, R. 2002. *The Protestant Ethnic and the Spirit of Capitalism.* New York: Columbia Press.

Cvetkovich, A. 2003. Aids Activism and the Oral History Archive. *Public Sentiments* [Online]. Available at: http://www.barnard.columbia.edu/sfonline/ps/cvetkovi.htm [accessed: 20 December 2008].

Drag Festival 2008. Homophober Überfall nach Drag-Festival. *Press Release*, 8 June.

Duggan, L. 2003. *The Twilight of Equality? Neoliberalism, Cultural Politics, and the Attack on Democracy.* Boston: Beacon Press.

Eicker, P. 2007. Küssen verboten? *Hinnerk*, 4 July, 16.

El-Tayeb, F. 2003. Begrenzte Horizonte. Queer Identity in der Festung Europa, in *Spricht die Subalterne deutsch? Migration und postkoloniale Kritik*, edited by H. Steyerl and E. Gutiérrez Rodríguez. Münster: Unrast, 129-45.

Fekete, L. 2006. Enlightened Fundamentalism? Immigration, Feminism and the Right. *Race and Class*, 48, 1-22.

Foucault, M. 1976. Society Must Be Defended, in *Lectures at the Collège de France, 1975-76* (transl. D. Macy), edited by M. Bertani and A. Fontana. London: Allen Lane (Penguin), 239-64.

Giddens, A. 1992. *The Transformation of Intimacy: Sexuality, Love and Eroticism in Modern Societies.* Cambridge: Polity.

Gordon, A. 1997. *Ghostly Matters: Haunting and the Sociological Imagination.* Minneapolis: University of Minnesota Press.

Grassmann, P. 2007. Migrantenkinder gegen Schwule: Homophobes Berlin. *Süddeutsche Zeitung*, 26 September, [Online]. Available at: http://www.sueddeutsche.de/panorama/artikel/965/134708/ [accessed: 20 August 2008].

Hall, S. et al. 1978. *Policing the Crisis: Mugging, The State and Law and Order.* London: Macmillan.

Haritaworn, J. 2008. Loyal Repetitions of the Nation: Gay Assimilation and the 'War on Terror'. *DarkMatter*, 3, Special Issue on Postcolonial Sexuality [Online]. Available at: http://www.darkmatter101.org. [accessed: 1 December 2008].

Haritaworn, J., Tauqir, T. and Erdem, E. 2008. Queer Imperialism: The Role of Gender and Sexuality Discourses in the 'War on Terror', in *Out of Place: Silences in Queerness/Raciality*, edited by E. Miyake and A. Kuntsman. York: Raw Nerve Books, 9-33.

Haritaworn, J. and Petzen, J. (forthcoming). Intersecting Assimilations: Tracing the German 'Muslim Homophobia' Discourse, in *Islam in its International Context: Comparative Perspectives*, edited by C. Flood and S. Hutchings. Cambridge: Cambridge Scholars Press.

Indymedia 2008. Homophober Angriff in Kreuzberg. *Indymedia*, 8 June, [Online]. Available at: http://de.indymedia.org/2008/06/219458.shtml [accessed: 20 August 2008].

Kelek, N. 2005. *Die fremde Braut. Ein Bericht aus dem Inneren des türkischen Lebens in Deutschland.* Cologne: Kiepenheuer & Witsch.

Klauda, G. 2007. Homophober Orient, toleranter Westen? *Inamo*, 52(13), 4-9.

Klesse, C. 2007. 'How to be a Happy Homosexual?!' Non-Monogamy and Governmentality in Relationship Manuals for Gay Men in the 1980s and 1990s. *Sociological Review*, 55(3), 571-91.

Kuntsman, A. 2009. *Figurations of Violence and Belonging Queerness, Migranthood and Nationalism in Cyberspace and Beyond.* Oxford: Peter Lang.

Lesben- und Schwulenverband in Deutschland (n.d.). Available at: http://www.community-gaymes.de/ [accessed: 1 March 2009].

LSVD (n.d.a), *Grundzüge der LSVD Arbeit, Lesben- und Schwulenverband Berlin-Brandenburg.* Available at: http://www.berlin.lsvd.de/cms/index.php?option=com_content&task=view&id=44&Itemid=108 [accessed: 10 August 2009].

LSVD LSVD (n.d.b). Available at: http://www.community-gaymes.de/ [accessed: 1 March 2009].

Maneo (ed.) 2007. *Gewalterfahrungen von schwulen und bisexuellen Jugendlichen und Männern in Deutschland.* Berlin: Maneo [Online]. Available at: http://www.maneo-toleranzkampagne.de/umfrage-bericht1.pdf [accessed: 1 April 2009].

Marx, K. 1968. *On Colonialism and Modernization* (ed. by S. Avineri). New York: Doubleday.

Massad, J. 2007. *Desiring Arabs*. Chicago: Chicago University Press.

Mbembe, A. 2003. Necropolitics. *Public Culture*, 15(1), 11-40.

OECD 2008. Employment Outlook – Edition 2008, *OECD Publishing* [Online]. Available at: http://www.oecd.org/dataoecd/33/54/40912588.pdf [accessed: 1 December 2008].

Patai, R. 1976. *The Arab Mind*. New York: Scribner.

Peter, C. and Schimkus, V. 2008. Moslems gegen Schwule. *Hamburger Morgenpost,* 21 April, 10-11. Available at: http://archiv.mopo.de/archiv/2007/20070421/hamburg/panorama/moslems_gegen_schwule.html [accessed: 20 August 2008].

Petzen, J. 2008. *Gender Politics in the New Europe: 'Civilizing' Muslim Sexualities*, unpublished PhD thesis. Seattle: University of Washington.

Puar, J. and Rai, A. 2002. Monster, Terrorist, Fag: The War on Terrorism and the Production of Docile Patriots. *Social Text*, 20(3), 117-48.

Puar, J. 2007. *Terrorist Assemblages: Homonationalism in Queer Times*. Durham: Duke University Press.

Randeria, S. 1999. Jenseits von Soziologie und soziokultureller Anthropologie. Zur Ortsbestimmung der nichtwestlichen Welt in einer zukünftigen Sozialtheorie. *Soziale Welt*, 50(4), 373-82.

Seidman, S. 1996. Introduction, in *Queer Theory/Sociology*, edited by S. Seidman. London: Blackwell, 1-29.

Simon, B. 2008. Einstellungen zur Homosexualität: Ausprägungen und psychologische Korrelate bei Jugendlichen mit und ohne Migrationshintergrund (ehemalige UdSSR und Türkei). *Zeitschrift für Entwicklungspsychologie und Pädagogische Psychologie*, 40, 87-99.

Spivak, G.C. 1999. *A Critique of Postcolonial Reason: Toward a History of the Vanishing Present*. Cambridge, MA: Harvard University Press, 284-311.

Sudbury, J. 2006. Rethinking Antiviolence Strategies: Lessons from the Black Women's Movement in Britain, in *The Color of Violence*, edited by Incite! Cambridge, MA: Southend Press, 13-24.

Theory, Culture and Society 1998. 15(3/4), Special Issue on *Love and Eroticism*.

Toprak, A. 2005. *Das schwache Geschlecht- die türkischen Männer. Zwangsheirat, häusliche Gewalt, Doppelmoral der Ehre*, Freiburg: Lambertus.

Toprak, A. 2008. Das Männlichkeitsbild türkischer Jugendlicher. *Jungle World*, 26 June, 4.

Weeks, J., Heaphy, B. and Donovan, C. 2001. *Same-Sex Intimacies: Families of Choice and Other Everyday Experiments*. London: Routledge.

Chapter 9

The Perpetual Redrawing of Cultural Boundaries: Central Europe in the Light of Today's Realities

Immanuel Wallerstein

In 1990, I was invited to participate in a small Franco-Polish colloquium in Warsaw that was devoted to the theme, "Central Europe: Reality, Myth, and the Stakes, 18th to 20th Centuries." The conference was being held just after the collapse of Communism in what had been the satellite states of the Soviet Union. It was a moment of much uncertainty about where things were heading and should be heading in this region. It led to considerable debate about how these areas should conceive of themselves culturally, and hence politically. Because of Poland's post-1945 history and because especially of the political and cultural impact of *Solidarnosc* throughout the region, the debate was in many ways most acute there.

I thought that the title of the colloquium was just right – reality, myth, and the stakes of cultural boundaries. My analysis was however at odds with what I saw to be the sense of most participants in the colloquium and most citizens in the region. The views of the majority were infused, I felt, with a combination of accumulated angers and wishful thinking which failed to take into account the real geopolitical constraints. However justified the angers and however glowing the utopian optimism, angers and wishful thinking do not necessarily lead to optimizing one's options. Looking back on my arguments almost 20 years later, and despite the great changes in the world-system since then, I still feel that my basic arguments about cultural identification were sound. So, what follows is a faithful translation of a paper that I wrote in French and published at the time.

***

If there exists something that may be called Central Europe, that means that there should exist a Western Europe (and also an Eastern Europe). Whether we give to Central Europe a largely Slavocentric or a largely Germanocentric definition, that still leaves quite a few European countries or peoples to its west. Take for example two countries that one seldom includes in Central Europe, Sweden and Portugal. Are these two both an integral part of Western Europe? These days, it is common to say so. You will allow me to be skeptical that these two countries are closer to each other than they are to Poland.

Geographically, Sweden and Poland are neighbors that have shared daily interactions for a very long time. Sweden and Poland have been at war with each other, and war is a very intimate relationship. Looked at from the point of view of their role in the world economy in the twentieth century, Poland and Portugal have somewhat similar structures in that there still exists in each a large peasant population. Furthermore, they are both Catholic countries. On the other hand, neither Sweden nor Poland has ever been an imperial power in what we call today the Third World, whereas Portugal was the last European power to undergo decolonization in the late twentieth century.

I could continue listing traits which fit two of the countries but not the third. It's hardly worth it. What is clear is that there is no obvious reason to put Sweden and Portugal in one cultural box and Poland in another. And if instead of Sweden I choose the case of the Netherlands, it wouldn't change much in this analysis. It is always quite possible to justify whatever classifications you offer, but they are never self-evident. So the question is on what bases, and when, and why we might be interested in (re)creating the concept of Central Europe, giving it a certain precise definition.

Which Central Europe are we talking of in 1990? Bronislaw Geremek recently made the observation that "the process of post-Communist democratization has led to an obvious convergence of interests between Poland, Czechoslovakia, and Hungary" (Geremek 1990, 2). That particular trinity is to be found in an increasing number of politico-intellectual discussions. But on what basis do we choose these three? Does the convergence of interests stop there? Why not include in the same group Romania, or Yugoslavia, or Lithuania? Some might say that they are ready to include them, but others might give me a list of clear reasons to exclude them. I am not trying to resolve this difference of views. I merely wish to assert that the decision is a function of present-day conditions, even very immediate ones, and has little to do with a common cultural tradition.

From the standpoint of cultural heritage, these three countries have relatively little in common. The languages are different. The religious situation is rather different, and to the degree they are similar, the similarities stretch beyond the three. These three countries were never part of the same political structure, unless one counts the Soviet pseudo-empire (and then once again this "empire" included others). Even in terms of their cultural relations with France or Germany, each has a different story. So why then this trinity?

I'll give one more example. If one insists on the label of Central European, it is done in order to reject the label of the past 40 years, East European. One can well understand that. The peoples of what is called Central Europe, *Mitteleuropa*, have wanted for 200 years to rid themselves of any identification with Russian "barbary". But will the world let them do it? Look at this discussion of another era. In 1925, Harold Temperley, an old-school British diplomatic historian wrote about the protocol of Troppau, which had been signed on 8 December 1820 by Austria, Prussia, and Russia, at a meeting at which both Great Britain and France took refuge in the category of observers. The three signatories proclaimed the doctrine that they would refuse to recognize any insurrectional government. They were referring to events then taking place in Spain, Naples, and Portugal. How does Temperley resume what was decided? He wrote, I remind you in 1925, that:

> The doctrine thus proclaimed was that revolution or insurrection, even if purely
> an affair of internal change, could never be recognized by the three military
> despots of East Europe (Temperley 1925: 23).

There's nothing you can do about it! Temperley lumped together Austria, Prussia, and Russia in the same camp. You may say that he was talking of 1820. I would say in turn, precisely. Long-term cultural realities have changed little since then, but today's geopolitical realities are simply not the same as in 1820.

My basic argument is thus quite simple. Historical cultural heritages, and especially the boundary lines of inclusion and exclusion, are at one and the same time deeply rooted – they constantly re-emerge when we thought them long dead – and incredibly ephemeral – they disappear rapidly under new circumstances or because of *force majeure*. It is as futile to rely on them as it is to ignore them completely.

It is more useful to try to figure out what cultural frontiers people want to recreate today, and to what ends? I pose three questions: a) Why not assume the simple label of European? b) Why not include the Balkans in Central European? c) Why want to call yourself European at all?

Note that I have not raised the question whether a reunified Germany is or is not part of Central Europe. Not that I don't think this is not a very hot issue, but I am sure it will not be neglected, whereas my other three questions may be less discussed.

Just European

You might say to me that you are obviously Europeans. So then I ask, why add a restrictive adjective? And you might respond, because everyone does it. There are Western Europeans, Mediterranean Europeans, Nordic Europeans. And I would answer, it is not at all so obvious that everyone does it. Scandinavians sometimes call themselves Nordics, sometimes Europeans, but rarely, at least these days, Northern Europeans. And you might respond, just a nuance. And I in turn might say, not an unimportant nuance. On the other hand, you often hear Greeks saying they are from Southern Europe. You occasionally hear Iberians saying it. You rarely hear an Italian saying it, and you almost never hear someone from France saying it. And what would an average Swiss say? And what would an average person from England say? (Note I talk of England, not Great Britain.)

This is not a child's game. If you add a restrictive adjective, you imply either a claim or a hesitancy. You might be claiming an equality to be achieved, or some assistance from your elders, or a full inclusion not permitted up to now. Or perhaps conversely, you might be rejecting such complaints in advance by using the label Western European.

Hence, in my opinion, this first question, why not just call yourself a European, is a question that is simultaneously a moral issue and one of political strategy.

Non-Balkan Central European

If you decide that, in the end, it is realistic to use a restrictive adjective with European – either because you have a common recent political history that is distinctive, or because you have more difficult economic problems than some others, or because you do not consider it possible to claim the same political tradition that other Europeans have known – why do you then feel the need to distinguish the Polish-Czech-Hungarian trinity from the Balkan countries? Obviously, it is in order to attach some further nuances to the label. Yes, we all were part of the same Soviet bloc, but our social structures are somewhat different, our economic problems are not really the same, the political traditions of the Northeast are more "Western" than those of the Southeast, etc. This is a way of putting yourself in a sort of middle rank in a European hierarchy, and to insist on the specific political claims that ensue from this middle rank. Furthermore, this claim has some plausibility. In any case, once again, it is simultaneously a moral issue and one of political strategy.

Why European at all?

You may be incredulous at this query. At a moment when the EEC is approaching its turning-point of 1992, and the Pope insists on the concept of Europeanity, and Gorbachev speaks of the "common house" of Europe, how can I raise such a question in relation to Poland, Czechoslovakia, and Hungary? It is obvious that these peoples wish to reclaim the past 50 years that seem to them lost. That is, they wish to climb back on the train, the European train, especially at a moment when it seems to them one that is rolling swiftly towards a healthier, richer future. Europe is constructing itself with difficulty, but beautifully. Why would not these three countries insist on being part of it?

I'm sorry, but all I can do is to remind you of the geopolitical context. In this post-Communist world which is also a post-American one, it seems to me rather clear that we are moving towards a new bifurcation (bifurcation, not polarization) between two large politico-economic complexes – a Pacific pole (Japan-United State-China) and a European pole (that includes Russia). These two poles are both part of the global North, each one seeking to maximize its share of the cake in the next major expansion of the capitalist world-economy. The two poles are competing with each other, and each is taking advantage of its links to particular parts of the South.

To claim to be European is to claim to be part of the North, in the great North-South divide. The fact is that Poland, Czechoslovakia, and Hungary are at the very most semiperipheral countries in the division of labor of the capitalist world-economy. They have, from many points of view, more in common with Brazil or Malaysia (to take some faraway examples) than with Austria. Obviously we live in a world structure that is not fixed and Poland can try to improve its comparative position within it. One way to do that is to link itself more closely with Europe. Are there other ways? Once again, this is a question that is simultaneously a moral issue and one of political strategy.

There are no formulaic answers to my questions. I am not criticizing anyone in the current situation. You are in a transitional situation that is very difficult, in which the decisions you have to take, seemingly so simple in the beginning, will become ever more difficult. I simply wish to raise some questions that I consider important and which have seemed to me (perhaps because I am poorly informed on internal debates in the three countries) not to have been much discussed heretofore.

References

Geremek, B. 1990. Pour l'Europe. *Liber*, II, March, 2ff.
Temperley, H. 1925. *The Foreign Policy of Canning, 1822-1827.* London: G. Bell & Sons.

PART IV
Border-Thinking

Chapter 10

Integration as Colonial Pedagogy of Postcolonial Immigrants and People of Colour: A German Case Study

Kien Nghi Ha

Pedagogical practices, engaging with a civilizing project, were intrinsic to most European colonial ambitions of cultural and political expansion. Historically, the idea and practice of teaching the Other provided a widely accepted legitimation to build powerful educational and disciplinary institutions for that purpose. As classical education implies a binary hierarchy between teachers and subordinates, it is not an accident that one trait of cultural colonialization relied upon this pedagogic role model to spread Western power to determine the worth and validity of knowledge, ethics, culture and identity. Therefore, colonial education was significant in the attempt to fabricate an ideological and cultural consent between colonial authority and its colonized subjects. On the other hand, it contributed to reinforcing the cultural, economic and political hegemony of the colonial power. By promoting racist stereotypes and colonial objectives, pedagogy as a modern cultural control technique of the self in the Foucauldian sense, effectively helped to shape colonial societies within a world system, where Eurocentrism was regarded in a teleological sense as a necessary civilizing mission.[1]

The internalization of the values and imaginations of the colonial culture through education created a phenomenon that W.E.B. Du Bois called the double consciousness of the oppressed. He described this ambivalent state of knowledge and self-perception as a "sense of always looking at one's self through the eyes of others" (Du Bois 1903: 3). Du Bois is an interesting starting-point here as he was one of the first postcolonial social scientists who actually challenged Western sociology from an African American perspective. He had anti-colonial sensibilities and a sense for injustices that resulted from racism and forced labour. In his famous book *The Souls of Black Folk* his understanding of the denied integration of Black Americans in the racially segregated United States is informed by the history and politics of exclusion,

1   I would like to thank Dorothea Herlyn for her generous help to translate a draft version of this chapter into English. I am also indebted to Encarnación Gutiérrez Rodríguez for her critical and insightful comments. For a general analysis see Altbach/Kelly 1992 and for the German context Adick 1996.

exploitation and cultural misrepresentation.[2] Ironically, Du Bois, who had studied in Berlin in the early 1890s, was despite political and theoretical differences also a personal friend of the eminent German sociologist Max Weber. Du Bois' and Weber's stances on race, power, nation state and migration represent contradicting approaches to sociology and reflect also their different subject positions in a predominantly white society. As a liberal nationalist Weber was for most of his life a prominent supporter of Germany's colonial ventures to secure national power ambitions on the global scale and also heavily involved in racist discourses claiming multiple dangers resulting from the alleged cultural and racial inferiority of Polish immigrants.[3] I understand Weber's position as a symbol for the unacknowledged double consciousness of Western colonial culture resulting in a politics of double standards. As a still highly admired European social scientist his work represents the best part of the supposedly enlightened dominant Western culture, that is completely convinced by its own liberal self-image and its virtue to protect democracy and freedom while at the time actively institutionalizing discriminating practices against racialized immigrants.

Taking Weber as a prevalent cultural and political symbol of Western colonial double consciousness I like to address how elements of colonial fantasies and discourses re-emerged in political debates around "integration". These debates are coupled to a range of political measures, conveyed into pedagogy. I am not simply arguing that old colonial practices are exactly reproduced in the current integration policies, but that awareness and critique of ideological similarities and discursive analogies are crucial to understand this power structure. I suggest analysing the integration courses as institutions of power imposed on People of Colour. The pedagogy model supporting these institutions rely on colonial paradigms. The integration courses as well as colonial education promise to transplant the superior Western rational knowledge, its more valuable culture and ultimately the enlightenment of liberal freedom to People of Colour, who are subjected to this knowledge transfer process. The recent legal and administrative intensification of Germany's views on integration is caused for a critical discussion on the debate. In view of the rising integration industry, there is a pressing need to question the ideas and practices associated with the term "integration" from a postcolonial perspective. Yet in the face of the recurrent demand for integration, I want (a) to analyse their repressive effects in terms of economic appropriation, cultural stigmatization and legal discrimination; (b) to understand the new paradigm of repressive integration as a ideological discourse and political practice, which is embedded in Germany's internal colonial history of Germanization, Anti-Semitism and racist immigration policies; and (c) to recognize the relationship between Germano-phile integrative programmes, Euro-centric hierarchies and racist practices of colonial education as a relevant topic.

---

2   In some way, a radicalization of this concept was presented by the Black Panthers in the 1960s, when they analysed the racist structures within the US society as internal colonialization. See for a discussion of the history of this concept Gutiérrez 2004.

3   See for more details Naber 2007.

Before analysing the political effects and ideological contexts of the German integration policies I like to provide some background information on the course system.

Although I will focus on the current German integration courses in this chapter, it is important to notice that compulsory integration policies with repressive sanctions are also established in other European countries like France, Austria, Denmark and the Netherlands.[4]

Like the German integration course system most of these restrictive policies are selectively applied to postcolonial and Muslim immigrants usually from Third World countries. This trend is disturbing since the effects of guided cultural assimilation, political examination and legal discrimination are inscribed in forceful integration laws.[5] Therefore it is necessary to look at their ideological presuppositions, logic and effects in order to examine how coercive integration is linked to colonial discourses and Eurocentrist thought patterns

Coercive Cultural Integration

On 1 December 2004, the social-democratic green federal cabinet passed the "Regulation on Integration Courses for Foreigners". Put into effect at the same time as the new Immigration Act, on 1 January 2005, the Regulation on Integration Courses (IntV), as defined by § 44a of the new Residence Act, in its essence prescribes not so much the right, but the obligation to take part in a rigorously controlled language and orientation course. By the end of 2006 more than 250,000 new and already settled immigrants have participated in 16,850 integration courses. This huge education system with more than 1,800 local co-operation partners is certified and centrally controlled by the Federal Office for Migration and Refugees. With the implementation of the National Integration Plan (NIP) in 2008 the courses were increased to 945 hours. The Regulation on Integration Courses describes the aim of the integration courses as "the acquisition of adequate German language proficiency"; they are further aimed at "familiarizing participants with everyday knowledge, the legal system culture and history of Germany. In particular immigrants should learn more about the democratic state system, the principles of the rule of law, equal rights, tolerance, and freedom of religion" (§3 IntV).[6] Thus within the Federal Republic's official political view, supervised integration functions as a national-pedagogical instrument, designed

---

4   There are also test requirements on language ability as well as cultural and political knowledge in order to apply for citizenship in many countries including the United States, Canada, United Kingdom and Germany.

5   See Joppke 2007.

6   Federal Ministry of the Interior: Ordinance on Integration Courses and its basic contents. http://www.en.bmi.bund.de/nn_148248/Internet/Content/Themen/Integration/DatenUnd Fakten/Ordinance_on_Integration_Courses.html [accessed: 14 October 2009].

to teach immigrants German culture and value systems. After the successful completion of their exams, they obtain the "Zertifikat Deutsch" language diploma, designed by the Goethe-Institute, while their political views are scrutinized in the standard Federal Orientation Course test. The yearly national budget to support this integration industry is approximately 264 million Euros in addition to the fees of the participants, who should pay nearly 40 percent of the course costs.

First of all it is important to consider that the integration courses are only obligatory for migrants from non-Western countries.[7] Citizens of the European Union living in Germany are at liberty to choose if they would like to attend. While citizens of the EU are granted privileges within the social, economical and political landscape, all other immigrants have to prove themselves worthy of a residence permit by actively displaying their integrative abilities. They also do not have to fear any sanctions, should they fail to pass the tests of the integration courses successfully. EU-citizens are in a position to decide, if these courses meet their self-defined interests and needs. Non-compulsory courses depend on a situation of negotiation and freedom of choice, where immigrants have to be treated as potential clients and not as inmates or objects of the administration. Due to this law design the repressive forms of integration affect mainly People of Colour from the postcolonial states of Africa, Asia and Latin America, in fact especially Muslim communities with Turkish or Arabic backgrounds. As an effect the regulation of integration and the restrictions of immigration, which are both executed by the predominantly white German administration, are shaped not only by economic and political arguments, but also by cultural-religious and ethnicizing views.

Instead of offering optional courses the politics of integration requirements chooses a different approach: to legitimate the repressive character this politics needs to make the claim that enforcement is necessary to prevent or to control socio-cultural and political threats for Germany. In this case the compulsory integration is strongly based on the collective constructions of negative stereotypes of non-EU immigrants from the dominant perspective of white German lawmakers. The newly introduced integration law defines a set of cultural and political criteria for different immigrant groups and specifies the need to meet them, for example, to extend the resident permit. For the first time certain immigrant groups, especially those with a postcolonial non-EU and Muslim background, are now subjected to specific regulations of the Residence Act (the former Aliens Act). Therefore I suggest analysing the obligation to integrate as a national-pedagogical instrument of power over the cultural (re-)socialization and political re-education of immigrants with non-EU backgrounds. In my analysis I want to point to the central function of the integration courses as cultural and political correction centres on an

---

7 There are efforts to subcategorise Non-EU citizens by privileging immigrants from Western orientated countries. For example, in the regulations for the immigration of family members (§ 30 AufenthG) citizens of the USA, Canada, Australia, New Zealand, Israel, Japan and South Korea are excluded from the obligation to obtain German language certificates of the Goethe-Institute.

administrative level for the purpose of selecting between those, who are regarded as "integration-willing" (integrationswillig) and those are regarded as not able to integrate (nicht integrationsfähig) into German mainstream society.

The differential distribution of rights and obligations – such as is manifested in the Residence Act and the Employment Promotion Act – further expands and reinforces the EU-centric and racial-centric hierarchy amongst immigrants. Since the measures of re-education are aimed specifically at migrants with postcolonial backgrounds, it is important to consider colonial contexts, analogies and configurations when analysing the concept of the regulation of integration. Both People of Colour and postcolonial migrants are frequently in contact with formerly colonized geographical regions or peripheral spheres, and are confronted with a tradition of racist-colonial stereotypes and a history of Western Orientalism and Islamophobia. Therefore, integration as a mass-effective sovereign act of political control, cultural surveillance and legal certification raises a host of questions, examining both the politics of identity instrumentalized by the dominant German culture in its strategies of self assurance, and the post-/colonial power relations articulated by the selective policies of migration and integration. Such asymmetric structures need to be analysed as to their effects. This will enable us to look for possible connections between migration, integration and the nation state within the context of its historical development and post-/colonial embedding.

No Integration

The processes of postcolonial migration transcend global borders. By encountering the global power structures of the past with those in the present it reveals the transformation of the "overlapping territories, intertwined histories" (Said 1994: 3) of the colonial landscape into the actual political and cultural economy of Western immigration societies in the era of globalization. As a social phenomenon, they raise questions about the topicality of colonial presences within and outside of Western societies. Therefore the question remains how far integration based on force, poses as a form of appropriation, an annexation of resources of productivity and culture of the postcolonial Other.

Integration as prescribed cultural nationalization does not only contain dis-integrating and deprecatory assumptions, but also repressive effects. These need to be taken into account when analysing nationalization as a discriminatory practise, revealing both the application of pedagogic practices analogous to colonial education and the objectification of migrants as exploitable "human resource" of the national inventory.[8] The recent discourse on immigration has shown that

---

8 In an earlier draft of the integration law the term "stock of foreigners" (Bestandsausländer) was used (see Prantl 2004). This term signifies a mercantile perspective in the trading of the commodified "human workforce", thus turning migrants into objects of a national inventory.

a majority of Germans mainly value an efficient and uncomplicated use of the profitable migrant workforce. To advance the nation's chances within the global competition, it is deemed necessary to modernize Germany into an immigrant society. Therefore the "Independent Commission on immigration" suggests selecting young, highly qualified and efficient VIP-applicants for immigration by a system of points.[9] A policy like this revitalizes colonial structures, divisions of the workforce and such patterns of thinking, which view the existence of the Other mainly as a service to metropolitan interests and needs. Functioning both as a form of incorporation and subjugation, the integration courses complement the aims of employment policies and national economies inscribed in the new Immigration Act. This law is meant to separate the "good" migrants, that is those who are obedient and willing to learn, from the "bad" migrants, that is those who are "resistant to" or even "incapable of" integration. The machinery of integration therefore presents itself as a praxis of national sanctions, aimed at the regulation of the processes of incorporation and exclusion of migrants.

Even though the obligation of integration is ripe with racist ambivalence and contradictions, there is only a very limited public discourse. The forceful integration into the nation does not only question the proclaimed aims of integration, that is to say the realization of this society's republican constitution, but also blatantly negates the migrants' cultural and political right to self-determination. In contrast, migrant subjects are viewed as obliging objects of administration, surrendered to national institutions. For what is the actual meaning of the seemingly embracing term of "integration" that is currently in use? As a leading German researcher formulates it,

> in the political debate, it [i.e. the term integration] is taken to mean assimilation, which means the departure from one's own cultural and linguistic roots and a total adjustment to German society (Meier-Braun 2002: 25-26 [own translation]).

The integration courses prescribe that for those "in need of integration", the right to exist within Germany is dependent on their successful performance in the official examination of integrative capacities. The newly formed "Federal Office for Migration and Refugees" plays an important role in the organization, execution and surveillance of this administered integration, functioning as a co-ordinator and director, particularly on regional and local levels. Due to the phenomena of "subtle registration system" and a "bureaucracy gone out of hand", political commentators, such as Heribert Prantl, coined the term "Integration Monstrosity" (Prantl 2004). The integration regime now has the power to use far-reaching measures of punishment on those wilful migrants, who do not obediently conform to the German course of integration. Negative sanctions can not only be evoked by a refusal to take part in integration courses, but also by insufficient test results. The punishment can take form in different shapes, from a refusal of citizenship, to

---

9   Unabhängige Kommission "Zuwanderung" (2001).

a cut in social benefits (§ 44a paragraph 3 AufenthG) up to restrictions in the right of residence (§ 8 paragraph 3 AufenthaltG), culminating in an order of eviction. The need for integration is turned into a juridical category of criminal law.

Within the structure of an integration course, apparently suspicious migrants find themselves in a protracted condition of systematic examination and questioning. Since integration is based on accusation, and not on society's willingness to accept diversity and legal-political equality, these involuntary integrative courses can turn into temporary detentions lasting 945 hours. The integration course can be understood as the reaction of the white German state to manage the risk as migration is perceived as a source of danger, which is affecting both global and national politics. In a time ruled by so-called anti-terror measures, by permanent security warnings and diffuse fears – of shapeless "sleepers", for example – in a time when civil liberties and constitutional principles (such as the presumption of innocence) are successively dismantled, the impervious, and sometimes imposed foreignness on the ethnicized and orientalized Other is stigmatized by dragnet investigations and general suspicion. Therefore, certain cultural-religious differences undergo a political instrumentalization: as soon as the dominant Western discourse of the recent years regards these differences as "Islamic" or "fundamentalist", Muslims are defined as security risks and are handed over to an enlightening process of intelligence gathering.

The poignant controversies within the nation about problems and threats caused by non-Western refugees and migrant groups have, thus, gained in political relevance. Several explosive topics were discussed within the public political debate in recent years: The Immigration Act; the way the media turned the lawsuit to evict the Islamic preacher Metin Kaplan into a scandal; the so-called head-scarf debate; the condemnation of misogynist forced weddings and "honorary murders"; the Rütli-School in Berlin-Neukölln or the arguments concerning the long awaited Anti-Discrimination Act. To different degrees all these events were marked by one-sided accusations of Muslim immigrant communities, who were often portrayed in the German discussion stereotypically as patriarchal, cultural backward leaning and threatening. Just how emotionally and irrationally the German condemnation debate was carried out, can be observed in the reactions to the murder of the Dutch film-maker Theo van Gogh in November 2004. Even though this incident has no direct connection to immigrant affairs in Germany, it was used as a reason to finally settle the scores with a multicultural practise that was viewed as doomed to fail, because it was supposedly too tolerant. This was curiously accompanied by a loss of reality and incidences of amnesia. German multi-cultural society was repeatedly proclaimed to have failed, therefore keeping up the pretence that the country had been struggling for such a liberal model for decades. In fact, apart from local initiatives, the notion of multi-culturalism had never been a part of the federal canon in Germany, nor of the exclusionary policy on foreigners. Headlines during those weeks read "Holland is Everywhere" warns Social-Democrat Dieter Wiefelspütz. The "Zeit" analysed the "Tricks of Tolerance", the "Welt" was daily staging the "Farewell to Multi-Culturalism" or even from the "Multi-Culti Trauma"

(Rosenkranz 2004). Immigrants, this is the conclusion, are in need of clearly drawn borders by a "fortified democracy", which is now meant to self-confidently defend its values. This rhetoric appeals to a German feeling of a racialized "Us" while staging German society as a victim of religious fundamentalism and the threat of expanding immigrant "parallel societies".

German Leitkultur in Historical Perspective

The special obligation of Non-European immigrants to participate in the integration courses creates an unsolvable contradiction to the official promotion of integration as an important tool to achieve social equality and cultural dialogue between partners as these immigrants groups are discriminated in their constitutional protected personality rights (see discussion in Avenarius/Nuissl von Rein 2005). Concentrating participants with a devaluated socio-cultural background is particularly problematic, because this separation can used as a source to continue their stigmatization.[10] As long as the German educational system failed dramatically in providing equal opportunities a compelling explanation is needed to regard the integration courses not as part of the institutional problems, but of the solution: The sobering results of the international PISA-study and the poor exam results of pupils with a migrant background have showed that many immigrants and their offspring experience the selective mechanism of the German school system often as a structure of social exclusion (see Lebenslagen in Deutschland 2004).

One reason why the official political discourse is unavailable to offer progressive answers lies in the avoidance to ask the right questions. Social realities, such as structural racism, institutionalized discrimination and the socio-cultural exclusion of postcolonial migrants from the German society, seem to be of little importance within the official integration (dis)course.[11] Since the racial inscriptions of this society are made invisible, important aspects of a power-critical view on migration, racism and integration are omitted. Instead, hegemonic discourses define the migrant Other as deficient in analogy to the colonial Other. There is a striking contrast between the positive connotations of the practised integration and its repressive and colonizing effects.

On the contrary, there is a growing impression that the imperative of integration is in fact a policy of cultural assimilation and social conformity, which is interested in securing the cultural and political hegemony of the so-called German "Leitkultur" (guiding culture or core culture). The regime of migration politics in

---

10   Besides new immigrants from Non-European states also immigrants who receive unemployment benefits can be obliged to participate.

11   The official National Integration Plan, which has a length of 200 pages, mentioned the word "racism" just once when it cited the name of a soccer fan project (p. 145). The politically more accepted term "discrimination" and its derivations are first used on page 65.

Germany endeavours to re-vitalise the imaginary foundations of a national culture and its identity, which is seen as being endangered by internal contradictions. As a self-evident norm of cultural socialization and subject constitution, nationalization attempts to assert itself through the politics of hegemony and identity. The accompanying discourse tries to preserve those ever-present and yet unverifiable images of a national "Leitkultur" as the norm for a society subjected to continuous structural changes in the course of global migration processes. In reaction to a seemingly inevitable modernization of German immigration laws that acknowledged the need for high-skilled immigrants to sustain economic growth, the demand for a "deutsche Leitkultur" became a hot debated political issue.[12] This ideological discourse seeks to strengthen national identity and German culture as fundamental and exclusive political values for the whole society. By actively constructing its own subject the call for the undefined "deutsche Leitkultur" not only takes the allegedly superior German core culture and the homogenous national identity for granted, at the same time it also excludes and marginalizes those immigrants and their socio-cultural affiliations who are not accepted as fellow citizens of the nationalized and culturally racialized society.

Like Samuel Huntington's "clash of civilizations" this discourse is based on one of the most sacred principles of European modernity: the idea of culture as almost static, separated and conflicting entities, which are hierarchically organized on the cultural level as racialized "civilizations" and on the political one as distinct nations. Both notions are present in the longing for "deutsche Leitkultur" as German culture and Germanness is understood to be rooted in the heart of Europe and its white European civilization. Within this discourse the notion of culture and cultural identity is fundamentally essentialized as national symbols. It has replaced the ideological function of race as biological marker for the hegemonic white Self and the devaluated Other (see for an extended analysis Pautz 2005), while still effectively racializing Germans as well as non-European and Muslim immigrants by a rigid cultural divide. Within this perspective the exclusion from society and the national body can only be solved by the failed immigrants: they are expected to abandon their problematic original cultural background and social deficits through assimilation into the dominant white European culture with its superior rational values.

In my view, the political will to create the "deutsche Leitkultur" should be analysed as a strategic reaction to the long-standing popular myth of uncontrollable

---

12   The Leitkultur debate was provoked by Friedrich Merz, then the chairman of the CDU parliamentary group in the Bundestag. In an article for the populistic "Bild am Sonntag" he demanded: "It is compulsory, that foreigners have to learn German and accept our customs and habits" (Spiegel Online 2000, own translation). First the term "deutsche Leitkultur" was heavy disputed, but in 2004 and 2007 conservative forces were more successful to establish this idea by intermingling this debate with questions of patriotism and basic political values. Both German conservatives parties have now implemented the call for "deutsche Leitkultur" in their declarations of political principles.

"Überfremdung" (domination by foreigners)[13] as consequence of non-temporary immigrant settlements and the widespread condemnation of multiculturalism by many white Germans. In this context the lamentation of the failed integration is not much more than a pretext to advocate tight control measures on immigration and, in effect, also to mobilize right-wing voters and neo-racist discourses by echoing dominant assumptions of the cultural and political inferiority of immigrants, especially those with Muslim and non-European backgrounds.

Interestingly, the ideological logic behind the notion of "deutsche Leitkultur" is linked to a political history and cultural tradition of anti-Semitic, racist and colonial discourses, which emerged in the era of Imperial Germany. One important discursive string is related to the term "Überfremdung".[14] In modern German cultural history "Überfremdung" was used in different contexts. It was probably first used to defend the predominance and purity of German language, later on as moral panic[15] to discredit German Jewry in the nineteenth century. Heinrich von Treitschke, a still famous German historian and at that time also an influential member of parliament (Reichstag) for the national-liberal party, claimed that there will be always Jewish Germans, who will remain "German speaking Orientals" (Treitschke 1879: 576 [own translation]). He initiated an anti-Semitic dispute with important impacts for the political culture of Imperial Germany and beyond (see Jensen 2005: 200-219 and Benz 2005: 149). The series of public discussions concerned with his essay "Unsere Aussichten" was later called the "Berliner Antisemitismusstreit" (1879-1881). The structural and metaphorical elements of his hostile argument towards Jewish Germans appeared to be partly translatable and have some analogies to the current Leitkultur-discourse. Both discourses relate the construction of racialized religious and cultural differences to specific immigration movements which are imagined as a threat to the nation.

It is significant to consider that there are a number of discursive figurations and cultural stereotypes, which discriminated Jewish people in the past, are now used to marginalize Muslim immigrants (see the discussions in Benz 2009 and Attia 2007). I suggest to understand Treitschke's infamous construction of Otherness, German self and the image of an unavoidable cultural conflict caused by "Überfremdung" as an persistent ideological point of view, that is also reflected by recent demands for "deutsche Leitkultur" and compulsory integration courses. I also suggest

---

13   Anti-immigration ideologies and movements came also in other Western countries into existence. In the United States nativism and the hegemony of White Anglo-Saxon Protestant culture excluded other European and even more effectively and long-standing Asian immigrants. White supremacist ideology were also important for the legislation of the "White Australia Policy", which was until its end in 1973 in favour of European immigrants. See also Samuel Huntington's much-debated book *Who We Are* (2004) for a recent defense of white nativism.

14   A useful overview is accessible in the German Wikipedia: http://de.wikipedia.org/wiki/%C3%9Cberfremdung, accessed 25 April 2009.

15   See Stanley Cohen (2002), who introduced this theory in 1973.

considering how anti-Semitism and anti-Slavic sentiments towards Polish-Germans and Polish immigrants are related to the rise of German colonial culture and politics. My interest is not to claim that intellectual German anti-Semitism and anti-Polish policies in the nineteenth century and Islamophobic anti-immigrant discourses in the presence are all the same or completely interchangeable. But they are defined as the Other of the dominant nation and despite important differences these alienating processes also share similarities.

More than 100 years ago, in a time when Imperial Germany became a colonial power, there was a strong political movement which perceived German and Jewish identity as incompatible and the latter as a general problem for German society. What Treitschke called "nationale Sonderexistenz" in regard to German-Jewish life-worlds is now belittlingly coined as Turkish "Parallelgesellschaft" in the dominant German discourse. Similar to the alienating framing of German Jewry in Imperial Germany non-European and Muslim immigrant communities are now suspected of being incapable of societal integration and cultural adaptation. As most nationalists throughout history Treitschke was obsessed by the idea that internal enemies of the German Empire could weaken the nation-state and accused German Jews to seek economic and cultural dominance (see Treitschke 1879: 573). Therefore he demanded that they strengthen their commitment to the nation and supported the rise of aggressive "natural Germanic feelings of the people against foreign elements, that occupied too much space in our life" (Treitschke 1879: 575 [own translation]). Contrary to the historical events, he regarded Germany as a safe haven that gave generously Jewish people political rights and citizenship as free gifts. Therefore he expected the Jewish community to be thankful and not only to deeply respect Christian customs and beliefs, but also to reverently accept the leadership of the German people. Like most conservatives today Treitschke strongly rejected the idea of multiculturalism and was afraid of "an era of German-Jewish mix-culture" (Treitschke 1879: 573).

One reason for Treitschke's disapproval was his belief, that German Jewry, unlike other Jewish communities in Western Europe, didn't descend from Spain, but had East European origins (Treitschke 1879: 573). His position repeated strong anti-Slavic sentiments in German society, which regarded East Europeans in general as racially and culturally inferior. He was especially afraid about those Jewish groups who were believed to be newly arrived as "Ostjuden" from East European countries. These groups, as he stated, were part of a never ending mass immigration from the Polish hinterland, and in his vision they allegedly represented a serious threat to the high standing German culture as well as national unity and security.[16]

---

16   See Treitschke 1879: 572f. It is not difficult to discover similarities in the presents discussion on established Muslim communities whose threatening potential are increased by links to "never-ending waves" of asylum seekers and the "invasion" of undocumented postcolonial migrants inside and outside of "Fortress Europe". One of the most present images for these scenario relate to events in October 2007 when several hundred Muslim

Another, but closely associated discourse string emerged with the introduction of the semi-state organized labour immigration policy in protestant Prussia in the early 1890s. Besides the economical benefits for the employers this policy was created to serve national interests. I have referred to this policy as driven by colonial ambitions to appropriate cheap human resources of mostly catholic Poles and other East Europeans.[17] Poorly protected by often discriminatory laws these immigrants were subjected to humiliating racial stereotypes, religious criticism, political prosecution and exploitation under harsh working conditions in the agriculture and mining industry. These discriminatory labour migration practices can be described as inversion of colonial expansion into the "innere Ausland", an internal foreign territory inhabited by excluded immigrants under the rule of the aliens act. The intention was to enhance the growth of the national economy in a global competition for power and wealth. These immigrants were also targeted by a powerful nationalist discourse against cultural, socio-economic and racial "Überfremdung", or "Polonisierung" as the famous sociologist Max Weber (1864-1920) put it.[18]

This sense is captured by another German term for undesired Otherness: "Fremdkörper", which can be translated as foreign body or alien object, is a racialized and anatomic metaphor for those, who cannot belong to the nation, due to their assumed physical appearance or other congenital features. It refers to the notion of the nation as biological and unchangeable entity and made racist exclusion a legitimate tool of citizenship policy.[19] The ideas of "Überfremdung" and "Fremdkörper" were in circulation to address the imagery of the conflicting Otherness of immigrants. One imagination derived from the colonial period is, for example, the perception of transnational immigration movements as natural catastrophe or military events. These associations to moral panic are sometimes still used in the German political debate and news coverage, where immigration has been portrayed as floods and invasions.

To solve the problem of racial and cultural Otherness two principles were introduced to German immigration policies from early on: in addition to the

---

and Black immigrants tried to overcome the fortified border fences of the North African outposts of the EU in Ceuta and Melilla.

17   For a more detailed analysis see Ha 2003: 56-107. There was even a serious political discussion in the parliament about the possibility to import Chinese natives from the German colony in the Jiaozhou Bay (Kiautschou) in order to exploit their labour force in the Prussian agrarian economy.

18   See his study "Die Verhältnisse der Landarbeiter im ostelbischen Deutschland" (1892).

19   This understanding is inscribed into law. For example, the regulation of German citizenship, is still based on a law from 1913. Even after the first modernization of this law in 2000 jus sanguinis (the right of blood) is still the leading principle that determine German citizenship. It is likely, that the widely supported understanding of the nationhood as endangered by racialized "Fremdkörpern" made it easier to accept violent solutions like "ethnic cleansing" and genocide as it happened later in Nazi Germany.

strict enforcement of temporary labour migration policy (and deportation when necessary) internal Germanization[20] was first applied on the Polish minority with German citizenship and later also on Polish immigrants.[21] One important element of the politics of internal Germanization was its governmental and pedagogical approach to control access to language and cultural identities by promoting German culture, history and language in state controlled institutions like schools and local administration and by discriminating against the mother tongues of racialized minorities and immigrants in public life.

If Germanization can be characterized as a politics of guided cultural assimilation by the dominant group then the recent politics of "deutsche Leitkultur" and compulsory integration courses to learn German language, history and political values is apparently related to this powerful ideology. As the name clearly indicates, the core idea of "deutsche Leitkultur" is to maintain the cultural, socio-economic and political privileges of essentialized Germanness in Germany. When the integration-as-assimilation approach was first proposed by federal agencies in the early 1980s it was criticised by several social scientist like Claus Leggewie, Franz Hamburger and Ahmet Bayaz as "Germanization" (Treibel 1990: 48). As long as integration is aimed at a broad scale Germanization of migrant identities, attempting to re-program cultural memory and diverse loyalties of migrants, it can well be viewed as an ideological project of nationalization and cultural homogenization.

Colonial World Views and Hierarchies

The current enactment of integration shows by its basic assumptions that migrant and Black subjects are defined as deficient and deviant objects within the German legal system of normalization and regulation. Here we can find obvious parallels and analogies to the antiquated German policy of foreigners and to colonial categorizations of the Other. Both the current concept of integration, and past strategies of "civilizing" and "missionizing" are based on a dualistic construction of differences, defacing the Other as entirely different (Fanon 1981: 31-4). The basic precondition for this perception is the creation of a dualism between within and without, subject and object, rational and irrational, good and evil. A definite line is drawn between the national, or rather Western "Us" and the categorical

---

20   The process of internal Germanization is closely associated to the long-lasting history of external Germanization in East Europe ("Ostkolonization" or "Ostsiedlung"), which used various practices to spread German language, settlements and ultimately also power into foreign regions. Language and other cultural elements were essential to strengthen Germanness abroad. Their peaceful or violent promotion made them powerful instruments to control territory, people and the society itself. See the articles in Bade 1993: 29-122.

21   See for example the accounts in Bullivant/Giles/Pape 1999 and Kleßmann 1984.

Other, constructing and stabilizing a hierarchy that is significant both intra-socially and trans-nationally.[22] First, the postcolonial Others are de-individualized, homogenized and negatively connoted, regardless of their inner complexities and heterogeneity. The collective characteristics, which have been ascribed, are then set into a counter-relation to those "Western" norms and values effective in the federal republic. This reproduces the perspective also prevalent in the overseas-administration's treatment of their colonized subjects. It views the Other not as a person with inalienable rights to individuality, nor as a political subject with a right to self-determination. Instead, the instruction of the colonized Other is based on the assumption of them being childlike and legally incapacitated. In the colonial perspective, their social existence and their becoming subjects are dependent on the degree to which the dominant power succeeds with its pedagogical, political and cultural socialization.

Although by different means, those People of Colour who want to immigrate are treated in a structurally similar way to inmates of colonial reformatories and penitentiaries: they are examined, corrected and selected both for the protection of German society and for their own "promotion". They are treated like infantile pupils, who are all – apart from a few strictly defined exceptions (§ 4 para 2 IntV) – in need of Western enlightenment and instruction in German culture and language. The stigma of "particular need for compulsory integration" conceptualizes them as incapacitated and helpless. Since they are unable to recognize or care for their own well-understood interests, the German state views itself not only as entitled, but obliged, to take charge of their function in society. We again find ourselves in a situation where it is the "burden of the white man" to force the "happiness" of integration onto the Other. Accordingly, German integration politics will in future comprise the notion of "demand and promotion" (Fordern und Fördern), which – as was shown by the "integration summit" on 14 July 2006 – is defined mainly as migrant self-commitment to the German Leitkultur.

The regulation of integration assumes that postcolonial and Muslim migrants – in contrast to the enlightened and fully civilized Germans – are not, or insufficiently, familiar with the principles of democracy, constitutional legality, equality, tolerance and freedom of religion. Working with such negative collective characteristics, integration politics suspect that all migrants have world views and behaviour which are authoritarian, sexist and fundamentalist. These politics obviously work with a concept of migrants as aliens and enemies, therefore providing acceptance for traditional racist and Orientalistic-Islamophobe stereotypes. As a result immigrants undergo two levels of devaluation: on the one hand, their cultural competence is negatively connoted, on the other hand the raging political accusations of extremism and religious fundamentalism are legitimized and generalized as a basis for governmental actions. The general suspicion is also evident by the plans for "belated integration" for long-established migrants. As objects of the dominant discourse about national interests, they are supposed

---

22   I have discussed this problem at length in Ha 2004.

to be available for arbitrary political notions. The objectifying language alone suggests that this form of integration does not aim at a politics of recognition and equality. The officially certified "need for integration" takes these negative signs of "Otherness" for granted. Migrants seem to have more need for integration, the more they are perceived as being culturally backward and threatening. However, the authoritarian and paternalistic threat of help can turn into an equally strict imperative of deportation as soon as an undefined limit of tolerability is crossed. In terms of laws and policies it is the Western nation state that defines the rules and methods to treat immigrants. Instead of making it the priority to dismantle the structural dynamics of discrimination[23] and to establish long-term equality, the political framework of rigid integration corroborates racist practices.

Ever since the enlightened age of European "discoveries" and expansion, the dualistic construction of differences has served to justify a claim to political and cultural superiority. Colonial pedagogic practices of the past centred around the forceful missionizing, civilizing and (under-)development of the Other. Within the still Western-dominated world politics it is suspected that neo-liberal and neo-imperial forces within international relations instrumentalize the notions of an instruction into values (such as capitalist economy, liberal democracy, human rights and women's rights, religious freedom etc.) to legitimize far-reaching interventions. In Germany's present discourse on integration, the dominant perspective is also effective in creating the notion of deficiency-compensation of immigrants, which the political agenda views as the primary aim of the instruction into democratic and cultural values. By means of general assumptions and dichotomous attributions, the discourse on integration defines in different shapes and nuances the racist and colonialist stigmata of a "conflict of cultures"[24] as one of the central problem of Western immigration societies. The discursive and social construction of fundamental differences and antagonisms in the relationship between "Germans" and "Foreigners" provides definite advantages for the dominant society. By means of its governmental defining power, it can establish a subordinate relationship between the German Leitkultur and those migrant practices, which are viewed as threatening or deficient, on all relevant levels. The assumed abnormality of migrants are frequently criminalized, fantasized and pathologized. In this way it is possible to apply to migrant subjects the administrative treatment deemed necessary, even against their will. Integration therefore becomes an instrument of social submission and cultural subordination.

---

23 For a summary of the international critique on institutionalized racism in Germany see Addy 2003: 36-49.

24 Çaglar (2002) wrote a thorough critique of this ideology for the German discussion.

Bibliography

Addy, D.N. 2003. *Diskriminierung und Rassismus. Internationale Verpflichtungen und nationale Herausforderungen für die Menschenrechtsarbeit in Deutschland.* Berlin: Deutsches Institut für Menschenrechte.

Adick, C. 1996. Kolonialpädagogik, in *Taschenbuch der Pädagogik*, vol. 3, edited by H. Hierdeis and T. Hug. Baltmannsweiler: Schneider, 952-64.

Altbach, P. and Kelly, G.P. (eds) 1992. *Education and the Colonial Experience.* New York: Advent Books.

Attia, I. (ed.) 2007. *Orient- und IslamBilder. Interdisziplinäre Beiträge zu Orientalismus und antimuslimischem Rassismus.* Münster: Unrast.

Avenarius, H. and Nuissl von Rein, E. 2005. Bildungspflicht für Erwachsene? Neue normative Anforderungen in Zeiten des lebenslangen Lernens. *Zeitschrift für Erwachsenenbildung*, 3/2005, 24-6.

Bade, K.J. (ed.) 1993. *Deutsche im Ausland: Fremd in Deutschland. Migration in Geschichte und Gegenwart.* München: Beck.

Benz, W. 2005. *Was ist Antisemitismus?.* München: C.H. Beck.

Benz, W. (ed.) 2009. *Islamfeindschaft und ihr Kontext. Dokumentation der Konferenz "Feindbild Muslim – Feindbild Jude".* Berlin: Metropol.

Bullivant, K., Giles, G. and Pape, W. (eds) 1999. Germany and Eastern Europe: Cultural Identities and Cultural Differences. *Yearbook of European Studies*, 13. Amsterdam: Rodopi.

Çaglar, G. 2002. *Der Mythos vom Krieg der Zivilisationen. Der Westen gegen den Rest der Welt.* Münster: Unrast.

Cohen, S. 2002. *Folk Devils and Moral Panics.* London: Routledge.

Die Bundesregierung 2007. *Der Nationale Integrationsplan. Neue Wege – Neue Chancen.* Berlin: Presse- und Informationsamt der Bundesregierung.

Du Bois, W.E.B. 1903. *The Souls of Black Folk.* Chicago: A.C. McClurg.

Fanon, F. 1981. *Die Verdammten dieser Erde.* Frankfurt am Main: Suhrkamp.

Financial Times Deutschland 2004. *Integrationskurse für Zuwanderer werden Pflicht*, [Online]. Available at: http://www.ftd.de/pw/de/1101904129913.html?nv=7dm [17 December 2004].

Gutiérrez, R.A. 2004. Internal Colonialism: An American Theory of Race. *Du Bois Review*, 1(2), 281-95.

Ha, K.N. 2003. Die kolonialen Muster deutscher Arbeitsmigrationspolitik, in *Spricht die Subalterne deutsch? Postkoloniale Kritik und Migration*, edited by E. Gutiérrez Rodriguez and H. Steyerl. Münster: Unrast, 56-107.

Ha, K.N. 2004. *Ethnizität und Migration Reloaded. Kulturelle Identität, Differenz und Hybridität im postkolonialen Diskurs.* Berlin: Wissenschaftlicher Verlag Berlin.

Huntington, S. 2004. *Who Are We ? – Die Krise der amerikanischen Identität.* Hamburg: Europa Verlag.

Jensen, U. 2005. *Gebildete Doppelgänger. Bürgerliche Juden und Protestanten im 19. Jahrhundert.* Göttingen: Vandenhoeck & Ruprecht.

Joppke, C. 2007. *Do Obligatory Civic Integration Courses for Immigrants in Western Europe further Integration?*, [Online]. Available at: http://www.focus-migration.de/index.php?id=2562&L=1 [accessed: 10 May 2009].

Kleßmann, C. 1984. Integration und Subkultur nationaler Minderheiten: das Beispiel der "Ruhrpolen" 1870-1939, in *Wanderarbeiter: Gastarbeiter. Bevölkerung, Arbeitsmarkt und Wanderung in Deutschland seit der Mitte des 19. Jahrhunderts*, vol. 2, edited by K.J. Bade. Ostfildern: Scripta Mercaturae, 486-505.

Lebenslagen in Deutschland. Der zweite Armuts- und Reichtumsbericht der Bundesregierung, Fassung für Ressortabstimmung und Beteiligung von Verbänden und Wissenschaft, Stand: 14.12.2004, [Online]. Available at: http://www.dbsh.de/Armutsbericht2004.pdf [accessed: 12 February 2005].

Meier-Braun, K.-H. 2002. *Deutschland, Einwanderungsland*. Frankfurt am Main: Suhrkamp.

Naber, G. 2007. "Ausgangspunkt einer deutschen Weltmachtpolitik" – Kolonialismus, Rassismus und Deutschtum bei Max Weber. *iz3w freiburg-postkolonial* [Online]. Available at: http://www.freiburg-postkolonial.de/Seiten/maxweber.htm [accessed: 10 May 2009].

Pautz, H. 2005. *Die deutsche Leitkultur. Eine Identitätsdebatte*. Stuttgart: Ibidem.

Prantl, H. 2004. Monstrum Integration. *Süddeutsche Zeitung*, 12 October 2004.

Rosenkranz, S. 2004. Die große Lüge von der Toleranz. *Der Stern*, 1 December, [Online]. Available at: http://www.stern.de/politik/deutschland/?id=532700 [accessed: 17 December 2004].

Said, E.W. 1994. *Culture and Imperialism*. New York: Vintage.

Spiegel Online 2000. *"Leitkultur": Merz gegen Kopftücher im Unterricht*, [Online]. Available at: http://www.spiegel.de/politik/deutschland/0,1518,106016,00.html [accessed 25 April 2009].

Treibel, A. 1990. *Migration in modernen Gesellschaften. Soziale Folgen von Einwanderung und Gastarbeit*. Weinheim: Juventa.

Treitschke, H. von 1879. Unsere Aussichten. *Preußische Jahrbücher*, vol. 44, 559-76.

Unabhängige Kommission "Zuwanderung" 2001. *Zuwanderung gestalten – Integration fördern*, [Online]. Available at: http://www.bmi.bund.de/cae/servlet/contentblob/150404/publicationFile/15101/ [accessed 13 September 2009].

Weber, M. 1892. *Die Verhältnisse der Landarbeiter im ostelbischen Deutschland*. Schriften des Vereins für Socialpolitik, vol. 55, Die Verhältnisse der Landarbeiter in Deutschland. Leipzig: Verlag Duncker & Humboldt.

Chapter 11

The Coloniality of Power and Ethnic Affinity in Migration Policy: The Spanish Case

Sandra Gil Araújo

This chapter presents an analysis of migration policies within a de-colonizing theoretical and empirical framework, an approach which has previously received little attention in Spain. Its objective is to analyze the complex factors that converge in the multiple processes of inclusion-exclusion encountered by postcolonial migrants settled in the centers of the world system.

In the following pages I explore the ties between the coloniality of power, migration policies, and the bases for national identity, taking Spain as a case study. First, I define core concepts and specify the assumptions that underlie the State's need to classify and differentiate populations. I also explore the links between the ways in which "nation" is imagined and the ways in which the immigrant presence is conceptualized and made an issue requiring state action. Second, I summarize some of the characteristics of contemporary immigration in Spain in order to then analyze the normative practices and discourses of integration for non-Communitarian immigrants in general, and more specifically, the criteria for accessing nationality in as much the instructions on the attributes necessary for belonging to the political community. In the Spanish case, the recent extension of the Law of Naturalization to Spanish-descended grandchildren, together with the preferential treatment awarded to immigrants from Brazil, Portugal, and the former Spanish colonies (except Morocco) have allowed the establishment of a link between citizenship, national identity, and ethnic/racial classifications. I close the chapter by offering some conclusions on the role of Spanish migration policy and citizenship as tools for the hierarchical ethnic/racial ranking of the population, and on the implications of narratives of affinity and cultural difference as expressions of the current validity of the coloniality of power. Finally I propose analyzing the field of migration studies itself from a de-colonial perspective, in as much as academic production defines, demarcates, and constitutes postcolonial subjects as objects needing regulation, redress, and analysis.

The Coloniality of Power, Ethnic Relations, and Migration Policy

For the modernity/coloniality network, the international division of work into center and periphery and the hierarchical ranking of ethnic/racial populations devised over centuries of European colonial expansion were not transformed with the actual end of colonial administration.

> Rather we are experiencing a transition from modern colonialism to global colonialism, a process which has certainly modified the forms of domination unleashed by modernity, but not the structure of the center-periphery relationship on a global scale (Castro Gómez and Grosfoguel 2007: 13).

From a de-colonizing perspective, the structures created during the sixteenth and seventeenth centuries play an important role in the present, even though the exclusions generated by the epistemological, racial, and gender hierarchies of modernity have been re-signified by contemporary global capitalism.

Following the work of sociologist Aníbal Quijano, the idea of the coloniality of power expresses one of the constitutive elements of contemporary patterns of power: "the imposition of an ethnic/racial classification on the world's population as a cornerstone for said pattern of power [which] operates on material and subjective planes, realms, and dimensions of social existence and on a societal scale" (Quijano 2000: 342).[1] The coloniality of power lies in the intersection of multiple and heterogeneous global hierarchies of sexual, political, epistemological, economic, linguistic, and racial domination, and it reconfigures the remaining structures of power in the world system.

Taking these positionings into account, migrations from Latin America, Asia, and Africa to Spanish territory should be analyzed within the more global framework of the migration of colonial workers to metropolitan centers to provide the latter with a cheap workforce. In a comparative analysis of the dynamics of inclusion/exclusion encountered by workers in Italy and Spain, Kitty Calavita (2005) invites us to think about the importation of workers from the periphery to the metropolis, the reconstruction of these workers into different "others", and the material utility derived from this otherness as an inverse colonialism, a *colonialism toward within*. Saskia Sassen (2007) has spoken of the *peripheralization of the core* to refer to the increasing use of a third world workforce to perform the services required to maintain *global cities*. Although the outsider status of (im)migrant workers in part results from permanent inequalities inherited from the colonial era, their peripheral condition is reproduced through migration policies, business strategies, gender relations, stigmatization, racialization, and other dominant visions and de-visions.

Many analyses of migration policy tend to take the existence of the nation-state as a given, as natural, without paying sufficient attention to the need States have to classify and differentiate populations. In this sense they lose sight of how the regulation of migrations contributes to the construction of the actual state-ness of the State (Torpey 2000). However, States' monopolization of the right

---

1 Ideas and systems of classification that originated 500 years ago: "With America, capitalism became world-reaching and Euro-centric, and coloniality and modernity solidified as the constitutive axes of a specific pattern of power" (Quijano 2000: 342).

to authorize and regulate migratory movements is consubstantial to the process by which nation-states have been constructed. In order to monopolize legitimate means of mobility, nation-states have been obliged to define who belongs and who does not, given that the *national form* (Balibar 1991) makes it necessary to create and maintain borders between nationals and non-nationals, as much in the demarcation of an exterior as in the identification of distinctions between the people who inhabit its territory.[2] A crucial aspect of this process is that individuals have also become dependent upon the State in terms of what is referred to as the possession of an identity.

The various forms of imagining the nation create space for distinct manners of thinking and acting with regards to the presence of immigrants (Gil Araujo, in press). What does this tell us about the principle of *ethnic affinity* applied to the governance of immigration? Given that via such norms and practices the State bestows a status of privileged migration or citizenship, invoking supposedly shared *ethnic* origins (Brubaker 1998, Joppke 2005), I propose conceptualizing policies of ethnic affinity as both the products and instruments of the coloniality of power. Analytically, it is important not to lose sight that these classifications, rather than reflecting objective distinctions, are utilized as weapons by the nation-state (and in certain cases by *nations without states*) in their attempts to define nationals and non-nationals and to privilege the migration of populations of determinate ethnic/racial origins. As Grosfoguel (2007, 10) recalls, "[t]he construction of national identity is interwoven with racial categories". The failure to question narratives of affinity and difference generated by the State not only bestows scientific legitimacy to such official visions and to the division of the social world, but it also makes it difficult to understand how and why states makes such claims, and with what consequences. In any case, the challenge is to uncover, in practices and discourses relating to immigration, the suppositions that help identify underlying models of nation.

Spain as a Country of Immigration: Introductory Notes

Over the past two decades, Spain has gone from being a typical country of emigration – directed primarily toward Latin American countries and more recently toward Northern and Western European ones – to being a territory which attracts immigrants, on the grounds of two determining factors: the characteristics of the labor market and Spain's incorporation into the European Union, which have decisively impacted both the intensity of the *phenomenon*; and the ways in which immigration has been conceptualized and administered (Agrela and Gil 2005). With the ends of justifying in the national political arena the importation of migration policies which were imposed by the EU but did not correspond to the scarce presence of immigrants in Spain, policy makers rapidly problematized

---

2   "As for structure, the national form produces a differentiation, and it perpetuates it and demands that this differentiation be defended" (Balibar 2003, 51).

immigration and profiled non-EU immigrants as a category demanding public policy intervention: " … it would not be an exaggeration to affirm that the social visibility of migrants and of the symbolic institution of the social formation that 'non-EU immigration' constitutes are, to a large extent, like the adjective of this revealing attribution, a product of EU migration policies" (Santamaría 2002: 105).

In this framework, since the mid-1980s, Spain came to be referred to as a *country of immigration*, in a context clearly divergent from that in which postwar migration occurred in Europe. The demand for labor was generated in sectors characterized by high seasonality and a lack of regulation. The model of economic growth established since then has been based on the extension of flexible, seasonal jobs. Policies geared toward expanding and redistributing employment have been replaced by the progressive de-regulation of the labor market. Some of the effects of these transformations include the growth of unemployment, the expansion of the informal economy, and the segmentation of the labor market. As in other European countries, decreases in unemployment have been associated with the proliferation of low-paying, seasonal jobs. Another key change has been the increasing incorporation of Spanish women into the workforce, which, together with a minimal sharing of reproductive tasks and the absence of public services has provoked a slow increase in the demand for domestic workers and caregivers. For Lorenzo Cachón (2002, 2006), the migration phenomenon in Spain has unleashed a lack of balance between: (a) an autochthonous workforce which has slowly increased the *level of acceptability* of employment (a product of economic development, increasing education levels, and the limited role of the State in terms of public welfare); and (b) a demand for labor in certain activities in the secondary labor market which native workers are unwilling to accept due to low salary levels and insecure, harsh working conditions. An elevated proportion of undocumented immigrants is the chronic, structural characteristic most defining Spain's immigration panorama (Arango 2004a, Cachón 2002). Some data suggest that this irregularity is a fundamental factor in the development of certain productive sectors characterized by high levels of irregularity, primarily those requiring intensive labor and with low production costs (Calavita 2005).

Far from a uni-directional migration, the Spanish migration process assumes a greater complexity than that which simple emigration versus immigration categorizations imply. This transition reflects the great heterogeneity of migration patterns, composed of at least five different, intertwined processes: (a) Spanish emigrants definitively settled in Latin American and Northern European countries, (b) guest workers who have emigrated from European countries but who generally return to their regions of origin once they retire, (c) the immigration of European retirees who settle in Spanish territory permanently or seasonally and who constitute an important part of EU immigration to Spain, (d) the immigration of workers from Northern countries who follow transnational capital, (e) the immigration of persons from non-EU countries of diverse origins and profiles, who increasingly are choosing Spain as their destination (Agrela and Gil 2005) and, within this last group, (f) the *returning* descendants of previous Spanish emigrants to Latin America. However, when reference is made to an "immigrant population" the implication is generally a reference to men and women (imagined as) poor and coming from poor countries (Santamaría 2002, Gil Araujo 2006a). Such conceptualizations have contributed to the framing of immigration from southern countries as problematic and to the camouflaging of immigration from other EU countries and of returning Spanish emigrants and their descendants. In the field of migration studies, little research has been produced either on EU immigrants in Spain or on contemporary processes of Spanish migration, which brings into focus the influence of "State Thought" (*pensée d'Etat*)[3] on the visions and de-visions constructed within academia.

In relation to the social and demographic profile of the immigrant population settled in Spain, Agrela and Dietz (2005) point out certain distinctive characteristics. On the one hand, its composition is exceedingly heterogeneous and there are notable differences between nationalities in relation to gender, skill sets, migration projects, and the types and grades of labor insertion. On the other hand, its geographic distribution is very diverse and its insertion into the labor market is limited to certain sectors, displaying a rapidly increasing tendency toward segmentation and ethnicization. The data signal a polarization of the types of jobs performed by these workers according to region of origin. EU citizens, North Americans, and Japanese are grouped into the most prestigious positions. In terms of low skilled labor in precarious and low paying positions, generally in the secondary labor market, we find concentrations of Maghrebi, Latin American, Asian, and African immigrants (Arango 2004b). Moreover, a majority of these immigrants endure work conditions decidedly worse than those found on average in the Spanish labor market, and they undertake the least desirable activities (Cachón 2002). Many work in the informal economy under irregular conditions, particularly women in domestic service and sex work (Gil Araujo 2006b). The stratifying effect of the articulation between certain migration policies, policies which discriminate on the basis of national origin and gender, and certain ethnically/racially/sexually segmented labor markets has led Spain to be defined as an ethno-fragmented society (Pedreño 2005). This ethno-fragmentation can be understood in the Spanish context as the expression of complex processes of international capital accumulation, and it is traversed by a racial/ethnic hierarchy with a global reach (Castro-Gómez and Grosfoguel 2007).

Immigration, Integration, and Nation Building: Practices and Discourses of Affinity and Difference

In the analysis I present in these pages, I start with the premise that forms of thinking and doing are not mere pieces of objective data but rather they represent

---

3   "a form of thinking which reflects, via its own (mental) structures, the structures of the state, which in this way takes shape" (Sayad 2002, 367).

a territory for exploration, as they are contingent products of multiple, interwoven, social, political, and economic processes, both from the past and in the present. While migration may be a universal phenomenon, there are important variations in the ways in which it is perceived and constructed according to its historical and geographic contexts. Therefore it must be scrutinized in concrete scenarios, without losing sight of its implications in on-going processes of national construction and reconstruction. Analyzing migration policies from this perspective presupposes examining the procedures through which the immigrant presence is problematized in a concrete historical moment. When Foucault (1985) maintains that we think from within the interior of an anonymous and constricting system of thought corresponding to a period and to a language, *state thought*, in the manner referred to by Abdelmalek Sayad (2002) is undoubtedly one of the basic and key structures of contemporary thought. This particular way of thinking lends form and content to multiple fields, from public policy and to even scientific activity, passing for the ways in which people conceive of themselves, but most especially, of the ways in which the immigrant presence is imagined.

In Spain, particularly since the year 2000, the process of regulating non-EU migration was accompanied by other initiatives and debates at the state, regional, and local levels about the *integration of the non-EU population* (Gil Araujo 2006a). Already by the mid-1990s, since its initial configuration as a field for public intervention, the integration/non integration of the immigrant population was thematically linked to the question of cultural distance or proximity. However the representation of immigrants in terms (or by gradations of) cultural similarity/ difference emerged with greater force at the start of the twenty-first century. Debates about the difficulties facing the *integration of non-EU immigrants*, in realms ranging from public policy to the mass media and academia, were organized around the narrow perimeter of cultural difference (Agrela 2002, Santamaría 2002, Gil Araujo 2002). *Non-communitarian immigration* slowly became a public issue, not only because of the aforementioned debates, but also because it became institutionalized as a social problem, the product of and motive for the creation of specific administrative initiatives, forums, programs, and integration plans, and the impetus for the proliferation of reports, research projects, publications, congresses and professional specializations in the study and management of immigration and immigrants.[4]

---

4   Some examples: the launching of the journal *Migraciones* in 1996, the organization of the First Congress on Migration in Spain (*I Congreso sobre inmigración en España)* in 1998, the initiation of the School for Social Mediators of Immigration (*Escuela de Mediadores Sociales para la Inmigración*) in 1998, the founding of the masters-level program Migrations and Intercultural Relations at the Universidad Autónoma of Madrid in 1999. Specific studies of international migrations in the Spanish context were not particularly prominent until the 1990s. One noteworthy exception is the general study conducted by the IOE Collective in 1987, which presented an analysis of the available data on immigration from so-called Third World countries and from Portugal, together with reflections on the

Since then, Latin American immigration has been configured – in discourse and policy making – as the desired immigration. Generally this preference has been supported by the existence of (what is defined as) a shared culture, principally in linguistic and religious terms, believed to facilitate the integration process.[5] However, Jessica Retis' (2006) empirical analysis of the construction of Latin American immigration in the Spanish press demonstrates that, when examined more closely, these perceptions reflect distinct grades of affinity for Latin Americans, according to nationality and phenotype.

At the same, the practice of Islam was crystallized as an obstacle to the integration of immigrants categorized as Muslim. In February, 2001, the spouse of Jordi Pujol, at that time President of the Catalan *Generalitat*, publicly expressed her preoccupation over the increasing number of mosques, which she considered to be a threat to Catholic identity. In May, 2002, Jordi Pujol himself defined the Muslim origins of the majority of immigrants to the Catalan region as an obstacle to their integration:[6]

> [Jordi Pujol] assured that immigration to Madrid from South America is easier to integrate, and it has little in common with that to Catalonia, composed largely of Maghrebis, Sub-Saharan Africans, and Pakistanis. "An Ecuadorean transplanted to Madrid feels like he's at home (…) he doesn't even notice".[7]

An insistence on the exogenous and "non-patriotic" (Moreras 2005, 234) nature of the Muslim population and their religious practices comes from diverse sectors, which has helped consolidate the perception of Islam and of Muslim immigrants as expressions of an absolute otherness. This vision is maintained through notions of *cultural incompatibilities* (constructed under the aegis of cultural difference

---

structural dimensions of the migration process. COLECTIVO IOE, "Los inmigrantes en España", *Revista de Estudios Sociales y de Sociología Aplicada*, No. 66, 1987.

5   In February 2000 the then-delegate of the Government for Immigration party, Enrique Fernández Miranda, pointed to a common language, a shared culture, and the practicing of Roman Catholicism as facilitators to foreign immigrant integration in Spain. A similar position was taken by the Public Ombudsman (*Defensor del Pueblo*) Enrique Múgica, who proposed that the State privilege Latin American immigration (Pedone and Gil Araujo, 2008).

6   However in the Catalan context, there are those who view Latin American immigration as a possible threat to the growth of Catalan language use: "I think it is common sense and acceptable that the nationalist process could find itself affected quite severely by the immigration of Castilian language speakers (mainly from Central and South American countries) without strategic political action" (Zapata-Barrero 2005: 22). On the Catalan Case: Gil Araujo 2007 and 2009.

7   "[Jordi Pujol] aseguró que la inmigración que recibe Madrid, proveniente de Sudamérica, es de más fácil integración y tiene muy poco que ver con la de Cataluña, formada por magrebíes, subsaharianos y pakistaníes. 'Un ecuatoriano trasplantado en Madrid se encuentra como en casa (...) ni se nota'" *El País*, 21 May 2002.

and the threshold for tolerance as these are found in the rest of Europe) and the consequent classification of immigrants as more or less capable of *integrating*, or as more or less *integrated*, according to their national origins and cultural practices. Also, in Spain, a large number of immigrants are subject to the racism of cultural difference, which since the 1970s constitutes a new geo-culture in the world capitalist system and which reinforces and legitimizes the subordinate positions of peripheral immigrants in metropolitan centers (Grosfoguel 2007). These diverse positionings express and perpetuate unequal political, economic, and social relationships between countries and populations, as well as the grades of similarity and difference between these peripheral subjects and the metropolis: those imagined as more or less similar/able to assimilate and those considered different/foreign.

However, empirically speaking, and contrary to logics of culturalism, so-called linguistic and religious affinity do not necessarily guarantee a satisfactory insertion process. Focusing on local and autonomous spaces, the pioneering work of David Cook and Anahi Viladrich (2009) offers some suggestive clues. Their reflections are based upon two case studies: (1) policies of preferential treatment or ethnic affinity with regards to returning emigrants, implemented by the *Junta* in Galicia, and (2) recruitment initiatives undertaken by a city council in a rural town in Aragon, targeting the descendants of Spanish emigrants residing in Argentina and Uruguay. In both cases, contrary to expectations, a familiar air did not guarantee insertion without conflict. Despite their relatively advantageous situation, in Galicia, Argentine migrants descended from Spanish emigrants found that their expectations and aspirations directly conflicted with those of natives, particularly in the realm of labor. They felt that, as citizens, they should have access to the same jobs and salaries that other Spanish enjoyed. However, they felt the jobs they were offered, according to their own criteria, were inadequate with regards to their abilities, experiences, and aspirations. At the same time, the local population categorized these immigrants' expectations as unrealistic and arrogant. In Aragon, migrant families accustomed to urban living could not adjust to the climactic, living, and work conditions they encountered, and they either returned to their places of origin or dispersed throughout Spanish territory. The local population, in turn, criticized the immigrants' perceived lack of a strong work ethic and, unexpectedly, they found that Rumanian immigrants more adequately covered, and at times surpassed, the town's labor needs. Therefore, members of the local population observed that, despite linguistic differences, the Rumanian immigrants were, in their work ethic and modest expectations, "more like us".

Imagining the nation: Ethnic affinity in the accessibility of nationality

How the nation is imagined is of upmost importance for understanding citizenship and the incorporation of migrants into the nation-state. Although the racialization of migrants is crucial to capturing the multiple ways in which immigrant populations are differentiated, a factor that is frequently undervalued is their racial/ethnic composition. How do narratives of nation influence the processes by which immigrants are identified and racialized? Is it possible to be both Spanish and Muslim? Put in another way: what implications do the foundation myths of the metropolitan nation have for postcolonial immigrants in terms of their access to rights and equal treatment (Grosfoguel 2007)? In this sense it seems opportune to pay attention to the norms for accessing nationality, such as instructional guides and the definition of the bases for national identity – that is, understanding the attributes necessary for belonging to the political community. In the Spanish case, until now, modifications to the law of naturalization have principally focused on extending the right to the foreign-born descendants of Spanish. The more recent extension of the right to nationality to the grandchildren of Spanish emigrants, together with the facilities awarded for the naturalization of immigrants from Brazil, Portugal, and the former colonies (except Morocco), permit the establishment of ties between citizenship, national identity, and ethnic/racial classification. Why do the majority of immigrants need ten years of residency to become naturalized, while those from former colonies need only two? Why, if Morocco is a former colony, are its nationals denied access to these prerogatives? Again, history offers some clues. In a study of the origins of the Spanish condition, historian Tamar Herzog (2006, 2007) notes that the first debates about the category "native of the Spanish kingdom" arose during the colonial enterprise and the emergence of a pan-Hispanic community. The condition "Spanish" arose before that of the modern "native" and was constructed on the basis of neighbor-ship or residency (*vecindad*). First in Castile, later in Hispano-America, and finally in the non-Castilian kingdoms of the peninsula, the notion of Spanish that came to the fore was that of the neighbor, that is, of individuals who integrated/formed part of the local community.[8]

In 1716 it was formally decreed that all neighbors of local communities were Spanish natives. The most important factor in being recognized as a native was loyalty. Certain actions and behaviors functioned as indicators of community integration and therefore of loyalty to the same, among these residency for ten years, matrimony with a local spouse, and the payment of taxes. However, the apparent openness of this conceptualization had its limits: (1) candidates had to

---

8   According to this doctrine, natives were those who loved the local community. However, given that love was something that indicated integration into the community, and integration was understood on the local level of residence and associated with other natives, with exercising rights, and with the fulfillment of obligations, persons had to refer to activities on the local level to demonstrate their integration and their qualification as neighbor. Later, authorities and members of communities were convoked to verify the integration of other individuals, often immigrants, and their declarations were fundamental to the recognition of these other individuals as neighbors and natives (Herzog 2007: 155). To a certain extent, ties to a community of residency as an instrument of demonstration and verification of integration still operate as part of regularization via settlement (*regularización por arraigo*).

Table 11.1   Latin American immigrants registered as Spanish nationals, by country of birth

Country of Birth	Registered in Spain	Spanish Nationals
Argentina	272,985	32%
Bolivia	200,749	2%
Colombia	291,676	10.5%
Cuba	83,121	43%
Ecuador	434,673	4.5%
Venezuela	130,630	59%
Uruguay	79,824	30.5%

Source: Based upon data at INE, Revised municipal registry, 2007. http://www.ine.es.

be Roman Catholic, and (2) they were also judged by their membership in certain social groups. Put in another way: native communities were defined in relation to religion and to integration and were elaborated around a discourse that excluded people who came from groups considered marginal. Because of their religion, Muslims, Jews, and Protestants could not attain the status of neighbor and native, regardless of whether they resided within Spanish kingdoms. Even Catholics, in the absence of their local integration, were considered to be foreigners born and raised in Spanish territory, something particularly clear in the case of the Gypsy people.

In 1812, the first liberal Constitution defined and distinguished between a Spaniard, and a Spanish citizen. The American territories were explicitly included within the Spanish nation. Citizenship was guaranteed to the Spanish in both territories and to the descendants of Spanish and American families who had their domicile in the Spanish kingdom. However, while the descendants of Africans could be Spanish, they were excluded from the category of citizen under the argument that their residency was the product of having been slaves and thus involuntary. Based upon certain legal opinions, Herzog (2007) noted that residency was always used by authorities to evaluate foreign integration. Precisely for this reason, if the majority of foreigners need to live in Spain for ten years to be naturalized, others can obtain it within a shorter period provided they can prove "special ties with Spain". This is the case for foreigners born in Spain, for those born of Spanish parents and grandparents, and for nationals of the previously colonized and evangelized territories of Latin America, Africa, and Asia. It does not apply to non-Catholic colonized populations such as Morocco, a country which, therefore, lacks a dual citizenship treaty with Spain.

Registration gives us an approximate estimate of the percentage of persons who, having been born outside of Spain, possess Spanish nationality. In a comparison of regions, 18 per cent of Latin American immigrants have Spanish nationality, compared with 14 per cent of those born in an Asian or African country. However, if we focus on differences between Latin American countries, the panorama becomes more complex. While on the one hand, between 30 to 59 per cent of Venezuelans, Cubans, Argentinians, and Uruguayan have Spanish nationality, on the other, only between 2 to 10 per cent of immigrants from Bolivia, Ecuador, and Colombia possess the same. While it is possible that an important portion of Argentinian, Venezuelan, Cuban, and Uruguayan immigrants have acquired Spanish nationality through residency or matrimony, the fact that the highest percentages exist within countries that were preferred by Spanish emigrants allows us to deduce that many of these *Spanish* are the now-returned descendants of these prior emigrants.

Taking into account the regulation of nationality for persons not born in Spanish territory, it is possible to establish a gradation of affinities, which are also reflected in the diversity of statutes that stratify the foreign population. In the first place we find the descendants of Spanish (children and, now, grandchildren), who together with nationality acquire the right to vote in all elections without ever having lived in Spain (through the strength of blood ties). If they decide to migrate to Spain, they will be considered *returned Spanish*. In the second place we find immigrants from Latin America, the Philippines, Brazil, Portugal, and the Republic of Equatorial Guinea, which thanks to their "special ties with Spain" acquire nationality (and its contingent political rights) after two years of continual residency in Spain. In most of these cases dual nationality accords are also in place. Finally, for the remainder of the immigrant population, including Moroccans, candidates must reside in Spain for 10 years before they can opt for nationality, and in most cases dual nationality is not permitted (due to cultural incompatibility?). In this case, the process of acquiring the necessary attributes for belonging to the national community has been prolonged, probably because it is presupposed that their "conversion" will take longer, due to a lack of *cultural* proximity.

This system of differentiated access to nationality on the basis of national origins makes manifest the strong ethnic/racial component of the Spanish national(ist) project. Roman Catholicism still operates (explicitly or implicitly) as a parameter for "evaluating" the integration capacity of those considered foreign. For Moreras (2005), the strength of Catholicism has less to do with its institutionalizing processes as it does with the recognition of this religion as part of the tradition, memory, and cultural expression of Spain itself. However, the law of naturalization also makes manifest the strength of *blood rights* in the ways in which nation is imagined and constructed. The extension of the right of naturalization to the grandchildren of Spanish under the framework of the Historical Memory Law (Ley de la Memoria Histórica), in force since 2009, can be interpreted as an immigrant selection policy.

Conclusions

The objective of this chapter has been to explore the potential of a de-colonizing vantage point in order to critically analyze the political discourses and migration policies of nationality/naturalization and its links to national identity, via the Spanish case.

One of the strongest myths of the twentieth century was the equation of the elimination of colonial administration with the de-colonization of the world. This mythology helped masque the continuity of the past colonial experience within present-day global racial hierarchies. Coloniality is still a fundamental part of capitalist world power systems, as it is based on the imposition of a racial/ethnic hierarchy on populations, a structure with its origins in "the idea that colonizer is ethnically and cognitively superior to the colonized" (Castro-Gómez 2007: 60). As these pages have shown, in the Spanish case, policies of ethnic affinity that generally favor Latin Americans, and more specifically the descendants of the Spanish, reproduce the idea of the superiority of the colonizer over the colonized, demonstrating the close links between immigration policies, citizenship, ways of imagining the nation, and the coloniality of power. The policy of *ius sanguis*, language, and religion are presented as the bases for belonging to the political community, which can only be accessed by nationality.

The application of the "returned emigrant" category to Spanish descended who were born and raised outside of Spain, and the use of the category "second generation" or "young immigrant" for the children of immigrants who possess Spanish nationality, reveal that the status emigrant/immigrant is not only a juridical category but also (and over all) a social and racial category. Policies of ethnic affinity also inform the initiatives of some regional governments toward those whom they consider *their* emigrants. This is a presently under-investigated theme which reveals how transnational practices can be either promoted or found suspect depending upon whether the populations practicing them are classified as nationals or as foreigners. A suggestive datum: the right to vote is awarded to emigrants and their descendants overseas, but denied to non-EU immigrants living in Spanish territory.

Narratives of cultural proximity between the autochthonous population with Latin American immigrants recreate the project of *Hispanidad* under Spanish domain, and it institutionalizes the so-called proximity of these (post)colonial subjects as the guarantee of their better integration. I am insistent upon this point: in no cases have discourses of similarity or affinity implied equality, particularly not in the frameworks in which the immigrant presence is problematized in terms of integration. The discourse of integration is, among other things, a discourse on forms of identification, both native and foreign, and more definitively, on the unequal power relations that these identifications imply. The notion of integration is interwoven with the paradigm of national construction utilized in the nineteenth and twentieth centuries to create unified national territories out of a patchwork of religions and groups of diverse natures, as was characteristic in Europe. The theoretical concept of social integration, which has as its premise the notion of a territorially delimited, historically rooted, and culturally homogenous society, underlies integration policy.

The application of the integration concept to the field of immigration is a recent adaptation of old ideas and instruments of domestication and social inclusion which operate in diverse areas such as education, moral and civic instruction, and social policy. This move was instigated via the identification of the social arena as a territory needing specific intervention to avert the dangers of social dis-integration (and not to overcome social inequalities). Some of the current positions taken on the integration of immigrants recall the technologies of moral training once applied to the laboring classes and their families as a key instrument of government. The term "integration" and its synonyms essentially point to all kinds of mechanisms and structures directed at reproducing a unified solidarity that overcomes the various fractures (class, gender, origin and race) that threaten the social and national order.

From the de-colonial perspective, the rapprochement of discourses of similarity illuminates something which, to my eyes, remains hidden: the strong global hierarchies of political, epistemological, economic, spiritual, linguistic, and racial domination which uphold ideas about *special ties*, *cultural proximity*, and *shared history* between Latin American immigrants and autochthonous Spanish. What kind of persons make up Latin American immigration to Spain? Women from the countryside and from the cities of the Dominican Republic who "discover" that they are "black"; Ecuadorians from coastal and sierra regions and indigenous Otavaleños; women from Cochabamba (Bolivia); Guaraní-speaking Paraguayans; newly impoverished, 'whitening' urban middle class from Argentina and Uruguay; men and women from diverse parts of Peru; families from Cali, Bogota, or Medellin; and young people from Cuba. Many are mestizo, some have university degrees, and a large portion are women. What is their common culture? Their colonial legacy? It is not as much about shared histories as it is about silent and denied histories. Narratives of the cultural proximity of Latin American immigrants evoke a colonized territory and population, Castilianicized, and evangelized by the Spanish imperium. At the same time, they ignore the diversity of populations, histories, geographies, trajectories, languages, ways of life, cosmovisions, racialization, genocides, defeats, and victories that inhabit Latin American territory. What emerges out of the discourse of *common culture* are homogenizing visions which colonize the plurality of positionings available to migrants from the periphery, expropriating their capacity for historical and political action.

Until now I have hoped to demonstrate that migration policy is a fundamental component of the construction of the immigrant as a social figure, as such policy operates as a tool by which populations are organized into hierarchies. Another crucial terrain, although much less explored, is the field of academic production. Postcolonial studies and the de-colonizing perspective have proven to be tools for the critical analysis, within the social sciences, of the factors which reproduce/ reinforce global ethnic-racial, sexual, and epistemological hierarchies. Migration studies have the potential to be a productive field in which to investigate the ways in which academic production defines, delimits, and constructs postcolonial immigrants as objects needing regulation, redress, and understanding.

In addition to being moulded by public and private administrations, research agendas are shaped by histories of national construction, cultural politics, and national idiosyncrasies, even more so when the *object of study* is the immigrant. If we allow ourselves to be guided by the research on immigrants in Spain, the group most frequently targeted as an object needing analysis has been the Moroccans, perhaps because they are perceived to be the most different (and therefore problematic?). Among Latin American immigrants, research (including doctoral dissertations) on (primarily feminine) Dominican immigration reached its peak in the mid-1990s, with later works focusing on Peruvians, then Ecuadorians, and more recently, although to a lesser extent, on Colombian immigrants.[9] It is suggestive that little knowledge has been produced on Argentinean immigration, despite being one of the oldest and most numerous populations; spanning a variety of intersections relating to administrative status, gender, age, skill level, moment of arrival, migration project, labor insertion; and bearing the very peculiar category of *returned Spanish*. Perhaps, and this is a hypothesis in need of greater exploration, the varied production of reflections and knowledge on (that is, the problematization of) the immigrant population according to country of origin reflects the ways in which the coloniality of power (made manifest by the distinct gradations of ethnic affinity between Spain and its multiple peripheries) transverse social scientific ways of thinking about and constructing the world. This hypothesis confirms the need to convert the academic realm itself into an object of study.

References

Agrela Romero, B. 2002. La política de inmigración en España: Reflexiones sobre la emergencia del discurso de la diferencia cultural. *Migraciones Internacionales*, 1(2), 93-121.

Agrela Romero, B. and Dietz, G. 2005. La Emergencia de regímenes multinivel y diversificación púbico-privada de la política de inmigración en España. *Migración y Desarrollo*, (4), 20-41.

Agrela, B. and Gil Araujo, S. 2005. Constructing Otherness: The Management of Migration and Diversity in the Spanish Context. *Migration. A European Journal of International Migration and Ethnic Relations* (43/44/45), 9-34.

Arango, J. 2004a. Inmigración, cambio demográfico y cambio social. *Información Comercial Española*, (815), 31-44.

Arango, J. 2004b. La población inmigrada en España. *Economistas*, (99), 6-14.

---

9 It is not insignificant to note that an important number of these investigations have been undertaken by social researchers from Latin American countries, such as: Gina Gallardo, Mirna Rivas, Claudia Pedone, Jessica Retis, Walter Actis, Natalia Moarés, Claudia Carrasquilla, Margarita Echeverri, Yulieth Hillón, Fernando Esteba, and Cecilia Jiménez Zunino, among others.

Balibar, E. 1991. La forma nación: historia e ideología, in *Raza, nación y clase*, edited by E. Balibar and I. Wallerstein. Madrid: IEPALA, 135-67.

Balibar, E. 2003. *Nosotros, ¿ciudadanos de Europa? Las fronteras, el Estado y el pueblo*. Madrid: Tecnos.

Brubaker, R. 1998. Migrations of Ethnic Unmixing in the "New Europe". *International Migration Review*, 32(4), 1047-65.

Cachón Rodríguez, L. 2002. La formación de la "España inmigrante": mercado y ciudadanía. *Revista Española de Sociología*, 97, (95)-126.

Cachón, L. 2006. De suecas a ecuatorianas y el retorno de la política, in *III seminario inmigración y Europa. Inmigración y derechos de ciudadanía*, coordinated by G. Pinyol. Barcelona: Fundación, Cidob, 47-65.

Calavita, K. 2005. *Immigrants at the Margins. Law, Race, and Exclusion in Southern Europe*. New York: Cambridge University Press.

Cook Martín, D. and Viladrich, A. 2009. The Problem with Similarity: Ethnic-Affinity Migrants in Spain. *Journal of Ethnic and Migration Studies*, 35(1), 151-70.

Castro-Gómez, S. 2007. El capitulo faltante del Imperio. La reorganización posmoderna de la colonialidad en el capitalismo posfordista, in *¿Un solo o varios mundos? Diferencia, subjetividad y conocimientos en la ciencias sociales contemporáneas*, edited by M. Zuleta, H. Cubides and M.R. Escobar. Bogotá: Universidad Central/Siglo del Hombre Editores, 69-88.

Castro-Gómez, S. and Grosfoguel, R. 2007. *El giro decolonial. Reflexiones para una diversidad epistémica más allá del capitalismo global*. Bogotá: Siglo del Hombre Editores.

Foucault, M. 1985. *Saber y verdad*. Madrid: La Piqueta.

Gil Araujo, S. 2002. Políticas públicas como tecnologías de gobierno. Las políticas de inmigrantes y las figuras de la inmigración, in *Políticas públicas y Estado de Bienestar en España: las migraciones*, edited by C. Clavijo and M. Aguirre. Madrid: FUHEM 147-90.

Gil Araujo, S. 2006a. Las políticas de integración de inmigrantes en el contexto español. Entre la normalización y el derecho a la diferencia, in *La exclusión social y el Estado de Bienestar en España. VI Informe FUHEM de Políticas Sociales*, edited by F. Vidal Fernández. Barcelona: Icaria, 441-78.

Gil Araujo S. 2006b. Construyendo otras. Normas, discursos y representaciones en torno a las mujeres inmigrantes no comunitarias, in *Mujeres migrantes: viajeras incansables*. Bilbao: Harresiak Apurtuz –Diputación Foral de Bizkaia, 95-116.

Gil Araujo, S. 2007. Discursos políticos sobre la nación en las políticas catalanas de integración de inmigrantes, in *Discursos sobre la inmigración en España. Los medios de comunicación, los parlamentos y las administraciones*, coordinated by R. Zapata-Barrero and T. Van Dijk. Barcelona: Fundació CIDOB, 223-68.

Gil Araujo, S. 2009. La gestión de la cuestión nacional: España y Cataluña en perspectiva, in *Políticas y gobernabilidad de la migración en España*, edited by R. Zapata-Barrero. Barcelona: Ariel, 227-46.

Gil Araujo, S. (forthcoming). *Las argucias de la integración. Políticas migratorias, construcción nacional y cuestión social.* Madrid: IEPALA.

Grosfoguel, R. 2007. Migrantes coloniales caribeños en los centros metropolitanos del sistema-mundo. Los casos de Estados Unidos, Francia, Los países Bajos y el Reino Unido. *Documento CIDOB Migraciones* (13), Barcelona: CIDOB.

Herzog, T. 2006. *Vecinos y extranjeros. Hacerse español en la edad moderna.* Madrid: Alianza Editorial.

Herzog, T. 2007. Communities Becoming a Nation: Spain and Spanish America in the Wake of Modernity (and Thereafter). *Citizenship Studies*, 11(2), 151-72.

Joppke, C. 2005. *Selecting by Origin: Ethnic Migration in the Liberal State.* Cambridge: Harvard University Press.

Moreras, J. 2005. ¿Integrados o interrogados? La integración de los colectivos musulmanes en España en clave de sospecha, in *La condición inmigrante. Exploraciones e investigaciones desde la Región de Murcia*, edited by A. Pedreño Canovas and M. Hernández Pedreño. Murcia: Universidad de Murcia, 226-40.

Pedone, C. and Gil Araujo, S. 2008. Los laberintos de la ciudadanía. Políticas migratorias e inserción de las familias migrantes latinoamericanas en España. *Revista Interdisciplinaria de la Movilidad Humana*, (31), 143-64.

Pedreño Canovas, A. 2005. Sociedades etnofragmentadas, in *La condición inmigrante. Exploraciones e investigaciones desde la Región de Murcia*, edited by A. Pedreño Canovas and M. Hernández Pedreño. Murcia, Universidad de Murcia, 75-103.

Quijano, A. 2000. Colonialidad del poder y clasificación social. *Journal of World-System Research*, VI(2), 342-386.

Retis, J. 2006. El discurso público sobre la inmigración latinoamericana en España. Análisis de la construcción de las imágenes de los inmigrantes latinoamericanos en la prensa de referencia. PhD Dissertation. Instituto Universitario de Investigación Ortega y Gasset – Universidad Complutense de Madrid, Madrid.

Santamaría, E. 2002. *La incógnita del extraño: una aproximación a la significación sociológica de la "inmigración no comunitaria.* Barcelona: Antrophos.

Sassen, S. 2007. *Una sociología de la globalización.* Buenos Aires: Katz.

Sayad, A. 2002. Immigrazione e "pensiero di stato", in *La doppia assenza. Delle illusioni dell'emmigrato alle sofferenze dell'immigrato.* Milán: Rafaello Cortina Editore, 367-86.

Torpey, J. 2000. *The Invention of the Passport. Surveillance, Citizenship and the State.* Cambridge: Cambridge University Press.

Zapata-Barrero, R. 2005. Construyendo una filosofía pública de inmigración en Cataluña: los términos del debate. *Revista de derecho migratorio y extranjería*, (10), 9-38.

Chapter 12

Not all the Women Want to be White: Decolonizing Beauty Studies

Shirley Anne Tate

Introduction

There is a myth which still circulates in feminist writing on beauty. That is, that all 'Black women want to be white' because white beauty is iconic. As such Black women are reproduced as possessors of damaged psyches, as pathological. This myth is part of the cultural melancholia of Black beauty with its origins in imperialism, slavery and postcolonial dependency within the USA, UK, Latin America and the Caribbean (Tate 2009). 'Black women want to be white' persists even in the face of twenty-first century beauty hybridities produced through stylization and identification.

I will trace the genealogy of this myth before looking at how it has been challenged by Black Nationalism and Black Atlantic diasporic beauty knowledge and practices. This will show there is no one beauty standard, white beauty is not iconic and there are different investments in beauty within the cultural circuits of the Black Atlantic diaspora. Through the example of aesthetic surgery and other race-ing stylizations I will also consider how thinking about 'race' and beauty as performative destabilizes this myth. The discussion highlights the necessity to consider racialized agency and 'race' performativity in theorizing beauty so as to de-center whiteness and re-center multiple Blacknesses in decolonizing beauty studies.

The Genealogy of the Myth

Common-sense views that 'beauty is in the eye of the beholder', 'beauty is skin-deep' and 'beauty comes from within' deny racialization. However, for Kant (1914) beauty is racialized as it is related to the norms of perfection of European, Chinese and Black people. In the twenty-first century we still read feminist work on beauty which does not look at 'race', does not see white beauty as racialized and misrepresents Black women's beauty practices as signs of psychic damage.

'Beauty studies' is writing mostly within Sociology and Cultural Studies which looks at beauty/ugliness (Tseelon 1995), beauty and racialization,[1] aesthetic surgery,[2] beauty and 'race' performativity (Tate 2007, 2009), beauty and misogyny (Jeffreys 2005) and the beauty industry (Black 2004; Wingfield 2008). Black antiracist feminists attend to the continuation of white beauty as iconic (Craig 2002; Hobson 2005), the assumption that if Black women internalize this value then whiteness will be the model they aspire to (Wingfield 2008; Collins 2004; Hunter 2005) and making it clear that there have always been multiple Black beauty models.[3] For many other writers on beauty Black women, if they are acknowledged, are put outside of the scope of the research (Black 2004) or reproduced as wanting to be white (Jeffreys 2005).

This reminds us that in order to position whiteness as more civilized, advanced and superior discourses on beauty continue to reproduce Africa and Black beauty as its ugly, inferior binary. Black ugliness/white beauty have been several centuries in the making. This racist legacy's permutations throughout the centuries has meant that the Black ugliness/white beauty binary of imperialism and slavery and Black Nationalist counter discourses on African-centered beauty has spawned a racialized beauty Empire. Empire is a deterritorializing system of rule which has no territorial power center or fixed boundaries (Hardt and Negri 2000). It incorporates the global as it manages hybrid identities, hierarchies and exchanges. A racialized beauty Empire operates at the level of the psyche, the social, the national, the global so that the myth that all Black women want to be white is a given even in the face of stylization and politics which speak otherwise. Further, different beauty identities are managed so that Black beauty's many stylizations and embodiments have an incommensurable Blackness or whiteness as their recognized ideal. Such incommensurability produced by both Black Nationalism and white supremacy is the guardian of the Black social skin. Even within the difference produced through everyday practices and discourses this legacy is shown in Sheila Jeffrey's (2005: 113) view that African American women have highlighted the racism of beauty standards in the USA that have white women bleaching their faces and straightening their hair and create impossible goals of emulating whiteness for black women:

> This has led to an industry of hair straighteners, and face whiteners, and other products designed to enable black women to approximate to a white ideal. Since it is unlikely that black women are somehow naturally excluded from the province of natural beauty, it is clear that what is beautiful is constructed politically and incorporates race, class and sex prejudices. When black women are chosen for their 'beauty' to be models, such as Iman from Somalia, or Waris Dirie, their faces and bodies are likely to conform to white ideals and not to

---

1   See Banks 2000; Brand 2000; Candelario 2000; Collins 2004; Cooper 2004; Craig 2002, 2006; Hobson 2005; Hunter 2005; Mercer 1994; Pinho 2006; Rooks 2000; White 2005.

2   See Davis 2003a, 1995; Gimlin 2002; Holliday and Sanchez Taylor 2006.

3   See Banks 2000; Craig 2006; Rooks 2000; Tate 2007, 2009.

resemble the commonest features of African American women's faces (Jeffreys 2005: 113).

She rightly states that beauty is racialized and politically constructed. However, rather damagingly for Black antiracist feminism, she places the idea of Black women wanting to be white within African American women's scholarship. This deflects our attention from her own point of view that beauty is about not 'looking Black'. We are also left wondering 'what are the commonest features of African American women's faces? What about Black women's ideas and beauty practices which run counter to this ideal? Why is "beauty" put in quotes when Jeffreys speaks about Iman and Waris Dirie?' It seems to me that these women are chosen *precisely* because they are *not* the white ideal as Alek Wek (2007: 138) affirms when she speaks about getting recognition 'because of, not in spite of, my African features – they wanted someone exotic who lived in a jungle'. Iman was also subjected to the white racist imaginary early in her career through denying her Blackness and making her a 'brown white woman' (Kuipers 2001). These examples make us notice that it is not a white ideal that is being emulated but there are different Black beauty models which have their own aesthetics, politics and race-ing stylization technologies (Tate 2009). Beauty is transformed both through activism and stylization.

There is a racist beauty habitus in the Black Atlantic where, 'beauty is to be found at the limits of the ugly, since it is the ugly which has so often been the sign under which the African has been read' (Nuttall 2006: 8). 'African ugliness' has been constructed through slavery and colonialism within the USA, Caribbean, UK and Latin America. The pigmentocracy of former slave societies means that 'light skin', 'good features' and 'straight hair' are still seen as necessary for Black feminine beauty which reflects the continuation of a racialized beauty hierarchy today (Pinho 2006).[4] This paradigm has been challenged by anti-racist critique, counter-discourses and bodily practices since at least the 1800s in the Black Atlantic diaspora.

Challenging the Myth: Masculinist Black Nationalism and Diasporic Beauty Knowledges/Practices

The argument for a beauty standard related to 'the African physiology' began in the United States in the nineteenth century as part of Black pride discourses to combat racist representations (Rooks 2000). During and following World War 1, African American writers and activists like J.A. Rogers, W.E.B. Du Bois and Marcus Garvey, spoke about the inherent beauty of African bodies. However, with regard to DuBois, Cesaire, Senghor and Fanon, Michelle Wright (2004) shows that feminist and queer re-readings of the Black Atlantic diaspora are necessary to

---

4   Also see Arrizón 2006; Banks 2000; Caldwell 2007; Candelario 2007; Collins 2004; Hobson 2005; hooks 1993; Hunter 2005; Jan Mohammed 2000; Mama 1995; Russell et al 1992; Weekes 1997.

counter the hetero-patriarchal discourse of nationalism where Black women do not exist. Wright (2004: 11) argues that, 'the counterdiscourses of Du Bois, Césaire, Fanon and Senghor speak of the Black subject as "he" and allocates to that subject full agency, leaving little room for (and even less discussion of) the Black female subject'. For Michelle Stephens (2005) early twentieth century Pan-Africanist Caribbean intellectuals and activists based in the USA (C.L.R. James, Marcus Garvey and Claude McKay) developed a masculinist diasporic global imaginary in which the battle was between African diasporic and 'western' masculinities and Black women were represented as 'the race's' passive nurturers.

The Rastafarian movement, inspired by Garvey, had its roots in 1930s Jamaica based in Pinnacle, Sligoville Road, St. Catherine. This African-centered movement in the then British West Indies decentered white beauty's iconicity. Its anti-colonialist, anti-racist aesthetics focused on natural hair (dreadlocks), praised darker Black skin, African features, Black self love and promoted a return to Africa (Barrett 1977). Its positive valuation of natural hair and dark skin continued in the United States based Black Power Movement which redefined Blackness in the 1960s/1970s with 'Black is beautiful'. Hair straightening and skin bleaching came to be equated with self-hatred while Afro hairstyles signalled political change and Black self love/knowledge (Weekes 1997).

At the beginning of the twentieth century Black women entrepreneurs like Madame C.J. Walker created alternative representations and straight hair became the signal of middle class status. Hair straightening was practiced by large numbers of Black women as part of the neat and tidy appearance (*boa aparêcia*) considered necessary in Brazilian society (Pinho 2006; Caldwell 2007). From the 1970s onwards Brazilian Afro-aesthetics emerged with the wearing of the Afro, dreadlocks and other Jamaican symbols such as Bob Marley (Pinho 2006). Contemporary Black Brazilians' beauty references in idealized images of African beauty counter associations of Blackness with ugliness, stench, criminality and the hegemonic standard of white or *mulata* beauty (Pinho 2006; Figueiredo 2002). Diasporic Africanness was constructed in Brazil by weaving together dress and hair styles to create Black anti-racist aesthetics through the crisscross of elements drawn from Jamaica, African Americans and an imagined Africa (Tate 2009).

According to the Black anti-racist aesthetics which developed in the diaspora through different expressions of Black Nationalism, racialized beauty standards weave racist assumptions into Black people's daily practices and inner lives and encourage them to accept their own ugliness (Taylor 2000). Black anti-racist aesthetics opposes the presumption that long straight hair is necessary for Black women's beauty and is opposed to skin bleaching (Taylor 2000). Instead Black antiracist aesthetics promotes the idea that Black people can be beautiful just as they are naturally because of the recognition that beauty is racialized (Taylor 2000). However, at the level of the everyday various writers have shown that in the Black Atlantic diaspora there is also an ongoing preference for white/light skin even if this is now differently nuanced (Candelario 2007; Hunter 2005).

Ginetta Candelario (2007) looks at identity formation in the Dominican Republic and amongst Dominicans[5] in the USA. For much of the Dominican Republic's history the national body has been defined as 'not Black'. 'Normative *white* Hispanic looks, therefore, are those that show some mixture of European, indigenous, or African ancestors but are somatically distant from the indigenous or African somatic norms' (Candelario 2007: 225). Dominicans continue to prefer a whiteness that indicates mixture and deploy 'Hispanic' as a marker of linguistic, somatic and cultural difference from Anglo whiteness and African American Blackness (Candelario 2000: 130). They do not use the language of *negrismo* – *negra, mulata* – as descriptions of themselves but use language which limits their 'racial' heritage to Europeans and the long since exterminated indigenous Taino population – *indio, indio oscuro, indio claro, trigueño, morena*. This erases Blackness and shows at the same time that whiteness is achieved (Candelario 2000), it is performative. The role of hair as racial signifier began in at least the late eighteenth century and for Dominicans hair still continues to be the main signifier of 'race' alongside facial features, skin color and ancestry (Candelario 2000). While lighter skin was generally valorized in New York skin that is too white is seen as unsightly and 'beautiful' refers to someone of color, the mestiza/mulata (Candelario 2000; 2007).

Within the racialized beauty Empire colonial domination still continues to haunt Black beauty's desires and practices. However, Black politics and Black Nationalist philosophies/movements in the Anglophone Caribbean, USA and UK, *Negrismo* the Black aesthetic and cultural movement in the Spanish speaking Caribbean (Arrizón 2006), *Négritude* in the French speaking Caribbean (Césaire 2000) and Brazilian Afro-aesthetics (Pinho 2006; Caldwell 2007), have impacted on beauty discourses and politics. Black politics and the discourse of white beauty iconicity aver that Black beauty cannot be assimilated into white beauty and vice versa. However, in everyday life there are beauty crossings either side of the 'racial' divide which trouble this incommensurability. Aesthetic surgery is one example in which the prohibition on beauty crossings is beginning to loose its grip. It is also an area in which the myth that Black women want to be white has its greatest purchase in the popular imagination.

Aesthetic Surgery and 'Wanting to be White': The Case of Lil' Kim

Aesthetic surgery on Black bodies is overwhelmingly viewed as 'wanting to be white'. What is worth bearing in mind is that white 'female bodies are racialized as well but this racialization is enacted in the assumption of de-racination, racial neutrality and naturalized invisibility' (Candelario 2000: 129). Aesthetic surgery on white bodies is thus 'race'-ing work even if this is not acknowledged or critiqued

---

5   This refers to people from the Dominican Republic rather than people from Dominica.

(Tate 2009). For Margaret Hunter (2005: 63) patients of color who have aesthetic surgery 'do not want to be white *per se*' but, in the United States white beauty is the ideal so even though women do not want to be white they are influenced by these cultural norms. Aesthetic surgery as a 'race'-ing technology can potentially reproduce what are seen to be 'white looks' on Black bodies in the same way that through collagen and implants it reproduces what are seen to be 'Blacker' lips and bottoms on white bodies (Tate 2009). However, the white body and face is only ever seen as enhanced and aesthetic surgery for white women is naturalized as free choice and a sign of socio-economic status.

Ray[6] highlights the relevance of aesthetic surgery for Black beauty when she says

> Yeah look at Lil' Kim. I don't know. She used to be really beautiful but now she's spoiled herself with having all that shit she's done to herself. She has had her breasts done, a nose job and now cheek implants or something. I didn't even know you could get cheek implants.

Ideas from Black anti-racist aesthetics continue into the twenty-first century because Lil' Kim was really beautiful before aesthetic surgery when she was 'natural'. I want to look at the assumptions inherent in understanding the African American rapper Lil' Kim's beauty and its imbrication with the white other. This may help us to see how Blackness and whiteness still operate with exclusionary categories even when we are aware of difference in Black beauty's shades, hair textures, facial features and body shapes in the Black Atlantic diaspora. That is, it will help us to see how the racialized beauty Empire still continues its work of keeping binaries in place. It is important to see how Lil' Kim's face and breasts have been constructed as problems in order to reaffirm Black antiracist aesthetics and white iconicity as guardians of the Black social skin. This emerges through accusations of 'psychic damage', 'white wannabe' and 'Eurocentrism' which reaffirm essentialist ideas of what Black beauty looks like. I see Lil' Kim as being involved in an analysis of the limits imposed on her and going beyond these in a USA where as Hunter (2005) states 'race', skin color, facial features and hair texture matter for social status and mobility. Her changed body questions Black *and* white aesthetics and the institutional practices that uphold them.

> Lil' Kim has said,
> I felt [surgery] would make me have more fun with my photoshoots and enhance my look a bit (Banter 2004: playahata.com).
> Bruce Banter's response is
> It's sad that she believes changing her nose, lip jobs, boob jobs, skin lightening and other changes will make her "more fun and enhance her" because that

---

6   This extract is from research done between 2005-2007 in the UK with Black women in their twenties. She was a 22-year-old student at the time of the interview.

feeling should come from within. Kim doesn't look the same (Banter 2004: playahata.com).

Like other women Lil' Kim talks about 'enhancing' herself as does the aesthetic surgery industry (Hunter 2005). It is not about looking 'the same' and she feels no shame about these procedures, 'I don't understand it. Is it because I'm a black girl from the hood that I get more criticism for it? I say you only live once, so whatever you want to do just do it without offending anybody' (awfulplasticsurgery.us 2006).

As a former working class 'hood' girl who has made good she is supposed to be 'authentic'. As a Black woman consumer of aesthetic surgery she treads the fine line between doing what she wants and causing offence. Offence is caused by what you do with your body as a Black woman and you can be called to account as 'race' and class traitor in a way that white women are not. People are offended because of Black anti-racist aesthetics's/white beauty iconicity's idea that changes Black women make to their bodies are affronts to the Black/white social and political skin. It is not about individual enhancement as for Jordan[7] but Black communal, cultural and political shame.

Lil' Kim is becoming a 'more doll-like European standard after succumbing to a white supremacy dynamic' (Banter 2004). She was even spoken about on 28 May 2008 as looking like 'a cat' (Consuela B. 2008). If we know that Black beauty is multiple, is Black *beauties*, then why this insistence that Lil' Kim is 'whitening herself'? In her 28 May 2008 picture at the premiere of 'Sex and the City' in New York she looked Black though not the same Lil' Kim of 2000 (Consuela B. 2008). She has shown us the potential of aesthetic surgery to change your looks so that you are not the same as you once were because color and known ancestry mean that 'race' is kept alive on her body. She is not passing for anything but herself, a Black woman. In this passing she decenters white beauty as iconic.

I do not share the view that women try to achieve normal bodies through aesthetic surgery so as to remove psychic pain when their defective bodies are 'fixed' (Davis 1995). There is nothing 'normal' about Lil' Kim as she is at pains to make sure we know. She is an active beautifier who creates distinction by constructing her body's cultural capital through her spending power. This removes her from where she started as a poor Black girl from the 'hood' and asserts her new class position. Lil' Kim's aesthetic surgery could equally be seen as a means to enhance status, economic rewards or cross-over value in the Hip Hop business.

She might not be at all engaged in producing the European doll image because this is to assert that she is creating a normalized body through aesthetic surgery. This is a position adopted by some feminists. For example, Kathy Davis (2003a, 2003b) is of the opinion that there is one ideal which is a white Western model which becomes the norm for everyone. Margaret Hunter (2005) also believes

---

7   Jordan is British glamour model and television personality Katie Price who spent £75,000 on aesthetic surgery in 2008.

that if you choose aesthetic surgery you want to be the same as everyone and as the ideal is white then that is what you are aiming to become. Ruth Holliday and Jacqueline Sanchez Taylor (2006) argue, however, that aesthetic surgery as consumption might produce a proliferation of difference. This proliferation of difference is shown by Lil' Kim who as a consumer actively re-makes her body.

Lil' Kim talks about what she has been doing as enhancement 'which does not suggest the transformation of the body of going from one thing to another, but rather working "with" the body' (Holliday and Sanchez Taylor 2006: 189). Lil' Kim is involved in reflexive body work and knows full well that her 'race' cannot be left behind, nor her community abandoned through her body shape, face, color shifting and hair extensions. Perhaps she is negotiating beauty post-Black anti-racist aesthetics in which the 'post' signals an attitude of doing what you like without offending anyone. Her post-Black anti-racist aesthetics attitude on enhancement signifies beauty agency. Nowhere is this more clearly marked than in Lil' Kim's selling of herself as a sex symbol, most obviously through her breast augmentation which hints at the hyper-sexuality contained in her lyrics. Her working class (originally), 'raced' and hyper-sexual body is unfavorably measured against middle class ideals of respectability in both Black and white communities. Lil' Kim is upfront in the creation of a hypersexualized Black woman's body so she is not 'passive but active and desiring (not just desirable)' (Holliday and Sanchez Taylor 2006: 191).

The discussion on Lil' Kim as consumer is significant given that more African Americans than ever before are having aesthetic surgery and one of the most common procedures is the nose job (Hunter 2005). Drawing on Kathyrn Pauly Morgan's (1998) analysis, Hunter states that cosmetic surgery is not about free choice but a colonization of the body by the coercive force to become more beautiful. In the USA this takes the form of procedures which do not enhance 'African, Indian or Asian ethnic features [but] instead [is aimed] toward minimizing them' (Hunter 2005: 59). I cannot deny minimization because that is the nature of the aesthetics and technology of surgery in which idealized white features are regarded as superior. However, what are 'African ethnic features' and what are 'idealized white features' when across the Black Atlantic diaspora our looks are varied? Further, why is 'ethnic' used here as a stand-in for 'racial'? The Black anti-racist aesthetics and white beauty iconicity polemic seeks to deny the existence of a variety of looks in the Black Atlantic diaspora. In this denial some Black women's bodies are marked as problems, as others to be silenced and removed from Black beauty's parameters. Some of this silencing occurs when like Hunter (2005) we insist that Black women are influenced by cultural norms of beauty which are *all* white. However, not *all* of *our* cultural norms of beauty are white. Further, what is seen as white beauty *does not* just naturally belong to white bodies but to Black bodies as well and whiteness is differently nuanced across the Black Atlantic diaspora.

In the twenty-first century Black beauty is a paradox. This is so because the imperative to valorize and perform a static 'natural' Black body beautiful coexists with the normalization of what is seen as 'unnatural' onto the Black body through stylization's race-ing technologies and practices, the rise of Black and Rasta 'chic' and the emergence of the global multicultural beauty, alongside the continuing iconicity of white beauty. These agonistic coexistences mean that the myth is destabilized because it becomes clear that both 'race' and 'beauty' are performative (Tate 2005, 2007, 2009).

Destabilizing the Myth: 'Race' and Beauty as Performative

For Lorraine[8] we are now at a point in our history when some people have changed and see Black beauty positively because they have embraced the idea of naturalness from Black anti-racist aesthetics. However

> Some people – they're trying to buy into like the Black that's white – not like the real Black. I suppose like the Black – Beyoncé like how she's got lighter. The idea of a Black girl now is probably light skin, straight hair, contacts if you can wear them, I reckon.

This observation points to 'hybrid beauty practices' because for Lorraine light skin, straight hair and contact lenses are grafted onto the Black body from elsewhere, from other bodies. Postcolonial beauty mimicry through race-ing stylization means that what was once considered artifice has become naturalized as part of Black beauty. This naturalization produces a wider versioning of Black beauty alongside the continuing place of Black anti-racist aesthetics in both Black beauty politics and stylization. Lorraine also talks about 'the real Black' as opposed to 'the idea of a Black girl now'. 'Real' relates to a Black original with no possibility of white within it, whilst 'idea' points to construction, desire, consumption and race-ing stylization. We know that 'the real Black' was never fixed once and for all and has no origin. However, although they were always shifting and varied in terms of looks and stylization practices 'the real Black' and 'the real white' still function as the beauty binary even in the twenty-first century.

Colonial domination and the racialized beauty Empire has meant that whiteness functions as spectacle and desire in capitalist production as well as being the central organizing core of European imperial conquest of non-white peoples and cultures (McClintock 1995). Hunter (2005) points to the 'racial' nature of the beauty industry where definitions of beauty and the discourse of the new multicultural global beauty serve a very powerful and exclusive 'racial' agenda. So hair coloring and the use of contact lenses are not 'innocent' but a variety of methods to emulate white women's aesthetics. Her point of view is based on Black anti-racist aesthetics in common with Lorraine's. What we need to remember is that white beauty –

---

8   Lorraine was a 21-year-old Black British student at the time of the interview in 2005.

Lorraine's straight hair, contact lenses and light skin – as capitalist commodity, can only ever be approximated by Black women, never possessed, because 'race' halts the slippage between dominant and subjugated bodies. Further, individuals in the Black Atlantic diaspora engage in 'borrowings' for reasons which are not based on wanting to be white but on Black generated beauty ideals as Carolyn Cooper (2004) shows.

Cooper sees a disturbing trend in the Caribbean today of Black women bleaching their faces and necks so as to approximate the 'light skinned' ideal and erase 'racial' identity. The 'mask of lightness' becomes a signifier of status in a racist society that still privileges lightness as a sign of beauty (Cooper 2004: 135). Cooper goes on to show skin bleaching as far more complicated than this in terms of how it is understood by its practitioners in her example of the skin-bleaching DJ. This man had what she came to realize is a 'practical sense of seasonal browning'[9] in which he knew that being browning was *not* an essential part of his identity but a fashion accessory (Cooper 2004: 137). Therefore skin bleaching is not about imitating a white ideal but about presenting the original 'browning' as a construction in a way which is meaningful to the bleacher and which in turn makes his Blackness clear. Relating this to dancehall women in Jamaica Bibi Bakere-Yusuf echoes my point of view in seeing skin bleaching 'as a superficial form of styling' which

> has little to do with a desire for dancehall women to become that which they
> are miming. As a superficial form of styling, bleaching can be thought of as
> another form of adornment, along the same lines as wearing green or pink wigs
> or wearing latex batty riders (Cooper 2004: 139).

Just so that we do not see Black women as having damaged psyches because they engage in this practice Amina Mire (2000) also makes clear that white and Asian (Japanese, Korean, Chinese) women bleach their skins with products from manufacturers like L'Oreal. Apart from the health risks which I am clear must be publicized to *all* communities,[10] why is there such a continuing emphasis on Black women bleaching their skin as wanting to be white when there are light skinned

---

9   Browning is both a sign for aesthetics and embodiment (Tate 2009). The etymology of the word 'browning' is unclear but it is more than likely derived from dancehall lyrics in Jamaica (Jan Mohammed 2000). One suggestion is that this term emerged in the1980s at a time in which there was greater political awareness about the growing imbalances in class in Jamaica (Jan Mohammed 2000). The word browning and its attendant aesthetics have spread from this island through the cultural routes of the Jamaican diaspora. See Tate (2009).

10   Amina Mire (2000) demonstrates how the chemical agents used in skin bleaching creams arrest the synthesis of melanin. This can lead to the complete destruction of the melanocytes. The creams themselves contain chemicals such as mercury, topical corticosteroids and are often carcinogenic. She also speaks about the sexism and racism of the Western medical profession who tend to see skin bleaching as a minor problem of some Black women hoping to pass as white.

Black beauty models available for emulation? This continuing emphasis serves to re-center the racialized beauty Empire's Black/white beauty binary in order to safeguard the Black/ white social skin as it increasingly becomes threatened by race-ing stylizations.

Black women from Lil' Kim to dancehall queens show us that beauty is performative and open to new stylizations. This means that new renderings of a specifically *Black* beauty have always been possible. I am not saying that we are now 'post-white beauty iconicity'. This would be to deny the effectiveness of the racialized beauty Empire aesthetic regimes in shaping what counts as beauty and how beauty is theorized. What I want to do instead is to shift the focus to discourses on and practices of Black beauty which are not centered on *becoming* white but rather on *being* different versionings of Black. A good example of this is the 'Black blonde'.

Black Blondes and the Possibility of Difference

Beauty theorists must move away from being focused on a white ideal and look instead at stylization and its transformational possibilities in terms of both politics and beauty norms. Homi Bhabha (1994) sees mimicry as a strategy of colonial power and knowledge. The colonizer requires that the colonized other adopts *his*[11] norms so as to produce mimic men. Bhabha also sees hybridity as an aspect of mimicry which produces something different from what was entailed through colonial discourse's construction of 'the other'. Hybridity involves beauty's *translation* and inscription onto bodies through the performativity of race-ing stylization which re-produces Black beauty with a difference.

Black beauty becomes translated, becomes *different* from what it once was because of the impact of new spaces and times (Hall 1996). For example, 'the Black blonde' like Beyoncé, has been critiqued since its ascendancy in Black style in the 1990s in Britain without giving a thought to those who are natural Black blondes. Black blondes are criticized for incorporating white norms. Whilst not denying that this might be the case I want to look at this through translation as an imitation which does not reinforce the original but rather displaces it (Bhabha 1990). 'Black blondes', whether natural or not, do not reinforce a white iconic 'original' but question it through locating 'blondeness' on the Black body. This stylization runs counter to the expected answer to discursive positions of hegemonic Black beauty produced through the discourse on white beauty as iconic and, its binary, that of Black anti-racist aesthetics. Within a racialized beauty Empire these discourses

---

11   Anne McClintock (1995) critiques Bhabha's work for its un-gendered mimicry which also ignores class in its focus on 'race'. His mimicry is a male elite strategy which does not distinguish between colonial and anti-colonial mimicry. I think that Bhabha's linkage of mimicry to hybridity makes its anti-colonial potential clear in terms of identifications, politics and ideology. It is this linkage which is the threat to colonial power.

produce hegemonic Black beauty which speaks of the impossibility of difference from the norm and its translation across beauty categories. However, stylization has other possibilities, because that which is seen as 'the other' is also appropriated and inscribed onto the surface of the body. As women like Beyoncé translate what are taken to be 'white looks' onto their bodies there is also a critique of Black anti-racist aesthetics's idea of 'the real Black'. Critique occurs because women's bodies point to these stylizations *as Black* and as *normalized artifice* which is recognized and valued as such. Disruptions of discourses on Black beauty through the translation of 'looks', like 'the Black blonde', occur in the moment of stylization.

There have always been a multitude of Black beauty models and there always will be (Craig 2006). Beauty stylization is something that women engage in with different motivations and politics. What is clear is that there is no 'real Black'. This is the challenge posed by race-ing stylization to white beauty as iconic and Black anti-racist aesthetics's view that changing our natural beauty means that we have internalized racism and despise ourselves. It is a challenge that is produced at every moment that women do something as everyday as having their hair styled and through this practice make Black beauty mobile. Black women's agency is thus central in a discussion of decolonizing beauty studies.

Conclusion: Racialized Agency and Decolonizing Beauty Studies

Decolonizing beauty studies is not aimed primarily at deconstructing Blackness and whiteness as 'racial' formations. Rather, it is about seeing beauty as a racialized discourse divided by performatively produced multiplicity which shapes and redirects Black beauty politics and embodiments in diverse ways. Decolonizing beauty studies means that we have to engage in a disidentification from normative discourses in order to decenter colonial ideas on Black beauty so that other Black *beauties* can be recognized. However, 'Black' as politics and consciousness of African ancestry is still central as twenty-first century 'race' consciousness forms the basis of this disidentification across the Black Atlantic diaspora. Within this 'race' consciousness we are aware that 'race' is performative but also worn on the body and Black cannot be solely equated with male, straight, middle class, national, citizen subjects. Further, 'race' consciousness is not based on Black Nationalist/white supremacist myths of discreetly bounded 'races'. We are now at a space and time in the Black Atlantic diaspora where we have to admit to different forms of collectivity, politics and a theoretical moment in which we can free ourselves from the bonds of raciology and compulsory raciality.

A twenty-first century 'race' consciousness does not imply we are now post-the necessity for 'race' (Ali 2003). We still need narratives of origination and authentication (Young 2000). However, in terms of beauty studies we should focus on the Black beauties that are performatively produced in the inscription of difference from Black/white hegemonic discourses on Black beauty. These Black beauties re-conceptualize Blackness, decenter racial essentialisms and remove beauty from its racialized, hermetically sealed boundaries. Further, Black beauties make use of and construct a hybrid dialogical subjectivity which subverts a politics of Blackness that relies on the self/other binary (Tate 2005, 2007, 2009).

Women's stylization is the performative creation of a decolonizing attitude and embodiment. This is simultaneously based on and constructs a decolonial imaginary which means that within the Black Atlantic diaspora we are inscribed within a Blackness where our dialogical subjectivities are mediated by differences of class, gender, sexuality, gender identity and nationality, for example. Admitting to *differences* challenges the patriarchal, heteronormative and middle class character of Black Nationalist ideologies of global Blackness and Euro/Anglo-centric othering as we engage with a specifically Black antiracist feminism. Such an engagement centers women's narratives and asserts the importance of difference in the construction of our Black Atlantic diasporic experiences and subjectivities in which Blackness must be understood as difference within unity.

References

Ali, S. 2003. *Mixed-Race, Post-Race: Gender, New Ethnicities and Cultural Practices.* Oxford: Berg.

Arrizón, A. 2006. *Queering Mestizaje: Transculturation and Performance.* Ann Arbor: The University of Michigan Press.

awfulplasticsurgery.us 2006. Lil' Kim's Skin Colouring is Disappearing Before our Eyes [Online]. Available at: http://awfulplasticsurgery.us/2006/01/lil_kim_html [accessed: 5 August 2008].

Banks, I. 2000. *Hair Matters: Beauty, Power and Black Women's Consciousness.* New York: New York University Press.

Banter, B. 2004. She's Got Served: The Impending Destruction of Lil' Kim. *playahata.com*, [Online]. Available at: http://www.playahata.com/pages/banner/lilkimdestruction.htm [accessed: 5 June 2008].

Barrett, L. 1977. *The Rastafarians: The Dreadlocks of Jamaica.* Kingston and London: Sangsters/Heinemann Educational Books Ltd.

Bhabha, H. 1990. The Third Space: Interview with Homi Bhabha, in *Identity, Community, Culture, Difference*, edited by J. Rutherford. London: Lawrence and Wishart.

Bhabha, H. 1994. Of Mimicry and Man: The Ambivalence of Colonial Discourse, in *The Location of Culture*, edited by H. Bhabha. London: Routledge.

Black, P. 2004. *The Beauty Industry: Gender, Culture, Pleasure.* London: Routledge.

Brand, P. 2000. Introduction: How Beauty Matters, in *Beauty Matters*, edited by P. Brand. Bloomington: Indiana University Press.

Caldwell, K.L. 2007. *Negras in Brazil: Revisioning Black Women, Citizenship and the Politics of Identity.* London: Rutgers University Press.

Candelario, G. 2000 Hair Raceing: Dominican Beauty Culture and Identity Production. *Meridians: Feminism, Race, Transnationalism*, 1(1), 128-56.

Candelario, G. 2007. *Black Behind the Ears: Dominican Racial Identity from Museums to Beauty Shops*. Durham: Duke University Press.

Césaire, A. 2000. *Discourse on Colonialism*, translated by J. Pinkham. New York: Monthly Review Press.

Collins, P.H. 2004. *Black Sexual Politics: African Americans, Gender and the New Racism*. London: Routledge.

Cooper, C. 2004. *Sound Clash: Jamaican Dancehall Culture at Large*. Basingstoke: Palgrave Macmillan.

Consuela, B. 2008. Lil' Kim Plastic Surgery. *Rightcelebrity*, [Online]. Available at: http://celebrity.rightpundits.com/?p=3797 [accessed: 5 June 2008].

Craig, M.L. 2002. *Ain't I a Beauty Queen? Black Women, Beauty, and the Politics of Race*. Oxford: Oxford University Press.

Craig, M.L. 2006. Race, Beauty and the Tangled Knot of Guilty Pleasure. *Feminist Theory*, 7(2), 159-77.

Davis, K. 1995. *Reshaping the Female Body: The Dilemma of Cosmetic Surgery*. London: Routledge.

Davis, K. 2003a. *Dubious Equalities and Embodied Differences: Cultural Studies on Cosmetic Surgery.* Lanham: Rowman and Littlefield.

Davis, K. 2003b. Surgical Passing: Or why Michael Jackson's Nose Makes 'Us' Uneasy. *Feminist Theory*, 4(1), 73-92.

Figueiredo, A. 2002. *Ebony Goddess: 24th Black Beauty Night-Ilê Aiyé*.

Gimlin, D.L. 2002. *Body Work: Beauty and Self-Image in American Culture*. London: University of California Press.

Hall, S. 1996. What is this Black in Black Popular Culture?', in *Stuart Hall: Critical Dialogues in Cultural Studies*, edited by D. Morley and K. Chen. London: Routledge.

Hardt, M. and Negri, A. 2000. *Empire*. Cambridge: Harvard University Press.

Hobson, J. 2005. *Venus in the Dark: Blackness and Beauty in Popular Culture*. Abingdon: Routledge.

Holliday R. and Sanchez Taylor J. 2006. Aesthetic Surgery as False Beauty. *Feminist Theory*, 7, 179-95.

hooks, b. 1993. *Sisters of the Yam: Black Women and Self-Recovery*. London: Routledge.

Hunter, M. 2005. *Race, Gender and the Politics of Skin Tone*. Abingdon: Routledge.

Jan Mohammed, P. 2000. 'But Most of All Mi Love Me Browning': The Emergence in Eighteenth and Nineteenth Century Jamaica of the Mulatto Woman as Desired. *Feminist Review*, 65(Summer), 22-48.

Jeffreys, S. 2005. *Beauty and Misogyny: Harmful Cultural Practices in the West*. London: Routledge.

Kant, I. 1914. *Critique of Judgement*, 2nd Edition, translated by J.H. Barnard. London: Macmillan and Co. Ltd.

Kuipers, D. (ed.) 2001. *I Am Iman*. New York: Universe Publishing.

Mama, A. 1995. *Beyond the Masks: Race, Gender and Subjectivity*. London: Routledge.

McClintock, A. 1995. *Imperial Leather: Race, Gender and Sexuality in the Colonial Contest*. London: Routledge.

Mercer, K. 1994. Black Hair Style/Politics, in *Welcome to the Jungle: New Positions in Black Cultural Studies*, edited by K. Mercer. London: Routledge.

Mire, A. 2000. Skin-Bleaching: Poison, Beauty, Power and the Politics of the Colour line. *New Feminist Research*, 3/4(28), 13-38.

Nuttall, S. 2006. Introduction: Rethinking Beauty, in *Beautiful Ugly: African and Diaspora Aesthetics*, edited by S. Nuttall. London: Duke University Press.

Pinho, P. 2006. Afro-aesthetics in Brazil, in *Beautiful Ugly: African and Diaspora Aesthetics*, edited by S. Nuttall. London: Duke University Press.

Rooks, N.M. 2000. *Hair Raising: Beauty, Culture and African American Women*. London: Rutgers University Press.

Russell, K., Wilson, M. and Hall, R. 1992. *The Color Complex: The Politics of Skin Color Among African Americans*. New York: Doubleday.

Stephens, M. 2005. *Black Empire: The Masculine Global Imaginary of Caribbean Intellectuals in the United States 1914-1962*. Durham and London: Duke University Press.

Tate, S. 2005. *Black Skins, Black Masks: Hybridity, Dialogism, Performativity*. Aldershot: Ashgate.

Tate, S. 2007. What's Shade Got to Do with It? Anti-Racist Aesthetics and Black Beauty. *Ethnic and Racial Studies*, 30(2), 300-19.

Tate, S. 2009. *Black Beauty: Aesthetics, Stylization, Politics*. Aldershot: Ashgate.

Taylor, P. 2000. Malcolm's Conk and Danto's Colors: or Four Logical petitions Concerning Race, Beauty, Aesthetics, in *Beauty Matters*, edited by P.Z. Brand. Bloomington: Indiana University Press, 57-66.

Tseëlon, E. 1995. *The Mask of Femininity: The Presentation of Woman in Everyday Life*. London: Sage Publications.

Weekes, D. 1997. Shades of Blackness: Young Black Female Constructions of Beauty, in *Black British Feminism: A Reader*, edited by H.S. Mirza. London: Routledge.

Wek, A. 2007. *Alek: Sudanese Refugee to International Supermodel*. London: Virago Press.

White, S.B. 2005. Releasing the Pursuit of Bouncin' and Behavin' Hair: Natural Hair as an Afrocentric Feminist Aesthetic of Beauty. *International Journal of Media and Cultural Politics*, 1(3), 295-308.

Wingfield, A.H. 2008. *Doing Business with Beauty – Black Women, Hair Salons and the Racial Enclave Economy*. Plymouth: Rowman and Littlefield Publishers.

Wright, M. 2004. *Becoming Black – Creating Identity in the African Diaspora*. Durham and London: Duke University Press.

Young, L. 2000. Hybridity's Discontents: Rereading Science and "Race"', in *Hybridity and its Discontents: Politics, Science, Culture,* edited by A. Brah and A.E. Coombes. London: Routledge.

PART V
Looking South

Chapter 13

South of Every North

Franco Cassano

The Solipsism of the Colonizer

In this chapter, I will briefly discuss the phenomena of fundamentalism, universalism, and inequality in order to show how a view from the South can help decolonize ruling understandings of these concepts in current sociology, that is to say, Northwestern sociology.

Etymologically speaking, the words "culture" and "colonization", take their roots from the Latin verb *colere*. The colonizer is convinced that his mission is to cultivate and render the earth productive and fertile, otherwise it will be condemned to sterility. The colonizer is the only one who has the right to appropriate land because only he knows how to cultivate land and make it fertile. It is only his culture that can bring about humanity's progress. In this world of colonies and still uncultivated land, the culture and rights of the other are inevitably eradicated. Whoever opposes this trajectory works against the progress of mankind – and history is full of graveyards where the enemies of "progress" have been buried.

If the colonizer is primarily a solipsist, for him the other is nothing more than a nuisance and hindrance. Decolonizing means above all overcoming solipsism, abandoning the false conviction that, from among all cultures that make up the world, only one culture has a license to truth. Decolonizing means breaking with the monologue of the colonizer, recognizing that the world and life can be observed from many different perspectives. The relationship between the colonizer and the colonized is illuminated by an old African myth involving two different masks. The European mask has a big mouth and small ears. The African mask, on the other hand, has a small mouth and big ears. The European mask speaks but fails to hear. The African mask cannot speak but is forced to hear. Decolonizing means transforming the two masks, giving each the same size mouth and the same size ears.

Decolonizing knowledge does not therefore mean impoverishing knowledge, but giving voice to those that the colonizer has long cast aside, and restoring the history of peoples whose stories have always been told by others. If modern colonialism has coincided with the assumption that the culture of the North is the only universally acceptable cultural standard, decolonizing must entail the radical deconstruction of this assumption. The cultures of the South are not vestiges of the past which humanity must rid itself of, but distinct voices that must continue to be heard. The South must not be seen merely as "backward", as a mixture of misery and superstition that needs to be superseded by the North. The South represents another way of looking at the world that is not obsessed with progress and competition. A world suffocated by unlimited growth needs to discover the wisdom of a way of life that does not seek to violate the Earth but rather recognizes the limits of exploitation. Progress does not mean becoming like the North, but recognizing the wisdom that exists in all cultures. Decolonizing means living in Babel without fear and anguish. It means not yearning for the unique language of the colonizer, but embracing all languages. Only by learning the difficult art of *translation* that presupposes the existence of the other can one overcome the solipsist worldview of the colonizer.

Western fundamentalism

Religious fanaticism in the guise of Islamic fundamentalism has become a ghastly spectre for the West. The West defends itself from acts of terror, but at the same time justifies its values by opposing them to the "intégrisme" of its adversaries. It opposes its values to a way of life that appears as both archaic and repressive, that is hostile to women's rights and every kind of liberty, and suspicious of any kind of civil independence from the religious sphere. While this glib and bleak vision of the enemy, upheld by the American neo-conservatives, has long held sway over the West's riposte to the events of 11 September, it is only perhaps now the United States has begun to delineate an alternative to the neo-con vision. We shall see.

Actually, the fight against fundamentalism is justifiable only on the condition that it is not instrumentalized. Criticism should be directed against all forms of fundamentalism and not as a blanket of criticism against other ways of life. Our notion is that the fight against fundamentalism should not be abandoned, but should be intensified. To proceed on this course, however, it is essential to arrive at a precise definition of fundamentalism. If it is not only a form of religious extremism, what is fundamentalism?

We would like to put forward the following definition. *Fundamentalism is an expansionist form of ethnocentricity.* Ethnocentricity can be defined as a particular type of belief that characterizes the culture of almost all peoples, or ethnic groups. Under the influence of ethnocentricity, peoples will see themselves as blessed with special qualities. They will see themselves as living at the centre of the universe, as being chosen by God, and as representing the highest and most perfect form of human life, as opposed to others peoples who constitute a poor and imperfect copy of Mankind. The clearest and most famous example of ethnocentricity is encapsulated in the Greek word "barbaro" and its onomatopoeic echo of the babble of speech of non-Hellenic peoples. The inability to understand a foreign tongue is transformed into the other's inability to speak except in terms of a pathetic babble. With one fell swoop, one's own limitations are cancelled and transformed into the limitations of the other. Clearly, disdain for the other is not only a monopoly of the ancient Greeks. Many cultures possess a similar word that both describes and in some way disparages the diversity of the other. This basic belief, which is common to all peoples, serves to reassure them before the incredible diversity of human life, just as the erroneous conviction of being placed by God at the centre of things has allowed man to endure the vastness of the universe.

If ethnocentrism can certainly induce one people, or ethnic group to insist on the conviction of its own superiority, and that of another ethnic group's inferiority, it might be thought of as a necessary, though not the sole condition for fundamentalism. *Fundamentalism is born when ethnocentrism becomes active* and begins to perceive in difference and diversity a constant danger and threat to its existence and the integrity of its beliefs. This fear changes the situation radically, since it is incompatible with pacifism and acquiescence. If the other constitutes a threat, the only solution is to eliminate it by propagating one's own values and beliefs and suppressing the evil the other represents by its mere existence. It is then that ethnocentrism begins its conquering march by promoting a world of uniformity and reducing the plurality of culture to a single culture, its own. This explains why fundamentalism is often accompanied by a strong ethnic impulse. The man on a mission from God is convinced he is working not just for his own but the good of the other; eradicating the diversity of the other coincides with his own salvation and liberation. Armed with such good motives, fundamentalism does not hear the cry of the other. It expropriates, represses and kills with sublime indifference.

If one accepts this broad definition of fundamentalism, it becomes impossible to deny that not only is Europe not immune to, but has been for centuries the greatest exponent of fundamentalism. It is worth remembering a famous episode illustrating this tendency. Hardly had he set foot in "India", than Columbus christened the island where he had landed, San Salvador. It simply did not occur to him that the land already had a name and a God. Those who lived on the land were "savages", beings of inferior stock, who, regardless of their consent, had to be converted to civilization and truth, or reduced without scruple and thought to slavery. The metaphor of "discovery" was nothing less than a concealment of the "conquest" of America by the Europeans. Once the "new" world was confiscated from its occupants, they were in turn obliged to accept a "new" language, "new" customs and "new" God. In this exclusive relationship with God one can see something almost sinister. From the Spanish conquerors to the Pilgrim Fathers, a dialogue was constructed to the exclusion of the other. The "indigenous" peoples were seen as part of a tiresome backdrop of resistance. The great narratives of the "Conquistadores" and settlers glorify Evangelization, discovery and progress where progress means to "go on" and "march" all over "native" lands. The march of "European progress" through the centuries after the conquest explains how the world, with the exception of China, became at the start of the twentieth century a mosaic of European provinces, a conglomerate of states whose borders were often defined by the European governments.

If it is now possible to define more clearly what we have called Western fundamentalism; fundamentalism takes its particular characteristics from a universalist ambition to absorb the entire world within itself and see every limit against its expansion as an unjustifiable opposition to truth and justice. If the form of this ambition can mutate, the ambition nevertheless remains to proclaim the good news, the so-called Evangelization of the world, by exporting the institutions and life style of the West. If one first exports truth, then civilization and finally wealth, the logic is that world government will fall into the hands of those who have invented these universal remedies. Even when it claims to be above any conditioning, the universalism of the West always comes back to a general and abstract idea of humanity that is in fact neither general nor abstract.

Universalism is therefore undermined by an incurable contradiction. If there is a centre from which truth emanates, the world will only have one version of the truth. It will always be a world arranged and organized by those arbiters of truth – while the truth is destined to be left on the margins of other cultures where it will – only later – be projected through chance copies of the original. The conviction that abstract values predominate in a universalized world masks the fact that universal values are really those of one particular culture. There are no universal principles, but only the universalistic disguises of principles of one lot of peoples.

All of this explains how, with the collapse of the colonial system, Western Fundamentalism has not just disappeared, but mutated. Now universalism is dressed up in terms of equality of opportunity and competition in the marketplace. All are invited to take part in the race of "progressive" nations. There are no more colonies and metropolis, inferior peoples and inaccessible hierarchies. Now there exist only differences in development, and historical backwardness in accessing wealth and welfare. In this new picture other peoples are formally independent, but must bow to the twin objectives of progress and modernization. Those nations who aspire to the same standards of living as the West must – of necessity – westernize by ridding themselves of their traditions and converting to the new religion of development and continuous growth. Cultures where profit and progress have been subordinated for thousands of years to values that cannot be expressed simply in economic terms have become, all of a sudden, obstacles to modernization – open air prisons run by satraps wielding the whip of superstition. The game appears open to all, but the trick is always the same. If some cultures are at the point of departure, others at the point of arrival, hierarchy has become impersonal. The "loser" nations can no longer impute their lack of success to the political, economic and military power of the "winners", but must look to themselves for answers.

Ultimately this process has gathered pace with the collapse of Communism and the advent of globalization. Movement of capital now knows no bounds; capitalism moves at high speed to invest as and where it wishes to realize its profits. Profit and competition have become the cornerstones of a global economy that fails to look beyond itself and begins to dump on the social and natural environment to pernicious effect. Political development has been entrusted to the International Monetary Fund and the World Bank, institutions that kow-tow to market fundamentalism (Stiglitz 2002, Soros 2002), and remain indifferent to its most obvious falsifications. Facing crisis and slump, some have even begun to preach the necessity of saving capitalism from the capitalists (Rajan and Zingales 2003). With a mix of ingenuity and cynicism it is maintained that capitalism is a near perfect, unquestionable system. It is only individual capitalists who make mistakes. The old magic trick of spinning dogma, dear to the church and Party System, is re-born under the shadow of the high prestige North and Western European universities.

If today a heavy blow has been inflicted on the hegemony of global capitalism, and its axioms no longer seem entirely safe, nothing can be taken for granted. Western fundamentalism possesses a remarkable capacity for transformation that allows it to reproduce in different shapes and guises. The task of provincializing Europe (Chakrabarty 2000) is a long-term project that requires unusual ways, the abandonment of old certainties and a singular appetite for change.

Towards a Critique of Universalism: Religion and Climate

If, as here argued, western fundamentalism goes hand in glove with his universalism, it becomes an obligation for the social scientist to de-colonize thought and deconstruct the universalist ambition. If universalism is seen for what it is, a sophisticated form of organizing hierarchy, the key point of critical analysis is to shed light on its non-universalist roots and expose the confidence trick by which it presents what is good for some as good for all.

As we have already seen, tribal customs posited as universal law have been used to consolidate hierarchical power. Cultures that do not adhere to the "universal" principle become at best stepping-stones on the way to building superior states where "universal" culture holds sway. The hierarchy is between those who remain true to themselves and those who undergo a radical transformation of customs and values. One team always plays at home; the other teams are always obliged to play away under the glare of hostile fans and referees biased in favour of the home crowd. The word *modernization*, widely employed in the social sciences from the fifties to the seventies, has come to legitimise this cultural genocide. How would you feel if someone turned up at your house to change all the rooms and furniture, then shoved you in the cupboard under the stairs and told you to come out only when he said?

The confidence trick, whereby a people's historically and geographically bound customs and practices are subsumed in the universal model can be shown for what it is by turning to a key reference point of European social science. If we follow Max Weber's argument linking capitalism and the pursuit of wealth to the ethics of Protestantism (Weber 1920-21), we can begin to see cracks in the argument of universalism. According to Weber, it is through Calvinist sobriety and the rationalization of daily life in terms of the profit motive that a privileged relationship has been forged with capitalism and shaped the means of production that have subsequently led to global hegemony. If one accepts Weber's argument, and allows that Protestantism has offered a springboard to the adventure of the spirit of modern capitalism, one can see that those countries with strong Protestant traditions are inevitably more advantaged than those with other religious traditions. In Protestant countries the pursuit of wealth is socially approved of since worldly success is seen as a sign of pre-destination and salvation.

It goes without saying that this point of departure imposes certain limits on the exportability of capitalism. Certainly the rapid development of Chinese capitalism, as many have argued, poses a threat to Weber's argument, pace the Euro-centric roots of capitalism. This, however, is to miss the point. While the success of Confucian capitalism clearly shows that other religious traditions have a part to play in capitalist expansion, the fact that both Confucian and Protestant versions of capitalism have succeeded does not mean that the development of capitalism is favoured by all religious traditions. If, as many have claimed, the axis of history is shifting gradually eastwards, from Manchester to Shanghai, this does not mean that all countries and all peoples are following suit. As inequality grows apace, some may well succeed, while others, already weak, are increasingly marginalized. If, as seems clear, the shift towards the East is making great waves after centuries of Western and European dominance, the rise in power and influence of China has served to complicate and widen the problem. Is the culture of progress, as proposed in these two very different forms, the only acceptable form of progress? What will happen to those peoples whose religious traditions in no way identify with capitalism? Must they live forever in the pocket of wealthy nations and see themselves consigned to the dustbin of history? Must they prepare for cultural extinction and colonization according to the sacred texts of some other tradition? Must the value of a culture only be seen in terms of its military and industrial power?

If therefore one accepts the Weberian argument and takes into account the necessary amendments to the general thesis regarding the role of religious tradition in the development of capitalism, one is struck by its effect in the division between the have and have-nots. Those nations condemned to living on the margins of the system live often with frustration and impotent rage at the prostitution of their culture and the spectre of organized crime that barely allows them to scrape a living within the global market.

The non-universalist roots of universalism, and the link between capitalism and a historically and geographically determined culture cannot only be seen in the influence of religious tradition, and the Calvinist glorification of profit as identified by Weber. As in a detective story, everything begins with a strange disappearance, that of the climate, and a near neglect in the social sciences of climate and its influence on practice and customs. Montesquieu's observations at the beginning of the Enlightenment in *Esprit des lois* are a famous if somewhat isolated case in point. Here the distinction is made between Northern and Southern peoples. If the former are seen as civilized, rational and hardworking, the latter are capricious and undisciplined, incapable of organization and work (Montesquieu 1949, Dainotto 2007). As Leopardi, a careful reader of Montesquieu, notes in an insightful passage from *Zibaldone*, however, modernity must be seen as a historical phase of transition from the Southern hegemony of Antiquity to the Northern hegemony of modern times (Leopardi 1988). The inference from this reading of Montesquieu is that the temperate climes of Northern Europe have acted as a kind of springboard for global hegemony, because the Northern climate promotes the rise of the work ethic. If this form of life becomes the universal standard of perfection, it is not difficult to understand how a hierarchy of peoples and countries has been constructed.

If, however, Montesquieu speaks frankly of climate and its influence, references to climate gradually disappear from social science literature to the point where we can speak of a total *"desaparecido"* of climate, and a complicitous silence hanging over the notion of climatic influence. At this point, the question becomes inevitable. Is this disappearance merely accidental, and due to absent-mindedness? Or are there powerful, unspoken reasons governing its neglect in social science textbooks? And if the answer is the latter, what are the motives? *Who has – so to speak – murdered climate?* The solution is simpler than that of a detective story. The murderer is all too clearly universalism – a universalism that sees in racial or climatic differences a possible obstacle in its necessary promotion of norms and universal values. To recognize the impact of climate would mean recognizing that the so-called Manchesterian vision of progress is possible only in the so-called Northern, temperate climes. Indeed, such efforts to export the system of production favoured by temperate climes to the Libyan desert, for example, or the Afghan hills or rainforests of South America, have often proved disastrous.

One sure effect of the disappearance of climate from social science discourse has been to posit the failure to modernize in terms of the cultural "weakness" of peoples from warmer climes. Together with this can be seen a kind of spiritualization of the concept of culture that dislocates it from the natural environment. If climate can only be manipulated through the extravagant use of technology and resources, it is much easier to attribute the failure to modernize and take off in the grand European style to cultural failings. Once the impact of climate is removed from discourse, everything depends on the capacity for cultural transformation. Every people must convert to the dominant culture and give itself up to the lifestyle of the developed world. Bearing the scars of these failed attempts to become more like the North, the South would appear to live in confusion and uncertainty. Like someone looking in at the goodies in the shop windows, either it accepts defeat or, as already pointed out, resorts to illegal means.

If the truth is that climate exerts a powerful influence on peoples and life style (Landes 1998), the underlying assumption in the social sciences that climate does not exist must be seen not only as a simple error, but what Freud would have called a form of *displacement*. Competition is apparently based on equality of opportunity, but in reality is always fixed in favour of those who, according to Montesquieu's definition of climate, are naturally born to discipline and rationality. In other words, this notion of competition has been determined by the strongest. In this race, the Southern character, which operates under a different climate and in a different value system and therefore appears to have none of the favoured attributes proposed by the Parsons' recipe for modernization (1966), has little or no role to play.

The great trick has been to structure universal criteria on Northwest European character traits, and then, with a sleight of hand, occlude the role of religion and climate in generating success. If – to use a metaphor – the gazelle manages to persuade the rest of the animals that speed is the criterion for winning, the gazelle nearly always wins. Winning becomes the norm for the gazelle, and losing is for the other "lesser" animals. The advantages of Protestantism and temperate climate are not for all nations. Universalism as we know it has been a fixed race from the very beginning.

Sophisticated Universalism

One source for a critique for Eurocentrism involving a more sophisticated universalism can be found in the work of Edward Said, whose *Orientalism* (1978) is a key text for comparative culture studies. Said's now famous argument is that the European view of other cultures, particularly oriental cultures, has exacerbated the conflict between East and West by constructing a body of literature, namely Orientalism. In this view, the East is identified with characteristics such as sensuality, mystery, intrigue, irrationality and mysticism that are nearly always in opposition to those of the West. Said rightly critiques this body of work, underlining the point that the East as depicted here perpetuates a cliché mix of exoticism and racism with its roots in the colonial experience that has rendered communication between cultures virtually impossible. Said takes with a pinch of salt an orientalism that by exulting cultural difference, ends up contributing to the clash of cultures. According to Said, the emphasis on cultural diversity, which characterizes postmodernism, ends up giving the keepers of tradition such power that it stands in the way of change. A relativist critique of universalism brings with it a serious risk – namely that of frustrating efforts to interpret and communicate between cultures.

Similar assumptions have inspired Amartya Sen's polemic regarding the supporters of the so-called "Asian values", which are seen in direct opposition to those of the West. As with Said, Sen also fears that insistence on cultural heterogeneity will end up legitimizing authoritarian regimes, keeping democracy out and opening up a cultural abyss between East and West. It comes as no surprise that Sen has recently taken a line against seeing culture as a clash of civilizations. In a lively debate with Huntington (1996) and Kagan (2003) regarding the invasion of Iraq, Sen argues against reducing the complexity and majesty of Islamic culture to a self referential warrior spirit (2006). Shedding light on the lay characteristics of Indian culture, notably its scepticism and rationalism (2005), he has also overthrown the orientalist image of mystics and castes, dear to many western intellectuals. The assumption of cultural heterogeneity and East-West polarity must be constantly refuted if it is to stop feeding into a spiral of incomprehension and retaliation.

The views of other important sociologists have also to some extent been shaped by a more sophisticated universalism (Goody 2006, Blaut 1993 and 2000). In his most recent work Goody, for example, has critiqued classical social thought and the emphasis on the cultural heterogeneity of the West, and its exclusive hold on progress and modernity. From other, more accurate studies, the thesis of radical difference and oneness of western tradition would appear more fragile than has previously been thought. Concepts of reason and liberty, mobility and secularization are not an exclusive product of the West. The fact that "cultural values" have been effectively "stolen" by the West has been steadfastly ignored. So it is:

> Many of those values such as humanism and charity so often considered a virtue
> of Christianity as well as the holy trinity of individualism, equality and liberty
> that have undeniably existed in other societies have been appropriated through
> an act of piracy by western democracy. (Goody 2006)

This can be seen as an authentic deconstruction of the old Eurocentrism, and an important if belated compensation for the thefts done by the West to non-Europeans.

The list of values expropriated by western culture may be long, but what interests us specifically is the difference between critique of Eurocentrism presented above and the Said-Sen critique. If, on the one hand, pluralism critiques the claim of *homo occidentalis* to present his culture as universal culture, the Said-Sen line critiques Eurocentrism in the name of a more sophisticated and rigorous universalism. With Eurocentrism, Europe and the West are presented as the safeguards of all constructive values to the exclusion of other cultures. This, however, is nothing more than a false, Manichaean version of reality, from which even the great sociologists such as Elias, Braudel and Weber with their emphasis on the exceptionality of Western culture are not immune.

The importance of this line of research cannot be denied, even if it does have its limitations. If the hope is to bridge the gap between civilizations, it can only be a one-sided exchange, since bias remains with the European tradition. While it shows that avowedly European values are present elsewhere, what happens when the values of other cultures aren't reflected in western tradition? Are the values extraneous to western tradition only an amalgam of backwardness, superstition and repression? Is there anything worth knowing and learning beyond these values?

In this critique of Eurocentrism it appears that only that which falls within the boundaries set by western culture is sought out for appraisal. While this allows for a degree of communication between the West and other cultures, the debate is set only in terms which suit western goals. There appears to be no real exchange; it is never asked, for example, if the West might have something vitally important to learn from other cultures. Convergence remains one way traffic, because the only meeting that really takes place is with some small pocket of non-European reality – one that invariably aspires to enter the universalist fold. If, therefore, we have before us a more sophisticated and generous version of universalism than the classical one, it is not wholly immune to the clarion call of Eurocentrism.

Inequality: South of Every Centre

From the perspectives discussed above one can divine two different critiques of Eurocentrism. In the first case (pluralistic way) Eurocentrism is accused of presenting Western values as universal values. In the second case, Eurocentrism is accused of eradicating all traces of the universal from other cultures and establishing a unique depository of values. If one is serious, however, about the task of building friendship and trust between cultures, one needs to take into account both perspectives. If pluralism allows us to accept diversity, one must recognize that a plurality of cultures cannot exist without constructing a network between cultures. *The universal values of the future can only be constructed if many hands are involved.*

This conclusion would be incomplete, however, without recognising the power differential between cultures and its influence on the mechanisms that determine their interaction. The paradigm of dependence between geographical areas was once widely accepted within social sciences. Accordingly, under-developed areas were not thought of as being merely behind more developed areas, but rather as victims of systematic exploitation and expropriation by more developed areas. Development and underdevelopment were not seen therefore as indicators of inequality between processes of modernization, but rather constituted two sides of the same coin. Progress and modernization in Europe would have been inconceivable without the subjugation of its colonies. Today, if this view is somewhat less influential, as much because its inherent pessimism has been discounted by the recent rise and success of the "Asian tigers", more sophisticated versions have come to the fore (Wallerstein 2004, Arrighi 2007).

While structural equality has been largely marginalized in recent social science studies, this has opened the way to the hegemony of the belated liberal view. In this reading, the confrontational, often tragic side of competition is blithely ignored. Differences in levels of development are reduced to levels of competitiveness between countries, as if all the competitors involved were running in straight lines without any interference from each other. Whichever nation occupies the top spot has not only invariably built on the back of other nations, but has no intention of yielding to those nations coming up behind. Economic doctrines do not concern themselves with the conflicts, and, for that matter, wars that accompany the struggle for the top spot, but are happy to delegate these problems and their disastrous consequences for intellectual learning to other disciplines. If, however, we wish to decolonize the social sciences, it means not just re-evaluating the gravity of external and internal conflicts, a theme that is palpably absent from the neoliberal view, but it also means re-evaluating the bitterness of inequality. This is perhaps the kernel of our argument. Whether inequality is consigned to the neoliberal paradigm of competition or to the postmodern paradigm of difference, it becomes almost as invisible as the power differential between countries and classes, and then it continues to grow.

If we can now bring our argument to a conclusion, the task of decolonizing European sociology and provincializing Europe is a long, complex process with many passages that need exploring. It cannot only be a theoretical process, but requires other voices, particularly those from the South to be heard. If at the moment these voices are weak, there is a reassuring sign and recognition of the fact that the South must reacquire its independence of thought (Cassano 1996, Mignolo 2005, De Sousa Santos 2000, Connell 2007). While it may be true that the struggle for independence is exacerbated by the unequal delineation of power between North and South which undermines solidarity and leads to political divisiveness and cultural prostitution, one perceives a new consciousness growing in the South.

Indeed, the very weakness of the South allows it to keep a clear mind and deconstruct Eurocentrism. If it fears the imposition of North-western values, and the new threat comes from the North-east, the South refuses to recognise this eventuality. It sees the conflict between Protestant Capitalism and Confucian Capitalism as a conflict that is of no concern to it, and as a war of succession between centres equally far from itself. The South is the bearer of a world that has not been colonized by production. Neither does it exalt Protestant austerity nor does it succumb to the Confucian pressures of the profit motive.

Finally, there remains a part of the European tradition that is not insensitive to the problems of the South, that refuses to defend the high and mighty, and sides with the poor and weak. There is much to be admired in this universalism that believes in the necessity of freedom and equality, *even against the West*. But this "generous" universalism, too, has to learn the South's lesson.

It has to be acknowledged, however, that – being that much closer to wisdom and tolerance and the eternal rhythms of everyday life then it is to vice-like grip of clock watching and time keeping that has condemned the rich and powerful – the South also has something to teach. A degree of equality for the South is not just an idle, Jacobin fancy, but a way to keep our feet firmly on the ground. The world needs the South more than it does the self-interest and historical universalism of the North. Only when the North realizes that to be saved from its pathological self, it must become more like the South, will mankind make real progress.

Bibliography

Arrighi, G. 2007. *Adam Smith in Beijing, Lineages of the Twenty-First Century.* London and New York: Verso.

Blaut, J.M. 1993. *The Colonizer's Model of the World: Geographical Diffusionism and Eurocentric History*. New York: Guilford.

Blaut, J.M. 2000. *Eight Eurocentric Historians*. New York: Guilford.

Cassano, F. 1996. *Il pensiero meridiano*. Roma-Bari: Laterza.

Chakrabarty, D. 2000. *Provincializing Europe. Postcolonial Thought and Historical Difference*. Princeton: Princeton University Press.

Connell, R. 2007. *Southern Theory. Social Science and the Global Dynamics of Knowledge*. Sydney: Allen & Unwin.

Dainotto, R.D. 2007. *Europe (in Theory)*. Durham and London: Duke University Press.

Goody, J. 2006. *The Theft of History*. Cambridge: Cambridge University Press.

Huntington, S. 1996. *The Clash of Civilizations and the Remaking of World Order*. New York: Simon & Schuster.

Kagan, R. 2003. *Of Paradise and Power. America and Europe in the New World Order*. New York: Knopf.

Landes, D.S. 1998. *The Wealth and Poverty of Nations*. New York and London: Norton.

Leopardi, G. 1988. Zibaldone di pensieri, in *Tutte le opere vol. II*, edited by W. Binni and E. Ghidetti. Firenze: Sansoni.

Mignolo, W.D. 1995: *The Darker Side of the Renaissance: Literacy, Territoriality, and Colonization*. Ann Arbor: University of Michigan Press.

Montesquieu, C. de. 1949. *Oeuvres complètes*. Paris: Gallimard.

Parsons, T. 1966. *Societies: Evolutionary and Comparative Perspectives*. Englewood Cliffs, New Jersey: Prentice-Hall.

Rajan, R.G. and Zingales, L. 2003. *Saving Capitalism from the Capitalists*. New York: Crown Business.

Said, E.W. 1978. *Orientalism*. New York: Pantheon Books.

Sen, A. 2005. *The Argumentative Indian: Writings on Indian History, Culture and Identity*. New York: Farrar, Straus and Giroux.

Sen, A. 2006. *Identity and Violence: The Illusion of Destiny*. New York and London: Norton.

Soros, G. 2002. *George Soros on Globalization*. New York and London: Public Affairs.

Stiglitz, J.E. 2002. *Globalization and its Discontents*. New York and London: Norton.

Wallerstein, I. 2004. *World-Systems Analysis: An Introduction*. Durham: Duke University Press.

Weber, M. 1920-21. *Gesammelte Aufsätze zur Religionssoziologie*. Tübingen: Mohr.

Chapter 14

From the Postmodern
to the Postcolonial – and Beyond Both

Boaventura de Sousa Santos

When, in the mid-1980s, I started using such phrases as "postmodern" and "postmodernity", my context was the epistemological debate. I had reached the conclusion that science in general, and not just the social sciences, was presided over by an epistemological paradigm and a model of rationality that were all but exhausted. The signs of exhaustion were so clear that we could even speak of a crisis of paradigm.

Although the then emerging cultural and social studies of science loomed large in my mind, my argument against this paradigm resided mainly in the epistemological reflection of the scientists themselves, of physicists in particular, which showed that the dominant paradigm had less and less to do with the scientists' scientific practice. This discrepancy, while giving credibility to the critique of the negative consequences of modern science, suggested as well a number of epistemological alternatives, pointing to an emergent paradigm that at the time I designated as postmodern science. As its very name indicates, in my conception, postmodern science had to do with privileging scientific knowledge, while arguing for a broader rationality for science. It implied superseding the nature/society dichotomy; taking into account the complexity of the subject/object relation; relying on a constructivist conception of truth; and bringing the natural sciences closer to the social sciences, and the latter closer to the humanities. It called for a new relation between science and ethics, requiring that science be applied not only in a technical, but also in an edifying way. Finally, it was based on a new, more balanced articulation between scientific knowledge and other forms of knowledge, with a view to transforming science into a new common sense. For this new articulation I proposed the concept of *double epistemological break*. In the years that followed, this epistemological proposition evolved and was consolidated with contributions from feminist epistemology and the cultural and social studies of science.

In the early 1990s, the crisis of capitalism, together with the crisis of socialism in the eastern European countries, led me to broaden the concept of postmodern/ postmodernity. Rather than a mere epistemological paradigm, it designated as well a new social and political paradigm. The next step was to conceive of social transformation beyond capitalism, as well as beyond the theoretical and practical alternatives to capitalism produced by western modernity. The epistemological transition and the social and political transition were conceived of as autonomous and subject to different logics, dynamics and rhythms, but as complementary, as well.

I advised from the start that the designation "postmodern" was inadequate, not only because it defined the new paradigm in the negative, but also because it presupposed a temporal sequence – the idea that the new paradigm could only emerge after the paradigm of modern science had completed its course. Now, if, on the one hand, that was far from happening, on the other, considering that development, whether scientific or social, was not homogeneous in the world, postmodernity could easily be understood as one more privilege of core societies, where modernity had been better fulfilled.

Going from the epistemological to the social and political field, it became evident that the concept of postmodernity I was proposing had little to do with the one that had been circulating in Europe and the United States. The latter's rejection of modernity – always conceived of as western modernity – implied the total rejection of modernity's modes of rationality and its values, as well as the master narratives that transformed them into the beacons of emancipatory social transformation. In other words, postmodernism in this sense included in its critique of modernity the very idea of the critical thought that modernity had inaugurated. As a consequence, the critique of modernity ended up paradoxically celebrating the society that modernity itself had shaped. On the contrary, the idea of postmodernity I subscribed to aimed to radicalize the critique of western modernity, proposing a new critical theory, which, unlike modern critical theory, would not convert the idea of an emancipatory transformation of society into a new form of social oppression. Such modern values as liberty, equality and solidarity have always seemed fundamental to me, as fundamental, indeed, as the critique of the violences committed in their name, and the denunciation of their poor concrete fulfilment in capitalist societies.

In order to counterpose my conception of postmodernity to celebratory postmodernism I designated it "oppositional postmodernism". My formulation was grounded on the idea that we live in societies confronted with modern problems – exactly those deriving from the lack of practical fulfillment of the values of liberty, equality and solidarity – for which there are no modern solutions available. Hence the need to reinvent social emancipation. Hence, as well, the fact that, in my critique of modern science, I never adopted epistemological or cultural relativism. For the theoretical reconstruction I proposed I drew, rather, on ideas and conceptions, which, while modern, had been marginalized by the dominant conceptions of modernity. I have specifically in mind the principle of community in the pillar of modern social regulation and the aesthetic-expressive rationality in the pillar of modern social emancipation. By the mid-1990s, however, it was clear to me that such reconstruction could only be completed from the vantage point of the experiences of the victims, that is to say, of the social groups that had suffered the consequences of the epistemological exclusivism of modern science, including the reduction of the emancipatory possibilities of western modernity to the ones made possible only by modern capitalism. Such a reduction, to my mind, transformed social emancipation into the double, rather than the opposite, of social regulation. My appeal for learning from the South – the South understood as a metaphor of the human suffering caused by capitalism – indicated precisely the aim to reinvent social emancipation by going beyond the critical theory produced in the North and the social and political praxis to which it subscribed.

For the past few years, I have come to realize that learning from the South, as a serious demand, requires some reformulation of the theory I have been proposing. As I said, I have never been happy with the designation "postmodern", if for no other reason, then because the hegemony of celebratory postmodernism virtually incapacitated its alternative – oppositional postmodernism. Furthermore, the idea of postmodernity points to the description that western modernity offers of itself, thus risking concealing the description that has been presented by those who have suffered the violence imposed on them by western modernity. This matricial violence had a name: colonialism. It was never included in self-representations of western modernity because colonialism was conceived of as a civilizing mission within the historicist boundaries of the West (historicism including both liberal political theory and Marxism), according to which European development pointed the way to the rest of the world. The question is, therefore, whether the "post" in postmodern means the same as the "post" in postcolonial. To put it another way: what are the limits of a radical critique of western modernity?

We are indeed living in a complex intellectual time that can be characterized in the following, somewhat paradoxical manner: culture, specifically western political culture is today as indispensable as inadequate to understand and change the world. Should a radical critique of such a culture imply both the radical nature of its indispensability and the radical nature of its inadequacy? Ultimately, what needs to be decided is whether this critique can be made from inside or if it presupposes the externality of the victims, that is to say, the victims that were part of modernity only by the exclusion and discrimination imposed by modernity itself. The issue of externality necessarily raises many problems. Those that argue for it (for example, Enrique Dussel, 1994, 2000) prefer to speak of transmodernity to designate the alternative the victims present to western modernity by way of resistance. In Dussel's view, the idea of being outside western modernity is crucial for formulating the concept of postcolonialism.

I submit that counterposing the postmodern and the postcolonial absolutely is a mistake, but also, by the same token, that the postmodern is far from responding to the concerns and sensibilities generated by postcolonialism.

By postcolonialism I mean a set of theoretical and analytical currents, firmly rooted in cultural studies but also present today in all the social sciences, sharing an important feature: in their understanding of the contemporary world, they all privilege, at the theoretical and political level, the unequal relations between the North and the South. Such relations were historically constituted by colonialism, and the end of colonialism as a political relation did not carry with itself the end of colonialism as a social relation, that is to say, as an authoritarian and discriminatory mentality and form of sociability. For this current, knowing to what extent we live in postcolonial societies is problematical. Moreover, the constitutive nature of colonialism in western modernity underscores its importance for understanding not only the nonwestern societies that were victimized by colonialism, but also the western societies themselves, especially as regards the patterns of social discrimination that prevail inside them. The postcolonial perspective draws on the idea that the structures of power and knowledge are more visible from the margins. Hence its interest in the geopolitics of knowledge, that is to say, its eagerness to problematize the question of who produces knowledge, in what context, and for whom.

As I have already suggested, many conceptions today claim to be postmodern. The dominant ones – including those of such important thinkers as Rorty (1989), Lyotard (1979), Baudrillard (1981), Vattimo (1995), Jameson (1984) – have the following characteristics in common: a critique of universalism and the master narratives on the linearity of history, as expressed in such concepts as progress, development or modernization while hierarchical totalities; renunciation of collective projects of social change, social emancipation being considered a myth without consistency; celebration, albeit melancholic, of the end of utopia, and celebration as well of skepticism in politics and parody in aesthetics; critique conceived of as deconstruction; cultural relativism or syncretism; emphasis on fragmentation, on margins and peripheries, on heterogeneity and plurality (of differences, agents, subjectivities); constructivist, nonfoundationalist and anti-essentialist epistemology.

This characterization, although necessarily incomplete, permits us to identify the major differences concerning the conception of the oppositional postmodernism I support. Rather than renouncing collective projects, I propose a plurality of collective projects, articulated in nonhierarchical forms by translation procedures, to replace the formulation of a general theory of social change. Rather than celebrating the end of utopia, I propose realistic, plural and critical utopias. Rather than renouncing social emancipation, I propose to reinvent it. In lieu of melancholy, I propose tragic optimism. In lieu of relativism, I propose plurality and the construction of an ethics from below. In lieu of deconstruction, I propose a postmodern critical theory, thoroughly reflective but immune to the obsession of deconstructing its own resistance. In lieu of the end of politics, I propose the creation of subversive subjectivities by promoting the passage from conformist action to rebellious action. In lieu of acritical syncretism, I propose *mestizaje* or hybridization, fully aware of the power relations that intervene in the process, that is, looking into who or what gets hybridized, in what contexts and with what purposes.

Oppositional postmodernism shares the following with the dominant conceptions of postmodernism: critique of universalism, the linearity of history, hierarchical totalities, and master narratives; emphasis on plurality, heterogeneity, margins or peripheries; constructivist, but not nihilist or relativist, epistemology.

It is not up to me to account fully for the convergences and divergences, let alone wonder if oppositional postmodernist may well turn out to be far more modernist than postmodernist.

The relation between the dominant conceptions of postmodernism and postcolonialism is complex. If not contradictory in itself, it is at least very ambiguous. The critique of universalism and historicism does put in question the West as the center of the world, thus allowing for the possibility of conceptions of alternative modernities, and allowing therefore for the affirmation and recognition of difference, namely historical difference. Furthermore, the idea of the exhaustion of western modernity helps to reveal the invasive and destructive nature of its imposition on the modern world, a revelation dear to postcolonialism. These two characteristics have been highlighted in particular by some of the varieties of postmodernism that have emerged in Latin America.

I believe, however, that these two characteristics are not enough to eliminate the western eurocentrism or ethnocentrism underlying dominant conceptions of postmodernism. First, the celebration of the fragmentation, plurality and proliferation of the peripheries conceals the unequal relation between North and South at the core of modern capitalism. The proliferation of the peripheries implies the proliferation of centers, which implies in turn the disappearance of the power relations between center and periphery that are constitutive of capitalism. In other words, the capitalist, colonial and imperial differences disappear. Secondly, dominant postmodernism often combines the critique of Western universalism with the claim of Western uniqueness, as when, for example, Rorty states that the idea of "human equality" is a western eccentricity, or that American democracy symbolizes and embodies the best Western values, thus concealing the dark face of US imperialism (1998). Lyotard, likewise, conceives of science as a western option as opposed to the traditional knowledge of nonwestern societies (1979). Actually, postmodern melancholy is full of north-centric stereotypes concerning the South, whose populations are viewed sometimes as immersed in despair without any way out. Finally, the conception of the postmodern as an exclusively Western self-representation is clearly present in Jameson, who conceives of postmodernism as the cultural feature of late capitalism (1984). Late capitalism, in Jameson's conception, is not belated capitalism, that is to say, a capitalism that arrives too late, but rather a more advanced form of capitalism. All in all, the question remains whether pronouncing the end of metanarratives and hierarchical totalities does not indeed amount to one more metanarrative, whose totality and hierarchy undermine the celebration of fragmentation and difference.

The conclusion, therefore, may be drawn that, even though postmodern and poststructuralist conceptions have contributed to the emergence of postcolonialism, they fail to give an adequate answer to its underlying ethical and political aspirations. Could the same be said of the oppositional postmodernism I have been arguing for? I don't think so, which does not mean that some reformulation of my reasoning is not in order. The postmodern conception I support is clearly linked to the conception of Western modernity that is my starting point. Herein lies some ambiguity concerning postcolonialism. I conceive of western modernity as a social and cultural paradigm that constitutes itself from the sixteenth century onwards and becomes consolidated between the late eighteenth and the early nineteenth century. In modernity I distinguish two pillars in dialectical tension: the pillar of social regulation and the pillar of social emancipation.[1] The way in which I conceive of each of these pillars seems to me to be adequate to European realities, particularly in the more developed countries, but not to those nonEuropean societies into which Europe has expanded. For example, social regulation as based on three principles – the principles of the State, the market, and the community – does not account for the forms of colonial (de)regulation in which the State is foreign, the market includes people among the merchandise (slaves), and the communities are devastated in the name of capitalism and the civilizing mission, and replaced by a tiny, racialized civil society, created by the State and made up of colonizers and their descendents, including as well tiny minorities of assimilated natives. On the other hand, I conceive of social emancipation as the historical process of increasing rationalization of the social life, institutions, politics, culture and knowledge, a process whose precise meaning and direction are summed up in the concept of progress. Here, too, I fail to thematize specifically the emancipation of the colonial peoples, and even less so their alternative rationalities, which were annihilated by the rationality of the cannons of the conquerors and the preaching of the missionaries.

Curiously enough, it is at the level of epistemology that colonialism gains more centrality in the conception of the oppositional postmodern I have been arguing for, as witness the distinction I draw between the two forms of knowledge sanctioned by western modernity – knowledge-as-regulation and knowledge-as-emancipation. Knowledge-as-regulation is a form of knowledge constructed along a trajectory between ignorance conceived of as chaos and knowledge conceived of as order; whereas knowledge-as-emancipation is constructed along a trajectory between ignorance conceived of as colonialism and knowledge conceived of as solidarity. Colonialist ignorance consists in refusing to recognize the other as an equal and converting the other into an object. Historically, this form of ignorance presupposes three distinct forms: the savage, nature, and the Orient. The gradual

---

1   The tension between social regulation and social emancipation is constitutive of the two major theoretical traditions of western modernity – political liberalism and Marxism. The differences between the two are significant. While political liberalism confines the possibilities of emancipation to the capitalist horizon, Marxism conceives of social emancipation in a postcapitalism horizon. Nevertheless, both traditions conceive of colonialism in the historicist framework of a temporal code that locates the colonial peoples in the "waiting room" of history, which is supposed to grant them the benefits of civilization in due time. It must be acknowledged, however, that, given the constitutively colonialist nature of modern capitalism, the postcapitalist horizon designed by Marxism is also a postcolonial horizon. No wonder, therefore, that, amongst all the European theoretical traditions, Marxism is the one that has contributed most to postcolonial studies, a fact that in part explains its new vitality.

overlapping of the logic of development of western modernity and the logic of development of capitalism led to the total supremacy of knowledge-as-regulation, the latter having recodified knowledge-as-emancipation in its own terms. Thus, the form of ignorance in knowledge-as-emancipation – colonialism – was recodified as a form of knowledge in knowledge-as-regulation – hence, colonialism-as-order. This is the process through which modern science, increasingly at the service of capitalist development, consolidates its epistemological primacy. In other words, the two contact zones between western modernity and nonwestern societies – the colonial and the epistemological zones – both characterized by drastic power inequalities, gradually turned into each other. The consequence of such a process of mutual fusion was that colonialism as a social relation survived colonialism as a political relation.

Colonialism is again still present in oppositional postmodernism in the way in which I conceive of the subjectivities capable of undertaking the paradigmatic transition in the social and political domains. I see them as emerging from three generating metaphors: the frontier, the baroque, and the South. They all connote the idea of margin or periphery: the frontier, as is obvious; the baroque, as a subaltern *ethos* of western modernity; and the South, understood as a metaphor of the human suffering caused by capitalist modernity. Through the South metaphor, I place the relations North/South at the core of the reinvention of social emancipation, explicitly demarcating myself from the dominant postmodern and poststructuralist thought (as in Foucault 1976), because it does not thematize the imperial subordination of the South *vis-à-vis* the North – as if the North were only "us", and not "us and them". As epistemological, political and cultural orientation, I propose, rather, that we defamiliarize ourselves from the imperial North in order to learn from the South. The caveat, however, is that the South itself is a product of empire, and thus learning from the South requires as well defamiliarization *vis-à-vis* the imperial South, that is to say, *vis-à-vis* all that in the South is the result of the colonial capitalist relation. Indeed, you only learn from the South to the extent that the South is conceived of as resistance to the domination of the North, and what you look for in the South is what has not been totally destroyed or disfigured by such domination. In other words, you only learn from the South to the extent that you contribute to its elimination while a product of empire.

Ever since the beginning of the current decade, I have been trying to give political consistency to this epistemological orientation, by analyzing globalization as a zone of confrontation between hegemonic and counter-hegemonic projects. The South emerges thereby as protagonizing counter-hegemonic globalization, whose most consistent manifestation is the World Social Forum, which I have been following very closely.

I may therefore conclude that, as opposed to the dominant currents of postmodern and poststructuralist thought, oppositional postmodernism aims to overcome western modernity from a postcolonial and postimperial perspective. It can be said that oppositional postmodernity places itself at the utmost margins or peripheries of western modernity to cast a new critical gaze on it. It is, however, obvious that it places itself inside, not outside, the margins. The postmodern transition is conceived of as an archeological task of excavation into the ruins of western modernity, in search of suppressed or marginalized elements or traditions, incomplete representations in particular, because less colonized by the hegemonic canon of modernity, capable of guiding us in the construction of new paradigms of social emancipation. Among such representations or traditions I identify, in the pillar of regulation, the principle of community; and, in the pillar of emancipation, aesthetic-expressive rationality. Herein lies my construction of the idea of a paradigmatic transition. I grant that, in fact, there are only post-factum transitions. While transitions are happening, the meaning of the changes occurring is ambiguous, if not opaque. In spite of that, however, it is worth speaking of transition to highlight the need of experimentation and interpolate the meaning of change, however unmanageable the latter may be. Ruins generate the impulse to reconstruct and allow us to imagine very distinct kinds of reconstruction, even if the materials available are no more than ruins and the imagination.

To a certain extent, the excavating process I propose justifies Walter Mignolo's view (2000) of my critique of modernity as an internal critique, which, because it does not step outside the margin, does not adequately incorporate the perspective of the victims of modernity, failing, therefore, to be a postcolonial perspective.[2]

---

2   While not agreeing with Mignolo's critique, I feel I have to reformulate or refine some aspects of my theoretical framework. My critical disagreement is based on four arguments.

My first argument is metatheoretical. In a relation of domination between oppressors and oppressed, the externality of the oppressed is to be conceived of only as an integral part of its subordinate integration – that is to say, exclusion – within the system of domination. In other words, in a dialectical relationship, the externality of the opposite is generated inside the relationship.

My second argument is theoretical. The genius of western modernity resides in the dialectics between regulation and emancipation, that is to say, in a dynamic discrepancy in one sole secular world between experiences and expectations. The result is a new conception of totality that includes all that modernity is and all that it is not, or is only as a potentiality. This voracity, this auto-and heterophagic hubris is what best characterizes western modernity, explaining as well why modernity has been conceived of in so many different ways, as many and as different as the alternative projects that have confronted it. Under these conditions, it is difficult to conceive of an absolute alterity or exteriority to western modernity, except in religious terms. This is perhaps why to confront religious fundamentalism you have to be inside western modernity.

The third argument is sociological. After 500 years of western global domination, it is difficult to perceive what is external to it, beyond what resists to it, and what resists to it, if resisting from the outside, is logically in transit from the outside to the inside.

Finally, the fourth argument concerns the characterization of my proposal. My proposal for the reconstruction of social emancipation from the South and by learning from the South allows for oppositional postmodernity to be legitimately conceived of as more postcolonial than postmodern. In other words, at the farthest margins it is even more difficult to

This said, I still think that some reformulation is necessary. As I refine my theoretical framework in order to deepen its postcolonial dimension, however, I feel compelled to question the dominant versions of postcolonialism. It seems, then, that I am condemned to being an oppositionist, going from the oppositional postmodern to the oppositional postcolonial.

My first point is that western modernity has been colonialist since its origin. In my description, this founding factor is not stressed enough. Furthermore, historically, I situate my characterization of modernity as social and cultural project between the end of the eighteenth and the middle of the nineteenth century in Europe. Excluded is, therefore, what Dussel (1973, 1994, 2000) and Mignolo (2000) designate as first modernity – Iberian modernity – that is precisely at the origin of the first colonial drive. If, as I have been arguing, Portuguese colonialism has very distinct characteristics from those of nineteenth-century hegemonic colonialism, my conception of modernity must include it, in its specificity, in the modern world system. Actually, as I will show further down, the specificity of Portuguese colonialism induces the specificity of postcolonialism in the geopolitical space encompassed by the former.

Second, in the past there has been colonialism, as a political relation, without capitalism, but since the fifteenth-century capitalism is not thinkable without colonialism, nor is colonialism thinkable without capitalism. In my characterization of western modernity, I have emphasized its relations with capitalism, but failed to pay attention to its relations with colonialism. Now, this needs to be done, not only to bring about strategies to analyze the South in such terms that will not reproduce its subordination *vis-à-vis* the North, but also to analyze the North in such terms that will encourage the North to reject such subordination as unfair. That is to say, the aim of the postcolonial perspective is not merely to allow for the self-description of the South, i.e., its abolishment as imperial South; it aims to ascertain as well to what extent colonialism prevails as a social relation in the colonizer societies of the North, even if ideologically concealed by the way these societies describe themselves. This analytical mechanism is particularly urgent in the geopolitical space of the Portuguese language, given the long duration of the colonial cycle, which, in the case of Africa and Asia, lasted until the last quarter of the twentieth century.

Although mutually constitutive, capitalism and colonialism are not to be confused. Capitalism may develop without colonialism as a political relation, as history shows, but not without colonialism as a social relation. This is what, after Anibal Quijano (2000), we may call coloniality of power and knowledge. As a possible characterization of colonialism, ample enough to contemplate all its many forms, I propose the following: the set of extremely unequal exchanges that depend on denying humanity to the weaker people in order to overexploit them or exclude them as being discardable. As a social formation, capitalism does not

---

distinguish between what is inside and outside the margin, and even if that were possible, it is doubtful that such a distinction would make any difference.

have to overexploit every worker and cannot, by definition, exclude and discard every population, but, by the same token, it cannot exist without overexploited and discardable populations. Granted that capitalism and colonialism are not to be confused, the anti-capitalist and the anti-colonial or postcolonial struggles are not to be confused either, but neither can be successfully undertaken without the other.

These two reformulations pose some theoretical, analytical and political challenges to the social theories that may want to use them. But before I go on to mention the challenges, I want to stress the oppositional nature of the conception of postcolonialism I am here presenting. As I have already said, the reformulations I propose engage in conflicting dialogue with the dominant versions of postcolonialism. In the following, I identify some of those conflicting points.

The first one concerns the culturalist bias of postcolonial studies. Postcolonial studies have been predominantly cultural studies, i.e. critical analysis of literary and other discourses, of social mentalities and subjectivities, ideologies and symbolic practices, which presuppose colonial hierarchy and the inability of the colonized to express themselves in their own terms, and which go on reproducing themselves, even after the colonial political link ends. This is a very important line of research, but if it remains confined to culture, it may run the risk of concealing or neglecting the materiality of the social and political relations that make possible, if not inevitable, the reproduction of those discourses, ideologies and symbolic practices. Without meaning to establish priorities among economic, social, political or cultural struggles – as far as I am concerned, they are all political when confronting power structures – I consider it important to develop analytical criteria to empower them all.[3]

The second point of conflict with the dominant conceptions of postcolonialism regards the articulation between capitalism and colonialism. The dominant conceptions tend to privilege colonialism and coloniality as explanatory factors of social relations. For example, Anibal Quijano (2000) maintains that all forms of oppression and discrimination in colonial capitalist societies – from sexual to ethnic to class discrimination – were reconfigured by colonial oppression and

---

3   The fact that some Eurocentric traditions – e.g. deconstruction and poststructuralism – are often too conspicuous in postcolonial studies tends to undermine the latter on the political level. To emphasize the recognition of difference without likewise emphasizing the economic, social and political conditions that guarantee equality in difference runs the risk of mixing radical denunciations with practical passivity regarding the required tasks of resistance. This is all the more serious because, under the current conditions of global capitalism, there is no effective recognition of difference (whether racial, sexual, ethnic, religious, etc.) without social redistribution. Moreover, structuralism pushed to the extreme may render invisible or trivialize the dominant forms of power, thus neutralizing all forms of resistance to them. To extreme poststructuralism, I prefer a pliable, plural structuralism, as when I identify six space-times in which are produced the six forms of power in contemporary capitalist societies: patriarchy, exploitation, unequal differentiation, fetishism of goods, domination, and unequal exchange.

discrimination, which subordinated all the others to its own logic. Thus, the fact that we were under a patriarchal society did not prevent the white woman from prevailing over a black or indigenous man. This stance parallels the classical Marxist conceptions that ascribe to capitalism and the class discrimination it produces a privileged explanatory role as regards the reproduction of the remaining forms of discrimination in capitalist societies. To my mind, even in colonial and former colonial societies, colonialism and capitalism are integral parts of the same constellation of powers; privileging one of them to explain practices of discrimination does not seem, therefore, to be adequate.[4] For the same reason, I think it is wrong for postcolonial criticism to focus more on western modernity than on capitalism. In this regard, I suggest two cautionary measures. First, all triumphant struggles against the cultural hegemony of western modernity must be considered illusory, if as a consequence the world is not less comfortable for global capitalism; second, we must not applaud the survival of capitalism beyond western modernity, unless we are sure that capitalism has not made an alliance with a worst barbarism.

The third dimension of the opposional nature of the kind of postcolonialism I propose concerns the provincialization of Europe, an insight of Hans-George Gadamer (1965) recently popularized by Dipesh Chakrabarty (2000). The phrase, provincialization of Europe, intends to designate the historical process – begun in 1914 and concluded by the end of the Second World War – of Europe's loss of cultural and political centrality in the modern world system and the subsequent crisis of the values and institutions that Europe has spread as universal from the nineteenth century onwards. This idea is central to postcolonialism and dear to postmodernism as well. I basically agree with it, but I suggest that the reflection it provokes calls for further probing. The dominant conceptions of postcolonialism provincialize Europe at the same time that they essentialize it, converting it into a monolithic entity that counterposes itself uniformly to nonwestern societies. Such essentialization always relies on the transformation of part of Europe into its whole. Thus, dominant postcolonialism universalizes colonial experience on the basis of British colonialism, and the emergent Latin-American postcolonialism somehow does the same, this time on the basis of Iberian colonialism. In both cases, the

---

4 I do not think, for example, that discrimination against women, even in colonial societies, is a product of colonialism. The importance of colonialism and coloniality to explain or understand social reality in societies that underwent colonialism is significant enough not to have to be dramatized beyond what is reasonable and may be refuted by the complexity of the societies in which we live. I do not think, for example, that class relations are always overdetermined by colonialism and coloniality, and always in the same way. Analytical tools that put in jeopardy the discovery of the wealth and complexity of societies must be avoided *a priori*. If this holds for colonial societies, it holds with a vengeance for colonizer societies. As regards the latter, it is important enough to acknowledge that, even long after it ends as a political relation, colonialism goes on impregnating some aspects of the culture, patterns of racism and social authoritarianism, and even the dominant outlooks of international relations.

colonizer is conceived of as representing Europe *vis-à-vis* the rest of the world. Now, not only were there several Europes, but there were and are unequal relations among the countries of Europe. Not only were there several colonialisms, but the relations among them were also complex; this being the case, something is surely wrong if such complexity is not to be present in the conceptions of postcolonialism themselves.

I propose, therefore, a reprovincialization of Europe that pays attention to the inequalities inside Europe and the ways in which they affected the different European colonialisms. It is important to show the specificities of Portuguese or Spanish colonialism *vis-à-vis* British or French colonialism, for they necessarily give rise to the specificities of postcolonialism in the geopolitical space of Spanish or Portuguese language, as opposed to postcolonialism in the geopolitical space of the English or French language. More important still, however, is to thematize the inequalities inside Europe among the different colonizer countries. For over a century, Portugal, the center of a colonial empire, was itself an informal colony of England; on the other hand, in the course of centuries, Portugal was pictured by the countries of Northern Europe as a country with similar social and cultural characteristics to those attributed by the European countries, including Portugal, to the overseas colonized peoples. These factors have necessarily had a specific impact on the conception of postcolonialism in the Portuguese geopolitical space, both in the societies colonized by the Portuguese and in the Portuguese society, past and present.

The provincialization, or decentering, of Europe must therefore take into account not only the different colonialisms, but also the different processes of decolonization. In this regard, the contrast between the American decolonization and the African or Asian decolonization must be considered. Since, with the exception of Haiti, independence in the Americas meant the handing over of the territories to the descendants of Europeans, the provincialization or decentering of Europe will have to imply the provincialization or decentering of the Americas, the colonial zone where there is more of Europe. Could it be mere coincidence that the postmodernist thesis is better received in Latin America than in Africa?

To conclude, the oppositional postcolonialism I support, emerging organically from the oppositional postmodernim I have been arguing for, forces us to go, not only beyond postmodernism, but beyond postcolonialism, as well. It urges a nonwestern understanding of the world in all its complexity, an understanding that will have to include the western understanding of the world, the latter being as indispensable as it is inadequate. These comprehensiveness and complexity are the historical, cultural and political ballast whence emerges counter-hegemonic globalization as the alternative constructed by the South in its extreme diversity. What is at stake is not just the counterposition between the South and the North. It is also the counterposition between the South of the South and the North of the South, and between the South of the North and the North of the North.

From this broad conception of postcolonialism, which includes internal colonialism as well, and from its articulation with other systems of power and discrimination that make up the inequalities of the world, there emerge the tasks of counter-hegemonic globalization, which, in turn, pose new challenges to the critical theory that is being constructed, from oppositional postmodernism to oppositional postcolonialism. In fact, the challenges of counter-hegemonic globalization push beyond the postmodern and the postcolonial in the transforming understanding of the world. On the one hand, the immense variety of movements and actions that integrate counter-hegemonic globalization are not contained in the decentering forms proposed by postmodernism *vis-à-vis* western modernity, or by postcolonialism *vis-à-vis* western colonialism. On the other, the gathering of wills and the creation of subjectivities that feature collective transforming actions require that the new critical thought be complemented by the formulation of new alternatives – and this the postmodern refuses to do, and the postcolonial does only very partially.

I identify the major challenges as follows.

The first one may be formulated thus: to think social emancipation without a general theory of social emancipation. Contrary to celebratory postmodernism, I maintain that social emancipation must continue to be an ethical and political exigency, perhaps more pressing than ever in the contemporary world. Contrary to some postcolonialism, I do not think that the term "emancipation" must be discarded for being modern and western. I do think, however, that it must be profoundly reconceptualized to integrate the emancipatory proposals formulated by the different movements and organizations that compose counter-hegemonic globalization, and that have little in common, as regards objectives, strategies, collective subjects and ways of acting, with the ones that historically constituted the western patterns of social emancipation.

The challenge of the reinvention of emancipation unfolds into many others. Here, I identify only one. It consists in credibly imagining social emancipation without recourse to a general theory of social emancipation. This is a difficult task, not only because not having recourse to a general theory is a total novelty in the western world, but also because not every movement agrees that a general theory is not needed, and there is ample debate among those who do not about the most adequate formulation of the general theory to be adopted. I believe, therefore, that a first step would be to come to a consensus on the uselessness, or impossibility, of a general theory. The fact that a general theory of social emancipation carries two results that are today considered unacceptable by the social groups that make up counter-hegemonic globalization, must be persuasively demonstrated. On the one hand, as a consequence of the general theory, some social struggles, objectives or agents will be put in the waiting room of history with the excuse that their time has not yet arrived; on the other hand, other social struggles, objectives or agents will be acknowledged as legitimate but integrated in hierarchical totalities that ascribe to them subordinate positions *vis-à-vis* other social struggles, objectives or agents.

To underscore the need for such a consensus expressing a certain negative universalism – the idea that no struggle, objective or agent has the overall recipe for the social emancipation of humanity – I have been suggesting that, in this phase of transition, what we do need, if not a general theory of social emancipation, is, at least, a general theory about the impossibility of a general theory. In lieu of a general theory of social emancipation, I propose a translation procedure involving the different partial projects of social emancipation. The work of translation aims to turn incommensurability into difference, a difference capable of rendering possible mutual intelligibility among the different projects of social emancipation, preventing any of them from subordinating in general or absorbing any other.

The second challenge consists in ascertaining to what extent Eurocentric culture and political philosophy are indispensable today for reinventing social emancipation. To the extent that they are, we need to know if such indispensability can go hand in hand with the recognition of their inadequacy, and hence with the search of an articulation with nonwestern cultures and political philosophies. What needs to be ascertained is to what extent some of the elements of European political culture are today common cultural and political heritage of the world. Take some of those elements as example: human rights, secularism, citizenship, the State, civil society, public sphere, equality before the law, the individual, the distinction between public and private, democracy, social justice, scientific rationality, popular sovereignty. These concepts were proclaimed in theory and often denied in practice; in colonialism, they were applied to destroy alternative political cultures. But the truth is that they were also used to resist colonialism and other forms of oppression. Moreover, even in the North, these concepts have been subjected to different kinds of critique, and they bear today very contrasting formulations, some more exclusive and Eurocentric than others, hegemonic and counter-hegemonic formulations, the latter being often integral part of emancipatory, postcolonial or anti-capitalist projects, coming from the South. Can these concepts be replaced by other, nonwestern concepts, to the benefit of the emancipatory struggles? I doubt that a general answer, whether affirmative or negative, can be given to this question. As a regulatory idea for research and practice in this regard, I suggest equal weight be given to the idea of indispensability and to the idea of inadequacy, that is to say, incompleteness. The third challenge consists in knowing how to maximize interculturality without subscribing to cultural and epistemological relativism. In other words, the point is to construct an ethical and political position without grounding it on any absolute principle, be it human nature or progress, since it was in their name that historically many emancipatory aspirations turned into forms of violence and atrocity, especially in the South. On the other hand, from the point of view of the pragmatics of social emancipation, relativism, with its absence of criteria for hierarchies of validity among different forms of knowledge, is an untenable position because it renders impossible any relation between knowledge and the meaning of social change. If anything is equally valid as knowledge, all projects of social emancipation are equally valid or, which amounts to the same, equally invalid.

It is within the scope of this challenge that ascertaining the inadequacy or incompleteness of the concepts of western political culture must encourage the search for alternative concepts from other cultures and the dialogue among them. Such dialogues, which I designate as diatopical hermeneutics, may conduce to regional or sectorial universalisms constructed from below, that is, to counter-hegemonic global public spheres – what I call subaltern cosmopolitism.

Finally, the fourth challenge can be formulated in the following way: is it possible to give meaning to the social struggles without giving meaning to history? Is it possible to think social emancipation without such concepts as progress, development, modernization? Postcolonialism has been making a radical critique of historicism. Based on what I designate as monoculture of linear time, historicism starts from the idea that all social reality is historically determined and must be analyzed according to the place of the period it occupies in a process of historical development conceived of as univocal and unidirectional. For example, in a period dominated by mechanized and industrialized agriculture, the traditional, subsistence peasant is probably considered anachronic or backward. Two social realities occurring simultaneously are not necessarily contemporaneous.

Historicism is criticized today both by postmodern and postcolonial currents. On the one hand, historicism conceals the fact that the more developed countries, far from showing the way of development to the less developed ones, block it, or only allow these countries to tread it in conditions that reproduce their underdevelopment. The conception of the stages of development always silences the fact that, when they started their developing process, the more developed countries never had to confront other countries already in more advanced stages of development than themselves. Besides discrediting the idea of alternative models of development, or even alternatives to development, historicism makes it possible to think that the less developed countries, in some specific characteristics, may be actually more developed than the more developed ones. Such characteristics are always interpreted according to the general stage of the society's development.

Given that this conception is hegemonic, imprinted in many ways in the scientific community, in the public opinion, in multilateral organizations and international relations, it is not easy to reply to the question I have formulated, the negative answer being in this case the most reasonable. How can an emancipatory meaning be ascribed to the social struggles if the very history in which they occur lacks direction towards social emancipation?

The critique of historicism and the temporal monoculture on which it is based renders impossible a metanarrative of social emancipation (be it socialism or any other), but its goal is to make possible the formulation and prosecution of multiple narratives of social emancipation as identified above. There is no emancipation, there are emancipations, and what defines them as such is not a historical logic, rather ethical and political criteria. If there is no historical logic that spares us the ethical questions caused by human action, we have no choice but to face the latter. And since there is no universal ethics, we are left only with the work of translation and diatopical hermeneutics, and the pragmatical confrontation of actions with their results. In ethical terms, the cosmopolitanism of the oppressed can only be the result of a conversation of humanity, as proposed by John Dewey (1966).

For the past ten years, the World Social Forum has been the embryo of such a conversation.

Conclusion

Can the work of a social scientist from a colonizer country contribute to postcolonialism other than being the object of postcolonial studies? This question must be asked, given a certain nativist essentialism that often contaminates postcolonialism. If it is hard to answer the question "Can the victim speak?", it is even harder to answer the question, "Who can speak for the victim?". Since I reject essentialism in any version, I do not hesitate to say that biography and bibliography are incommensurate, even though they may influence each other. All knowledge is contextual, but context is a social, dynamic construction, the product of a history that has nothing to do with the arbitrary determinism of origin. Such context is of interest to us in a way that transcends by far individual issues. Two notes on the sociology of knowledge are therefore in order.

The scientific, social and cultural space of official Portuguese language bears two characteristics that grant it, at least potentially, some specificity in postcolonial studies as a whole. The first one is that, given the fact that the imperial cycle lasted until thirty years ago, there are still fortunately today, acting in this space, many intellectuals, social scientists and political activists that participated in the struggle against colonialism in its most consistent sense, i.e. as a political relation. The duration of Portuguese colonialism until the twentieth century is a historical anachronism, but it interests us today as a sociological fact, whose part in our contemporaneity is still to be assessed. In the anticolonial struggles there were important solidarities and complicities between those fighting in the colonies and those fighting in the "metropolis," and such solidarities and the way they evolved are still to be assessed as well. While in other spaces colonialism as a social relation dominates postcolonial studies, in the space of official Portuguese language, at least as concerns Africa and East Timor, political colonialism is still crucial for understanding and explaining contemporaneity, in its broadest sense, both as regards the colonizer and the colonized society, from the State to public administration, from educational politics to identities, from social-scientific knowledge to public opinion, from social discrimination inside the countries that compose this space to the international relations among them. Put it another way, in this space, the decolonization processes are part of our political actuality, and they, too, include specificities that run the risk of being devalued or neglected, if the canon of hegemonic postcolonialism (i.e. British) manages to prevail acritically. By way of illustration, only two cases waiting for social scientists in this space. Goa is the region in the world that was subjected to effective colonial occupation for the longest, between 1510 and 1962, and also the only one that did not give way to independence (even if India thinks otherwise). East Timor, in turn, colonized for very long, semi-decolonized following the April 1974 Revolution, then recolonized by Indonesia, finally gains independence by the sheer will of its people and with the help of an unprecedented international solidarity, in which must be highlighted the extraordinary solidarity, first of the people and then of the government of the former multisecular colonial power.

The second note of sociology of knowledge was already announced above. It concerns the challenges that the specificity of Portuguese colonialism brings and how it reflects itself in the postcolonial studies of this geopolitical and cultural space, and in a way also in the construction of the scientific community gathered together here today. I mentioned above that the conception of the oppositional postmodern I have been arguing for positions itself ideologically at the extreme margins of western modernity, even if inside them. Such positioning was perhaps facilitated by the context in which the conception was constructed, in view of the social and political reality of one of the least developed countries of Europe, a country that for a short while led the first modernity in the sixteenth century, rapidly to enter a process of decadence. If this decadence dragged along the decadence of the colonies, it also opened up spaces for colonial relationships that have little to do with those that prevailed in hegemonic colonialism. As I said above, the impact of this specificity in postcolonial studies is still to be examined. This is, to my mind, our task. It is a complex task for, no matter what theme of social research we engage in, we study it from the point of view of theoretical and analytical frameworks that were constructed by the hegemonic social sciences in geopolitical spaces other than ours. That is to say, the deficit of proper representation that is inherent to the colonized, as post colonial studies have amply demonstrated, seems to involve, in our case, both the colonized and the colonizer, which suggests the need for a new kind of postcolonialism. Be it as it may, I suspect that for a while our research, whatever the topic, will be concerned with identity. Ours is therefore the contingency of living our experience in the reverse of the experience of the others. If this contingency is lived with epistemological awareness, it may ground a new cordial cosmopolitanism, which does not emerge spontaneously, as Sérgio Buarque de Holanda wanted, but which can be constructed as an eminently political and cultural task, under historical and sociological conditions which, being proper to us, are propitious to it.

Bibliography

Baudrillard, J. 1981. *Simulacres et simulations*. Paris: Galilée.

Chakrabarty, D. 2000. Universalism and Belonging in the Logic of Capital. *Public Culture*, 12(3), 653-78.

Dewey, J. 1966. *Democracy and Education: An Introduction to the Philosophy of Education*. New York: The Free Press.

Dussel, E. 1973. *Para una etica de la liberacion latinoamericana*. Mexico DF: Siglo Veintiuno, 2 volumes.

Dussel, E. 1994. *1492: El encubrimiento del otro, hacia el origen del "mito de la modernidad"*. La Paz: Plural Editores y Universidad Mayor de San Andrés.

Dussel, E. 2000. Europa, modernidad y eurocentrismo, in *La colonialidad del saber: eurocentrismo y ciencias sociales – perspectivas latinoamericanas*, edited by E. Lander. Buenos Aires: CLACSO, 41-53.

Foucault, M. 1976. *La Volonté de Savoir*. Paris: Gallimard.

Gadamer, H.-G. 1965. *Wahrheit und Methode*. Tübingen: J.C.B. Mohr.

Jameson, F. 1984. Postmodernism, or the Cultural Logic of Late Capitalism. *New Left Review*, 146, 53-92.

Lyotard, J.-F. 1979. *La Condition Postmoderne: rapport sur le savoir*. Paris: Editions Minuit.

Mignolo, W. 2000. *Local Histories/Global Designs: Coloniality, Subaltern Knowledges, and Border Thinking*. Princeton: Princeton University Press.

Quijano, A. 2000. Colonialidad del poder y classificacion social. *Journal of World-Systems Research*, 6(2), 342-86.

Rorty, R. 1998. *Achieving Our Country: Leftist Thought in Twentieth Century America*. Cambridge: Harvard University Press.

Vattimo, G. 1995. *Más allá de la interpretación*. Barcelona: Paidós /ICE-UAB.

Chapter 15

Critical Geopolitics and the Decolonization of Area Studies

Heriberto Cairo

I would like to begin this reflection with the question asked by Jean Genêt (1960) in *Les nègres*: "Mais, qu'est-ce que c'est donc un noir? Et d'abord, c'est de quelle couleur?"[1] (quoted in Wallerstein 1991: 128). Immanuel Wallerstein points out that Genêt tries to make us realize that "the definition of the universal is a particular definition of a particular system – the modern world-system – and that, within that system, the definition of the particular has no particularities but is a universal of that system" (1991: 128), because this is what happens when we talk, for example, of Sub-Saharan Africa, the Middle East, Eastern Europe or Latin America. We like regions to be clearly defined, either naturally or historically, but they only make sense within the current modern world-system that has constructed, defined and maintained them; they can only be studied epistemologically if we accept as a premise the system that created them. But we might also ask ourselves why other possible regions are not so successful academically speaking; there are relatively few practitioners of Atlantic Studies, Mediterranean Studies or Central Asian Studies. Why is this? Why do we not study any spatial grouping? Is the Latin European area any less representative than that of Latin America, for example?

The fact is that in the modern world-system the differences that exist between different regions of the world are expressed as a global hierarchical classification (Agnew 2003), in which Europe, or rather the West, is situated at the top, both in terms of power (economic and military) and knowledge. Social sciences in particular are fully immersed in this hierarchy: theories, models, research techniques, authors, as well as objects of study – in this case areas or regions of the world – all have their origin in Europe, or the West in its broader sense, and spread later to the rest of the world.

In his seminal book on Eurocentrism, James Blaut analyses what constitutes, in the literal sense, "the colonizer's model of the world" and argues that this is not just a set of beliefs but "a structured whole" (Blaut 1993: 10). The "supertheory" of this model is "Eurocentric diffusionism", whose essential features are defined by an inside (Europe) and an outside (the rest of the world), in which the most important interaction is "the inner-to-outer diffusion of innovative ideas, people, and commodities" (1993: 42). The "advancement" of Europe cannot be understood

---

1   "What is a Negro? And, first of all, what colour is he?"

without colonialism; neither can its success in world domination be understood without the spread of Eurocentric diffusionism.

But the capacity to determine what form of knowledge is hegemonic, and which objects of investigation are legitimate and which are not, does not only come from the desires and plans of the ruling classes at the core; the ruling classes on the peripheries who gradually become incorporated into the world-system are also a decisive factor in this process. It is generally not possible to understand the control exerted by ruling classes without reference to the "collaboration" with ruling classes on the periphery (Taylor and Flint 2000), particularly in the field of knowledge.

In this study I will attempt to show how in recent years the development of critical geopolitics (in the sense of John Agnew, Gearóid Ó Tuathail and Simon Dalby) has permitted a different approach to the study of world regions from that of *area studies*, which had their origins in the United States (and other Western countries) after the Second World War. This way makes it possible to understand the spatial practices and representations that enable a region to be constructed, and the underlying forces and interests that benefit from it. In other words, it permits the reconstruction of the region, which is the first step towards decolonizing studies on it.

Area Studies

Right from their beginnings, area studies have been defined by a very marked Eurocentrism (or Western Centrism), which has led to regions always being studied in comparison with a developed, democratic and more advanced West. This has given rise to a binary geography, typifying the vision of the modern world that began to evolve with the European Renaissance before spreading worldwide. This is one of the fundamental elements of the coloniality of knowledge.

Precursors of present-day area studies have existed since the nineteenth century, when the bases of the present division of labour were established in the university (Wallerstein 1991), but it was only after the Second World War that such studies became generalized, in very different university contexts and with reference to a great diversity of regions. Schueller (2007) describes their early vicissitudes in some detail. Already during the Second World War there was a demand for specialists on the different regions involved in the conflict and the end of the war only served to increase this. In 1946 the army established language learning programmes at Princeton and the universities of Indiana, Michigan and Pennsylvania, and area studies were funded by numerous foundations. It was the Cold War, however, that was responsible for their true recognition:

> The launching of the first Sputnik in 1957 propelled Congress to pass the National Defense Education Act (NDEA). Under Title VI of the NDEA, area studies centers were funded in universities, thus formalizing the material and

political basis for the relationship between area studies and the state (Schueller 2007: 44).

The Cold War provided the perfect breeding ground for area studies. Eastern European Studies in particular were consolidated in this period for obvious reasons, but other regions of the world were also objects of scrutiny. "Dangerous" regions were given the priority attention deemed necessary, although, in theory, any region was open to scrutiny.

As more regions became defined, Europe and the West were also defined (and redefined) and connected in a permanent relationship. As Stenning puts it, with respect to Eastern European Studies:

> [D]espite focusing on Eastern Europe, constructs geographies which call attention to the presence of the East in the West and the West in the East, which recognize the 'transition' in the East as a process which also reshapes the West, which reflect on the binary politics of the Cold War (and earlier histories) that shaped these East–West geographies. And, overall, "which locate the student (be that us or our undergraduates) in these spatialities (Stenning 2005: 382).

While the end of the Cold War marked the end for some things, others that had resulted from its logic were adapted to the new situation. For example, the western military alliance, the North Atlantic Treaty Organization (NATO) not only continued to exist but was enlarged, absorbing many of its former enemies and extending its operational bases, although it obviously had to revise its objectives and mode of action.

Something similar happened with area studies. Not only did they not disappear but many organizations, like the Latin American Studies Organization (LASA), are still thriving. An attempt to readjust objectives was also made here. In September 2003, the United States Subcommittee on Education passed H.R. 3077, the International Studies in Higher Education Act, which authorized the creation of a consultative council, nominated by the Secretary of the Department of Homeland Security, to oversee the curricula of area studies centres receiving official funding which "needed to better reflect the needs of national security" (Schueller 2007: 41). One of the experts whose testimony was valued by the Subcommittee was Stanley Kurtz of the Hoover Institution and editor of the National Review. He expressed his alarm at the "anti-Americanism of post-colonial theory", particularly in Middle East Studies, which

> singled out the pernicious consequence of the writings of Edward Said and recommended federal oversight over these centers. His recommendations: balance and diversity (Schueller 2007: 41).

Put briefly, at the present time area studies continue to have a geostrategic orientation. Indeed, a driving force in area studies has been Samuel Huntington, the well-known author of various works that attempt to readjust the role of the United States in the world (or rather attempt to readjust the world to the United States), while the events of 11 September 2001 have evidently left their mark on the way such studies are pursued.

If it is true that area studies are decidedly interdisciplinary, embracing sociology, geography, history, economy and political sciences as well as other recognized disciplines, and that as such they open up ways to exceed the limitations of traditional approaches in social sciences, it is also true that if they are to be reformed, it is necessary to decolonize them, in other words, to overcome the Eurocentrism/Western Centrism we have already referred to.

Critical Geopolitics

The critical geopolitics that has developed in recent years may be useful for this task as it permits a different approach to studying the regions of the world from that of area studies. Critical geopolitics is closely tied to the pioneering work done by John Agnew, Simon Dalby and Géaroid Ó Tuathail, among others. The expression "critical geopolitics" was actually coined by Ó Tuathail (1988) and Dalby (1990a, 1990b). The latter proposed the development of a "critical theory of geopolitics", which he defined as "the investigation of how a particular set of practices comes to be dominant and excludes other sets of practices. Where conventional discourse simply accepts the current circumstances as given, 'naturalized', a critical theory asks questions of how they came to be as they are" (1990a: 28).

For Dalby, it is all about overcoming the "realist" approach of power politics and the "crude interpretations of international affairs"; in other words, he rejects using as a starting point the bases of some of the more important approaches to the analysis of international relations. He finds a way around this by researching the "ideological dimension", not only in terms of perceptions, but fundamentally by studying how the actors understand and pursue their roles. In this sense, his aim is to reconceptualize geopolitics as "discourse"; in effect, "[t]he analysis thus focuses attention on how these discourses are used in politics; it thus focuses on their 'discursive practices', or, in other words, how the discourse is constructed, and used" (Dalby 1990a: 40). Scholars in political theory and international relations, following the pioneer work of Richard Ashley (1987), which asked not "to leave the tradition to the conservatives", have as well developed a spatial account of political relations between communities and states, insofar as they consider that the scenario in which the actions take place is not merely a support but forms an inseparable part of these actions. In this context, Richard Walker, William Connolly and Michael Shapiro should also be mentioned.

Critical geopolitics shows that we currently see the world in a way that was established in the Renaissance. The development at that time of a cartography that recovered Ptolemy's map of the world was highly significant as it enabled the world to be seen as a structured whole; likewise, the discovery of perspective that "allows a framing or 'field of projection' of particulars as elements in an ordered whole" (Agnew 2003: 21). The observer who looks at the world this way in effect moves to an "off-stage" position and becomes a supposedly neutral spectator of "objective" facts, represented on maps and analysed by science. We find ourselves in the same position that Santiago Castro-Gómez (2007a; 2007b) calls "the hubris of point zero", because, "like God, the observer [modern western science] observes the world from an unseen observation platform in order to obtain a truthful observation that leaves no room for doubt [...] [but] when mortals want to be like the gods, but lack the capacity to be so, they commit the sin of hubris [the sin of excess] [...], that is, claiming a point of view that is superior to other points of view, but without that point of view being considered a point of view" (Castro-Gómez 2007b: 83). From here on, it can be clearly understood that knowledge generated from area studies is a "determined" point of view which is Westerncentric in origin, but, precisely for this reason, it can be decolonized to incorporate other knowledge that permits a breaking away from the episteme "in order to *come down* from point zero" (Castro-Gómez 2007b: 89).

There are two ways of breaking with the episteme, which are clearly complementary: one is the incorporation of traditional and modern forms of knowledge that are excluded from scientific rationalism, and the other is the legitimization of research on subaltern narratives and silenced knowledges. In this sense, one of the fundamental characteristics of critical geopolitics is that spatial reflection on the relations of power cannot be limited – as occurs in traditional geopolitics – to those that exist between states while the countless flows taking place on the margins are forgotten. Such a reductionist way of operating would limit "the political" to "the State". Consequently, there is also a need to develop what Paul Routledge (1998) calls "anti-geopolitics", in other words, spatial practices and representations of the space of social movements, peoples' organizations and dissident intellectuals that resist the geopolitics of states in many different ways.

The reconceptualization of geopolitics as discourse contributes to a cultural construction of the global geopolitical map. If critical geopolitics is centred on discourse, this will require reflection in order to clarify some fundamental questions, including its relationship with the material and symbolic aspects that shape a region such as Latin America, or the study of how other regions are not shaped. The concept of "geopolitical discourse" has been used to refer to statements on the geographical disposition of state foreign policies, and on occasions to the whole set of procedures that generate and organize such discourse in state government élites, that is to say, both the geopolitical statements and their enunciation. A precise definition of geopolitical discourse has been drawn up by Agnew and Corbridge, who consider that it alludes to "how the geography of the international political economy has been 'written and read' in the practices of foreign and economic policies during the different periods of geopolitical order. By written is meant the way geographical representations are incorporated into the practices of political élites. By read is meant the ways in which these representations are communicated" (1995: 46). In other words, it could be said that the notion of

geopolitical discourse refers to the way in which the intellectuals of statecraft
– that heterogeneous group of both university and institutional "theorists" and
military and diplomatic "practitioners" – spatialize world politics.

This way of defining geopolitical discourse avoids a double simplification:
the idealistic, associated with textualist approaches that attempt to explain social
practices as epiphenomena of language, and the deterministic, which reduces
discourse to mere ideology, or a set of ideas determined by social practices (often
economic) or serving a representational function. In this sense, geopolitical
discourse would be based on the dialectic relationship between "representations
of space" and "spatial practices" claimed by Lefebvre (1974). Spatial practices
refer to specific places and interrelated spatial groupings organized for economic
production and social reproduction in a given social formation. Representations
of space imply the signs, codes and "understandings" that are needed to make
spatial practices intelligible. And the concept – also Lefebvrian – of "spaces of
representation" is useful for understanding the relationships between geopolitical
discourses and social identification processes, in particular the elements favouring
their hegemony and the resistances undermining them.

Spatial representation will only be dominant in the long term if there is
sufficient overlap with dominant spatial practices, but resistances are generated
in its very development, along with spaces of representation that may transform
these practices. Discourse is subjected to a series of exclusion procedures through
which real production regimes are established (Foucault 1971); for it to be at
all effective, a set of "conditions of existence" or "conditions of possibility" are
necessary, which at the same time contribute to its creation. Edward Said (1993)
appeals for the need to situate text and language in the world. Cultural products are
inseparable from the historical circumstances that gave rise to them.

In short, geopolitical discourses are inseparable from and constituted by
geopolitical representations and geopolitical practices. In order to construct a
critical geopolitics for any region of the world, not only must the spatial practices
and representations of states be addressed, but also the spatial practices and
representations of social movements must be considered as a real possibility
for challenging the geopolitical power of states and the representations of
state intellectuals; in other words, exploration of the spatial constitution of the
mechanisms of power in the region and the mapping of resistances to this power
are core components of regional critical geopolitics.

Why do Some Regions "Exist" (and are Studied) and Not Others?

From this perspective there are clearly no natural regions; any spatial grouping
is the result of geopolitical discourse – that is, of geopolitical representations and
geopolitical practices – but what we now need to explore are the mechanisms that
make some regions "exist" while "hiding" others; in other words, the conditions
of possibility for the "existence" and maintenance of a region. To demonstrate

this we shall consider two cases: Latin America and Southern or Latin Europe. The underlying hypothesis is that "Southern Europe" "is not" a region – that is, in the hegemonic vision of the world, we do not consider it to be a region – whereas "Latin America" *does* constitute a region in this vision of things. A search on one of the Internet's biggest search engines, though not precise,[2] gives an initial approximation that is useful for illustrating tendencies. We conducted our search for references to the various denominations for geographical regions (the simplest and broadest at the same time) in Europe and America[3] using Google General Search, and obtained the following results:

"Southern Europe":	2,330,000 results
"Northern Europe":	4,750,000 results
"Western Europe":	27,600,000 results
"Eastern Europe":	43,100,000 results
"Central Europe":	10,200,000 results
"Latin America":	122,000,000 results
"North America":	184,000,000 results
"South America":	94,800,000 results
"Central America":	201,000,000 results
"East America":	93,100 results
"West America":	140,000 results

Taking into account that the search for "Europe" yielded 579 million results and "America" 678 million results, showing a certain balance between references to these two "parts" of the world, the imbalance between references to subregions of America and Europe is somewhat surprising. The reasons may lie in a much wider perception that America is more subdivided than Europe, but the fact that the difference is so marked still seems odd.

What it shows us with respect to the divisions is also interesting: "America" is divided into North and South, while "Europe" is divided between East to West. "Southern Europe" and "Northern Europe" are hardly discernible as regions with a geographical entity, while "East America" and "West America" are virtually non-

---

2   It should be taken into account that not only is it imprecise in itself, but there may be a variation in different searches of the same object with a few minutes difference. For this reason we tried to carry out all the searches on Google in the shortest possible interval of time (over a period of one hour on 19 April 2009) and under the same conditions. Searches were made in English.

3   There are also geopolitical constructs that intersect with both regions, such as "Iberoamérica" (with almost 3,000,000 hits from the Google search). This is clearly a "reality" based on common languages or, according to some authors, civilizational identity; its meaning is usually interpreted in hegemonic terms (Cairo 2005), but it can also be used counter-hegemonically (Cairo and Bringel, pending publication).

existent. It is also worth noting, for example, that "Central Europe" appears to be a much greater entity than "Southern Europe", although there are references to this.

It seems, therefore, that the data only permit a partial corroboration of the hypothesis: "Latin America" clearly exists, while "Southern Europe" is much more open to doubt. We then asked ourselves if this vision of the world translated to academic interests. To check this, we first went to a specialized search engine, Google Scholar, and searched for the exact references to these regions in academic articles, obtaining the following results:

"Southern Europe":	2,470 results
"Northern Europe":	3,119 results
"Western Europe":	15,800 results
"Eastern Europe":	56,700 results
"Central Europe":	15,100 results
"Latin America":	105,000 results
"North America":	115,000 results
"South America":	22,400 results
"Central America":	14,700 results

The results leave no room for doubt: "Latin America" is a consolidated object of study, like "North America", but almost no one seems interested in studying "Southern Europe". In fact, the main regional object of study in Europe is "Eastern Europe".

These data were corroborated by a visit to the library of a major university in Southern Europe which has a distinct Latin Americanist "vocation": the Complutense University of Madrid. A search for key words using the same terms[4] as before yielded the following results:

1. *"Europa Meridional"* (88) + *"Europa del Sur"* (95): 183 books found [Southern Europe]
2. *"Europa Nórdica"* (3) + *"Europa del Norte"* (223): 226 books found [Northern Europe]
3. *"Europa Oriental"* (997) + *"Europa del Este"* (326): 1323 books found [Eastern Europe]
4. *"Europa Occidental"* (681) + *"Europa del Oeste"* (166) 97 books found [Western Europe]
5. *"Europa Central"* (696) + *"Europa del Centro"* (166): 862 books found [Central Europe]
6. *"América Latina"* (8230) + *"Latinoamérica"* (321): 8551 books found [Latin America]

---

4   This time searches were made in Spanish.

7. "*América del Norte*" (661) + "*Norteamérica*" (687): 1348 books found
   [North America]
8. "*América del Sur*" (761) + "Sudamérica" (72)
   + "Suramérica" (14): 847 books found
   [South America]

If Southern Europe does not constitute a regional framework of common reference, it will be of even less interest to researchers. The case of Latin America is completely the opposite: it is a regional framework of common reference and, moreover, is a highly attractive object of study for researchers. What are the factors that influence this contrast in the geopolitics of knowledge? Is it that one is more homogeneous than the other? Or is it older?

The answers are clearly neither easy nor direct; they can only be tackled indirectly with a multiple approach to the process of construction (or non-construction, or aborted construction) of these two geopolitical representations. The outstanding study by Walter Mignolo (2005), *The Idea of Latin America,* in which he highlights the milestones in the socio-political-ideological structure of Latin America, is a good model to follow, except that in the case of Southern or Latin Europe this should be done in reverse, in other words, we should show the milestones during its "disappearance", although here we are going to outline only some conditions of possibility.

There is consensus among authors that the idea of Latin America had its origins in the second half of the nineteenth century, and insofar as it was the result of a French geostrategy set up in opposition to Great Britain, the dominant power at the time, we should assume that the construction of a Latin Europe was also mooted. Mignolo (2005 [2007: 101]) thinks this idea had already been laid to rest by the mid nineteenth century but, quoting the same author on whom he bases his argument, it is not clear that it was not still an issue at that time: "France is the guardian of the destiny of all Latin nations on the two continents. Only she can prevent that family of peoples from succumbing to the simultaneous advance of the Germans, the Saxons or the Slavs" (Michel Chevalier, 1836, quoted in Mignolo 2005 [2007: 102]). The geopolitical representation of Latin Europe therefore existed in the mid nineteenth century and the French developed spatial practices for its effective construction. Only later would the paths taken by Latin America and Latin Europe fork.

An examination of two geopolitical texts written by American authors in the twentieth century – the century of United States hegemony after the transcendental changes in world order – will perhaps shed some light on the matter. These are: *The New World* by Isaiah Bowman (1924), written after the First World War, and *The Clash of Civilizations* by Samuel Huntington (1996), written after the end of the Cold War. Latin America appears in both books but the profiles of Europe are different. If Huntington includes Western Europe together with the United States, Canada, Australia and New Zealand in a civilization he calls "Western", in Bowman's work there is nothing that might lead us to conclude that the European countries and the United States are in the same boat. Bowman focuses his attention on the great powers, and in this respect it is true that the United States and the imperial nations of Great Britain and France had an equal standing, but however much Europe was talked about, any references were more geophysical than geopolitical. This leads us to conjecture that the construction of Western Europe as Europe, and therefore part of the West, would take between the First World War and the end of the Cold War.

The "non-existence" of Southern or Latin Europe

In order to construct this "reality" we need to examine any possible basic narratives. We find three geopolitical representations which can be grouped into: Mediterranean Europe, as opposed to continental and insular (Anglo-Saxon) Europe, Latin Europe, as opposed to Slav, Germanic and Anglo-Saxon Europe, and Catholic Europe as opposed to Orthodox and Protestant Europe. While it is true that the spatial groupings comprising each of these regions are not exactly the same, they all bear out the existence of a differentiated region in the south and south-west of Europe.

The narrative of Mediterranean Europe has been used at times in a non-academic context. It is widely used as a figure of speech in travel agencies and tourist brochures, but, as I pointed out earlier, it is not differentiated as a region in the hegemonic vision of the world. In academic circles, the most significant study is perhaps that of Fernand Braudel. It is true that the Mediterranean that Braudel speaks of "runs [...] from the first olive tree one encounters when coming from the north to the first palm groves that appear with the desert" (Braudel 1985 [1989: 19]); in other words, it includes the northern European shore and the southern African shore of the Mediterranean Sea. But it is no less true that the "trinity of foods" that characterizes the region – olive oil, wheat bread and wine – is only complete on the European side. The splendour of the region continued well into the seventeenth century, or, to be more exact, 1620, according to Braudel, "when the English and Dutch took control of the distant outlets of the Mediterranean and invaded its very space" (1989: 74).

In a rhetorical context, the Latin Europe narrative is anchored more in the legacy of Rome and covers the area that Rome not only conquered but integrated. We have already mentioned that the geopolitical representation of a Latin Europe, as distinct from the Germanic or Slav Europes, was given a decisive boost by France in the nineteenth century (Mignolo 2005). This country was instrumental in bringing together Portugal, Spain, Belgium, Italy and even Romania as part of a geopolitical exercise to challenge the hegemony of Great Britain.

Catholic Europe is not the Europe of Christianity in general but that of the Counter-Reformation, led from the Vatican, and championed by Spain under the Hapsburgs; it is perhaps the one that most "strays out of the frame" as it includes countries like Poland and Austria; these hardly fit in with previous narratives, but it is an element that is usually included with them.

In this way, the three narratives are practically interwoven in the same geopolitical representation: "Rome was and continues to be the core of that old universe, first Latin and then Catholic, that extends as far as the Protestant world, as far as the ocean and the North Sea, the Rhine and the Danube, throughout which the Counter-Reformation planted its baroque churches like so many watchful sentinels" (Braudel 1985 [1989: 142]).

Other elements have also given a certain presence to the region: the dictatorships that were in force until the 1970s in Spain, Portugal and Greece (with Italy sometimes included because of its fascist experience with Mussolini, although it has been a democracy since the Second World War). These made the region an object of research for "transitologists" (see, for example, Linz and Stepan 1996). For some, the importance of leftist movements, including communist parties, in those four countries in the late Seventies gave rise to a regionalism generated from below (see, for example, Hadjimichalis 1987).

If narrative fundamentals for the existence of a Southern or Latin Europe exist and have existed, and if conditions in the mid nineteenth century made the existence of such a region possible, why is it that Latin Europe and Latin European studies not "exist" as such? In my opinion, it was the appearance of the Soviet Union at the beginning of the twentieth century, followed by the geopolitical East-West division of Europe after the Second World War that led to an alignment of the Latin European-Mediterranean political élites with the dominant core of the world-system, the vortex of which was still in north-west Europe in 1917 but would later pass to the United States.

The recent history of Spain illustrates this well. In the early years of General Franco's dictatorship there was a move to develop a geopolitical representation in the form of a Hispanic (and, by extension, Hispano-American) spiritual Catholic empire opposed to both the communist and the European capitalist world (in particular, the Anglo-Saxon world, that of "fair Albion"); in other words, the position of Spain was in opposition to both Eastern and Western Europe. The outcome of the Second World War on the one hand, and the impossibility of consolidating an autarchic development on the other, led the regime to sign agreements with the United States in 1953, which put the country decisively in the "West"; in fact, the rhetoric about the "'last bastion' of the West" was common to all three dictatorial regimes in Spain, Portugal and Greece. Following the end of Francoism, there was a period of ambiguity with respect to Spain's geopolitical position and a brief flirtation with the Non-Aligned Movement, during which friendly meetings were held between Adolf Suárez and leaders such as Yasser Arafat. The triumph of the self-vision of Spain as a western European country, however, was brought about by the majorities making up the ruling classes and political élites, of both the left and the right, who applied for and obtained membership of the European Community, as it was called at that time. Spain then joined the North Atlantic Treaty Organization following a referendum in which the President of the Government, Felipe González, Secretary General of the

Spanish Socialist Workers' Party (PSOE),[5] used his own determination and the State propaganda machine to show that outside Europe and the West there was only chaos and poverty. He obtained the support of just 52.5 per cent of the voters, with 39.8 per cent voting against. Since then, the Europeanness, Westernness and centrality of Spain have been difficult to question.

At the time the so-called "political transitions" were taking place in the 1970s in Southern Europe (Portugal, Spain and Greece), conditions of possibility were ripe for the development of another political discourse and other practices and spatial representations which could have strengthened the links between Southern Europe and the global South. I think the changes brought about by the Carnation Revolution in Portugal illustrate this point. In 1974, Portugal was a semi-peripheral country governed by an anachronistic authoritarian regime mired in an endless colonial war. The colonial troops, tired of war and to a certain extent identifying with the "subversive enemy", succeeded in bringing down the regime. In the process that followed, not only was independence conferred on the colonies but the 1976 Constitution declared self-determination to be a universal principle for all, and in particular the Portuguese. In 1975 there had been a real possibility of a Portugal linked to the global South, but the experiment led by captains like Otelo Saraiva de Carvalho soon came to an end at the hands of socialists and social democrats, supported by the United States and European NATO countries (particularly the United Kingdom), but also at the hands of the Portuguese Communist Party, with support from the Soviet Union. It was this context of the Cold War that "forced" the East-West partition of Europe.

The "existence" of Latin America

The Iberian countries began their European expansion in the fifteenth and sixteenth centuries, across a world that they ended up organizing entirely to suit their own needs and interests. In this way, the Europeans set about "inventing" new regions that responded to this logic of European domination. Sixteenth century America was one of those "inventions" of the Spanish and Portuguese that played a fundamental role in the construction of modernity, although it should be noted that, as Walter Mignolo (2005) rightly points out, this process was a constituent of the first modernity, while the invention of Latin America, which was a product of French cultural geopolitics and English economic geopolitics on the continent, took place during the second modernity, led by inhabitants of the countries of north-west Europe. This not only destroyed the first modernity but ended up subjugating, if only informally, the countries that had been leaders in the first modernity. As a consequence, Spain historically played ambivalent roles in the modern world-system, and therefore in Latin America: it was an imperial country in the first modernity and a subaltern country in the second.

---

5   A position he had assumed with strong support from Willy Brandt and Olof Palme, in other words, with the support of German and Nordic European social-democracy.

But Latin America is not a region defined only from outside. There have been at least two attempts at developing an endogenous logic of unity: immediately after independence, when Bolivar tried to achieve unity of the recently created states, and in the twentieth century, particularly the first half, with the attempt from the left to construct "Our America" in the face of United States imperialism.

The aspiration of Simón Bolivar was that sooner or later the states created by the *criollos* would form a strong natural federation. In this Bolivarian utopia, the *criollos* of Hispanic origin would govern the autonomous states of the Latin American federation, according to the republican ideals of the French Revolution and liberal Bolivarian patriarchism. For a short time, Bolivar got to govern the territory which today makes up the four South American countries of Venezuela, Colombia, Peru and Bolivia. He wanted to bring all the Latin American countries together in a sort of political federal community, and not only for idealistic reasons: for Bolivar, the unification of Latin America was also necessary for the administrative structure of the political institutions, destroyed during the Wars of Independence, to re-emerge and resist any plans for Reconquest by the European Holy Alliance and the burgeoning expansionism of the United States. Bolivar's first, and at the same time last, attempt to bring about union was the organization of the Congress of Panama in June, 1826, when Colombia invited the American nations to take part in this meeting (Pakkasvirta and Cairo 2009). Not long afterwards, Greater Colombia broke up and the Bolivarian dream came to an abrupt end, leaving the *criollo* states to fall within the orbit of informal British imperialism.

"Our America" was an expression of José Martí that broke with Greece and Rome. It derived from Martí's attempt to construct a geopolitical representation on the foundations of the continent's pre-Colombian civilizations (Mignolo 2005). Later on, José Carlos Mariátegui (and currently Enrique Dussel) would become involved in a similar project. Such autonomous projects are minority undertakings in the region, although at certain times they have been able to mobilize broad sectors of the population.

> The question of what it means to be Latin American is changing at the beginning of the twenty-first century; answers that were once convincing have ceased to exist and doubts have been raised about the usefulness of continental compromises. The number of voices taking part in this debate has grown [...] At the same time, national states [...] have become diminished by globalization. The uncertainties and economic and political regressions at the end of the twentieth century put an end to many expectations. Those who only showed a commitment to nation states or the market or mass media when it came to Latin American development and integration learnt that none of these points of reference are what they were.

With these words, García Canclini (2002: 18) begins to raise a series of doubts in *Latin Americans Looking for a Place in this Century*, which examines the viability of Latin America in a globalized world. The essay touches on both the elements that globalize the region and those that enhance its special features, but the motive question asked is significant: "Who wants to be Latin American?" From his own perspective, García Canclini is relatively cautious with respect to the response, although he reminds us that the story of Latin America has to be polyphonic.

His essay concludes with the enumeration of a series of objectives "that could contribute to the reconstitution of Latin America as a region, making it more creative and competitive in global exchanges" (García Canclini 2002: 94-5). These include: the identification of strategic areas of development; the development of multi-cultural and participatory socio-cultural practices that promote technological advance; the redeployment of cultural practices between the endogenous and the international, and the cultivation and protection of Latin American diversity. In short, García Canclini recommends greater negotiation of the place of Latin America in a globalized world, at the same time taking its cultural peculiarities into consideration.

In Conclusion

The comparison between what was to become of Latin America and Latin Europe as geopolitical representations has given us a glimpse of how, from the end of the nineteenth century onwards, the intelligentsias of both regions were subordinated to the core of the world-system in different ways: in Latin America, the *criollos* colonized themselves and considered themselves Latin Americans (Mignolo 2005), while in Latin Europe the ruling classes were linked as a semi-periphery annexed to a core formed by North-West Europe, a process in which some parts of this region actually became part of the core itself. By the mid nineteenth century, conditions were such that the "existence" of both regions was possible. This might have meant the coming into being of a Latin Europe, perhaps similar to Eastern Europe, which would have led to the existence of solid studies on Latin or Southern Europe.

Maybe it is no longer the right moment for taking up García Canclini's proposal, or creating a series of antihegemonic Latin European studies, given the weight of what is "European" in the region in its present form. As Walter Mignolo points out in the conclusion of *The Idea of Latin America*: "for the future continental imaginary, a complete reordering of the continent is not a solution. Changing the content without questioning the logic sustaining it is necessary, but it falls very short of being sufficient. An 'epistemology of the South' would be a second step to erase the memory of a planet divided into four continents and help promote a process of critical frontier thinking" (Mignolo 2005 [2007: 181]). In the words of Boaventura de Sousa Santos (2007), this thinking could only be "post-abyssal", that is to say, able to overcome the monopoly of western science in distinguishing between true and false and the exclusion of knowledge that comes from "the other side of the line".

Perhaps – and only perhaps – this is the right moment for "dismantling" the idea of Latin America, which was created as "part of the universal process of expansion [of the second modernity]" (Mignolo 2005 [2007: 217]), and for constructing an "After Latin America", as part of the global South, from which there is no reason to exclude Latin or Southern Europe, despite the desires and interests of its ruling classes and élites.

Bibliography

Agnew, J. 2003. *Geopolitics: Re-visioning World Politics*. London: Routledge, 2nd Edition.

Blaut, J.M. 1993. *The Colonizer's Model of the World: Geographical Diffusionism and Eurocentric History*. New York: Guilford Press.

Bowman, I. 1924. *The New World: Problems in Political Geography*. London: George G. Harrap (Revised Edition).

Braudel, F. 1985. *La Méditerranée. L'espace et l'histoire*. Paris: Flammarion [Translated into Spanish: *El Mediterráneo. El espacio y la historia*. México D. F.: Fondo de Cultura Económica, 1989].

Cairo, H. 2005. Discursos geopolíticos y construcción de identidades supranacionales en América Latina, in *Von Wäldern, Städten und Grenzen: Narration und kulturelle Identitätsbildungsprozesse in Lateinamerika*, edited by E. Rodrigues-Moura (Yearbook ¡Atención! Jahrbuch des Österreichischen Lateinamerika-Instituts, vol. 8). Frankfurt am Main: Brandes & Apsel/ Südwind, 315-37.

Cairo, H. and Bringel, B. (forthcoming). Articulaciones del Sur global: afinidad cultural, internacionalismo solidario e Iberoamérica en la globalización contrahegemónica, in *Descolonizar la modernidad, descolonizar Europa. Un diálogo Europa-América Latina*, edited by H. Cairo and R. Grosfoguel. Madrid: IEPALA Editorial.

Castro-Gómez, S. 2007a. *La hybris del punto cero. Ciencia, raza e Ilustración en la Nueva Granada (1750-1816)*. Bogotá: Editorial Pontificia Universidad Javeriana (first reprint).

Castro-Gómez, S. 2007b. Decolonizar la Universidad. La hybris del punto cero y el diálogo de saberes, in *El giro decolonial: Reflexiones para una diversidad epistémica más allá del capitalismo global*, edited by S. Castro-Gómez and R. Grosfoguel. Bogotá: Siglo del Hombre Editores/Pontificia Universidad Javeriana/Universidad Central, 79-91.

Dalby, S. 1990a. *Creating the Second Cold War*. London: Pinter.

Dalby, S. 1990b. American Security Discourse and Geopolitics. *Political Geography Quarterly*, 9(2), 171-88.

Foucault, M. 1971. *L'ordre du discours*. Paris: Gallimard.

García Canclini, N. 2002. *Latinoamericanos buscando lugar en este siglo*. Buenos Aires: Paidós.

Hadjimichalis, C. 1987. *Uneven Development and Regionalism: State, Territory and Class in Southern Europe*. London: Croom Helm.

Huntington, S.P. 1996. *The Clash of Civilizations and the Remaking of World Order*. New York: Simon & Schuster.

Lefebvre, H. 1974. *La production de l'espace*. Paris: Anthropos.

Linz, J.J. and Stepan, A. 1996. *Problems of Democratic Transition and Consolidation: Southern Europe, South America, and Post-Communist Europe*. Baltimore: Johns Hopkins University Press.

Mignolo, W. 2005. *The Idea of Latin America*. Oxford: Blackwell [Translation to Spanish: *La idea de América Latina. La herida colonial y la opción decolonial*. Barcelona: Gedisa, 2007].

Ó Tuathail, G. 1988. *Critical Geopolitics: The Social Construction of Space and Place in the Practice of Statecraft*. Unpublished PhD Thesis, Syracuse University.

Pakkasvirta, J. and Cairo, H. 2009. Introducción. Estudiando América Latina en la escuela de investigación de AMELAT XXI, in *Estudiar América Latina: retos y perspectivas*, edited by H. Cairo and J. Pakkasvirta. San José de Costa Rica: Alma Mater/Universidad de Costa Rica/Universidad Complutense de Madrid/ Universidad de la República de Uruguay, 11-22.

Routledge, P. 1998. Antigeopolitics. Introduction, in *The Geopolitics Reader*, edited by G. Ó Tuathail, S. Dalby and P. Routledge. London: Routledge, 245-55.

Said, E. 1993. *Culture and Imperialism*. New York: Knopf/Random House.

Santos, B. de Sousa. 2007. Beyond Abyssal Thinking: From Global Lines to Ecologies of Knowledges. *Review*, 30(1), 45-990.

Schueller, M.J. 2007. Area Studies and Multicultural Imperialism: The Project of Decolonizing Knowledge. *Social Text*, 25(1), 41-62.

Stenning, A. 2005. Out There and In Here: Studying Eastern Europe in the West. *Area*, 37(4), 378–383.

Taylor, P.J. and Flint, C. 2000. *Political Geography: World-economy, Nation-state and Locality*. London: Wiley.

Wallerstein, I. 1991. *Unthinking Social Science: The Limits of Nineteenth-Century Paradigms*. Cambridge: Polity Press.

Index